W9-DCG-650

Relational Database:

Selected Writings

C. J. Date

ADDISON-WESLEY PUBLISHING COMPANY

Reading, Massachusetts • Menlo Park, California • Don Mills, Ontario
Wokingham, England • Amsterdam • Madrid
San Juan • Bogatá • Sydney • Santiago
Singapore • Tokyo

Library of Congress Cataloging-in-Publication Data

Date, C. J.
  Relational database.

  Bibliography: p.
  Includes index.
  1. Data base management.   I. Title.
QA76.9.D3D3724   1986   005.75′6   85–22907
ISBN 0–201–14196–5

Copyright © 1986 by Addison-Wesley Publishing Company, Inc.

All rights reserved. No part of this publication may be reproduced, stored in a retrieval system, or transmitted, in any form or by any means, electronic, mechanical, photocopying, recording, or otherwise, without the prior written permission of the publisher. Printed in the United States of America. Published simultaneously in Canada.

DEFGHIJ-HA-8987

I dedicate this book to the desert
and the spirit of the desert

Preface

The purpose of this book is to bring together into one place all those of my database papers from the period 1974–1985 that seem to me to be worth preserving. Most of those papers were originally published in one of the professional database journals or in the proceedings of one of the technical database conferences (see below), and I am grateful to all concerned for permission to republish them in this fashion. I have of course taken the opportunity to make a number of small improvements and corrections in the versions printed here, but apart from such minor changes the papers are all essentially as originally published. However, I have also included a couple of papers that have not previously been published at all.

In a collection of this kind there is inevitably a certain unevenness of style—some of the papers are fairly formal in nature, others (marked generally by the use of the first person singular) much less so. There is also inevitably a certain amount of repetition. I have edited out the worst overlaps, but otherwise have generally tried to keep each paper reasonably self-contained.

The book is arranged into four principal parts:

I. Relational Database Management
II. Relational vs. Nonrelational Systems
III. The SQL Language
IV. Database Design

There is also an afterword, containing the text of an interview I gave to *Data Base Newsletter* in 1983.

Part I consists of a collection of papers on the relational model and relational systems in general. Part II is concerned with various aspects of the differences between relational and nonrelational systems. Part III contains a detailed critique of what is rapidly becoming the de facto standard in the relational field, namely the "Structured Query Language" SQL, and proposes a number of extensions and revisions to that language. Finally, Part IV presents a detailed methodology for relational database design. The sequence of papers within each part is very largely arbitrary.

Acknowledgments: As usual, I am delighted to acknowledge my debt to the many people involved, directly or indirectly, in the production of this book. First, as already stated, I am grateful to the copyright holders of the original papers for permission to republish those papers in this manner. Second, I am also grateful to the numerous reviewers of those original papers; individual acknowledgments to those reviewers appear within the papers themselves. Third, I am very pleased to acknowledge the encouragement I received from numerous close friends and colleagues while working on this book. Last, I am (as always) grateful to my editor, Elydia Siegel, and to the staff at Addison-Wesley for their assistance and professional expertise.

Saratoga, California   C.J.D.

Contents

CHAPTER 3
Why Every Relation Should Have Exactly One Primary Key   33

CHAPTER 4
Referential Integrity   41

CHAPTER 5
On the Performance of Relational Database Systems   65

CHAPTER 6

Some Relational Myths Exploded (AN EXAMINATION OF SOME POPULAR MISCONCEPTIONS CONCERNING RELATIONAL DATABASE MANAGEMENT SYSTEMS) **77**

CHAPTER 7

A Formal Definition of the Relational Model **125**

CHAPTER 8

The Relational Model and Its Interpretation **143**

PART II   RELATIONAL VS. NONRELATIONAL SYSTEMS

CHAPTER 12
Why Is It So Difficult to Provide a Relational Interface to IMS?   **241**

PART III   THE SQL LANGUAGE

CHAPTER 13
Some Principles of Good Language Design (WITH ESPECIAL REFERENCE TO THE DESIGN OF DATABASE LANGUAGES)   **261**

CHAPTER 17

Updating Views 367

CHAPTER 18

A Note on the Parts Explosion Problem 397

PART IV   DATABASE DESIGN

CHAPTER 19
A Practical Approach to Database Design   **417**

AFTERWORD: THE RELATIONAL FUTURE

## PART I

RELATIONAL DATABASE MANAGEMENT

1

Relational Database: An Overview

(AN INTRODUCTION TO RELATIONAL SYSTEM CONCEPTS, USING SQL/DS AS A CONCRETE EXAMPLE)

ABSTRACT

The aim of this paper is to present a brief and very informal description of relational database systems, using SQL/DS as a vehicle for purposes of illustration. Codd's pioneering paper on the relational model [3] was published in June 1970. SQL/DS, IBM's first fully supported relational database program product, was announced in January 1981 [10]. A secondary objective of the present paper is to give some guidance to the vast body of literature that has grown up on the subject in the intervening years (a Fur-

Originally published in *Proc. GUIDE 53,* Atlanta, Georgia (May 1981); *Proc. SEAS Spring Meeting,* Noordwijkerhout, Netherlands (April 1983); *Proc. 10th Australian Computer Conference,* Melbourne, Australia (September 1983); and elsewhere. Also published (in considerably revised form) as *Relational Data Base System Concepts Using SQL/DS*, copyright 1984 Auerbach Publishers Inc. Data Base Management.

ther Reading section is included at the end of the paper). The paper consists primarily of a distillation of material from the author's book *An Introduction to Database Systems: Volume I* [1].

COMMENTS ON REPUBLICATION

This brief overview, though inevitably rather superficial, still seems to me a useful introduction to relational concepts in general. SQL/DS, like most other current relational products, does not in fact support the full underlying theory (i.e., the relational model) in every last respect; nevertheless, it can reasonably be regarded as a fairly typical example of relational systems as currently implemented. For more information on the underlying theory, see the subsequent papers in this part of the book, especially the next paper ("An Informal Definition of the Relational Model").

Note: When this paper was first written, SQL/DS was available only for the DOS/VSE operating system. IBM subsequently made available both (a) a version of SQL/DS for VM/CMS and (b) a companion product called DB2 for MVS/370 and MVS/XA. Most of the paper applies with little change to those other systems also.

INTRODUCTION

SQL/DS is a relational database management system running under the IBM DOS/VSE operating system.[1] It can coexist with both CICS/DOS/ VS and DL/I DOS/VS; that is, a SQL/DS application program can optionally use CICS for access to terminals and/or DL/I for access to DL/I databases. The function of SQL/DS is to provide access, via the "Structured Query Language" SQL (usually pronounced "sequel"), to a relational database by one or more users concurrently. A *relational database* is simply a database that is perceived by the user as a collection of *tables—* where a table is *an unordered set of rows* ("relation" is just a mathematical term for such a table). An example, the suppliers-and-parts database, is shown in Fig. 1.1. Note that each table (relation) can be thought of as a *file*, with the rows representing records and the columns fields.

As already indicated, all access to tables such as those of Fig. 1.1 is via the language SQL (see Fig. 1.2). SQL can be used both (a) from a terminal (via ISQL—"Interactive SQL"), in which case retrieved data is displayed directly at the terminal, and (b) embedded in a COBOL, PL/I, or Assem-

---

[1] As mentioned in the "Comments on Republication," a version of SQL/DS for VM/CMS and a companion product called DB2 for MVS/370 and MVS/XA have both subsequently been released by IBM.

```
     --   -----   ------  ------                      --  --  ---
S    S#   SNAME   STATUS  CITY               SP       S#  P#  QTY
     --   -----   ------  ------                      --  --  ---
     S1   Smith       20  London                      S1  P1  300
     S2   Jones       10  Paris                       S1  P2  200
     S3   Blake       30  Paris                       S1  P3  400
     S4   Clark       20  London                      S1  P4  200
     S5   Adams       30  Athens                      S1  P5  100
                                                      S1  P6  100
     --   -----   -----   ------   ------             S2  P1  300
P    P#   PNAME   COLOR   WEIGHT   CITY               S2  P2  400
     --   -----   -----   ------   ------             S3  P2  200
     P1   Nut     Red         12   London             S4  P2  200
     P2   Bolt    Green       17   Paris              S4  P4  300
     P3   Screw   Blue        17   Rome               S4  P5  400
     P4   Screw   Red         14   London
     P5   Cam     Blue        12   Paris
     P6   Cog     Red         19   London
```

Figure 1.1   The suppliers-and-parts database (sample values)

bler Language application program, in which case retrieved data is fetched into an input area named in the statement (":SC" in Fig. 1.2).

Figure 1.1 of course represents the database as it appears at some specific time. The database *definition* is shown in Fig. 1.3. It is important to note that the SQL statement "CREATE TABLE" shown in that figure is *executable* (like all SQL statements) and can be issued at any time. Thus, for example, a new table can be added to an existing database at any time, without interfering with the work of existing users at all. (The effect of CREATE TABLE is to build a new, empty table. Data can subsequently be entered into the table via the SQL INSERT statement or via a bulk loading utility.) Similarly, it is possible to add a new field (column) to an existing

Interactive:

```
                                           ------
     SELECT CITY             Result:   CITY
     FROM   S                              ------
     WHERE  S# = 'S4'                   London
```

Embedded in PL/I (could be COBOL or Assembler):

```
                                               ------
EXEC SQL SELECT CITY INTO :SC      Result:   SC
         FROM   S                              ------
         WHERE  S# = 'S4' ;                   London
```

Figure 1.2   SQL retrieval example

```
CREATE TABLE S   ( S#      CHAR(5),
                    SNAME   CHAR(20),
                    STATUS  SMALLINT,
                    CITY    CHAR(15) )

CREATE TABLE P   ( P#      CHAR(6),
                    PNAME   CHAR(20),
                    COLOR   CHAR(6),
                    WEIGHT  SMALLINT,
                    CITY    CHAR(15) )

CREATE TABLE SP  ( S#      CHAR(5),
                    P#      CHAR(6),
                    QTY     INTEGER  )
```

Figure 1.3 SQL data definition example

table at any time, again without affecting existing users, via the SQL statement ALTER TABLE.

USER PERSPECTIVE

The tables seen by the user in SQL/DS come in two varieties, *base tables* and *views*. A base table is a "real" table—i.e., a table that physically exists, in the sense that there exist physical stored records, and possibly physical indexes, in one or more VSAM data sets, that directly support that table in storage. By contrast, a view is a "virtual" table—i.e., a table that does not exist in physical storage, but looks to the user as if it did. Views are defined, in a manner to be explained later, in terms of one or more underlying base tables.

(The foregoing paragraph should not be interpreted as saying that a base table is physically *stored* as a table—i.e., as a set of physically adjacent stored records, with each record consisting simply of a direct copy of a row of the base table. There are numerous differences between a base table and its storage representation. The point is, users can always *think* of base tables as "physically existing," while not having to concern themselves with how those tables are actually implemented in storage.)

Like base tables, views can be created at any time. (The same is true of indexes.) Similarly, base tables and views (and indexes) can be "dropped" (i.e., destroyed) at any time. With regard to indexes, however, note carefully that although the user is responsible for creating and destroying them, using the SQL data definition statements CREATE INDEX and DROP INDEX, the user is *not* responsible for saying when those indexes should be used. Indexes are never mentioned in SQL data manipulation statements such as SELECT. The decision as to whether or not to use a particular index in responding to (say) a SELECT operation is made by the system, not by the user.

The user interface to SQL/DS is the SQL language. We have already indicated (a) that SQL is available in both interactive and embedded environments, and (b) that it provides both data definition and data manipulation functions (in fact, as we shall see later, it provides certain "data control" functions as well). The major data definition functions (CREATE/DROP/ALTER TABLE and CREATE/DROP INDEX) have already been discussed. The major data manipulation functions are SELECT, UPDATE, DELETE, and INSERT. Figure 1.4 gives additional examples of SELECT and UPDATE to illustrate another point, namely the fact that SQL data manipulation statements typically operate on entire sets of records, instead of just on one record at a time. Languages having this characteristic are sometimes described as "nonprocedural": Users specify WHAT, not HOW (i.e., they say what data they want, without specifying a procedure for finding it). The process of "navigating" around the physical database to locate the desired data is performed automatically by the system, not manually by the user.

```
                                            --
SELECT  S#                       Result:  S#
FROM    SP                                --
WHERE   P# = 'P2'                         S1
                                          S2
                                          S3
                                          S4


UPDATE  S                        Result:  STATUS doubled
SET     STATUS = 2 * STATUS               for S1 and S4
WHERE   CITY = 'London'
```

Figure 1.4 SQL data manipulation examples

SYSTEM STRUCTURE

SQL/DS consists of two major components, the Database Storage System (DBSS) and the Relational Data System (RDS). The DBSS is basically a powerful multiuser access method: It handles all physical level details, providing such functions as Boolean logic searching, automatic index maintenance, and in particular full locking and recovery support. The user of the DBSS is not a human user, however, but rather *compiled SQL code*, produced by the SQL/DS preprocessor (part of the RDS). The *human* interface—i.e., the tabular data structure and the corresponding SQL operators—is supported by the RDS, which divides in turn into two pieces, a preprocessor and a runtime component. Consider an application program, written in PL/I say, that includes one or more SQL statements. What happens to such a program is the following:

- The preprocessor strips out the SQL statements, replacing them by PL/I CALL statements to the RDS runtime component.

- It then *compiles* those SQL statements into machine code (including, in particular, machine code calls on the DBSS). The compilation process involves choosing an *access strategy* (e.g., choosing whether or not to use a particular index) for each SQL request, and then reflecting that strategy in the generated code. The total set of all such generated code for all SQL statements in the program—the *access module* for the program—is stored in the SQL/DS database.

- The modified PL/I source program is compiled and link-edited in the usual way.

- At execution time, the first call from the program to SQL/DS causes the runtime component to fetch the access module and pass control to· it. (On subsequent calls, of course, the fetch step is unnecessary.) The access module then executes, invoking the DBSS as appropriate, and the desired database operations are performed.

The procedure just outlined raises another point. Since SQL statements are compiled, not interpreted, it is possible that decisions made at compile time (e.g., the decision to use a certain index X) may no longer be valid at execution time (index X may have been dropped). If the runtime component discovers at the time it fetches the access module that that module relies on some object (such as index X) that no longer exists, then it automatically *recompiles* the original SQL statements to generate a new access module (incorporating a different access strategy), before continuing with execution. This process is totally invisible to the user.

It follows from the foregoing that users are quite independent of the presence or absence of indexes in the physical database. Such "physical data independence" is typical of relational systems in general (though most systems achieve it by interpretation rather than as described here; SQL/DS uses a compilation approach for reasons of performance). Relational systems stress, to a much greater degree than nonrelational systems, the distinction between externals (what the user sees) and internals (what physically exists). As a result, it is not necessary to change programs when a change in the physical database structure occurs. User productivity is thus greatly enhanced.

Note that SQL statements are *always* compiled, not interpreted, even in the case of Interactive SQL (ISQL). Experience with System R, the prototype forerunner of SQL/DS, suggests that, even in the interactive case, compilation almost always results in better overall performance than interpretation [17].

DATA MANIPULATION

The SQL data manipulation statements (SELECT, UPDATE, DELETE, INSERT) are quite typical of relational manipulative operators in general. This section therefore gives a number of examples of those statements. The basic *retrieval* statement is SELECT - FROM - WHERE, illustrated in Fig. 1.5. Note: The symbol " ~ =" in that figure stands for "not equals."

```
SELECT DISTINCT COLOR, CITY        Result:  COLOR   CITY
FROM   P                                    ------  ------
WHERE  WEIGHT > 10                          Red     London
AND    CITY ~= 'Paris'                      ---Red-----London---
ORDER  BY COLOR DESC                        ---Red-----London---
                                            Blue    Rome

                                   (2nd and 3rd records
                                   eliminated if user
                                   specifies DISTINCT)
```

Figure 1.5   The basic "SELECT - FROM - WHERE"

Notice that the result of the SELECT is another table (one that is derived from an existing table, not one that is stored in the database). Several points arise in connexion with this example:

- If DESC (descending) is omitted, ASC (ascending) order is assumed.
- If the entire ORDER BY clause is omitted, the result appears in unpredictable order.
- If the entire WHERE clause is omitted, all records of the FROM table qualify.
- If DISTINCT is omitted, the result may contain duplicate records (in the example, four records will be returned if DISTINCT is omitted, two if it is included).

Join

One feature that, almost more than any other, distinguishes relational from nonrelational systems is the availability of the *join* operator. Loosely speaking, what this means is that it is possible to select data from multiple tables in a single SELECT statement. An example is given in Fig. 1.6. The term

Problem: For each part supplied, retrieve part number and names of all cities in which there is located a supplier who supplies the part.

```
        --  --  ---           --      ------           --  ------
   SP   S#  P#  ...       S   S#  ... CITY             P#  CITY
        --  --  ---           --      ------           --  ------
        S1  P1  ...           S1      London           P1  London
        S1  P2  ...  PLUS     S2      Paris     ==>     P2  London
        .   .   .             .       .                 .   .
        .   .   .             .       .                 .   .
        .   .   .                                       .   .
        S2  P1  ...                                     P1  Paris
        .   .   .                                        .   .

              SELECT  SP.P#,  S.CITY
              FROM    SP, S
              WHERE   SP.S# = S.S#
```

Figure 1.6   Example involving join

"join" arises from the fact that (in the example) tables SP and S are conceptually being *joined* on their common S# column.

The point about this example is that the user can join the two tables *regardless* of whether any special access paths (e.g., indexes on S.S# and SP.S#) have physically been established in the database prior to the time of the request. The system will use such access paths if available (and suitable), but does not insist on their presence. By contrast, nonrelational systems typically allow a single user request to refer to two or more records simultaneously *only* if a physical connexion (e.g., a parent-child pointer) exists linking those two records together. Thus, once again, the relational user is independent of the physical structure of the database.

Built-In Functions

SQL provides a set of special built-in functions: COUNT, SUM, AVG, MAX, MIN, and COUNT(*) (the "*" refers to an entire row of the table concerned). Examples are given in Fig. 1.7 (opposite page). The last example also illustrates the GROUP BY clause, which is used to divide a table up (conceptually) into groups so that a function such as SUM can be applied to each of those groups.

Accessing the Catalog

SQL/DS automatically maintains a set of tables that constitute the *system catalog*. The catalog contains descriptions of all objects (tables, indexes, access modules, users, ...) known to the system. For example, there is a catalog table called SYSCOLUMNS that includes an entry (i.e., row) for

```
                                                          Result:

Number of suppliers:    SELECT  COUNT(*)                      5
                        FROM    S

Number of suppliers     SELECT  COUNT(DISTINCT S#)            4
supplying parts:        FROM    SP

Total quantity of P2:   SELECT  SUM(QTY)                   1000
                        FROM    SP
                        WHERE   P# = 'P2'
                                                   --  -------
                                                   P#
                                                   --  -------
Part number and total   SELECT  P#, SUM(QTY)       P1      600
quantity for each       FROM    SP                 P2     1000
part supplied:          GROUP   BY P#              P3      400
                                                   P4      500
                                                   P5      500
                                                   P6      100
```

Figure 1.7 SQL built-in function examples

every column of every table in the database (including the catalog tables themselves), giving the name of the column (CNAME), the name of the containing table (TNAME), the data type of the column (COLTYPE), and so on. Users can use SQL SELECT statements to interrogate the catalog tables, just like any other tables in the database. An example ("List all tables containing a column called S#") is shown in Fig. 1.8.

```
                                                   -----
SELECT  TNAME                  Result:   TNAME
FROM    SYSCOLUMNS                       -----
WHERE   CNAME = 'S#'                     S
                                         SP
```

Figure 1.8 Example of catalog access

Data Modification

The data modification statements are UPDATE, DELETE, and INSERT. Examples are given in Fig. 1.9 (overleaf).

Application Programming

We include this topic under the heading of data manipulation for convenience. However, it should be stressed that *any* SQL statement—not just data manipulation statements but data definition and data control statements

```
UPDATE  P
SET     COLOR = 'Yellow',
        WEIGHT = WEIGHT - 10
WHERE   CITY = 'Paris'

DELETE
FROM    S
WHERE   CITY = 'London'

INSERT
INTO    P ( P#, PNAME, COLOR, WEIGHT, CITY )
VALUES  ('P7','Grommet','Black',24,'Athens')
```

Figure 1.9 SQL data modification examples

also—can be embedded in application programs. But of course it is the data manipulation statements that are most generally useful in this context.

SQL statements in an application program are prefixed with EXEC SQL, so that they can easily be recognized by the preprocessor. They can include references to host language variables; such references are prefixed with a colon, again for purposes of recognition. An example has already been given (see Fig. 1.2).

The major difference between interactive and embedded SQL lies in the treatment of SELECT. SELECT returns a whole table, i.e., a *set* of (typically) many records. Host languages such as PL/I are however not well equipped to deal with sets. What is needed, therefore, is a mechanism for stepping through such a set and picking off the records one by one; and *cursors* provide such a mechanism. A cursor is an embedded-SQL object that is associated (via a declaration of that cursor) with a specific SELECT operation. To access the records corresponding to that SELECT, the user must: (a) OPEN the cursor, which (conceptually) causes the SELECT to be executed and hence identifies the corresponding set of records; (b) use FETCH repeatedly on the opened cursor, which (on each execution) steps that cursor to the next record in the SELECTed set and then retrieves that record; and finally (c) CLOSE the cursor when all required records have been processed. Special forms of UPDATE and DELETE are also provided for updating or deleting the record on which the cursor is currently positioned. An example is given (in outline) in Fig. 1.10.

VIEWS

A view is a virtual table—i.e., a table that does not "really exist" but looks to the user as if it did. Views are not directly supported by stored data; instead, their *definition* in terms of other tables is stored in the system catalog. An example of a view definition is given in Fig. 1.11.

```
EXEC SQL DECLARE C CURSOR FOR
           SELECT S#, QTY
           FROM    SP
           WHERE   P# = 'P2'
           FOR UPDATE OF QTY ;

DECLARE X CHAR(5) ;
DECLARE Y FIXED BIN(31) ;
DECLARE Z FIXED BIN(15) ;

EXEC SQL OPEN C ;
DO WHILE more records to come ;
   EXEC SQL FETCH C INTO :X, :Y ;
   process X and Y ;
   EXEC SQL UPDATE SP
              SET    QTY = QTY + :Z
              WHERE  CURRENT OF C ;
END ;
EXEC SQL CLOSE C ;
```

Figure 1.10   Example of the use of a cursor

```
CREATE VIEW LONDON_SUPPLIERS
    AS SELECT S#, SNAME, STATUS
       FROM    S
       WHERE   CITY = 'London'
```

Figure 1.11   CREATE VIEW (example)

The view LONDON_SUPPLIERS acts as a "window," through which the user can see the S#, SNAME, and STATUS fields (only) of records in base table S for which the CITY value is London (only). The SELECT defining this view is *not* executed when the view is created but is merely stored in the catalog. But to the user it now appears as if a table called LONDON_SUPPLIERS does really exist in the database. Figure 1.12 shows an example of a retrieval against that table. The preprocessor will *merge* the SELECT of Fig. 1.12 with the SELECT of Fig. 1.11 (from the catalog) to give the modified SELECT in Fig. 1.13).

```
                                         --
SELECT S#                       Result:  S#
FROM   LONDON_SUPPLIERS                  --
WHERE  STATUS < 50                       S1
                                         S4
```

Figure 1.12   Retrieval against a view (example)

```
                                          --
SELECT  S#                    Result:     S#
FROM    S                                 --
WHERE   STATUS < 50                       S1
AND     CITY = 'London'                   S4
```

Figure 1.13 Merged SELECT statement

The modified SELECT can now be compiled and executed in the normal way. In other words, the original SELECT on the view is converted into an equivalent SELECT on the underlying base table. Data modification statements are handled in a similar fashion; however, modification operations on views are subject to a number of restrictions, the details of which are beyond the scope of this paper. Simplifying matters somewhat, a view can be modified only if it represents a simple row-and-column subset of a single underlying base table (for example, it is not a join).[2]

More examples of views (nonupdatable) are given in Fig. 1.14.

```
CREATE VIEW PQ ( P#, SUMQTY )
    AS SELECT P#, SUM(QTY)
       FROM    SP
       GROUP   BY P#

CREATE VIEW CITY_PAIRS ( SCITY, PCITY )
    AS SELECT S.CITY, P.CITY
       FROM    S, SP, P
       WHERE   S.S# = SP.S# AND SP.P# = P.P#
```

Figure 1.14 Additional view examples

From this short discussion it should be clear that views can simplify still further the user's perception of the database, e.g., by concealing irrelevant data or by joining distinct tables together into a single table. In fact, they can help to insulate the user from changes in the *logical* (as opposed to physical) structure of the database: "logical data independence." We have already mentioned the fact that users are unaffected by *growth* in the logical structure; that is, new tables and new fields can be added at any time without affecting existing users (one aspect of logical data independence). Views can protect the user against another aspect: *rearrangement* of the logical structure. Suppose, for example, that the database designer decides to move field F from table T1 to table T2. A user of the old T1

---

[2]See the paper "Updating Views" (elsewhere in this collection) for a fuller discussion of this topic.

can be given a *view* in which the new T1 is joined with field F from the new T2, thus making it look to that user as if F is still in T1.

Another advantage of views is that they provide an important measure of data security (see the next section).

SECURITY

There are two aspects to security in SQL/DS: the view mechanism, and the GRANT and REVOKE statements. First, views can be used to hide sensitive data from unauthorized users. Some examples of views that might be used in this way are shown in Fig. 1.15 (where the database is assumed to include a table called EMP, with fields EMP#, DEPT#, MGR#, JOB, and SAL). The first reveals information only for employees in department D3; the second reveals information only for employees who have the user of the view as their manager; the third conceals all salary information; and the fourth gives salary per department, but no individual salaries. Note: "SELECT *" is shorthand for a SELECT that names all fields of the table—i.e., a SELECT that accesses the entire row (for all rows satisfying the WHERE clause).

```
CREATE VIEW D3EMPS AS
        SELECT * FROM EMP WHERE DEPT# = 'D3'

CREATE VIEW MYEMPS AS
        SELECT * FROM EMP WHERE MGR# = USER

CREATE VIEW SALHIDDEN AS
        SELECT EMP#, DEPT#, MGR#, JOB FROM EMP

CREATE VIEW AVGSALS ( DEPT#, AVGSAL ) AS
        SELECT DEPT#, AVG(SAL) FROM EMP GROUP BY DEPT#
```

Figure 1.15　Using views to hide data (examples)

GRANT and REVOKE

To perform any SQL operation, the user must hold the appropriate *access privilege* for the operation and operand concerned. Examples of access privileges are SELECT, UPDATE, DELETE, INSERT (privilege to perform the indicated operation on the base table or view concerned—in the case of UPDATE, the privilege can be restricted to specific fields); INDEX (privilege to create an index on the base table concerned); RESOURCE (privilege to create a base table); and DBA ("database administrator"—i.e., unconstrained authority).

At system installation time, at least one user must be designated as holding the DBA privilege. That user can then choose to delegate authority, or not, as the case may be. Any user creating a table is automatically granted all applicable privileges on that table, "with the GRANT option." Any user holding a privilege "with the GRANT option" can selectively and dynamically grant that privilege to another user, and moreover can optionally pass "the GRANT option" on to that other user (so that that user in turn can go on to grant the privilege to a third party, and so on). Similarly, a user who has granted a privilege can if desired subsequently revoke that privilege (and revocation cascades appropriately). These functions are performed by means of the SQL "data control" statements GRANT and REVOKE. Some examples are shown in Fig. 1.16.

```
GRANT INSERT, DELETE, UPDATE ON SP TO JONES

GRANT SELECT ON SP TO BLAKE WITH GRANT OPTION

GRANT UPDATE ( STATUS ) ON S TO CLARK

GRANT DBA TO SMITH, ADAMS


REVOKE DELETE ON SP FROM JONES, BLAKE

REVOKE DBA FROM ADAMS
```

Figure 1.16   Examples of GRANT and REVOKE

CONCLUSION

This has been a necessarily very superficial look at some aspects of relational systems, using SQL/DS as a concrete example of such a system. Numerous topics have not been discussed at all, among them transactions and recovery, locking and concurrency, physical storage structures, system internals, system installation, and operational aspects. Although it is true that relational and nonrelational systems will probably differ somewhat in such areas, it is also true that those differences will tend to be less directly visible to the user. To put it another way, those areas are typically *less directly influenced* by the fact that the system is relational rather than nonrelational. Such topics have therefore been omitted from consideration in this brief paper.

For similar reasons, we have also not discussed any performance issues, at least not in any depth. Indeed, it is a major objective of relational systems to *separate* functional and performance questions so that they can be addressed independently of one another. Such separation allows simplicity and ease of use at the external (user) level—a primary emphasis in relational systems—while simultaneously providing a high degree of freedom at the internal (system) level. Performance then becomes a matter of (a) whether the system supports the necessary storage structures at the internal level and (b) whether it can translate high-level external requests into sequences of internal operations that are "as good as hand-code." There is no *intrinsic* reason why a relational system should perform any worse than any other type of system, in general.

There is, however, one "externals" topic that has also not been touched on at all, namely the problem of *relational database design*. How does the designer decide what tables should exist and what fields they should contain? Again, space precludes any detailed discussion of this question here; we therefore content ourselves with the following observations. First, designing a relational database is typically somewhat easier than designing some other kind of database (though in complex situations it is still a nontrivial problem). Second, theoretical work on "normalization" provides guidelines and discipline that can be used to advantage in practical applications. For more information, see the Further Reading section.

FURTHER READING

General

1. C. J. Date, *An Introduction to Database Systems*: *Volume I*, 4th edition (Reading, MA: Addison-Wesley, 1985).

2. C. J. Date, *An Introduction to Database Systems*: *Volume II* (Reading, MA: ·Addison-Wesley, 1982).

The Relational Model

3. E. F. Codd, "A Relational Model of Data for Large Shared Data Banks," *CACM* 13, No. 6 (June 1970).
   The classic original paper that first propounded the relational approach, introducing the notions of relational data structure and relational algebra.

4. E. F. Codd, "Relational Completeness of Data Base Sublanguages." In *Data Base Systems*: Courant Computer Science Symposia Series, Vol. 6 (Englewood Cliffs, NJ: Prentice-Hall, 1972).
   Contains a formal definition of relational algebra and relational calculus.

5. E. F. Codd, "A Data Base Sublanguage Founded on the Relational Calculus," *Proc. 1971 ACM SIGFIDET Workshop on Data Description, Access and Control* (November 1971).
   An informal introduction to the relational calculus of [4].

6. E. F. Codd, "Extending the Database Relational Model to Capture More Meaning," *ACM TODS* 4, No. 4 (December 1979).

Indicates how the relational model might be extended to incorporate more "semantic" notions such as entity types and subtypes, associations, properties, and characteristics.

7. E. F. Codd, "Relational Database: A Practical Foundation for Productivity," *CACM* 25, No. 2 (February 1982).

The paper that Codd presented on the occasion of his receiving the 1981 ACM Turing Award.

8. Reference [1], Chapters 11–14.

These chapters provide a tutorial treatment of relational data structure, relational integrity rules, relational algebra, and relational calculus, respectively.

Normalization Theory

9. E. F. Codd, "Further Normalization of the Data Base Relational Model." In *Data Base Systems:* Courant Computer Science Symposia Series, Vol. 6 (Englewood Cliffs, N.J: Prentice-Hall, 1972).

Contains a formal treatment of first, second, and third normal forms. A tutorial treatment of the same material is given in [10].

10. E. F. Codd, "Normalized Data Base Structure: A Brief Tutorial," *Proc. 1971 ACM SIGFIDET Workshop on Data Description, Access and Control* (November 1971).

11. R. Fagin, "Normal Forms and Relational Database Operators," *Proc. 1979 ACM SIGMOD International Conference on Management of Data* (May 1979).

The "last word" on normal forms obtainable via the relational algebra operations projection and (natural) join.

12. W. Kent, "A Simple Guide to Five Normal Forms in Relational Database Theory," *CACM* 26, No. 2 (February 1983).

An informal description of first, second, ..., fifth normal forms.

13. Reference [1], Chapter 17.

Provides a thorough tutorial treatment of normalization and related matters, up to and including the "projection/join normal form" of [11].

Comparison of the Relational Approach with Other Approaches

14. R. Rustin, ed. "Data Models: Data Structure Set vs. Relational," *Proc. 1974 ACM SIGMOD Workshop on Data Description, Access and Control,* Vol. II (May 1974).

The proceedings of a debate between proponents of the "data structure set" (i.e., network) and relational approaches to database management. (The two papers by Codd and Date are included in Part II of the present volume.)

System R

The IBM research prototype System R was the forerunner of the SQL/DS and DB2 products.

15. M. M. Astrahan et al., "System R: Relational Approach to Database Management," *ACM TODS* 1, No. 2 (June 1976).
A description of the overall system as originally planned.

16. M. W. Blasgen et al., "System R: An Architectural Overview," *IBM Sys. J.* 20, No. 1 (February 1981).
A description of the system as finally implemented.

17. D. D. Chamberlin et al., "A History and Evaluation of System R," *CACM* 24, No. 10 (October 1981).

SQL/DS and DB2

18. IBM Corporation, *SQL/Data System General Information*. IBM Form No. GH24-5012.

19. IBM Corporation, *IBM Database 2 General Information*. IBM Form No. GC26-4082.

20. Reference [1], Chapters 4–9, 18, and 19.
A greatly expanded version of the present paper (but expressed in terms of DB2 rather than SQL/DS).

An Informal Definition
of the Relational Model

ABSTRACT

This paper provides a brief tutorial on the theory underlying relational systems such as SQL/DS and DB2—namely, the relational model. The relational model is *a way of looking at data*; it can be regarded as a prescription for how data might be represented and how that representation might be manipulated. More specifically, the model is concerned with three aspects of data: data *structure*, data *integrity*, and data *manipulation*. The paper examines each of these three aspects in turn.

COMMENTS ON REPUBLICATION

As indicated in the "Comments on Republication" of the previous paper, products such as SQL/DS and DB2 typically do not support the relational model in its entirety. This tutorial is therefore included here as a more complete (and somewhat more theoretical) introduction to relational ideas. A

Based on Appendix A (pp. 265–275) of *A Guide to DB2,* by C. J. Date, copyright 1984 Addison-Wesley, Reading, Massachusetts. Reprinted with permission.

much fuller and more exhaustive treatment of the same material can be found in *An Introduction to Database Systems: Volume I,* 4th edition (Addison-Wesley, 1985). See also the paper ''A Formal Definition of the Relational Model,'' published later in this collection.

Note: The paper deliberately makes use of certain formal relational terms—most especially *relation* instead of table, *tuple* instead of record or row, and *attribute* instead of field or column. It uses the same sample database (suppliers and parts) as the previous paper. However, examples are generally expressed in terms of DB2 rather than SQL/DS (where it makes any difference).

RELATIONAL DATA STRUCTURE

The smallest unit of data in the relational model is the individual data value. Such values are considered to be *atomic*—that is, they are nondecomposable so far as the model is concerned. A *domain* is a set of such values, all of the same type; for example, the domain of supplier numbers is the set of all valid supplier numbers, the domain of shipment quantities is the set of all integers greater than zero and less than 10,000 (say). Thus domains are *pools of values*, from which the actual values appearing in attributes (columns) are drawn. The significance of domains is as follows: If two attributes draw their values from the same domain, then comparisons—and hence joins, unions, etc.—involving those two attributes probably make sense, because they are comparing like with like; conversely, if two attributes draw their values from different domains, then comparisons (etc.) involving those two attributes probably do not make sense. In SQL terms, for example, the query

```
SELECT  S.*, SP.*
FROM    S, SP
WHERE   S.S# = SP.S# ;
```

probably does make sense, whereas the query

```
SELECT  S.*, SP.*
FROM    S, SP
WHERE   S.STATUS = SP.QTY ;
```

probably does not.[1]

Note that domains are primarily conceptual in nature. They may or may not be explicitly stored in the database as actual sets of values. But

---

[1]Note, however, that SQL has no notion of domains in the sense of this paper. Both of the SELECT statements shown are legal queries in SQL.

they should be specified as part of the database definition (in a system that supports the concept at all—but most systems currently do not); and then each attribute definition should include a reference to the corresponding domain. A given attribute may have the same name as the corresponding domain or a different name. Obviously it must have a different name if any ambiguity would otherwise result (in particular, if two attributes in the same relation are both based on the same domain; see the definition of relation below, and note the phrase "not necessarily all distinct").

It is now possible to define the term "relation." A *relation* on domains *D1, D2, ..., Dn* (not necessarily all distinct) consists of a *heading* and a *body*. The heading consists of a fixed set of *attributes A1, A2, ..., An*, such that each attribute *Ai* corresponds to exactly one underlying domain *Di* ($i = 1,2,...,n$). The body consists of a time-varying set of *tuples*[2] where each tuple in turn consists of a set of (attribute-name : attribute-value) pairs ($Ai:vi$) ($i = 1,2,...,n$), one such pair for each attribute *Ai* in the heading. For any given pair ($Ai:vi$), *vi* is a value from the unique domain *Di* that is associated with the attribute *Ai*.

As an example, let us see how the supplier relation S of the suppliers-and-parts database (see Fig. 2.1) measures up to this definition.

The underlying domains for relation S are the domain of supplier numbers (D1, say), the domain of supplier names (D2), the domain of supplier status values (D3), and the domain of city names (D4). The heading of S

S	S#	SNAME	STATUS	CITY
	S1	Smith	20	London
	S2	Jones	10	Paris
	S3	Blake	30	Paris
	S4	Clark	20	London
	S5	Adams	30	Athens

P	P#	PNAME	COLOR	WEIGHT	CITY
	P1	Nut	Red	12	London
	P2	Bolt	Green	17	Paris
	P3	Screw	Blue	17	Rome
	P4	Screw	Red	14	London
	P5	Cam	Blue	12	Paris
	P6	Cog	Red	19	London

SP	S#	P#	QTY
	S1	P1	300
	S1	P2	200
	S1	P3	400
	S1	P4	200
	S1	P5	100
	S1	P6	100
	S2	P1	300
	S2	P2	400
	S3	P2	200
	S4	P2	200
	S4	P4	300
	S4	P5	400

Figure 2.1   The suppliers-and-parts database

---

[2]Usually pronounced to rhyme with "couples."

consists of the attributes S# (underlying domain D1), SNAME (domain D2), STATUS (domain D3), and CITY (domain D4). The body of S consists of a set of tuples (five tuples in Fig. 2.1, but this set varies with time as updates are made to the relation); and each tuple consists of a set of four (attribute-name : attribute-value) pairs, one such pair for each of the four attributes in the heading. For example, the tuple for supplier S1 consists of the pairs

```
( S#     :  'S1'      )
( SNAME  :  'Smith'   )
( STATUS :  20        )
( CITY   :  'London'  )
```

(though it is normal to elide the attribute names in informal contexts). And of course each attribute value does indeed come from the appropriate underlying domain; the value 'S1', for example, does come from the supplier number domain D1. So S is indeed a relation according to the definition.

Note carefully that when we draw a relation such as relation S as a table, as we did in Fig. 2.1, we are merely making use of a convenient method for representing the relation on paper. A table and a relation are not really the same thing, though in informal contexts it is convenient to assume that they are. For example, the rows of a table clearly have an ordering (from top to bottom), whereas the tuples of a relation do not (a relation is a mathematical *set*, and sets do not have any ordering in mathematics). Likewise, the columns of a table also have an ordering (from left to right), whereas the attributes of a relation do not.

Notice, too, that the underlying domains of a relation are "not necessarily all distinct." For an example of one where they are not, see the relation in Fig. 2.2, which includes two attributes both defined on the domain of city names (it is the relation resulting from the query "Find all pairs of cities such that a supplier in the first city supplies a part stored in the second city").

The value *n* (the number of attributes in the relation, or equivalently the number of underlying domains) is called the *degree* of the relation. A relation of degree one is called *unary*, a relation of degree two *binary*, a

```
------   ------
S.CITY   P.CITY
------   ------
London   London
London   Paris
London   Rome
Paris    London
Paris    Paris
```

Figure 2.2 Relation with two attributes sharing a common domain

relation of degree three *ternary*, ..., and a relation of degree *n n-ary*. In the suppliers-and-parts database, relations S, P, and SP have degrees 4, 5, and 3, respectively. The number of tuples in the relation is called the *cardinality* of that relation; the cardinalities of relations S, P, and SP of Fig. 2.1 are 5, 6, and 12, respectively. The cardinality of a relation changes with time, whereas the degree does not.

RELATIONAL DATA INTEGRITY

One important consequence of the definitions in the previous section is that *every relation has a primary key*. Since the body of a relation is a set, and sets by definition do not contain duplicate elements, it follows that (at any given time) no two tuples of a relation can be duplicates of each other. Let R be a relation with attributes $A1, A2, ..., An$. The set of attributes $K = (Ai,Aj,...,Ak)$ of R is said to be a *candidate key* of R if and only if it satisfies the following two time-independent properties:

1. *Uniqueness*:
   At any given time, no two distinct tuples of R have the same value for Ai, the same value for Aj, ..., and the same value for Ak.
2. *Minimality*:
   None of Ai, Aj, ..., Ak can be discarded from K without destroying the uniqueness property.

Every relation has at least one candidate key, because at least the combination of all of its attributes has the uniqueness property. For a given relation, one candidate key is (arbitrarily) designated as the *primary* key. The remaining candidate keys (if any) are called *alternate* keys.

Example: Suppose that supplier names and supplier numbers are both unique (no two suppliers have the same number or the same name). Then relation S has two candidate keys, S# and SNAME. Suppose S# is chosen as the primary key; SNAME then becomes an alternate key.

Now consider attribute S# of relation SP. It is clear that a given value for that attribute, say the supplier number S1, should be permitted to appear in the database only if that same value also appears as a value of the primary key S# of relation S (for otherwise the database cannot be considered to be in a state of integrity). An attribute such as SP.S# is said to be a *foreign key*. In general, a foreign key is an attribute (or attribute combination) of one relation $R2$ whose values are required to match those of the primary key of some relation $R1$ ($R1$ and $R2$ not necessarily distinct). Note that a foreign key and the corresponding primary key should be defined on the same underlying domain.

It is now possible to state the two integrity rules of the relational model. Note: These rules are *general*, in the sense that any database that conforms to the model is required to satisfy them. However, any specific database will have a set of additional specific rules that apply to it alone. For example, the suppliers-and-parts database may have a specific rule to the effect that shipment quantities must be in the range 1 to 9999, say. But such specific rules are outside the scope of the relational model *per se*.

1. *Entity integrity*:
   No attribute participating in the primary key of a base relation is allowed to accept null values.[3]

2. *Referential integrity*:
   If base relation *R2* includes a foreign key *FK* matching the primary key *PK* of some base relation *R1*, then every value of *FK* in *R2* must either (a) be equal to the value of *PK* in some tuple of *R1* or (b) be wholly null (i.e., each attribute value participating in that *FK* value must be null). *R1* and *R2* are not necessarily distinct.

The justification for the entity integrity rule is as follows:

1. Base relations correspond to entities in the real world. For example, base relation S corresponds to a set of suppliers in the real world.

2. By definition, entities in the real world are distinguishable—that is, they have a unique identification of some kind.

3. Primary keys perform the unique identification function in the relational model.

4. Thus, a primary key value that was null would be a contradiction in terms—in effect, it would be saying that there was some entity that had no *id*entity (i.e., did not exist). Hence the name "entity integrity."

As for the second rule ("referential integrity"), it is clear that a given foreign key value must have a matching primary key value in some tuple of the referenced relation if that foreign key value is nonnull. Sometimes, however, it is necessary to permit the foreign key to accept null values. Suppose, for example, that in a given company it is legal for some employee to be currently assigned to no department at all. For such an employee, the department number attribute (which is a foreign key) would have to be null in the tuple representing that employee in the database.

---

[3]A *base relation* corresponds to what SQL calls a base table—i.e., it is an independent, named relation (as opposed to, e.g., a view or the result of a retrieval). A *null value* is a value representing "information missing" or "property does not apply."

RELATIONAL DATA MANIPULATION

The manipulative part of the relational model consists of a set of operators known collectively as the *relational algebra*, together with a relational assignment operator which assigns the value of some arbitrary expression of the algebra to another relation. We discuss the algebra first.

Each operator of the relational algebra takes either one or two relations as its operand(s) and produces a new relation as its result. In his paper "Relational Completeness of Data Base Sublanguages" (published in *Data Base Systems*, Courant Computer Science Symposia Series, Vol. 6, Prentice-Hall, 1972), Codd originally defined eight such operators, two groups of four each: (1) the traditional set operations union, intersection, difference, and Cartesian product (all modified slightly to take account of the fact that their operands are relations, as opposed to arbitrary sets); and (2) the special relational operations select, project, join, and divide. The eight operations are shown symbolically in Fig. 2.3. Note: Despite what was said in the section on relational data structure, we assume in what follows that the left-to-right order of attributes within a relation *is* significant—not because it is necessary to do so, but because it simplifies the discussion.

Traditional Set Operations

Each of the traditional set operations takes two operands. For all except Cartesian product, the two operand relations must be *union-compatible*—that is, they must be of the same degree, n say, and the ith attribute of each ($i = 1,2,...,n$) must be based on the same domain (they do not have to have the same name).

- Union

  The union of two (union-compatible) relations A and B is the set of all tuples t belonging to either A or B (or both).
  SQL example:

```
SELECT S# FROM S
UNION
SELECT S# FROM SP ;
```

- Intersection

  The intersection of two (union-compatible) relations A and B is the set of all tuples t belonging to both A and B.
  SQL example:

```
SELECT S# FROM S
WHERE   EXISTS
      ( SELECT S# FROM SP
        WHERE   SP.S# = S.S# ) ;
```

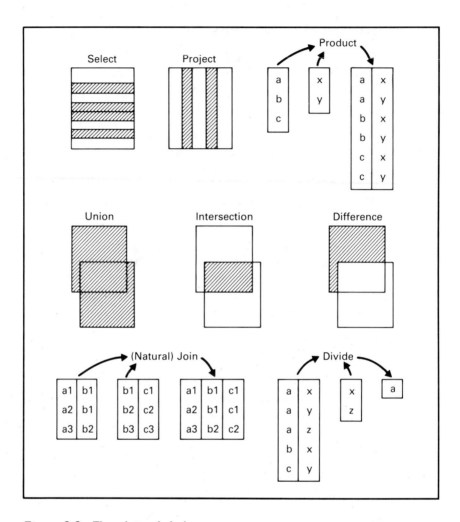

Figure 2.3 The relational algebra

- Difference

The difference between two (union-compatible) relations *A* and *B* is the set of all tuples *t* belonging to *A* and not to *B*.
SQL example:

```
SELECT S# FROM S
WHERE  NOT EXISTS
     ( SELECT S# FROM SP
       WHERE  SP.S# = S.S# ) ;
```

- Product

The product of two relations *A* and *B* is the set of all tuples *t* such that *t* is the concatenation of a tuple *a* belonging to *A* and a tuple *b* belonging to *B*.

SQL example:

```
SELECT  S.*, SP.*
FROM    S, SP ;
```

Special Relational Operations

- Selection

Let *theta* represent any valid scalar comparison operator (for example, $=$, $\sim=$, $>$, $>=$, etc.). The theta-selection of relation *A* on attributes *X* and *Y* is the set of all tuples *t* of *A* such that the predicate "*t.X theta t.Y*" evaluates to *true*. (Attributes *X* and *Y* should be defined on the same domain, and the operation *theta* must make sense for that domain.) A constant value may be specified instead of attribute *Y*. Thus, the theta-selection operator yields a "horizontal" subset of a given relation—that is, that subset of the tuples of the given relation for which a specified predicate is satisfied. Note: "Theta-selection" is often abbreviated to just "selection." But note that "selection" is not the same as the SELECT operator of SQL.

SQL example:

```
SELECT  *
FROM    S
WHERE   CITY ~= 'London' ;
```

- Projection

The projection operator yields a "vertical" subset of a given relation— that is, that subset obtained by selecting specified attributes and then eliminating redundant duplicate tuples within the attributes selected, if necessary.

SQL example:

```
SELECT DISTINCT COLOR, CITY
FROM    P ;
```

- Join

Let *theta* be as defined under "Selection" above. The theta-join of relation *A* on attribute *X* with relation *B* on attribute *Y* is the set of all tuples *t* such that *t* is the concatenation of a tuple *a* belonging to *A* and a tuple *b* belonging to *B* and the predicate "*a.X theta b.Y*" evaluates to *true*. (Attributes *A.X* and *B.Y* should be defined on the same domain, and the operation *theta* must make sense for that domain.)

SQL example:

```
SELECT  S.*, P.*
FROM    S, P
WHERE   S.CITY > P.CITY ;
```

If *theta* is equality, the join is called an equijoin. It follows from the definition that the result of an equijoin must include two identical attributes. If one of those two attributes is eliminated (which it can be via projection), the result is called the *natural* join. The unqualified term "join" is usually taken to mean the natural join.

- Division

In its simplest form (which is the only form discussed in this paper), the division operator divides a relation of degree two (the dividend) by a relation of degree one (the divisor), and produces a result relation of degree one (the quotient). Let the dividend (A) have attributes X and Y, and let the divisor (B) have attribute Y. Attributes $A.Y$ and $B.Y$ should be defined on the same domain. The result of dividing A by B (the quotient) is the relation C, with sole attribute X, such that every value x of $C.X$ appears as a value of $A.X$, and the pair of values (x,y) appears in A for *all* values y appearing in B.

SQL example:

```
SELECT DISTINCT S# FROM SP SP1
WHERE   NOT EXISTS
     ( SELECT P# FROM P
       WHERE   NOT EXISTS
            ( SELECT * FROM SP SP2
              WHERE  SP2.S# = SP1.S# AND SP2.P# = P.P# ) ) ;
```

In this example, the dividend is the projection of relation SP over attributes S# and P#, and the divisor is the projection of relation P over attribute P#. The quotient is a relation with one attribute (S#) that lists supplier numbers for suppliers that supply all parts.

It is worth mentioning that, of these eight operations, only five are primitive, namely selection, projection, product, union, and difference. The other three can be defined in terms of those five. For example, the natural join is a projection of a selection of a product. In practice, however, those other three operations (especially join) are so useful that a good case can be made for supporting them directly, even though they are not primitive.

Turning now to the relational assignment operation, the purpose of that operation is simply to allow the value of some algebraic expression—say a join—to be saved in some more or less permanent place. It can be simulated in SQL by means of the INSERT ... SELECT operation. For example, suppose relation XYZ has two attributes, S# and P#, and suppose also that it is currently empty (contains no tuples). The SQL statement

```
INSERT INTO XYZ ( S#, P# )
       SELECT S.S#, P.P#
       FROM   S, P
       WHERE  S.CITY = P.CITY ;
```

assigns the result of the SELECT (namely, a projection of a join) to the relation XYZ.

SUMMARY

By way of conclusion, Fig. 2.4 summarizes the major components of the relational model.

Data structure

  domains (values)
  n-ary relations (attributes, tuples)
  keys (candidate, primary, alternate, foreign)

Data integrity

  1. primary key values must not be null
  2. foreign key values must match primary key values
    (or be null)

Data manipulation

  relational algebra
    union, intersection, difference, product
    select, project, join, divide
  relational assignment

Figure 2.4 The relational model

3

Why Every Relation Should Have Exactly One Primary Key

ABSTRACT

The relational model requires every relation to have a single distinguished primary key. It has sometimes been proposed instead that relations should be permitted to have any number of (effectively interchangeable) "unique keys." The present paper argues against that proposal.

COMMENTS ON REPUBLICATION

This paper was originally written at the request of IBM, at a time when X3H2 (the American National Standards Database Committee) was considering incorporating primary key support into the SQL language. The views expressed are my own, however, not necessarily IBM's, and I take full responsibility for them.

Originally published under the title "Why Relations Should Have Exactly One Primary Key" as *American National Standards Database Committee (X3H2) Working Paper X3H2-84-118* (October 1984). Reprinted with permission of IBM.

33

DEFINITIONS

It is convenient to begin with definitions of the relevant portions of the relational model, in order to establish a precise framework for subsequent discussion. Note: I deliberately use the formal terms *relation*, *attribute*, and *tuple* in these definitions.[1] Informal equivalents: relation = table, attribute = column, tuple = row.

Primary, Candidate, and Alternate Keys

Let R be a relation with attributes $A1$, $A2$, ..., An. The set of attributes K = (Ai, Aj,..., Ak) of R is said to be a *candidate key* of R if and only if it satisfies the following two time-independent properties:

1. *Uniqueness*:
   At any given time, no two distinct tuples of R have the same value for Ai, the same value for Aj, ..., and the same value for Ak.
2. *Minimality*:
   None of Ai, Aj, ..., Ak can be discarded from K without destroying the uniqueness property.

   Every relation has at least one candidate key, because at least the combination of all of its attributes has the uniqueness property. For a given relation, one candidate key is (arbitrarily) designated as the *primary* key. Then the remaining candidate keys (if any) are called *alternate* keys.

Foreign Keys

A foreign key is an attribute (or attribute combination) in one relation $R2$ whose values are required to match those of the primary key of some relation $R1$ ($R1$ and $R2$ not necessarily distinct).

Integrity Rules

The relational model includes two general integrity rules, expressed in terms of primary and foreign keys. The rules are general in the sense that every database that claims to conform to the relational model is required to satisfy them.

1. *Entity integrity*:
   No attribute participating in the primary key of a base relation is allowed to accept null values.

---

[1]The definitions are taken from the previous paper ''An Informal Definition of the Relational Model.''

2. *Referential integrity*:

   If base relation *R2* includes a foreign key *FK* matching the primary key *PK* of some base relation *R1*, then every value of *FK* in *R2* must either (a) be equal to the value of *PK* in some tuple of *R1* or (b) be wholly null (i.e., each attribute value participating in that *FK* value must be null). *R1* and *R2* are not necessarily distinct.

Note that the rules refer specifically to *base relations* only.

A NOTE ON TERMINOLOGY

The term "primary key" should NOT be abbreviated to just "key." The term "key" has far too many meanings already. I would vote for *always* qualifying it, by primary, foreign, candidate, alternate, hash, index, parent, child, master, native, secondary, search, ordering, encryption, decryption, etc., as appropriate. However, if any of that multiplicity of keys does deserve to be called THE key, it is clearly the primary key. Unfortunately "key" (unqualified) is already used in many systems to mean something else.

WHY PRIMARY KEYS ARE IMPORTANT

Why are primary keys important? The answer is that they provide *the sole tuple-level addressing mechanism within the relational model*. That is, the *only* system-guaranteed way of pinpointing some individual tuple is via the combination (R,k), where R is the name of the containing relation and k is the primary key value for the tuple concerned. Primary key values are used elsewhere in the database (as values of foreign keys) to serve as *references* to the tuples identified by those values. It follows, therefore, that primary keys are *absolutely fundamental* to the operation of the overall relational model, for exactly the same reason that main memory addresses are fundamental to the operation of the underlying machine. It also follows that a system that has no knowledge of primary keys is bound to display behavior on occasion that is not "truly relational."

Note, incidentally, that primary keys are crucial to the database design process. The database *design* will include explicit primary (and foreign) key specifications. It is therefore desirable that the database *definition* should do likewise.

Furthermore, note that an understanding of primary keys (and foreign keys) is required in order to support the updating of views correctly. (Most systems' rules for updating views are pretty ad hoc at present.) It follows that a general integrity support mechanism (along the lines of CREATE

CONSTRAINT, "assertions," etc.) is probably not adequate for primary and foreign key support.

THE CURRENT X3H2 POSITION

It is apparently the current X3H2 position that relations should be permitted to have any number (including zero, I presume) of effectively interchangeable "unique keys." For example, given the relation:

```
EMP ( EMP#, SS#, ENAME, DEPT#, SALARY )
```

where EMP# and SS# (social security number) are both "unique," it should be permissible to use those two attributes interchangeably as the addressing mechanism for EMPs—in particular, to allow a given foreign key referencing EMPs to do so via either EMP# values or via SS# values, as in the following examples:

```
JOBHIST ( EMP#, DATE, JOB )

BENEFIT ( SS#, DATE, PAYMENT )
```

It is also argued that security constraints may prohibit users of job history information from even seeing social security numbers and likewise users of benefits information from seeing employee numbers. Thus it is suggested that allowing "multiple unique keys" provides both more flexibility and more function than the original relational model.

Note: From this point forward, I will use the term "principal key" to mean a "unique key" that can be used as the addressing mechanism for a given relation (I most definitely want to avoid the terminology "multiple primary keys," which only serves to muddy a term that is currently well-defined). In the relational model the only principal key is the primary key. The X3H2 proposal is that any candidate key can be a principal key, and that a relation is not limited to having just one.

POSITION STATEMENT

It is my position that every relation should have exactly one principal key, namely the primary key. (Of course, if that position is accepted, the "principal key" terminology just introduced can immediately be dropped again.)

JUSTIFICATION

Note 1: Although it is my belief that every relation should have (a) at least one principal key and also (b) at most one, the main purpose of this paper is to argue only the second of these two points.

Note 2: I should mention that I have discussed the arguments that follow in some detail with Dr. Codd, originator of the relational model, and he is in full support of my position.

1. The X3H2 proposal is introducing a new concept and therefore requires a new term ("principal key" or something equivalent). In fact, it presumably also needs a term for a candidate key that is not a principal key ("non-principal key"?)—or does the proposal require that *all* candidate keys be considered principal keys? Either way, the existing (well-defined) relational terms—viz., primary key and alternate key—should *not* be taken over and their meanings bastardized. Thus, one (minor) argument in favor of my position is simply that it involves fewer terms.

2. Second, note that Integrity Rule 1 (entity integrity) would have to be extended to apply to all principal keys. The argument is exactly the same as the argument that justifies the rule for the primary key in the first place (see below): If a principal key is allowed to take on null values, then it isn't an addressing mechanism (i.e., it isn't a principal key). For example, consider the two EMP tuples shown below (assuming for the moment that there is only one principal key, namely EMP#):

```
          ----   -----   -----   ------
  EMP     EMP#   ENAME   DEPT#   SALARY
          ----   -----   -----   ------
          E1     e       d            s
          null   e       d            s
```

The example illustrates the denotation problem that Integrity Rule 1 was designed to avoid: Is there one employee here or two? (Answer: Don't know. As a result, the SQL query "SELECT COUNT(*) FROM EMP" would not be guaranteed to return the correct number of employees.) And note too that the same problem arises, in a more extreme form, if we replace E1 in the example by null. Therefore we do not allow EMP# to accept null values.

Note, moreover, that a rule to the effect that *at least one* principal key must have a nonnull value (in any given tuple) also does not work. For consider the following example:

```
          ----   ----   -----   -----   ------
  EMP     EMP#   SS#    ENAME   DEPT#   SALARY
          ----   ----   -----   -----   ------
          E1     null   e       d            s
          null   S1     e       d            s
```

One employee or two?

Note finally that in the real world social security numbers *can* be null (you don't have to have one). Moreover, it is also possible to have more than one! In other words, the standard example supporting the "multiple principal keys" position in fact breaks down.

3. A little philosophy: Databases are supposed to represent real-world entities. Entities in the real world are distinguishable (i.e., uniquely identifiable); thus, their representatives in the database must also be distinguishable. In the relational model the unique identification function is performed by primary keys. The discipline of using the same symbol to identify a given entity everywhere it is referenced in the database is a sound one: It allows the system to recognize the fact that those references do in fact all refer to the same thing. In particular, it allows operations such as join (which of necessity must work by matching *symbols*) to behave as if they actually matched *entities*—i.e., they can more closely reflect the true semantics of the underlying situation. To illustrate this point, consider the EMP#-SS# example again. Note that although JOBHIST and BENEFIT both include references to employees—i.e., are both related to employees, and therefore are related to each other—they cannot be directly joined without going through EMP as an intermediary.

4. Following on from the previous point: Consider the query (or "meta-query"):

Which relations refer to employees?

(a simple example of a query that might be issued by a user who is trying to discover the structure of the database). If employees are identified uniformly throughout the database by employee number, the query can be expressed as a simple catalog interrogation: "Which relations include an EMP# attribute?" If, on the other hand, they are identified by employee number in some relations and social security number in others, the catalog interrogation becomes correspondingly more complex. In general, the user in the example would have to know *all* principal keys for employees.

Note, too, that the query "Find all references in the database to employee *x*" also becomes quite complicated (even if we know that *x* is an employee number and not a social security number, or the other way around; it becomes much worse if it might be either). In fact, the phrase "employee *x*," in and of itself, tends to suggest that entities naturally have some single, well-defined identifier in the real world.

5. The security argument (more philosophy): It seems to me extremely unreasonable to suggest that a given user might be allowed to know that some entity is represented in the database, might even be allowed to see that ent-

ity's representative in the database, but might *not* be allowed to see that entity's primary identifier. If (for example) some user is to be allowed to see employees but not their social security numbers, then that fact in itself is precisely an argument for not choosing "social security number" as the primary key. And if *every* candidate key for a given relation needs to be hidden from some legitimate user of that relation, then an "artificial" (surrogate, freely visible) primary key can and should be introduced.

A real-world example to support the foregoing argument: There are certainly situations—for example, in a court case—where the identity of a witness, let us say, needs to be concealed while the existence of that witness, and certain properties of that witness, are certainly not concealed. But then what we do is invent a name ("Mr. X") for that witness, so that we can refer to him (or her). And that invented name is precisely a surrogate in the sense of the previous paragraph. Indeed, a good case could be made that familiar identifiers such as "employee number," "part number," "license number," etc., are all in fact nothing but surrogates in this sense: They are assigned by the system, have (or should have) no intrinsic meaning, are carefully controlled to ensure that they are unique and nonnull, etc.—except that today the "system" that exercises all these necessary controls is typically not a DBMS but some manual system.

Finally, it is virtually impossible—I would argue that it is *completely* impossible—to talk about some person or thing without a name for that person or thing.

6. The foregoing paragraphs show why it is my belief that insisting on a single primary key does not really take any representational power away from the user (equivalently, that allowing multiple principal keys does not really add any such power). Occam's Razor (peculiarly appropriate in this context, incidentally: its original formulation was "Entities should not be multiplied beyond necessity"!) would therefore argue in favor of single primary keys.

Note, too, that if we can agree on single primary keys now, there is always the possibility of extending to multiple principal keys (if desirable) at some future time. And note, moreover, that this argument does not apply in the opposite direction: Once we are committed to a standard that says systems must allow multiple principal keys, a system that permits only a single primary key will forever be nonconforming. Requiring support in a proposed standard for multiple principal keys therefore seems inappropriate—and also rather unwise, since as yet we do not fully understand all the implications of such support (for example, what are the effects on the updatability of views?).

In conclusion: A good general principle is: Don't complicate the model (or system) out of proportion to the increase in function gained. The complexity affects everybody, not just the few people who can benefit. In the case at hand, the increase in functionality seems marginal, to say the least; the increase in complexity, by contrast, is significant, and indeed its full extent is certainly unknown.

4

Referential Integrity

ABSTRACT

The problem of referential integrity is discussed and a proposal for dealing with it in a relational framework is described in some detail. The proposal is consistent with a more general integrity scheme also sketched briefly in the paper. The referential integrity aspects of DBTG are analyzed in terms of this proposal.

COMMENTS ON REPUBLICATION

The preceding papers in this collection have referred several times already to the concept of referential integrity. That concept has always been an integral part of the relational model. However, relational products have historically always been rather weak in this area; at the time of writing, moreover, they still are (for the most part), though some signs of improvement are beginning to appear.

The original intent of this paper was thus to provide a basis for implementing referential integrity in a relational system. I now feel that the concrete approach proposed is perhaps a little *too* general-purpose, for rea-

Copyright 1981 IEEE. Reprinted, with permission, from *Proc. 7th International Conference on Very Large Data Bases* (Cannes, France, September 9–11, 1981), pp. 2–12.

sons that are explained in the paper (in the form of added footnotes). However, I believe the ideas are still reasonably valid overall. I also feel that the paper is worth republishing as documentation of the evolution of the foreign key concept, from its first definition in Codd's original paper to its final accepted form.

Regarding the "signs of improvement" alluded to above: I regret that (so far as I am aware) there is still no system that does a completely adequate job on referential integrity:

- First, there is apparently no system that permits all the combinations of options that seem to be necessary in practice.

- Second, I know of only one or two systems that place the support where it logically belongs, which is down in the base DBMS, at the level of the base relation definitions. Other systems attempt to place it at some higher level—bundling it with the view definition mechanism, or implementing it as part of a data entry subsystem, or providing application generator options to allow the construction of user applications that will in turn enforce the constraints. While each of these approaches is better than nothing, the fact remains that they are all architecturally unsound. (The basic problem in every case is that users can enter the system at a lower level and thus bypass the constraints. There is also the point that it may be more difficult at this higher level to avoid the specification of conflicting constraints.)

- Third, even the few systems I know that do place the support at the correct level (a) do not adequately distinguish referential integrity from other kinds, and (b) do not provide for the specification of the various compensating actions (cascade delete, etc.) that are needed in practice.

Note: A concrete proposal for supporting referential integrity in SQL specifically is outlined in the paper "A Practical Approach to Database Design" in Part IV of this book.

INTRODUCTION

We are concerned in this paper with the problem of referential integrity in a relational database. The problem of referential integrity is the problem of ensuring that the database in question satisfies a set of predefined *referential constraints*, and is an important special case of the general database integrity problem. Generally speaking, referential constraints arise whenever one relation includes references to another, as for example in the case of an EMPLOYEE relation that includes references, via its DEPT# attribute, to some DEPARTMENT relation; the constraint in this example would typically be that every value of the DEPT# attribute appearing in a tuple of the EMPLOYEE relation must occur as the value of the DEPT# attribute in some corresponding tuple of the DEPARTMENT relation.

The referential integrity problem is of course well known, and partial solutions to it have been provided in various nonrelational systems. In IMS, for example, certain referential constraints are built into the hierarchic data structure itself, and others can be specified by means of the so-called logical database insert/update/delete rules [10]. The "set type" construct together with the notion of membership class performs a similar function in DBTG [1]. While it is true that these solutions *are* only partial, and the approach of building constraints into the data structure itself can lead to problems of its own [11], it is a fact that these systems do at least tackle the problem, whereas most relational systems (at the time of writing) do not. Various proposals have been made for dealing with *completely general* constraints in a relational framework (see, e.g., reference [9]), but (a) little has been done to implement such proposals, and (b) such proposals typically do not recognize the significance of referential integrity as an important special case. The purpose of this paper, then, is to examine this special case in some depth, and in particular to present a specific language in which referential constraints can be expressed in a relational environment—at the same time not losing sight of the fact that referential integrity *is* only a special case.

STRUCTURE OF THE PAPER

The overall structure of the paper is as follows. We begin by examining the general concept of referential integrity in the relational model. Codd, in reference [3], proposed a rather abstract "principle of referential integrity" as an integral component of the basic relational model (that is, a database is required to conform to that principle in order to qualify as "fully relational"). Our examination of these ideas falls into three parts:

1. An explanation of Codd's original proposal;

2. Some criticisms of that proposal, followed by a correspondingly revised formulation (this revision, the result of several discussions between Codd and the present writer, is also given in [6], but without the rationale);

3. Certain further comments on the revision. These further comments in turn fall into three broad categories:

(a) An additional criticism of the proposal, considered purely as an abstract principle;

(b) Some further criticisms from a more pragmatic viewpoint;

(c) An identification of certain important features that, though legiti-

mately excluded from the abstract formulation, are nevertheless required in any concrete realization of the principle.

The foregoing analysis is then followed by the most significant part of
the paper, namely, a concrete proposal for a language for dealing with referential integrity in a relational framework, which overcomes the objections identified under 3(a) and 3(b) above on the one hand, and meets the
requirements identified under 3(c) above on the other. The proposal is compatible with a more general scheme, also sketched briefly in the paper, for
expressing integrity constraints of arbitrary complexity. The paper concludes with a short discussion of the *reference graph* and (for interest) a
brief analysis of the referential integrity aspects of DBTG [1] in terms of
the proposal.

Readers are assumed to be familiar with relational database concepts,
in particular with the notions of *relation*, *domain*, *attribute*, *tuple*, *primary
key*, and *candidate key*. A tutorial treatment of this material can be found
in [6].

REFERENTIAL INTEGRITY IN THE RELATIONAL MODEL

Codd's original formulation of a principle of referential integrity [3] runs
as follows. First, we define a *primary domain* to be any domain on which
some single-attribute primary key is defined. For example, consider a database concerning suppliers (S), parts (P), and shipments (SP), with definition:

```
DOMAIN S#        ...
DOMAIN NAME      ...
DOMAIN STATUS    ...
DOMAIN LOCATION ...
DOMAIN P#        ...
DOMAIN COLOR     ...
DOMAIN WEIGHT    ...
DOMAIN QTY       ...

RELATION S ( S#        : DOMAIN S#,
             SNAME     : DOMAIN NAME,
             STATUS    : DOMAIN STATUS,
             CITY      : DOMAIN LOCATION )
         PRIMARY KEY ( S# )
         ALTERNATE KEY ( SNAME )

RELATION P ( P#        : DOMAIN P#,
             PNAME     : DOMAIN NAME,
             COLOR     : DOMAIN COLOR,
             WEIGHT    : DOMAIN WEIGHT,
             CITY      : DOMAIN LOCATION )
         PRIMARY KEY ( P# )

RELATION SP ( S#       : DOMAIN S#,
              P#       : DOMAIN P#,
              QTY      : DOMAIN QTY )
          PRIMARY KEY ( S#,P# )
```

In this database, S# and P# are the (only) primary domains. Note that the database definition includes a specification of primary and alternate keys. (An alternate key is a candidate key that is not the primary key.) By definition, no attribute that participates in the primary key of a base relation is allowed to take on null values.

Now we require all relations in the database to obey the following rule.

Referential integrity (Codd)
Let relation R1 have a multiattribute primary key. If attribute A of that multiattribute primary key is defined on primary domain D, then, at all times, for each value k of A in R1 there must exist a relation R2 in the database with primary key K defined on D, such that k occurs as a value of K in R2.

A relation such as R1 in this rule is a *referencing* relation, a relation such as R2 is a *referenced* relation. Attribute R1.A is a *referential attribute*.[1] Given the suppliers-and-parts database, for example, relation SP is a referencing relation, relations S and P are referenced relations; every value of the referential attribute SP.S# must occur as a value of the primary key of S (i.e., S.S#), and every value of the referential attribute SP.P# must occur as a value of the primary key of P (i.e., P.P#).

As suggested earlier, however, the foregoing version of the referential integrity rule is unsatisfactory for a number of reasons. We therefore proceed to make a number of modifications to that rule, indicating our reasons as we go.

- First, we allow a referential attribute to be *any* attribute that is defined on a primary domain, not just one that is a component of a multiattribute primary key. The reason for this change is that the original definition does not cater for cases such as the EMPLOYEE – DEPARTMENT example quoted earlier (attribute EMPLOYEE. DEPT# is not a component of the primary key of EMPLOYEE, which is EMPLOYEE.EMP#).

- Second, we change the definition of primary domain (slightly). A given domain may *optionally* be designated as primary if and only if there exists a relation in the database with (single-attribute) primary key defined on that domain. Thus we may *choose* to designate domains S# and P# as primary (by explicitly stating PRIMARY in their definitions):

```
DOMAIN S# ... PRIMARY
   ...
DOMAIN P# ... PRIMARY
```

---

[1]The preferred term is *foreign key*. However, we stay with the term "referential attribute" here, since that was the term used in the paper when it was first published.

To illustrate the need for this change, we extend our example to include

```
DOMAIN PERCENT ...

RELATION CITYTAX ( CITY   : DOMAIN LOCATION,
                   TAX    : DOMAIN PERCENT )
           PRIMARY KEY ( CITY )
```

with the meaning that shipments by suppliers in the indicated city are subject to the indicated tax (i.e., percentage markup on the shipment value; to make the example more complete we ought perhaps to include a SHIPMENT-VALUE attribute in the SP relation). We also suppose that many cities have a markup of zero, and therefore choose to include tuples in CITYTAX only for cities for which TAX is nonzero; thus, in general, there may be CITY values in relation S that do not appear in relation CITYTAX. (We do not mean to suggest that this is a good design, only that it is a feasible one.) We therefore choose not to designate LOCATION as a primary domain, because otherwise relation S would violate the referential integrity rule (modified as indicated in the preceding paragraph).

- Third, we allow the referential attribute to take on null values (in the absence of any explicit constraint to the contrary; if the referential attribute is in fact a component of the primary key, then of course that fact in itself prohibits the appearance of nulls). Then we require only that *nonnull* values of the referential attribute R1.A occur as values of the primary key (R2.K) in relation R2. The reason for this change is that, e.g., not every employee need be assigned to a department, and we therefore need some way of handling those that are not. As another example, suppose that the EMPLOYEE relation also includes a MGR# attribute (manager number); then the value of MGR# within any given tuple is required to be equal to the value of EMP# in some other tuple of the relation, *except* for the case of the tuple representing the president of the company, for which MGR# will be null. Note, incidentally, that in this latter example the referencing relation and the referenced relation are one and the same.

Thus we wind up with the following rule.

Referential integrity (Codd, modified)
Let attribute A of relation R1 be defined on primary domain D. Then, at all times, each value of A in R1 must be either (a) null, or (b) equal to k, say, where k is the primary key value of some tuple in some relation R2 (R1 and R2 not necessarily distinct) with primary key K defined on D.

To handle
recursion,
(Prerequisite
courses),

Note that at least one such R2 must exist, by the definition of primary domain. Note, too, that the constraint is trivially satisfied if A is the primary key of R1. An attribute such as A is sometimes called a *foreign key*. Note, however, that this definition of foreign key is not quite the same as that originally given by Codd.[2]

Codd proposed that his referential integrity rule (which we now take to be modified as indicated above) be considered a component of the basic relational model, just as the relational data structure and the relational algebra are components of that model [3]. That is, a database that does not conform to the rule cannot be considered "fully relational" in the sense of [3]. However, the rule is very general, just as (for example) the definition of relational data structure is very general. For any specific database, a more specific set of rules is obviously needed, just as a specific definition of the relations actually in that database is also needed. Also, the general rule still suffers from a further intrinsic limitation (1. below) and two additional shortcomings (2. and 3. below) when viewed in a purely pragmatic light:

1. First, there may be situations in which the referential attribute R1.A is itself the primary key of R1 and we wish to insist that there exist a *distinct* referenced relation R2 (as pointed out earlier, if R1.A is the primary key of R1, then the rule is trivially satisfied, but that may not be enough). As an example, consider the CITYTAX relation introduced earlier, in which CITY is the primary key. Suppose that we also have

```
RELATION C ( CITY   : DOMAIN LOCATION,
             ...    : ..... )
         PRIMARY KEY ( CITY )
```

---

[2]Nor is it quite the same as the preferred current definition. For the record, Codd's original definition [2] was as follows (paraphrasing slightly):

"An attribute or attribute combination of relation R is called a *foreign key* if it is not the primary key of R but its elements are values of the primary key of some relation S (the possibility that R and S are identical is not excluded)."

The preferred current definition is actually quite close to the original in spirit:

"An attribute or attribute combination of base relation R is called a *foreign key* if and only if, for all time, its nonnull elements are required to be values of the primary key of some base relation S (R and S not necessarily distinct)."

Note that this definition includes no mention of primary domains. Note, too, that it requires there to be a *single* corresponding relation S; it does not merely say that for each value of the foreign key there must exist *some* relation containing a matching primary key value. The proposals described later in this paper are less demanding than this current definition, but (as indicated in the "Comments on Republication") I now feel that those proposals were probably a little *too* general in this respect.

and suppose that every CITY value appearing in CITYTAX is required to appear in relation C also.

2. Second, the general rule insists that each referenced relation have a single-attribute primary key (i.e., "references" can be made only to relations having such a primary key). Thus, for example, given the relations

```
COURSE    ( COURSE#, TITLE )
          PRIMARY KEY ( COURSE# )

OFFERING ( COURSE#, OFF#, DATE, LOCATION )
          PRIMARY KEY ( COURSE#, OFF# )

STUDENT   ( COURSE#, OFF#, EMP#, GRADE )
          PRIMARY KEY ( COURSE#, OFF#, EMP# )
```

(domain specifications omitted for brevity), the rule handles references from OFFERINGs to COURSEs but not from STUDENTs to OFFERINGs.

Aside: While it may be good discipline to insist that all primary keys be single-attribute (i.e., to insist that an "artificial" single-attribute primary key be introduced whenever the "real" primary key is composite), the fact is that many databases do not adhere to such a discipline today.

3. Third, the general rule relies on the notion of domain, which, important though it is for relational theory, is unfortunately not supported in most current implementations.

As for the question of the need for more specific rules in any specific situation:

4. Given a referencing relation R1, the general rule states merely that a referenced relation R2 must exist—it does not *identify* that relation. Indeed, it actually allows there to be more than one such, to cater for the situation where, for example, suppliers are represented by several distinct relations, one for each supplier city, and shipments can refer to any of them; in other words, a given referencing relation may be allowed to have *alternative* referenced relations. But of course in any specific database it is essential to know exactly which relations are referenced by a given referencing relation.

5. The general rule does not specify what the system should do in the face of an attempted violation. For example, suppose that (a) some user attempts to change the DEPT# value in some tuple of the DEPARTMENT relation, (b) there exist one or more EMPLOYEE tuples having the current value as the value of their DEPT# attribute, and (c) the system is aware of the EMPLOYEE – DEPARTMENT reference. Then there are three possible courses of action:

- Reject the update;
- Accept the update and "cascade" it to the corresponding EMPLOYEE tuples (i.e., update the DEPT# attribute in those tuples accordingly);
- Accept the update but set the DEPT# attribute in the corresponding EMPLOYEE tuples to null.

Which action is required will of course depend on the policy of the organization that the database is serving.

We therefore propose a specific language for the formulation of specific referential integrity rules that overcomes objections 1., 2., and 3., and also satisfies requirements 4. and 5. Before getting into details, however, we give in outline a scheme for expressing integrity rules of arbitrary complexity, in order to establish a framework for our proposal.

A LANGUAGE PROPOSAL FOR GENERAL INTEGRITY RULES

The integrity rule proposal outlined in this section is taken from [8]. It is loosely based on the language UDL [7], in particular in its use of *cursors*. A cursor in UDL is an object whose value is (normally) the address of some specific record in the database. (UDL uses the terms *record* and *field* rather than *tuple* and *attribute*.) The cursor is said to *point to* the record concerned. The expression "C→R" refers to the specific instance of record type R that cursor C is currently pointing to; similarly, the expression "C→R.F" refers to the specific instance of field type F within that specific record. Each cursor is constrained to point to records of exactly one record type. Each record type has exactly one *default* cursor (identified in the declaration of that record type); the expressions "C→R" and "C→R.F" can be abbreviated to just "R" and "R.F", respectively, in which case the default cursor for R is assumed to be the qualifying cursor in each case.

Aside: Within the proposal at hand, in fact, cursor-qualified references such as C→R and C→R.F appear only as *bound variables* or parameters. See [7] for more details of cursors in UDL, both in their role as explicit position-holders in the database and in their role as bound-variable designators.

For purposes of reference, we first give a grammar for our general integrity rule proposal, and then follow it with some examples. The grammar makes use of the convenient "commalist" notation introduced in [11]; loosely speaking, the syntactic category "*xyz*-commalist" (for arbitrary *xyz*) represents a list of *xyz*'s separated by commas. The reader may like to skip the grammar on a first reading. Further details and additional examples are given in [8].

Note: The concrete syntax used in this paper was chosen purely to illustrate the concepts, and can legitimately be criticized on a number of points of detail. An actual implementation may of course choose to modify it in any of a variety of ways.

```
integrity-rule
    ::=  label : [ trigger-condition-commalist : ]
                   constraint
                 [ ; ¦ ELSE violation-action ]

trigger-condition
    ::=  WHEN COMMITTING
         ¦ BEFORE before-change
         ¦ AFTER  after-change

before-change
    ::=  INSERTING record-name [ FROM structure-name ]
         ¦ UPDATING record-parameter [ FROM structure-name ]
         ¦ UPDATING field-parameter [ FROM [ structure-name .]
                                             element-name ]
         ¦ DELETING record-parameter

after-change
    ::=  INSERTING record-name
         ¦ UPDATING record-parameter
         ¦ UPDATING field-parameter
         ¦ DELETING record-parameter

record-parameter
    ::=  [ cursor-name -> ] record-name

field-parameter
    ::=  [ cursor-name -> ] record-name . field-name

constraint
    ::=  predicate    (Ex. <,>,=, <?, etc),

violation-action
    ::=  executable-unit
```

Examples

The examples in this section are intended to illustrate general integrity constraints, not referential ones. The first four should be broadly self-explanatory.

```
EX1 : AFTER INSERTING SC->S,
      AFTER UPDATING SC->S.STATUS
      /* i.e., after either of the foregoing operations */ :
      SC->S.STATUS > 0
      ELSE
          DO ;
              append return code meaning "rule EX1 violated"
                              to RETURN_CODES ;
              reject operation ;
          END ;
```

If cursor SC is the default cursor for S and if we make some fairly obvious assumptions regarding default trigger-conditions and default violation-actions, then we can abbreviate rule EX1 to simply

```
EX1 : S.STATUS > 0 ;
```

In the remaining examples we omit as much explicit specification as possible.

```
EX2 : P.CITY IN ('London','Paris','Rome') ;

EX3 : BEFORE DELETING SP :
      SP.QTY = 0 ;

EX4 : BEFORE UPDATING S.STATUS FROM NEW_STATUS :
      NEW_STATUS > S.STATUS ;
```

Purely for purposes of illustration, we give an example of a *deferred* rule—"the sum of all QTY values in relation SP must be less than $10**7$" (perhaps not a very realistic example, because it could equally well be specified as a nondeferred rule):

```
EX5 : WHEN COMMITTING :
      SETSUM (SP.QTY) < 10**7 ;
```

Rule EX5 is checked at commit time (i.e., "end of transaction") for any transaction that creates, destroys, or changes an instance of SP.QTY.

KEY CONSTRAINTS

Example 6 below specifies that attribute S# is the primary key for relation S.

```
EX6 : BEFORE INSERTING S    FROM NEW_S,
      BEFORE UPDATING  S.S# FROM NEW_S.S# :
      ~ EXISTS (S WHERE S.S# = NEW_S.S#)
      AND ~ IS_NULL (NEW_S.S#) ;
```

The constraint part of this rule can be read as "There does not exist an S tuple such that the S# value in that S tuple is equal to NEW_S.S#, and furthermore NEW_S.S# is not null." It is clear that this formulation is rather clumsy (albeit precise). For both usability and ease of implementation, therefore, we choose to "special case" primary key constraints, specifying them as shown earlier by means of a PRIMARY KEY clause in the definition of the relation concerned. However, that clause should be seen merely as a shorthand for a formulation such as that in the example above. Similar remarks apply to the ALTERNATE KEY clause.

REFERENTIAL CONSTRAINTS

We give an example to show how referential constraints might be expressed in the general syntax shown so far (all cursors now shown explicitly for clarity).

```
EX7A : AFTER INSERTING SPC->SP,
       AFTER UPDATING  SPC->SP.S# :
          EXISTS (SC->S WHERE SC->S.S# = SPC->SP.S#) ;

EX7B : BEFORE DELETING SC->S,
       BEFORE UPDATING SC->S.S# :
          ~ EXISTS (SPC->SP WHERE SPC->SP.S# = SC->S.S#) ;
```

These rules state that:

(a) When an SP tuple is created or the S# attribute of an SP tuple is updated, there must already exist an S tuple having an S# value equal to the new SP.S# value;

(b) When an S tuple is deleted or the S# attribute of an S tuple is updated, there must not exist any SP tuples having an S# value equal to the old S.S# value.

If either (a) or (b) is violated, the offending operation is rejected (default violation-action for rules EX7A and EX7B). As indicated earlier, however, other violation-actions might be desirable in some situations; rules EX7A and EX7B can be reformulated to handle these cases if required. We do not go into details here.

(Note: Rules analogous to EX7A and EX7B are of course also required relating to the referential attribute SP.P#.)

We give another example in order to illustrate the case in which "R1 and R2 are not distinct" (see the modified version of Codd's rule, earlier).

```
EX8A : AFTER INSERTING E1->EMPLOYEE,
       AFTER UPDATING  E1->EMPLOYEE.MGR# :
          EXISTS (E2->EMPLOYEE WHERE E2->EMPLOYEE.EMP#
                                   = E1->EMPLOYEE.MGR#) ;

EX8B : BEFORE DELETING E2->EMPLOYEE,
       BEFORE UPDATING E2->EMPLOYEE.EMP# :
          ~ EXISTS (E1->EMPLOYEE WHERE E1->EMPLOYEE.MGR#
                                     = E2->EMPLOYEE.EMP#) ;
```

Note that rule EX8A as formulated here does not permit EMPLOYEE.MGR# to be null; if this were to be allowed we should have to add the specification "OR IS_NULL (E1→EMPLOYEE.MGR#)" to the constraint in EX8A. (It does however permit a given tuple to have the same value for EMP# and MGR#, so that the "company president" tuple could show the president as reporting to him- or herself.)

As with key constraints (discussed earlier), the general syntax does the job but is very clumsy. Again, therefore, we introduce a special-case syntax,[3] both to improve usability and to improve the chances of the system special-casing the implementation (probably important for such an important case):

```
referential-constraint
    ::=  label : dependency
                [ nulls-rule ]
                [ delete-rule ]
                [ update-rule ]

dependency
    ::=  referential-attribute IDENTIFIES referenced-spec

referential-attribute
    ::=  attribute-spec

attribute-spec
    ::=  relation-name . attributes

attributes
    ::=  attribute-name ¦ ( attribute-name-commalist )

referenced-spec
    ::=  primary-key ¦ [ quantifier ] ( primary-key-commalist )

primary-key
    ::=  attribute-spec

quantifier
    ::=  EXACTLY ONE OF ¦ AT LEAST ONE OF ¦ ALL OF

nulls-rule
    ::=  NULLS [ NOT ] ALLOWED

delete-rule
    ::=  DELETING effect

effect
    ::=  CASCADES ¦ NULLIFIES ¦ RESTRICTED

update-rule
    ::=  UPDATING effect
```

Explanations

These explanations are deliberately intended to be comprehensive and may not be fully understood on a first reading. The reader may like to skip straight to the examples that follow.

---

[3]This portion of the paper differs on a number of points of detail from the version originally published.

1. A referential-constraint consists of a label, a dependency, an optional nulls-rule (default NULLS NOT ALLOWED), an optional delete-rule (default DELETING RESTRICTED), and an optional update-rule (default UPDATING RESTRICTED).

2. A dependency consists of a referential-attribute and a referenced-spec, separated by the keyword IDENTIFIES. The referential-attribute designates a referential attribute in a referencing relation; referential attributes are allowed to be composite. The referenced-spec designates either the primary key of a single corresponding referenced relation, or a set of primary keys (corresponding to a set of referenced relations) preceded by an optional quantifier (default EXACTLY ONE OF). Referential-attributes and primary-keys are each specified as a relation-name, followed by a period (separator), followed by either a single attribute-name or a list of attribute-names separated by commas and enclosed in parentheses. Within a given dependency, all such specifications must contain the same number of attribute-names; the first attribute nominated in the referential-attribute (in left-to-right order) corresponds to the first nominated in each primary-key, the second to the second, and so on.

   Note: Attribute-names refer to simple attributes only. A composite attribute is designated by listing the names of all of its constituent simple attributes.

3. The nulls-rule indicates whether nulls are allowed for the referential-attribute. NULLS ALLOWED means that, in any given instance of the referential-attribute, either every constituent attribute value must be null or every constituent attribute value must be nonnull. NULLS NOT ALLOWED means that, in any given instance of the referential-attribute, every constituent attribute value must be nonnull.

4. The delete-rule defines the effect of attempting to delete a tuple of a referenced relation. It applies to all referenced relations identified (via a primary-key) on the right-hand side of the dependency. CASCADES means that matching tuples in the referencing relation are deleted also. NULLIFIES means that the referential attribute in those tuples is updated to null. RESTRICTED means that the delete will fail if any such matching tuples exist. For both CASCADES and NULLIFIES the original tuple is deleted *after* the referencing tuples have been deleted or updated (as applicable); if a failure occurs while deleting or updating those tuples, the entire operation fails and the database remains unchanged.

5. The update-rule defines the effect of attempting to update the primary key value in a tuple of a referenced relation. It applies to all referenced relations identified (via a primary-key) on the right-hand side of the dependency. CASCADES means that matching tuples in the referencing relation are updated correspondingly. NULLIFIES means that the referential

attribute in those tuples is updated to null. RESTRICTED means that the update will fail if any such matching tuples exist. For both CASCADES and NULLIFIES the original tuple is updated *after* the referencing tuples have been updated; if a failure occurs while updating those tuples, the entire operation fails and the database remains unchanged.

6. If a given dependency includes multiple primary-key specifications on the right-hand side, then it also includes a quantifier (explicitly or by default). The possibilities are EXACTLY ONE OF (default), AT LEAST ONE OF, and ALL OF. The three cases are indistinguishable if there is only one primary-key mentioned; for simplicity, however, we treat this case as EXACTLY ONE OF.

Note, incidentally, that a given referential-attribute can appear on the left-hand side of any number of dependencies.

7. No syntax (other than the nulls-rule) is provided for specifying any rules concerning the insertion of a tuple into a referencing relation or the update of a referential attribute within such a tuple. Instead, such operations are always governed by the following rule. On completion of any transaction that includes such an operation (i.e., at commit time for such a transaction), the referential attribute in question must satisfy the following constraint (otherwise the transaction is rejected):

- Let the referential attribute, which for generality we assume to be composite, consist of simple attributes $A1, A2, \ldots, An$, and let the values of these attributes in the inserted or updated tuple be $k1, k2, \ldots, kn$. These n values must either all be null or all nonnull (of course, they must all be nonnull if NULLS NOT ALLOWED is specified).

- Let each referenced relation corresponding to the referencing relation have attributes $K1, K2, \ldots, Kn$ corresponding (in order) to $A1, A2, \ldots, An$. (The combination $(K1, K2, \ldots, Kn)$ constitutes the primary key for each such relation. We assume without loss of generality that all such primary keys have the same attribute names.)

- Then, assuming that $k1, k2, \ldots, kn$ are all nonnull:

  (a) If the applicable quantifier is EXACTLY ONE OF, there must exist a tuple in exactly one of the referenced relations having $K1 = k1$, $K2 = k2, \ldots, Kn = kn$.

  (b) If the applicable quantifier is AT LEAST ONE OF, there must exist a tuple in at least one of the referenced relations having $K1 = k1$, $K2 = k2, \ldots, Kn = kn$.

  (c) If the applicable quantifier is ALL OF, there must exist a tuple in every one of the referenced relations having $K1 = k1$, $K2 = k2$, $\ldots, Kn = kn$.

There are two reasons, to be discussed later, for deferring the foregoing check until commit time. Of course, the implementation could make a note of the tuples concerned at the time of the insert or update operation, if that would make the subsequent commit-time check more efficient.

Examples

```
RX1 : SP.S# IDENTIFIES S.S# ;
```

Explanation: This constraint may informally be read as "Given an SP tuple with value x for SP.S#, there exists an S tuple having that value x for S.S#." Deleting an S tuple or updating an S.S# value is allowed only if there are no corresponding SP tuples. Inserting an SP tuple or updating an SP.S# value is allowed only if the new SP.S# value is not null and an S tuple exists (by commit time) with S# value equal to that new value.

```
RX2 : SP.S# IDENTIFIES S.S#
      NULLS NOT ALLOWED
      DELETING RESTRICTED
      UPDATING CASCADES ;
```

This is similar to the previous example, except that the nulls and delete rules have been made explicit and the update rule has been changed so that updating an S.S# value cascades to the corresponding SP tuples. Let us consider this update rule in a little more detail. An expanded version of that rule is

```
BEFORE UPDATING S.S# FROM NEW_S# :
UPDATE SP.S# FROM NEW_S# WHERE SP.S# = S.S# ;
```

Note, however, that updating corresponding SP tuples as indicated will temporarily cause those tuples to violate the referential constraint (there will be no matching S tuple until the original S tuple has also been updated). This is one of the reasons for postponing the check on updating a referential attribute until commit time (see paragraph 7 of the explanations given above).

```
RX3 : SP.P# IDENTIFIES P.P# ;
```

Example RX3 is similar to example RX1 above.

For the sake of the next example, suppose that relation S is partitioned into a set of (disjoint) supplier relations L_S, P_S, R_S, A_S (one for each of the supplier cities London, Paris, Rome, Athens):

```
RX4 : SP.S# IDENTIFIES EXACTLY ONE OF
                ( L_S.S#, P_S.S#, R_S.S#, A_S.S# ) ;
```

As another example, suppose that relation S is replaced by its projections SN(S#,SNAME), ST(S#,STATUS), and SC(S#,CITY). Then we have the following dependency:[4]

Vertical

```
RX5 : SP.S# IDENTIFIES ALL OF (SN.S#, ST.S#, SC.S# ) ;
```

Some further examples:

```
RX6 : EMPLOYEE.MGR# IDENTIFIES EMPLOYEE.EMP# ;
RX7 : EMPLOYEE.MGR# IDENTIFIES EMPLOYEE.EMP#
      NULLS ALLOWED
      DELETING NULLIFIES
      UPDATING CASCADES ;

RX8 : OFFERING.COURSE# IDENTIFIES COURSE.COURSE#
      NULLS NOT ALLOWED
      DELETING CASCADES
      UPDATING CASCADES ;

RX9 : STUDENT.(COURSE#,OFF#) IDENTIFIES
                             OFFERING.(COURSE#,OFF#)
      NULLS NOT ALLOWED
      DELETING CASCADES
      UPDATING CASCADES ;
```

For a final example, we return to departments and employees, and extend the DEPARTMENT relation to include an ADVISOR# attribute, identifying an employee (by employee number) who is the advisor to the department in question. We thus have a cycle:

```
RX10 : EMPLOYEE.DEPT# IDENTIFIES DEPARTMENT.DEPT# ;
RX11 : DEPARTMENT.ADVISOR# IDENTIFIES EMPLOYEE.EMP# ;
```

Suppose also that neither of the referential attributes DEPT# and ADVISOR# is allowed to be null. A moment's reflexion will show that this example provides another reason for postponing the check on inserting a referencing tuple to commit time (see paragraph 7 of the explanations given earlier).

---

[4]We also have the dependencies

```
RX5A : SN.S# IDENTIFIES ST.S# ... ;
RX5B : ST.S# IDENTIFIES SN.S# ... ;
RX5C : SN.S# IDENTIFIES SC.S# ... ;
RX5D : SC.S# IDENTIFIES SN.S# ... ;
RX5E : ST.S# IDENTIFIES SC.S# ... ;
RX5F : SC.S# IDENTIFIES ST.S# ... ;
```

Note the permutations.
Too general!

This fact is one of the reasons that I now feel that the proposals of this paper are a little too liberal. It seems better to insist that, for any given type of entity, there is a single "master" relation that lists all entities of that type.

THE REFERENCE GRAPH   *[handwritten: Table of Integrity Rules]*

A system that implements referential integrity will require an internal representation (part of the system catalog) of all referential constraints. The *reference graph* is such a representation. For expository purposes let us assume that no relation can have a primary key involving more than three attributes. Then we can define the reference graph as the combination of two relations RGX and RGY, as follows (domain specifications elided for brevity):

```
RELATION RGX ( LABEL   : ... ,
               R1      : ... ,
               A1      : ... ,
               A2      : ... ,
               A3      : ... ,
               COUNT   : ... ,
               QFIER   : ... ,
               NRULE   : ... ,
               URULE   : ... ,
               DRULE   : ... )
        PRIMARY KEY ( LABEL )


RELATION RGY ( LABEL   : ... ,
               SEQNO   : ... ,
               R2      : ... ,
               K1      : ... ,
               K2      : ... ,
               K3      : ... )
        PRIMARY KEY ( LABEL , SEQNO )
```

[handwritten annotation: Referencing]

[handwritten annotation: Referenced]

Within a given tuple of RGX, LABEL represents the label of a referential constraint; R1 represents the referencing relation and (A1,A2,A3) the referential attribute within that relation (which cannot involve more than three components, by our simplifying assumption); COUNT represents the number of referenced relations in the constraint; QFIER represents the applicable quantifier; and NRULE, DRULE, and URULE represent the applicable nulls, delete, and update rules. If COUNT has the value n in some given RGX tuple, then there will be n corresponding tuples in relation RGY, with the same LABEL as that RGX tuple and with SEQNO values $1,2,...,n$. Within each of those RGY tuples, R2 represents a referenced relation and (K1,K2,K3) represents that relation's primary key.

Note: We include K1, K2, K3 in relation RGY for clarity. However, this information is presumably redundant; that is, we presume that elsewhere in the catalog is the specification of the primary key for any given relation. We also assume that the number of attributes constituting the primary key is given elsewhere (if it is less than three in some particular case, then unused K's and A's for that relation in RGX and RGY will be null).

Example

We show reference graph entries for certain of the examples from the previous section. For reasons of space we abbreviate EMPLOYEE to EMP, COURSE to CSE, OFFERING to OFF, STUDENT to STU, EMP# to E#, MGR# to M#, COURSE# to C#, and OFF# to O#. Other abbreviations should be obvious.

```
Relation RGX
-----   ---   --  --  --  -----  -----  -----  -----  -----
LABEL   R1    A1  A2  A3  COUNT  QFIER  NRULE  DRULE  URULE
-----   ---   --  --  --  -----  -----  -----  -----  -----
RX1     SP    S#  --  --    1    exact  no     restr  restr
RX3     SP    P#  --  --    1    exact  no     restr  restr
RX6     EMP   M#  --  --    1    exact  yes    nullf  casc
RX8     OFF   C#  --  --    1    exact  no     casc   casc
RX9     STU   C#  O#  --    1    exact  no     casc   casc
RX4     SP    S#  --  --    4    exact  no     restr  restr
RX5     SP    S#  --  --    3    all    no     restr  restr
```

```
Relation RGY
-----   -----   ---  --  --  --
LABEL   SEQNO   R2   K1  K2  K3
-----   -----   ---  --  --  --
RX1       1     S    S#  --  --
RX3       1     P    P#  --  --
RX6       1     EMP  E#  --  --
RX8       1     CSE  C#  --  --
RX9       1     OFF  C#  O#  --
RX4       1     L_S  S#  --  --
RX4       2     P_S  S#  --  --
RX4       3     R_S  S#  --  --
RX4       4     A_S  S#  --  --
RX5       1     SN   S#  --  --
RX5       2     ST   S#  --  --
RX5       3     SC   S#  --  --
```

We note in passing that relations RGX and RGY could be used to drive a utility program to produce a pictorial representation of the interrelation dependencies in the database.[5]

REFERENTIAL INTEGRITY IN DBTG

It may be useful to analyze the referential integrity features of DBTG [1] in terms of the concepts discussed so far. To do this, let us consider a DBTG

---

[5]It is worth pointing out that relational implementations that do not support referential integrity at the user interface must nevertheless include some *internal* support for the concept, because it is needed to maintain the integrity of the system's own catalog. In the catalog structure of the IBM product DB2, for example, attribute TBNAME of the catalog relation SYSCOLUMNS is a foreign key matching attribute NAME (primary key) of the catalog relation SYSTABLES.

"set type" S_SP, with owner S and member SP, which is a DBTG representation of the relationship between suppliers and shipments:

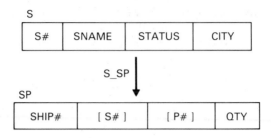

For the sake of the example we introduce an "artificial" single-attribute primary key SHIP# for shipments, in order to allow the attribute SP.S# to take on null values. (Note: Attribute SP.S# is present only if S_SP is "inessential"—see below—which is why we show it in square brackets in the figure. Similarly for attribute SP.P#, of course.)

We consider two versions of set type S_SP:

(a) An *essential* version, in which shipments (SP tuples) do not include an S# attribute; and

(b) An *inessential* version, in which they do and the system is aware of the constraint that, within a given S_SP set occurrence, the value of S# in the owner must be equal to the value of S# in all of the members [4]. This latter constraint is expressed in DBTG by means of a CHECK clause in the definition of S_SP [1].

As indicated earlier in the paper, the notion of *membership class* (of SP with respect to S_SP) is relevant here. Membership class is specified as a combination of *insertion* class (AUTOMATIC or MANUAL) and *retention* class (FIXED or MANDATORY or OPTIONAL). We consider each in turn.

■ Insertion class has meaning only at the time of creating a new SP tuple. It thus does not correspond precisely to anything we have been discussing in our relational proposal, which is completely time-independent. However: AUTOMATIC means that the new SP tuple will be connected to a corresponding S tuple at the time of creation, MANUAL means that it will not. Therefore:

(a) If set type S_SP is essential, AUTOMATIC corresponds approximately to a relational rule that SP.S# must have NULLS NOT ALLOWED and must be equal to some existing S.S# value, and MANUAL corresponds to a (hypothetical) relational rule that SP.S#

must have NULLS ALLOWED and *must in fact be null*—both rules being interpreted as applying to the creation of a new SP tuple *only*.

(b) If set type S_SP is inessential, AUTOMATIC is as for the essential case; MANUAL, however, allows the new SP.S# value to be *anything* (not null, because DBTG does not support null values, but any nonnull value—regardless of whether an S tuple having that S# value exists or not).

- The following table shows which of the nine possible combinations of delete rule and update rule (in the terminology of this paper) are handled by the concept of retention class.

DRULE	URULE	S_SP essential	S_SP inessential
casc	casc	FIXED	–
casc	nullf	–	–
casc	restr	–	FIXED
nullf	casc	OPTIONAL	–
nullf	nullf	–	–
nullf	restr	–	OPTIONAL(*)
restr	casc	MANDATORY	–
restr	nullf	–	–
restr	restr	–	MANDATORY

*Deleting an S tuple causes the corresponding SP tuples to be disconnected, but SP.S# values remain unchanged instead of being set to null.

It is interesting to note that, for a given set type, only three of the nine possibilities can be handled. We also observe that DBTG cannot handle the case where (for example) suppliers in different cities are represented by different record types, and shipments can refer to any of them ("alternative owners").

SUMMARY

In this proposal we have presented a framework for dealing with referential integrity within the relational model. The following are the highlights of this proposal.

- It accords well with intuition.

- It is consistent with a more general proposal for dealing with arbitrary integrity constraints.

- It is decoupled from the concept of domain (though the two concepts could easily be recoupled if the system in question does provide domain support).

- It is *not* decoupled from the notion of primary key (though such decoupling could be provided if it were considered desirable).[6]
- A given referenced relation can have multiple referencing relations. (In DBTG terms, one owner type can own multiple set types, and therefore have multiple member types—very loosely speaking.)
- A given referencing relation can have multiple referenced relations—i.e., *associations* [3] can be handled. (In DBTG terms, one member occurrence can have multiple owner occurrences, one in each of a given set of owner types—very loosely speaking.)
- *Alternative* referenced relations can be handled. That is, a given referential attribute can have multiple referenced relations, and values of that attribute can be constrained to match EXACTLY ONE OF, AT LEAST ONE OF, or ALL OF those relations. (DBTG cannot handle these cases.)
- Referential attributes (and matching primary keys) can be composite.
- A referential attribute can itself be a primary key.
- Cycles can be handled; in particular, a relation can include references to itself.
- A variety of violation-actions can be specified to handle attempted violations.

ACKNOWLEDGMENTS

I am grateful to Ted Codd for several discussions on the referential integrity aspects of his extended relational model RM/T [3], which led directly to the proposals outlined herein, and for his helpful comments on an earlier draft of this paper. I would also like to thank my colleagues Ron Fagin, Bill Kent, Bill McGee, and Phil Shaw for numerous constructive comments, both on the proposal itself and on the manner of its exposition.

REFERENCES

1. CODASYL Programming Language Committee, *Data Base Task Group Report* (April 1971).

2. E. F. Codd, "A Relational Model of Data for Large Shared Data Banks," *CACM* 13, No. 6 (June 1970).

---

[6]It is definitely not desirable, in my opinion. See the paper "Why Every Relation Should Have Exactly One Primary Key" (previous paper in this collection).

3. E. F. Codd, "Extending the Database Relational Model to Capture More Meaning," *ACM TODS* 4, No. 4 (December 1979).

4. E. F. Codd and C. J. Date, "Interactive Support for Nonprogrammers: The Relational and Network Approaches" (in this volume).

5. C. J. Date and E. F. Codd, "The Relational and Network Approaches: Comparison of the Application Programming Interfaces" (in this volume).

6. C. J. Date, *An Introduction to Database Systems: Volume I,* 3rd edition (Reading, MA: Addison-Wesley, 1981).

7. C. J. Date, "An Introduction to the Unified Database Language (UDL)" (in this volume).

8. C. J. Date, *An Introduction to Database Systems*: *Volume II* (Reading, MA: Addison-Wesley, 1982).

9. K. P. Eswaran and D. D. Chamberlin, "Functional Specifications of a Subsystem for Data Base Integrity," *Proc. 1st International Conference on Very Large Data Bases* (September 1975).

10. IBM Corporation, *IMS/VS System Application Design Guide.* IBM Form No. SH20-9025.

11. ANSI X3.53-1976. American National Standard Programming Language PL/I (1976).

5

On the Performance
of Relational
Database Systems

ABSTRACT

Contrary to popular belief, relational systems are capable of performing at least as well as, and quite possibly better than, older (nonrelational) systems. This paper explains why this is so.

COMMENTS ON REPUBLICATION

Since this paper was first written, IBM has published the results of a number of performance tests comparing IMS and DB2[1] (see the remarks on this

---

[1] See "IBM Database 2 Performance Measurements," by Chris Loosley, published in *InfoIMS* 5, No. 1 (First Quarter 1985), available from PO Box 20651, San Jose, CA 95160.

This paper is based in part on material (pp. 258–262) from *A Guide to DB2,* by C. J. Date, copyright 1984, Addison-Wesley, Reading, Massachusetts; reprinted with permission. An earlier version appeared in *Computerworld* (February 13, 1984) under the title "Practice and Theory: How Relational Systems Perform," copyright 1984 by CW Communications, Inc., Framingham, Massachusetts 01701; reprinted with permission.

topic toward the end of the paper). This is not the place to review those results in detail; suffice it to say that the DB2 figures were very encouraging. For a typical IMS-type workload, it seems that DB2 was a factor of between 1.65 and 2.35 times slower than IMS (i.e., if IMS could handle 15 transactions per second, then DB2 could handle somewhere between 6 and 9 transactions per second). These figures indicate that, for many installations, DB2 could already serve as a perfectly adequate production system. It is certainly not just an "Information Center" (i.e., ad hoc query) product, as many people have tried to suggest on many occasions.

In addition, of course, it should be stressed that:

1. The previous point notwithstanding, DB2 is of course highly suitable as an Information Center product also (which IMS is most certainly not).

2. These performance results relate to *the first release* of DB2. Future releases are almost certain to show performance improvements. (It would be interesting, incidentally, to compare the DB2 figures with corresponding figures for the first release of IMS.)

In short, the IBM figures provide practical evidence to support the somewhat theoretical arguments made in the paper.

INTRODUCTION

A number of misconceptions have grown up in the DP world over the past few years concerning relational systems, and many of those misconceptions have to do with performance. Two very commonly heard opinions are the following:

> "Relational systems are all very fine for ad hoc query, but they will never achieve the performance needed for production systems (or transaction processing systems or ...)."

> "Relational systems require a breakthrough in hardware technology (e.g., hardware associative memory) before they will be able to achieve acceptable performance."

The contrasting opinion (that of the present writer, needless to say) is as follows:

> There is no intrinsic reason why a relational system should perform any worse than any other kind of system.

The intent of this paper is to justify this latter opinion.

PERFORMANCE OF AN INDIVIDUAL TRANSACTION

In this section let us agree to ignore the interference effects introduced by the fact that multiple transactions can run in parallel, and concentrate rather on the performance of some given transaction considered in isolation. The two principal factors determining the performance of such a transaction are of course the number of I/O operations and the pathlength (amount of CPU processing). Let us consider each in turn.

Pathlength

The IBM products DB2 and SQL/DS [1] are compiling systems: User-level database statements are compiled prior to run time into appropriate machine code instructions. At the time of writing, most other systems, relational or otherwise, are interpretive; but the advantages of compilation are widely recognized, and several other relational systems—for example, ORACLE [2] and INGRES [3]—are believed to be moving (either totally or partially) toward the compiling approach. For the sake of the present discussion, therefore, let us concentrate on compiling systems. The purpose of compiling is, precisely, to reduce the runtime pathlength! To be specific, all of the following operations—

- parsing the original user request
- detecting and reporting on syntax errors
- mapping logical-level names to physical-level addresses
- choosing an access strategy
- checking authorization
- generating machine code

—are removed from the runtime path. (Of these operations, easily the most significant from the performance standpoint is choosing an access strategy—in a word, optimization. See Fig. 5.1.) The runtime pathlength is thus considerably shorter than it would otherwise be. What is more, the generated code is tightly tailored to the original request, and may thus be more efficient than more generalized, interpretive code. Moreover, the performance benefits of compilation can be achieved without any corresponding loss of flexibility in operation: If recompilation becomes necessary (e.g., if an index is dropped), then the system can perform that recompilation automatically, thanks to an ingenious technique (now known as "automatic bind" [1]) pioneered in the IBM Research prototype System R.

Note, incidentally, that compilation in the above sense (i.e., *optimized* compilation) would not even be feasible in a record-level system, because the system would not be able to capture the user's intent in the same way.

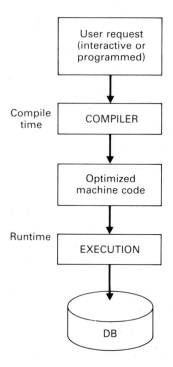

Figure 5.1   Optimized compilation reduces the runtime pathlength

Thus it is conceivable that a relational system may ultimately involve *shorter* pathlengths than a nonrelational system (especially if the nonrelational system always has to interpret requests at run time).

I/O Operations

The number of I/O operations required to satisfy a particular request is a function of the *physical* structure of the database, not the logical structure; it has nothing to do with how the database is perceived by its users, i.e., as relations or as some other logical structure. (Of course, I am assuming here that the system does make a genuine distinction between the physical and logical levels, as a relational system does.) See Fig. 5.2.

The question of how much I/O is needed in a relational system can therefore be broken down into two subsidiary questions:

1. Are the physical structures supported by the system capable of providing the kind of I/O performance needed?

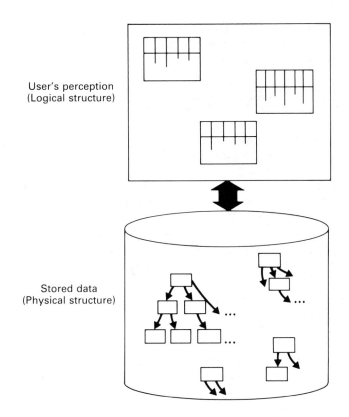

Figure 5.2   Logical vs. physical data structure in a relational system

2. If the answer to the first question is "Yes," then is the system capable of accepting high-level relational requests (e.g., a SQL SELECT statement or a QUEL RETRIEVE statement) and converting them into operations on those physical structures that are "as good as hand code"— i.e., as good as the code that would be produced by a skilled programmer working directly at the physical level?

Regarding Question 1, most relational systems today support B-tree indexes. A few systems support hashes, etc., in addition—for example, INGRES does [3]—but B-trees are far and away the structure most often encountered in practice; in fact, there is little doubt that if a single physical structure has to be chosen, then B-trees are the obvious choice. Now, B-trees are certainly capable of providing adequate performance for many applications (this statement must be true, or nobody would use VSAM). On the other hand, it is also true that there are some applications that simply have to use (say) hashing to meet their performance requirements. Thus, the answer to the first question in most current systems is "Yes" if indexes are acceptable for the application in hand, "No" otherwise. (In the latter case, of course, the answer may still be "Yes" for some other system.)

Assuming that the answer to Question 1 is "Yes," let us now consider Question 2 (Can the system produce code that is as good as hand code?). The short answer is "Yes, it can" (in many cases but not all). The function of the system optimizer is precisely to convert user-level statements into optimized machine code—where "optimized" means, basically, that the generated code employs the best strategy it can for satisfying the original request. In DB2, for example, the optimizer will always try to make use of a "clustering index" if one exists that matches the requirements of the user-level statement. Of course, the optimizer does *not* produce the best possible code for every possible request—but then nor do most human programmers.

Note, moreover, that we are talking here about products that are (for the most part) only at the stage of a first or second release—products, what is more, that are based on a brand-new technology. It is reasonable to expect continuing improvements in the area of optimization throughout the lifetime of those products. Indeed, the field of database optimization today may be likened to the field of programming language optimization as it was some fifteen or twenty years ago: Numerous researchers are investigating the problem, at universities and elsewhere, and the fruits of that activity will no doubt eventually find their way into implemented products. Moreover, such enhancements can be made without in any way affecting the form of the external interface (that is what data independence is all about).

As a matter of fact, it is even conceivable that the optimizer might produce code that is *better* than hand code. It may well be the case that the optimizer has information available to it—regarding, for example, physical data clustering, table sizes, index selectivities, and so on—that a hand coder typically would not have. Moreover, that information may change with time. If it does, then reoptimization may become necessary. Such reoptimization is trivial in a relational system (it simply involves a recompile, and quite possibly an automatic one at that); it would be very difficult in a hand-coding system (it would require a program rewrite).

One final point (related to the previous one) regarding optimization: There is another reason why relational systems may in fact outperform non-relational systems in some cases. The point is precisely that those relational systems are optimizing systems. High-level relational operations are optimizable precisely because they are high-level—they carry a lot of semantic content, and the optimizer is therefore able to recognize what it is that the user is trying to do and can respond in an optimal way. By contrast, in a nonrelational system, in which the user operates at the record level instead of at the set level, access strategies are chosen by the user; and if the user makes a wrong choice, then there is little or no chance that the system will be able to optimize that user's code.

As an example of the foregoing, suppose the (nonrelational) user is trying to compute the join of two tables A and B. There are two basic strategies: (a) For each record of A in turn, find all matching records in B; (b) for each record of B in turn, find all matching records in A. Now, depending on such considerations as the relative sizes of A and B and (especially) their physical clustering characteristics, one of these strategies is likely to outperform the other by several orders of magnitude; and (as stated previously) if the user chooses the wrong one, then there is really no way that the system can convert it into the other, because the user's choice is expressed as a sequence of low-level operations instead of as a single high-level operation.

PERFORMANCE OF THE OVERALL SYSTEM

It is sometimes suggested (see, e.g., reference [4]) that a relational system must necessarily perform poorly *as a system*, regardless of its efficiency with respect to any individual transaction. The argument is that relational systems will be running a mixture of planned transactions and ad hoc queries (short-running activities and long-running activities, to use the terminology of [4]), and that those two kinds of activity are mutually disruptive.

.Now, it is true for *any* system (not just a relational one) that these two kinds of activity may tend to interfere with each other somewhat, and there is no harm in drawing attention to that fact. But to suggest that relational systems will therefore have significantly worse performance than less flexible (hierarchic or network) systems is completely unwarranted, for at least the following two reasons:

- First, it is an apples-and-oranges comparison. It is extremely difficult to perform any kind of ad hoc activity at all on hierarchic and network databases, with the result that those systems are almost invariably (de facto) devoted to planned activities. This fact does not mean that users would not like to be able to perform ad hoc access to those databases if they could.

- Second, there is no *requirement* to mix the two kinds of activity in a relational system. It is ridiculous to suggest, as reference [4] does, that controls cannot be imposed in the relational environment. Of course they can, if the installation requires them. The authorization subsystem—which tends to be much more sophisticated in relational than in nonrelational systems, incidentally—provides one obvious example (not the only one) of an appropriate control mechanism. In INGRES, for example, it is perfectly feasible to restrict ad hoc queries to specified hours of the day and/or days of the week [3].

Moreover, even if such controls do prove necessary in some installations, the user will still enjoy all the other advantages of relational technology (ease of use, speed of application development, resilience to change, etc.), and in addition will be able to perform ad hoc access at controlled times. Furthermore, there will be many installations where such controls will not be necessary, because the overall performance requirements will be less stringent. Balancing the requirement for ad hoc data availability vs. the control needed to guarantee specific levels of performance is a tradeoff like any other.

FURTHER CONSIDERATIONS

From all of the foregoing, I conclude that there is absolutely no reason why a relational system that is implemented on perfectly conventional hardware using perfectly conventional software techniques should not perform perfectly acceptably. A hardware breakthrough is *not* required (though if, e.g., cheap large-capacity associative memory ever did become a commercial reality, it would certainly be easier to take advantage of it in a relational system than in a nonrelational one).

Of course, I should emphasize the point that the foregoing discussions are all very general! I am *not* saying that a system like DB2 today is able to perform as well as a long-established system such as IMS today. In the case of DB2 in particular, it is probably too early even to give any kind of performance figures as yet, though it is a safe bet that any such figures would be substantially less attractive than the corresponding figures for IMS.[2] There is little doubt that *for a given application*, where the data structures and the transaction patterns are very well understood ahead of time, an established system like IMS can be customized and configured to produce more impressive performance than a system like DB2 can—today. On the other hand:

(a) That customized system may not look so impressive when other applications are added to it. Implementing application B on a system that is customized to application A is rather like cutting wood against the

---

[2]But see the remarks on this point in the "Comments on Republication."

grain—extraneous considerations keep getting in the way. And note that these comments apply, not only to system performance, but also to the logical structure of the system as perceived by the user (that is, application B will probably be more awkward to write as well). Logical data structures in a nonrelational system tend to be biased toward some applications and against others, precisely because they closely reflect the physical data structure. Logical data structures in a relational system, by contrast, are more neutral: The application bias shows, not in the logical data structure, but in the manipulative operations, which by definition are far more flexible than the comparatively static data structure. (The bias will of course also show in the *physical* data structure.)

(b) To amplify point (a) somewhat: Consider the standard departments-and-employees database, and consider two typical transactions:

(T1) Find a specified department and all of its employees;

(T2) Find all departments.

In IMS, the data would typically be organized as a two-level hierarchy, with (say) index access to departments and pointer access from each department to its employees (see Fig. 5.3). This arrangement gives good performance for transaction T1 but poor performance for transaction

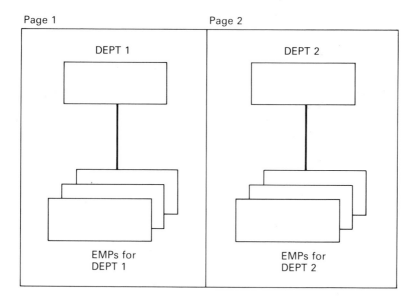

Figure 5.3 Departments and employees in IMS (physical structure)

T2. In a relational system, the data could be physically arranged *either* as in IMS, *or* (perhaps more usually) as two physically separate sets of records, each with a corresponding index (see Fig. 5.4). The first of these arrangements would give essentially the same performance as IMS for both T1 and T2; the second would give somewhat worse performance than IMS for T1 (typically four I/O operations instead of two) but *much* better performance than IMS for T2 (basically N times fewer I/O operations, where N is the number of records per page).

(c) One reason for the performance advantage of nonrelational systems is simply that those systems have been running for ten or fifteen years

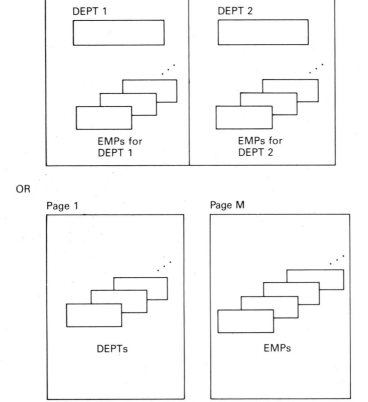

Figure 5.4   Departments and employees in a relational system (physical structure)

and have been constantly improved and tuned throughout that time. Relational systems will improve too over the next few years. Moreover, it is not clear that further significant improvements are even possible in a nonrelational system, whereas (as indicated earlier) the field is wide open for such improvements in the relational case.

(d) Even if the nonrelational system provides superior runtime performance, the value of that benefit has to be balanced against the amount of time it takes to get the system operational in the first place (not to mention the amount of time spent in subsequent maintenance). The installation's investment will be recovered more quickly with a relational system than with a nonrelational one, because applications will be running sooner. The ultimate return on investment may be higher too, if the application lifetime is less than the time it takes for the non-relational version to "catch up," economically speaking, with the relational one (see Fig. 5.5).

But let me repeat that all of the above is somewhat theoretical. As stated earlier, a system like DB2, today, is extremely unlikely to achieve the performance level of a system like IMS, today. The tradeoff that must be considered today is *performance vs. usability*—or, to put it another way,

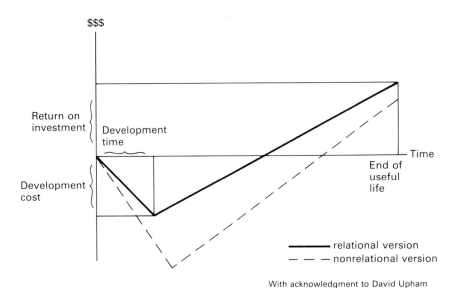

With acknowledgment to David Upham
of Relational Database Associates, Seattle

Figure 5.5   Costs and returns on a hypothetical application

machine productivity versus people productivity. Now, it is a truism that people costs are rising (fast) and machine costs are falling (also fast); as a result, people productivity is very rapidly becoming the dominating factor in many applications (indeed, in many cases it already is). For such applications, relational systems are obviously ideally suited, even at their present level of performance. However, there are also many applications in which raw machine performance is still the overriding concern. Thus, systems like IMS will have a major role to play for several years to come. And even if relational systems do eventually achieve parity in performance (as I for one am convinced they will), the huge investment in nonrelational systems is sufficient to ensure the continued existence of those systems for the foreseeable future. Human beings are notoriously reluctant to expend the effort needed to learn something new, even when the advantages of doing so are manifestly obvious: Witness the fact that, *even today*, some applications are still written in assembler language instead of COBOL or some still higher level language. This is clearly one reason why DB2 is viewed by IBM—at least at the time of writing—as complementing IMS, not replacing it, and why the two products are designed to work together in harmony as a single cooperating system.[3]

REFERENCES

1. Information on DB2 and SQL/DS is available from IBM Corporation, Armonk, New York.

2. Information on ORACLE is available from Oracle Corporation, Menlo Park, California.

3. Information on INGRES is available from Relational Technology Inc., Alameda, California.

4. William H. Inmon, "What Price Relational?" *Computerworld* (November 28, 1983).

---

[3]See the further remarks on this subject in the "Comments on Republication."

6

Some Relational Myths Exploded

(AN EXAMINATION OF SOME POPULAR MISCONCEPTIONS CONCERNING RELATIONAL DATABASE MANAGEMENT SYSTEMS)

ABSTRACT

Relational database management is a key technology for the 1980s, yet the field still suffers from a great deal of misunderstanding and misrepresentation. Misconceptions abound. The purpose of this paper is to correct some of those misconceptions.

COMMENTS ON REPUBLICATION

This paper was originally written in 1984 in response to a number of articles that appeared in the trade press at about that time—for example, an article

This paper originally appeared in two parts. Part I was published in *InfoIMS 4,* No. 2 (2nd Quarter 1984); Part II was published in *InfoIMS 4,* No. 3 (3rd Quarter 1984). Reprinted with permission.

in *Computerworld* entitled "What Price Relational?", by William H. Inmon, dated November 28, 1983 (reference [20] in the present paper), and another in *Datamation* entitled "What, If Anything, Is a Relational Database?", by Frank Sweet, dated September 1984 (not explicitly referenced). However, articles continue to appear in many publications that grossly misrepresent the relational approach. This "myths" discussion is still needed and still timely.

Note: The discussion under Myth No. 16 regarding database language standardization activity is as of approximately mid 1984. The current status (late 1985) is as follows:

- The database committee (X3H2) has dropped work on RDL per se and is instead proposing a language that is essentially identical to IBM SQL in all major respects.

- The public review period for that proposed standard concluded in September 1985. All comments received during that period, together with the committee's responses to those comments, must now be submitted along with the proposed standard to the parent committee X3, whose responsibility it is to decide whether the proposed standard should be adopted.

I have removed a slightly confusing parenthetical remark from the discussion of third normal form under Myth No. 20; otherwise the paper as reprinted here is more or less still as originally published.

INTRODUCTION

Relational systems are here to stay. Ample evidence (if evidence is needed) in support of this claim can be found in the great number of relational products now available—well in excess of fifty at last count (but the number is increasing almost daily), and running on machines that range all the way from quite small micros to the largest mainframes. It is of course true that those products will probably not all survive; ordinary market forces will presumably see to that. Taken en masse, however, the large array of relational products clearly represents not just some passing fad, but rather a state of affairs that will endure for the foreseeable future. And the reason for that state of affairs is, of course, that there is a solid theoretical foundation underlying those products—namely, the relational model.

Despite all of this activity, however, the field of relational technology is still very poorly understood by a great many people (see, for example, references [20] and [22]). Indeed, the number of misconceptions—one might almost say "myths"—that have grown up in the past few years concerning relational systems is truly amazing. The purpose of this paper is to correct some of those misconceptions.

The various "myths" (I adopt the term for convenience) discussed in what follows are not all equally significant, of course. I have left it to the reader's judgment to decide which are major and which minor. Also, they overlap one another to some extent, as is only to be expected; I have tried to treat them in a reasonably coherent manner, but it is sometimes difficult to impose an appropriately logical structure on such a diffuse collection. The structure of the paper is thus a trifle arbitrary in places.

Note: Some of the "myths" discussed in what follows do have a grain of truth in them, or are even entirely true, *in the form in which they are stated*; see, for example, Myth No. 2 below. "Myth" is thus not an entirely appropriate term in all cases. But it seemed best to state each misconception in the form in which it is most commonly encountered, even when that form does not truly capture the essence of the situation; the subsequent discussion makes it clear what the true state of affairs is (and what the "myth" is) in each case. Such an approach appeared preferable to the alternative of indulging in unnatural circumlocutions merely for the sake of ensuring that each myth was in fact false as stated.

For convenience the various myths are collected together below.

- Myth No. 1: A relational database is a database in which the data is physically stored as tables.
- Myth No. 2: A relation is just a flat file.
- Myth No. 3: The relational model is just flat files.
- Myth No. 4: "Join" is just the relational version of the parent-child links found in hierarchic and network systems.
- Myth No. 5: Relational systems must necessarily perform poorly.
- Myth No. 6: The data must be hierarchically clustered for good performance.
- Myth No. 7: Hierarchic clustering requires pointers.
- Myth No. 8: The relational model presupposes (or requires) content-addressable memory.
- Myth No. 9: Relational databases use more storage than other kinds of database.
- Myth No. 10: The relational approach is intended purely for query, not for production systems.
- Myth No. 11: Automatic navigation does not apply to application programs, because such programs are forced to operate on one record at a time.
- Myth No. 12: Control is not possible in a relational system.

- Myth No. 13: Relational systems provide no data integrity.
- Myth No. 14: A relational system that included all necessary integrity controls would be indistinguishable from a hierarchic or network system.
- Myth No. 15: Data has a naturally hierarchic structure.
- Myth No. 16: Relational systems do not conform to the official database standard.
- Myth No. 17: Hierarchic and network structures are more powerful than relational structures.
- Myth No. 18: Relational databases involve a lot of redundancy.
- Myth No. 19: The relational model is "just theory."
- Myth No. 20: Relational databases require "third normal form."
- Myth No. 21: The primary key concept is unnecessary.
- Myth No. 22: The relational model is only suitable for simple data (i.e., numbers and character strings).
- Myth No. 23: SQL (or QUEL or ...) is a panacea.
- Myth No. 24: Database design is unnecessary in a relational system.
- Myth No. 25: Third normal form is a panacea.
- Myth No. 26: The relational approach is a panacea.

Without further ado, let us examine these myths in detail.

MYTH NUMBER 1: *A relational database is a database in which the data is physically stored as tables.*

This misconception, still regrettably all too common even today, betrays a severe confusion between the physical and logical levels of the system. In fact, it is precisely the *separation* of those two levels that is one of the principal objectives of the relational model. That separation is the direct basis for the high degree of data independence found in relational systems; in addition, it allows the twin problems of logical and physical database design to be separately addressed, in itself a significant contribution (see Myth No. 24).

The true state of affairs is as follows: A relational database is a database in which the data is *logically perceived* as tables. Tables are the *logical* data structure in a relational system, not the physical data structure. At the physical level, in fact, the system is free to use any or all of the traditional techniques—physical ordering (sequential files), indexing (several varieties), hashes, pointer chains, compression (both data and index), record clustering (both inter- and intra-file), and so on—provided only that it can map those structures into tables at the logical level. *All* of those traditional techniques are supported by one or another of today's relational products. Within a given system, moreover, different files can typically use different physical structures, and the physical structure of a given file can typically be changed dynamically, without having any effect on the logical level at all.

MYTH NUMBER 2: *A relation is just a flat file.*

This is one of the "myths" that does have a grain of truth in it. A relation does resemble the familiar "flat file" (or table) in many respects—indeed, one of the strongpoints of the relational model is precisely that its data structures are very familiar and easy to understand. It is very important that a data model should have a simple and universally understood conceptual representation for its fundamental data structures, in order to facilitate the process of reasoning about the effects of operations on those structures [7]. But a relation should be regarded not as "just a table," but rather as a *disciplined* table—to be specific, a table in which:

- All records (rows) are of the same type.
- The columns (fields) have no particular order, left to right.
- The records (rows) have no particular ordering, top to bottom—or at most are ordered according to values of some field or field combination within those records. (Note that this type of ordering is "inessential." See Myth No. 17.) Other types of ordering, such as time-of-arrival or (application-)program-controlled, are specifically disallowed.
- Every field is single-valued (i.e., repeating groups are not allowed).
- The records have a unique identifier field (or field combination) called the *primary key*. As a consequence, no two rows of the table are duplicates of each other.

This discipline results in a considerable simplification in the data structures the user has to deal with. In fact, it is a characteristic of relational data structure that *all* data is represented in exactly the same way—namely, as field values (i.e., values of columns within rows of tables). That fact leads in turn to a tremendous simplification in the *operators* the user has to deal with (see the discussion under Myth No. 3 below, also Myth No. 17). In other words, the discipline is a help, not a hindrance.

MYTH NUMBER 3: *The relational model is just flat files.*

The relational model is the theoretical foundation on which relational systems are built. It may be defined, informally, as *a way of looking at data*—that is, a prescription for (1) how data can be represented and (2) how that representation can be manipulated. Note this second point carefully: The model does *not* consist of data structure alone (although numerous writers have tried to suggest that it does, and indeed still do). Data structure alone is not particularly interesting, or useful: If there are no operators, there is nothing that can be done with the data (as reference [6] puts it, considering structure alone and ignoring the operators is like trying to understand the way the human body functions by studying anatomy and ignoring physiology). In particular, it is not sufficient when comparing the relational model with other models to compare structural aspects alone; the operators *must* be taken into account also.

Actually, the relational model consists of three parts, not just two: a structural part, a manipulative part, and an *integrity* part. The structural part consists of *n*-ary relations (loosely speaking, tables of *n* columns). The manipulative part consists of a collection of operators, and is discussed below. The integrity part is discussed later in this paper (see Myths No. 13 and 14).

The manipulative part of the model, in turn, consists of two parts: (1) a set of operators (such as join) known collectively as the *relational algebra*, together with (2) a *relational assignment* operator that allows the value of some arbitrary expression of the algebra, such as a join of two relations, to be assigned to another relation. The operators of the relational algebra are as follows:

SELECT (also known as RESTRICT)	UNION
PROJECT	INTERSECT
JOIN	DIFFERENCE
DIVIDE	CARTESIAN PRODUCT

A detailed explanation of these operators is beyond the scope of this paper; such an explanation can be found in many places (see, for example, reference [4], where they were first defined). The point to be made here is that the operators were not chosen arbitrarily. On the contrary, they were defined specifically to provide exactly the same expressive power as the well-understood (that is, mathematically well-understood) "first-order predicate calculus," as applied to relations. What this means in practical terms is that, if a system supports all of the algebraic operators, then we *know* from the theory precisely what that system is functionally capable of. The system is predictable; there are no surprises (at least for a user who understands the model).

Having thus sketched the components of the model, I am now in a position to define exactly what is meant by the term "relational *system*." The point here is that *not all aspects of the model are equally important*;

some of course are crucial, but others may be regarded as features that are merely "nice to have," comparatively speaking. In his Turing paper, therefore (reference [7]), Codd proposed that a system may fairly be defined as relational if and only if it supports at least the following:

- Databases that are logically perceived as tables (and nothing but tables—in particular, there must be no user-visible navigation links connecting those tables);

- The operators SELECT, PROJECT, and JOIN of the relational algebra, without requiring any predefinition of particular physical structures to support those operations. (Note: JOIN here means, specifically, the *natural* join [4].)

Note carefully that a system does not have to support SELECT, PROJECT, and JOIN *explicitly* in order to qualify as relational. It is only the functionality of those operators we are talking about here. For example, DB2 and SQL/DS [1] provide the functionality of all three, and more besides, via the SELECT statement of the "Structured Query Language" SQL. (It is unfortunate that the SQL statement and the algebraic operator have the same name, incidentally—they certainly do not perform the same function. In fact, the SELECT statement of SQL includes *all* of the functionality of the algebra.) More important, note that a system that supports relational databases but not these three operators does not qualify as a relational system; nor does a system that allows (say) the user to SELECT records on the basis of the value of some field only if that field is indexed (because it is requiring predefinition of some particular physical structure).

The justification for the proposed definition is as follows.

1. Although SELECT, PROJECT, and JOIN are less than the full algebra, they are an extremely useful subset. There are comparatively few practical problems that can be solved with the algebra that cannot be solved with those three operators alone.

2. A system that supports the relational data structure but not the relational operators does not provide the ease-of-use and productivity features of a truly relational system.

3. A system that supports the relational operators but requires predefinition of certain physical structures to support those operators does not provide the data independence of a truly relational system.

4. To do a good job of implementing the operators (at least in a large mainframe environment) *requires* the system to do some optimization. That is, the system must be able to take a user-level request, represented (effectively) as some kind of algebraic expression, and "navigate" through the

database to the target data in some efficient way. Thus, to implement a system that realizes the potential of the relational model in an efficient manner is a technically nontrivial task. This is one of the reasons, incidentally, why it has taken so long for relational products to appear, even though the theory has been around for so many years.

Note therefore that in relational systems (in contrast to nonrelational ones) it is the system that does the navigating, not the user. For this reason, relational systems are sometimes described as "automatic navigation" systems.

There are a number of systems on the market today that advertise themselves as "relational" that do not meet the proposed criteria. As I have tried to suggest, those criteria are useful as a means of drawing a sharp line between systems that are indeed genuinely relational and those that are merely "relational-like." "Relational-like" systems do not provide the full benefits of the relational model.

MYTH NUMBER 4: *"Join" is just the relational version of the parent-child links found in hierarchic and network systems.*

There is a simple general principle that can usefully be applied when trying to decide whether two concepts A and B are the same: Simply ask yourself "Is every instance of A an instance of B?" and, conversely, "Is every instance of B an instance of A?" Only if the answer is "Yes" to both questions is it true that A and B are identical. Applied to the case in hand, this test alone is sufficient to show right away that this "myth" is indeed a myth. But there is a great deal more that needs to be said on the subject.

First, a table with *n* columns represents an *n*-ary relationship among the *n* objects represented by those *n* columns (which is why it is called a relation). For example, the table

```
EMP   ( EMP#, ENAME, DEPT#, SALARY )
```

represents a relationship among employee numbers, employee names, department numbers, and salaries. Likewise, the table

```
DEPT ( DEPT#, DNAME, MGR_EMP#, BUDGET )
```

represents a relationship among department numbers, department names, managers' employee numbers, and department budgets. *In a relational system, tables are the ONLY explicit way of representing relationships.* But, of course, the database does contain a large number of *implicit* relationships also. Here are some examples of implicit relationships in the EMP/DEPT database:

1. "Works_In": Certain employees work in certain departments. For a given employee, the value of DEPT# in that employee's EMP record identifies the DEPT record for the corresponding department.

2. "Well_Paid": Some employees may have a salary that is greater than the entire budget of some departments. The fact that a given employee is "well paid" in this sense is represented by the fact that the value of SALARY in the EMP record for the employee concerned is greater than the value of BUDGET in some DEPT record.

3. "Manages": Certain employees are the immediate manager for certain other employees. For a given manager, the value of EMP# in that person's EMP record identifies the DEPT record (via the MGR_EMP# field) for the department managed by that person, and the DEPT# field in that record in turn identifies the EMP records for the employees who work in that department (and who are therefore managed by that person).

Such implicit relationships can be made explicit by constructing tables for them. And that is precisely what the relational operators do; in particular, that is what "join" does. (Logically speaking, at any rate; the constructed table does not always have to be materialized, at least not in its entirety. But that is an optimization question and is beyond the scope of the present discussion.) For example, the three implicit relationships described above can be made explicit as follows (using SQL syntax):

1. "Works_In":

```
SELECT EMP.*, DEPT.*
FROM    EMP, DEPT
WHERE   EMP.DEPT# = DEPT.DEPT# ;
```

The effect of this operation is to join the EMP and DEPT tables on the basis of matching department number values. The resulting table consists of all possible rows of the form

```
( EMP#, ENAME, DEPT#, SALARY, DEPT#, DNAME, MGR_EMP#, BUDGET )
```

such that the "EMP" portion comes from the EMP table, the "DEPT" portion comes from the DEPT table, and, in every row, the two DEPT# positions contain the same value. For any given row in this table, the employee represented by the first four fields works in the department represented by the last four fields.

2. "Well_Paid":

```
SELECT EMP.*, DEPT.*
FROM    EMP, DEPT
WHERE   EMP.SALARY > DEPT.BUDGET ;
```

The effect of this operation is to join the EMP and DEPT tables on the basis of a "greater-than" comparison between employee salaries and department budgets. The resulting table consists of all possible rows of the form

```
( EMP#, ENAME, DEPT#, SALARY, DEPT#, DNAME, MGR_EMP#, BUDGET )
```

such that the "EMP" portion comes from the EMP table, the "DEPT" portion comes from the DEPT table, and, in every row, the SALARY value is greater than the BUDGET value. For any given row, the employee represented by the first four fields is "well paid" by comparison with the department represented by the last four fields.

   3. "Manages":

```
SELECT  MGR.*, EMP.*
FROM    EMP MGR, DEPT, EMP
WHERE   MGR.EMP#   = DEPT.MGR_EMP#
AND     DEPT.DEPT# = EMP.DEPT# ;
```

There are two joins here: first a join of "MGR" (i.e., EMP) and DEPT on the basis of an equality match between EMP# and MGR_EMP#, and then a join of the result and EMP on the basis of an equality match between DEPT# and DEPT#. This example illustrates the important point that, because the result of any relational algebra operation (in particular, the result of a join) is another table, it is always possible to go on to perform further algebraic operations on it. In the example, the sequence of operations yields a final table of the form

```
( EMP#, ENAME, DEPT#, SALARY, EMP#, ENAME, DEPT#, SALARY )
```

in which, for any given row, the employee represented by the first four fields is the immediate manager of the employee represented by the last four fields.

   As the examples make clear, join is an operator (*not* a parent-child link!—see below) that builds a new table from two given tables by concatenating records from those two tables. The two original tables are not necessarily distinct. The new table contains a record for every pair of records (one from each of the two given tables) that satisfy the condition—the "join predicate"—specified as part of the operation. Note that (a) the join operator is not restricted to matching on columns with the same name, and (b) neither is it restricted to matching on equality (though the "natural" join *is* so restricted).

   Aside: Although, as we have seen, the term "join" strictly refers to an *operation*, it is commonly used also to refer to the *table* that results from that operation. This usage is convenient, though sometimes a little confusing. It will not be employed in this paper.

Now let us turn our attention to parent-child links. The hierarchic or network analog of the EMP/DEPT database given earlier would typically look like this:

DEPT (DEPT#, DNAME, MGR_EMP#, BUDGET)

| DEPTEMP

EMP (EMP#, ENAME, SALARY)

Notice that the DEPT# field has been eliminated from the EMP record, and the parent-child link DEPTEMP has been added in its place. DEPT is the parent in this link and EMP is the child. *The DEPTEMP link is both a logical and a physical construct*: logical, because it is explicitly visible to users (hierarchic and network user languages include operators that explicitly refer to such links); and physical, because such links are always supported by some specific physical structure (typically a pointer chain that runs from each parent instance through all of the corresponding child instances). If the physical support is removed, logical operators that refer to the link will no longer work.

Note 1: It would theoretically be possible to build a system in which references to links functioned correctly even if the physical support for those links were removed. But then what would be the point of exposing links at the logical level of such a system at all? They would not provide any additional logical function, only additional complexity (see Myth No. 17, later). In any case, the point is purely academic: No system actually behaves in such a fashion today.

Note 2: DEPTEMP is an example of what is called an *essential* link, because the DEPT# field has been removed from the EMP record. If the DEPT# field were reinstated in that record, the link would become *inessential*. The distinction between essential and inessential links is discussed in more detail under Myth No. 17, later.

So the first point to make is that join is an operator (and therefore dynamic), whereas a link is a data structure (and therefore static—very much so). Furthermore, join is a *logical* operator, and a link is a *physical* structure. So it is clearly not the case that joins are "the same as" links. However, it is true that links may be an appropriate data structure (at the physical level, of course) in a relational system under certain circumstances—in particular, a link *may* be a good structure when the linked tables frequently appear as the operands of an operation that joins them together. For example, it may well be that a physical link between (the stored form of) the DEPT table and (the stored form of) the EMP table could provide an efficient basis for implementing the "Works_In" example discussed above.

(The physical link in question may be essential or inessential. Either way, of course, it will be invisible at the logical level. See Myth No. 17.) But note carefully that:

- Such a link does not have to exist for the join to work.

- Other physical structures (for example, indexes) may provide a more efficient basis for other joins.

- Still other joins may be performed so infrequently that it is not worth the overhead of maintaining a specific physical structure in order to make them efficient. This is a physical design tradeoff like so many others—except that in a relational system the designer is allowed the luxury of being wrong (see Myth No. 24, later).

- The physical structure is always invisible to the user, regardless of whether it is a link or something else. Users and user programs therefore do not depend on that structure, and it can be altered at any time in a totally transparent manner.

- A link corresponds to a one-to-many relationship, whereas a join may correspond to a many-to-many relationship; e.g., see the "Well_Paid" example earlier. A many-to-many relationship cannot possibly be represented by a link (it may be represented by a combination of two links, however).

- Even in the case of one-to-many relationships, it is extremely unlikely that all such relationships would be represented by physical links, if only because there are so many of them.

One final point on this subject: It is sometimes argued that links are a usability feature (as well as a performance feature) in hierarchic and network systems, in that they constrain the user to just those relationships that "make sense," logically speaking. Now, this argument is clearly not 100 percent accurate: As already suggested, there may well be relationships that users need to exploit that are not represented by links. Let us ignore that proviso for the moment, however. The point is, the same constraining effect can be achieved (if desired) in a relational system via that system's *view* mechanism. In fact, any table that can be derived from the given tables of the database via an expression of the relational algebra—in particular, via a join—can be predefined as a view, if desired. Thus, the need for the user to perform explicit join operations (etc.) can be easily and significantly reduced. Furthermore, the system's authorization mechanism can then be used to constrain users to just those "prejoined" tables—once again, assuming such constraints are desirable.

MYTH NUMBER 5: *Relational systems must necessarily perform poorly.*

I include this myth here for completeness. It is one of the commonest myths of all. But there is so much to say about it that it seemed best to devote a separate paper to it [16]. However, a few specific aspects of performance are addressed explicitly in the present paper—see Myths Nos. 6, 7, 8, and 10 below.

MYTH NUMBER 6: *The data must be hierarchically clustered for good performance.*

The suggestion here is that data *must* be physically interleaved on the disk (as it commonly is in hierarchic and network systems) in order to achieve satisfactory performance. But what is generally overlooked when such claims are made is that such interleaving biases the database *toward* some applications but *against* others. To see that this is so, consider the EMP/DEPT database again, and consider two typical transactions against that database (example taken from [16]):

T1. Find a specified department and all of its employees.

T2. Find all departments.

In a hierarchic or network system, the database would typically be organized as a two-level hierarchy, with index or hash access to departments and pointer (link) access from each department to its employees. (We are talking about the physical organization here, of course.) Furthermore, all of the employee records for a given department would typically be stored on the same physical page as the corresponding department record (this is what is meant by hierarchic clustering). This arrangement gives good performance for transactions of type T1 but bad performance for those of type T2.

In a relational system, by contrast, the data could be physically arranged *either* as in the hierarchic/network case, *or* (perhaps more usually) as two physically separate sets of records, each with a corresponding index (and/or hash). The first of these arrangements would give essentially the same performance as the hierarchic/network system for both T1 and T2; the second would give somewhat worse performance for T1 (two or four I/O operations—depending on whether hashing or indexing applies—instead of one or two, respectively), but *much* better performance for T2 (N times fewer I/O operations, where N is the number of records per page). So the question is simply which class of transaction, T1 or T2, is the more important. Furthermore, of course, the designer does realistically have a choice in the relational case, and moreover the physical structure can be changed at a later time if the answer to the question (as to which of T1 and T2 is the more important) changes, without logically impairing any existing applications.

MYTH NUMBER 7: *Hierarchic clustering requires pointers.*

Assume for the sake of the discussion here that hierarchic clustering is desirable for performance reasons for some particular set of data. Because today's hierarchic and network systems typically use pointer chains as the basis for their physical storage structure, and because that storage structure in turn provides hierarchic clustering (see Myth No. 6 above), the notion has grown up that such clustering *requires* such a pointer-based storage structure. On this (shaky!) basis it is then suggested that relational systems that are currently index-based, such as DB2 and SQL/DS [1], will need major surgery before they will be able to provide such clustering.

It should be readily apparent that this conclusion is mistaken, at least from a theoretical point of view, because hierarchic clustering requires only that certain records be stored physically near one another—there is no requirement that those records be connected by pointers. In fact, there is at least one relational system, namely ORACLE [2], that supports such a "store near" facility without involving pointers at all. The EMP/DEPT example would look something like this in ORACLE:

```
CREATE  CLUSTER DEPTEMP
        DEPT#  ...

ALTER   CLUSTER DEPTEMP
        ADD TABLE DEPT
        WHERE DEPT# = DEPTEMP.DEPT#

ALTER   CLUSTER DEPTEMP
        ADD TABLE EMP
        WHERE DEPT# = DEPTEMP.DEPT#
```

Now ORACLE will automatically store each DEPT record on a separate page and each EMP record on the same page as the corresponding DEPT record. (Each page will physically contain the applicable DEPT# value once only, incidentally, which is a form of data compression.) The performance of join operations between DEPT and EMP over matching DEPT# values will automatically benefit from this arrangement.

Analogous effects can be achieved in DB2 and SQL/DS (but at present in a less than fully supported manner) by judicious use of the database load utility.

MYTH NUMBER 8: *The relational model presupposes (or requires) content-addressable memory.*

This is another myth—and an extraordinarily widespread one it is, too—that probably has its origin in the "logical/physical" confusion touched on several times already in this paper. It is true that the relational model does involve associative addressing (and indeed no other kind) at the logical level—but, as already explained, the relational model as such is concerned *only* with the logical level. It does *not* follow that associative addressing hardware is required at the physical level. Systems such as INGRES [3] have demonstrated that perfectly good performance can be achieved without such hardware, and indeed that often such hardware does not even help [19]. On the other hand, it is true that: (a) If such hardware were available (and useful), then it would be easier to take advantage of it in a relational system (think of the absurdity of having to support CODASYL-style manual navigation with such a device!); (b) any such hardware would almost certainly itself be based on the relational model, for a variety of reasons that there is no room to discuss here (see reference [14] for such a discussion).

MYTH NUMBER 9: *Relational databases use more storage than other kinds of database.*

This is yet another myth that derives from the logical/physical confusion—though in fairness it must be admitted that there is some truth in this one, so far as most current systems are concerned. In principle, a relational database could use exactly the same physical storage structure as one of today's hierarchic or network databases, in which case of course the storage requirements would be exactly the same. But in most current relational systems, tables map into (uncompressed) stored files, and those files in turn are heavily indexed—in other words, most relational systems today can be regarded as "inverted list" systems at the physical level. And inverted list databases do tend to take up more space than other kinds, for either or both of the following reasons: (a) They provide more entry points into the data (equivalently, more access paths); (b) data fields often take up more space than pointers.

Aside: Inverted list structures stand to gain a great deal (in terms of space reduction) from compression techniques, both for the indexed files and for the indexes themselves. The use of such techniques might easily reduce space requirements to the point where they are essentially the same as, or even less than, those for other structures. As it is, however, it is true that most relational databases today will tend to occupy more storage than their hierarchic or network counterparts.

MYTH NUMBER 10: *The relational approach is intended purely for query, not for production systems.*

Another myth that is encountered all too frequently! There are several (overlapping) aspects to this one. Among other things, it is claimed that:

1. Relational systems cannot achieve the performance needed for production systems.

2. Relational systems clearly *are* good for query, and query and production systems have historically always been distinct; therefore, relational systems cannot be intended for production work.

3. The relational algebra operators are intended for interactive (i.e., query) users, not for programmers.

4. The relational algebra operators are all retrieval operators, and hence relational systems are effectively read-only (i.e., query) systems.

5. Tight control is needed in a production environment to prevent some greedy transaction from hogging system resources, and such controls cannot be imposed in a relational system.

Of these points, the first is (as explained earlier) the subject of a separate paper (reference [16]), and the last is addressed in detail under Myth No. 12 later in the present paper. The remainder are discussed below.

First, it is certainly true that relational systems are good for query. Indeed, one of the original objectives for the relational model was to provide high-level (non-navigational) operators, in order that end-users could get directly to their data without having to wait for the DP department to write a program for them [7]. But matters did not stop there. By making those same operators available to the DP department as well, application programmers could be made more productive too. Thus, the operators of the relational algebra were intended to form the basis for both interactive (query) access *and* programming access to the same database. Furthermore, the optimization features of the system (discussed earlier in this paper) obviously apply to both kinds of access; thus, transactions in the conventional sense—that is, applications that are intended to be executed repeatedly and for which good performance is therefore highly desirable—can certainly be accommodated in a relational system.

As for the observation that query and production systems have historically always been distinct: There are two reasons for this state of affairs. The first is that, for technical reasons, it has always been rather difficult—not necessarily impossible, of course—to build satisfactory query interfaces for the old-style hierarchic and network systems. That problem does not exist in relational systems. Second, it is true—and may still be true for relational systems—that the two kinds of activity, query and production, do tend to interfere with one another (purely from a performance perspective, of course), and that therefore a "data extract" approach may sometimes provide the most satisfactory solution. But in a relational environment the "extracted-from" system and the "extracted-to" system can be one and the same (though production and extract activities may perhaps be performed at different times of the day); furthermore, the extract process itself is almost trivial, thanks to the high-level relational operators.

Turning now to the notion that the operators of the relational algebra are purely retrieval operators, and hence that relational systems are effectively read-only systems: This is a misconception of a different kind. The operators are *not* purely intended for retrieval (though it is true that most examples of the use of those operators in textbooks and similar works— see, e.g., [11]—do tend to be examples of queries). Rather, those operators are intended to be used for *writing expressions*. Those expressions in turn are intended to serve a variety of purposes, including retrieval of course, but certainly not limited to that function alone. The following is a list (taken from [14]) of some of the applications for such expressions:

- Retrieval—i.e., defining the set of data to be retrieved as the result of a query;

- Update—i.e., defining the set of data to be modified or deleted via an update operation;

- Virtual data—i.e., defining the set of data to be visible through a view;

- Access rights—i.e., defining the set of data over which authorization of some kind is to be granted;

- Stability requirements—i.e., defining the set of data that is to be the scope of a locking or other concurrency control operation;

- Integrity constraints—i.e., defining some specific rule that the database must satisfy, over and above the general rules that are part of the model and apply to *every* database (see Myth No. 13);

and certainly others besides.

MYTH NUMBER 11: *Automatic navigation does not apply to application programs, because such programs are forced to operate on one record at a time.*

It is of course true for conventional application programming languages such as PL/I and COBOL that the programmer is forced to operate on one record at a time, because most such languages are not capable of treating an entire set of records as a single operand. Relational systems provide a variety of approaches to this problem. In EQUEL (the programming version of the database language used in INGRES [3]), for example, the programmer writes a RETRIEVE statement, followed by a set of host language statements enclosed in curly brackets—e.g.:

```
##    RETRIEVE ( X = EMP.SALARY, Y = DEPT.BUDGET )
##    WHERE      EMP.DEPTNO = DEPT.DEPTNO
##    AND        DEPT.LOCATION = Z
##    {
      process X and Y
##    }
```

(The ## markers are flags for the EQUEL preprocessor.) The host language statements—"process X and Y," in the example—are executed once for each record in the set returned by the RETRIEVE statement; from the program's point of view, therefore, they do certainly constitute record-at-a-time processing. But note carefully that this does not mean that the program is performing manual navigation to get to its target data. The result returned by the RETRIEVE statement *is* the target data, and that RETRIEVE statement is optimized and executed by the system in the usual way. In other words, it is still the system that chooses the access paths by which the data is to be accessed; the navigation is thus still automatic, as in the interactive case.

MYTH NUMBER 12: *Control is not possible in a relational system.*

This myth is related to Myth No. 10, concerning the purpose of relational systems. The contention is that (as stated before) "Tight control is needed in a production environment to prevent some greedy transaction from hogging system resources, and such controls cannot be imposed in a relational system"—hence that either (a) such systems must be intended for query only, or (b) they must necessarily perform poorly, because of the mutual disruption caused by running jobs simultaneously that have conflicting requirements. The contention is justified with statements such as the following (all taken from reference [20]):

- "The user is able to operate free-form at a terminal. . . . The very essence of the relational environment is user freedom. Imposing restrictions on the user (even if they make sense) goes against the relational philosophy."

- "The relational environment, in its attempt at user friendliness, does not make a distinction between long-running and short-running jobs."

- "The relational movement is founded in a batch mentality. . . . In a relational environment (typified by SQL), it is normal and natural to scan entire databases."

- "Relational systems, by fiat of their ease of use, do not place restrictions on the user. The user is as likely to scan databases averaging account balances as the user is to seek information about a single account.''

- ''The nonprocedural nature of the relational environment is such that system requests are handled interactively, not in a precompiled mode.''

- ''Given the syntax of a language like SQL, it is very difficult if not impossible to separate requests. . . . Until the request goes into execution, it cannot be determined whether it will be short-running or long-running.''

- ''There is a price to [pay for] the flexibility of relational systems, and unfortunately the vendors of relational software often choose to ignore that price.''

It is difficult to know how to respond coherently to all of these accusations, but I will try. First, it obviously is possible, and desirable, to impose restrictions ''if they make sense.'' It is ridiculous to suggest otherwise. Some examples of the kind of controls available in systems today are given at the end of this discussion. But even if such restrictions do prove necessary in some environments, users will still enjoy all the other advantages of relational systems—ease of use, speed of application development, resilience to change, etc.—and in addition will be able to perform ad hoc access to the database at controlled times. Furthermore, there will be many installations where such controls will not be necessary, because the overall performance requirements will be less stringent. Performance vs. user freedom is a tradeoff like any other.

Next, it is of course true for *any* system (not just a relational one) that long-running and short-running jobs will tend to interfere with one another, and there is no harm in drawing attention to that fact. But to suggest that relational systems do not and cannot distinguish between them ''until the request goes into execution''—furthermore, to suggest that ''it is normal and natural [in a relational system] to scan entire databases''—displays an ignorance both of the controls referred to above and of the way relational systems are typically implemented: specifically, of their optimization capabilities. Let me amplify this point somewhat.

- It is not 100 percent true that ''requests are handled interactively, not in a precompiled mode.'' In almost every system I know, relational (i.e., high-level) requests may be issued *either* interactively *or* from an application program; and many systems do employ some kind of ''precompiled mode,'' at least for the case of requests that emanate from an application program, and sometimes for interactive requests too. In the IBM systems DB2 and SQL/DS, in particular, requests are *compiled* into optimized machine code before execution; in the interactive case, of course, the compilation has to be done at the time the request is entered, but in the application programming case it can be and is done ahead of time (in fact, as is normal with compilation, the program is typically compiled *once* but executed many times, possibly many thousands of times).

- Note the word "optimized" in the previous paragraph. As explained earlier, relational systems typically include an optimizer component, whose function is to choose an efficient strategy for navigating through (the relevant portion of) the database to satisfy the user's request. Needless to say, the optimizer will try extremely hard *not* to have to "scan entire databases": It will do its best to take advantage of any hashes, primary and secondary indexes, etc., that exist, just as a good hand-coder would. Indeed, as pointed out in [16], the optimizer may even produce code that is *better* than hand code, because it may have information available to it that a hand-coder typically would not have.

  Although the field of optimization in this sense is still fairly new, it is a fact that several of today's products do generate quite good strategies in many cases already. Moreover, optimization techniques are bound to improve with time. Reference [16] discusses all of these points in more detail.

- Given that optimization must precede execution (even in a non-compiling system, and even when the request is entered interactively), it *is* possible *in all cases* to determine whether a given request will be long- or short-running before that request is executed. The optimizer knows whether the request will use a hash or an index, it knows how selective indexes are, it knows how complex the search condition is (in particular, whether any ANDs or ORs are involved), it has statistics regarding table sizes and data distributions, it is aware of physical clustering characteristics, etc. From all of this information it should be possible to make an estimate of the time the request will take to execute. It is true, however, that most systems today do not attempt to make such an estimate, or at least do not pass that estimate on to the user; in fact, so far as I am aware, only one system, namely SQL/DS, currently makes any such attempt (see below). But this is another area where we can expect to see improvements in future releases.

- Finally, it is true that "there is a price to pay for the flexibility of relational systems," but the price is not that the installation must give up all control—rather, it is simply that the installation must be aware of the fact that control may be needed, and may have to exercise such control in some situations.

To conclude this discussion, here is a short (and certainly incomplete) list of control features in existing relational products. Note: These are all features of the *database* system. It is conceivable that the operating system might include some relevant features as well—for example, the ability to control the times at which a given user is allowed to log on to the system. It is also to be expected that further controls will be added to the database systems themselves as those systems evolve.

- Time estimates (SQL/DS): Before an interactive request is executed, the system will inform the user of the estimated execution time for that request. The user then has the option of proceeding with execution or canceling the request.

- Views (most systems): As already described under Myth No. 4, the view mechanism can easily be used to constrain users to predefined operations and predefined access paths, if desired.

- "Explain" (SQL/DS): EXPLAIN is a special statement that can be used in SQL/DS to obtain information regarding the implementation (and therefore the performance) of a specified SQL operation. The information is placed in a set of user-provided database tables. The information includes:

estimated execution time

estimated result size

access path(s) chosen

tables and fields referenced

estimated selectivities for search predicates

estimated number of executions for each subquery

sort and index utilization

All of this information is obviously useful in capacity planning and similar activities.

- Authorization (most systems): The authorization mechanism can clearly be used to prevent ad hoc access by specified users, or even all ad hoc access of any kind, to performance-sensitive data. However, such restrictions will be too severe in many cases. A more flexible scheme is provided in INGRES, whereby such access can be restricted to specified users (or all users) *at specified times of day and/or at specified terminals. For example:*

```
DEFINE PERMIT RETRIEVE            /* operation       */
              ON EMP              /* table           */
            ( EMP#, ENAME, DEPT# ) /* fields          */
              TO JOE              /* user            */
              AT TTA1             /* terminal        */
              FROM 8:00 TO 17:00  /* time constraints */
              ON SAT TO SUN       /* weekends only   */
              WHERE DEPT# != "D23" /* exclude EMPs in */
              AND   DEPT# != "M27" /* DEPTs D23 & M27 */
```

- Data partitioning (all systems): If query and production data are disjoint, there is clearly no question of performance interference at all. This is a very simple control, of course, doubtless too simple for many environments. But where it does apply, the installation still enjoys the benefits of running one DBMS instead of two, and of course all of the other relational advantages still apply also.

- Data extract (all systems): A special case of the previous paragraph. As pointed out earlier in this paper, "data extract" may still be a useful approach in a relational environment; also (again as mentioned earlier), the extract process itself is almost trivial in a relational system, compared with what typically has to be done to extract data from some other kind of system.

MYTH NUMBER 13: *Relational systems provide no data integrity.*

It is unfortunately the case that this "myth" is very largely true in current systems. To suggest that those systems provide no integrity at all is an exaggeration, to be sure, but the statement is nevertheless broadly true in its intended interpretation. That interpretation is, specifically, that today's systems do not support *primary and foreign keys* properly (in fact, in most cases they do not support those concepts at all). To understand what this statement means, consider the EMP/DEPT database once again:

```
EMP  ( EMP#, ENAME, DEPT#, SALARY )
DEPT ( DEPT#, DNAME, MGR_EMP#, BUDGET )
```

In this database, field EMP# is the *primary key* for the EMP relation: Every EMP record has a unique value for EMP#. Likewise, field DEPT# is the primary key for the DEPT relation. Furthermore, field DEPT# in the EMP relation is a *foreign key* matching the primary key of relation DEPT: Every value of DEPT# appearing in a record of EMP must also appear as the value of DEPT# in some record of DEPT. Likewise, field MGR_EMP# in the DEPT relation is a foreign key matching the primary key of relation EMP. We can represent this situation diagrammatically as follows:

EMP (EMP#, ENAME, DEPT#, SALARY)

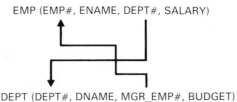

DEPT (DEPT#, DNAME, MGR_EMP#, BUDGET)

Constraints such as those illustrated by this example—for instance, the constraint that if the database shows employee Joe as belonging to department D23, it ought also to show that department D23 exists—are known generically as *foreign key constraints*. They have a variety of implications for INSERT, DELETE, and UPDATE operations on the relations involved (see [17] for a thorough discussion). But, as already indicated, most relational systems today do not support these concepts at all.

Let us go back to the relational model for a moment. As explained under the discussion of Myth No. 3, the relational model has three parts— a structural part, a manipulative part, and an integrity part. The structural and manipulative parts have already been discussed. The integrity part consists of two general integrity rules, viz:

1. The primary key of a base relation is not allowed to accept null values.

2. If base relation R2 includes a foreign key FK matching the primary key PK of base relation R1 (R1 and R2 not necessarily distinct), then every value of FK appearing in R2 must either (a) appear as the value of PK in some record of R1, or (b) be null. (Case (b) allows for the possibility that—for example—a given employee may currently be assigned to no department at all.)

These rules capture, in a more or less formal manner, the generic aspects of the real-world constraints sketched in the EMP/DEPT example above. The rules are *general*, in the sense that every database that claims to conform to the relational model must satisfy them. Of course, any given database may additionally have integrity rules that are specific to it alone; for example, the EMP/DEPT database might have a rule that salaries must be less than $100,000—but we are not concerned with such specific rules in this discussion. Again, see reference [17] for a thorough treatment of all of these ideas.

So we see that, so far as foreign key constraints are concerned, it is not the *model* that is lacking; rather, it is current systems, which have failed to implement the integrity part of the model. *I regard lack of support for foreign keys as the biggest single deficiency in relational systems today*—a deficiency that, I hasten to add, can and soon will be remedied; indeed, signs of such remedies are already beginning to appear in some products. But as matters stand at present, there is no question that users are left to fend for themselves in this area in most systems. For some suggestions as to exactly how users might "fend for themselves," the reader is again referred to [17].

In conclusion, I should stress the point that I do not consider this problem to be any kind of showstopper. It is true that users may have to do more work than they would otherwise have to, also that in some cases users' freedom of access to the database may have to be curtailed somewhat—but these drawbacks are outweighed (in my opinion) by all of the other advantages that relational systems already offer.

MYTH NUMBER 14: *A relational system that included all necessary integrity controls would be indistinguishable from a hierarchic or network system.*

This is another very common myth, also a somewhat subtle one. The suggestion is that, when foreign key support is added to a relational system, the resulting databases will be essentially indistinguishable from network databases (from now on I will shorten "hierarchic or network" to just "network," for brevity). Another way of stating this myth is that the simplicity of relational databases derives from the fact that they do not include any (foreign key) integrity constraints—in other words, the simplicity is spurious, and derives from an over-simplified view of the real world.

This myth arises from a confusion between (logical) data structure diagrams, on the one hand, and what might be called *reference diagrams*, on the other. Consider the following example:

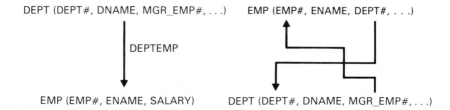

The diagram on the left is the link structure from Myth No. 4. It represents the logical data structure for a network database. Users of that network database see both the records, DEPT and EMP, *and the link DEPTEMP that connects them.* User operations are formulated in terms of all three of those constructs. The user language includes operators (such as CONNECT and DISCONNECT) that explicitly manipulate instances of the DEPTEMP link.

The diagram on the right, by contrast, is a reference diagram for a relational database (it is the diagram used in the discussion of Myth No. 13). It represents the (sole) data objects in that database, namely the DEPT and EMP relations, and shows which of those objects reference which others; in other words, it shows foreign keys and their corresponding primary keys.

Now, it is true that the diagram on the right does superficially resemble the one on the left (except that the arrows go the other way), *but the interpretation of the two diagrams is quite different.* The relational user still operates on relations, and nothing else; no additional operators are needed for manipulating "references." For example, to specify that employee Joe is in department D23, the user simply sets the DEPT# field of Joe's EMP record to the value D23; there is no need for an explicit CONNECT operator to "connect" that EMP record to the corresponding DEPT record.

Of course, it *is* true that the relational operation will fail if there is no DEPT record for D23 (assuming now that the system is enforcing that foreign key constraint), just as the CONNECT will fail under similar circumstances in the network case. But the point is that no additional data structure is needed to enforce such constraints, and nor are any additional operators. The simple relational structure is sufficient, and all of the consequent advantages of that simplicity still apply.

To sum up: Links can be used in a network system to enforce certain "referential integrity constraints" that would be handled by foreign keys in a relational system, and the corresponding network data structure diagrams do superficially resemble a relational system's "reference diagrams." But note that in a network system:

- Not all integrity constraints will be handled by links (in general, it is likely that not even all *referential* constraints will be handled by links).

- Links perform other functions in addition to integrity enforcement. In particular, they provide user-visible navigation paths. This "functional bundling" leads to a number of problems that have been discussed in detail elsewhere [8]. The basic problem is that it is not possible to add a new (link-enforced) referential constraint to the database without at the same time adding a new navigation path. (Furthermore, adding a link is itself a nontrivial operation [11].)

MYTH NUMBER 15: *Data has a naturally hierarchic structure.*

For some data, this "myth" clearly does contain an element of truth (though it could be argued that the phrase "naturally hierarchic" does not have a very precise meaning). For example, the EMP/DEPT database is "naturally hierarchic" (if it is the case that, at any given time, each employee must be in exactly one department). However, the inference that hierarchies are therefore a good data structure is *false*, even for "naturally hierarchic" data. The point is, not all processing—not necessarily even most processing—against the data will conform to the "natural" structure. For example, suppose the EMP/DEPT database is represented as the obvious hierarchy, with employees subordinate to departments, and consider the following two queries (which are of course inverses of each other):

Q1. Find the employees for a specified department.

Q2. Find the department for a specified employee.

The given hierarchy is fine for Q1 but not for Q2. (I am assuming that the system provides operators for entering the hierarchy at the top and then traversing it top-down, as is customary in such systems. Even if the system provided operators for entering the hierarchy at the bottom and traversing it bottom-up as well, those operators would necessarily be different from the top-down ones—whereas the English-language versions of the two queries display no such artificial distinctions.) In other words, although the original queries are symmetric, their hierarchic formulations are certainly not, precisely because the data structure itself is not symmetric. The hierarchic structure is biased in favor of certain applications, and therefore against others.

An equivalent relational database, by contrast, displays no such bias but rather is completely symmetric. (At the logical level, that is. There may be a bias at the physical level. We should certainly not expect a corresponding symmetry in *performance*.) Here are relational (SQL) versions of the two queries; notice how the natural symmetry is preserved.

```
Q1. SELECT  *
    FROM    EMP
    WHERE   DEPT#  IN
          ( SELECT DEPT#
            FROM   DEPT
            WHERE  DNAME = given value ) ;

Q2. SELECT  *
    FROM    DEPT
    WHERE   DEPT#  IN
          ( SELECT DEPT#
            FROM   EMP
            WHERE  ENAME = given value ) ;
```

It is sometimes argued that hierarchies can still be a good data structure, provided that different applications can be allowed to see different hierarchic views over the same data. (This is the raison d'être for the logical database facility of IMS, of course.) If Q2 were allowed to see the EMP/DEPT database with departments subordinate to employees, for example, the asymmetry referred to above would be avoided.

The problem with this approach is that the number of hierarchic views grows exceedingly quickly. Even if we restrict ourselves to "straight-line" hierarchies only, in which each parent record-type has only a single child record-type, N record-types lead to N! (N factorial) possible hierarchies: 2 record-types lead to 2 hierarchies, 3 record-types to 6 hierarchies, 4 record-types to 24, 5 to 120, etc. If we admit IMS-style hierarchies, in which a parent record-type can have multiple child record-types, the number grows faster still. And all of these views have to be predefined in some way. It seems preferable to have a data structure that is rather neutral (as the relational structure is), and then to provide *operators* that allow applications to traverse that structure dynamically in any fashion they choose.

MYTH NUMBER 16: *Relational systems do not conform to the official database standard.*

It is sometimes claimed that CODASYL systems conform to "the official standard" for DBMSs, and hence by implication that relational systems do not and should therefore be avoided. The fact is that no such standard exists (at least in the USA). The body responsible for standards in the USA is the American National Standards Institute (ANSI). Within ANSI, the committee responsible for data processing standards is X3, and X3 in turn has a committee called X3H2 whose charter is to develop database standards in *two* areas, namely network systems *and relational systems*. The current situation in X3H2 with regard to those two activities is as follows.[1]

- *Network*. The committee has a draft document [24], dated January 1984, defining a proposed standard network database language called NDL that is *very loosely* based on the old CODASYL specifications. The committee hopes to go to public review with (a revised version of) this proposal later this year (over 13 years after the final CODASYL report!).

- *Relational*. The committee has another draft document [25], also dated January 1984, defining a proposed standard relational database language called RDL that is (again) *very loosely* based on the IBM SQL language. The committee hopes (again) to go to public review with a revised version of this proposal later this year (only two years after the committee started work on it, incidentally; it is interesting to speculate as to why NDL took 13 years and RDL only two).

Quite apart from the X3H2 activity, numerous vendors, both hardware and software, have independently decided that SQL is going to be a de facto standard anyway. As a result, there are at the time of writing some 15 or 20 products available in the marketplace that support some dialect of the SQL language. In particular, of course, IBM has adopted SQL as the primary user language for its family of relational products DB2, SQL/DS, and QMF. There can thus be no doubt that SQL systems will become widespread in the 1980s, regardless of whether SQL is ever accepted as an official standard (or whether anything else is, come to that).

---

[1]See the remarks on this topic under the "Comments on Republication."

MYTH NUMBER 17: *Hierarchic and network structures are more powerful than relational structures.*

This myth definitely *is* a myth! The fact is:

- *There is nothing that can be represented by hierarchies and networks that cannot be represented by relations.*

To put this another way (the following statement is slightly over-simplified, but it does capture the essence of the situation): A relational structure consists of nothing but records, whereas hierarchic and network structures consist of records and links, and links cannot represent anything that records cannot. The links add *complexity* but no additional *power*. See [10] or [11] for an extensive discussion of this point, with many examples.

Earlier in this paper, I used the phrase "the relational philosophy" (in a quote from [20]), without however attempting to define what that philosophy was. I am not aware that anyone ever has defined such a philosophy, at least not in writing. But one aspect of that philosophy is certainly *simplicity* (for the user, that is). Given that (a) every known data structure involves records (possibly other constructs as well), and that (b) records by themselves are adequate to represent every known collection of data, then why not (c) eliminate all other constructs? (Apply Occam's Razor, in other words.) Records are all you need.

This simplification or reduction of the data structure to a single representational construct has repercussions and ramifications throughout the system. Specifically, it leads to a corresponding simplification in the *operators* that must be supported by that system (and that must be documented, taught, learned, understood, remembered, and applied by the user). And by "operators" here I mean, not only the ones that are obviously needed for data manipulation, but all of the other operators as well: for example, the declarative operators, the integrity operators, the security operators, the storage mapping operators, and in particular the exception-handling operators. In regard to the last of these, incidentally, note that the more complicated the system is, then the more ways there are for things to go wrong, and the more difficult application maintenance becomes.

- *Example* (slightly contrived). In a network system, links carry information. They must therefore be subject to the system's security mechanism, just as records are. For instance, a given user of the EMP/DEPT database (network version) may be allowed to see DEPT records and EMP records but may not be allowed to know which employees are in which departments. The DEPTEMP link would therefore have to be placed out of bounds for that user. (It is therefore unfortunate that the DEPTEMP link may well provide the only access path to EMP records!

—that is, it may not even be possible to provide access to EMP records without providing access to the DEPTEMP link also. See the comments regarding functional bundling under Myth No. 14 above.)

Let us consider the data manipulation operators specifically in a little more detail. Because there is fundamentally only one way of representing data in a relational system—namely, as values of fields within records within tables—relational languages basically need only four manipulative operators, one for each of the four basic manipulative functions (retrieve, change, insert, delete). For example, SQL has SELECT, UPDATE, INSERT, and DELETE; QUEL has RETRIEVE, REPLACE, APPEND, and DELETE; Query-By-Example [1] has P. ("print"), U., I., and D.; and so on. In fact, it is an axiom that, if there are *n* ways to represent data in a given system, then 4*n* operators are needed to manipulate data in that system. (Systems may not always provide all 4*n* operators explicitly, but that simply means that users sometimes have to "program their way around" the missing ones.) And, as already stated, the additional structures and additional operators do not provide any additional power, only additional complexity.

This is a good point at which to discuss the notion of *essentiality* [8]. A data object is *essential* if its loss would cause a loss of information. For example, in the relational version of EMP/DEPT:

```
DEPT ( DEPT#, DNAME, MGR_EMP#, BUDGET )
EMP  ( EMP#, ENAME, DEPT#, SALARY )
```

everything is essential in that sense. Likewise, in the network version:

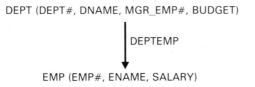

in which the field EMP.DEPT# has been removed and the link DEPTEMP inserted in its place, everything is again essential. But what about the following revised network:

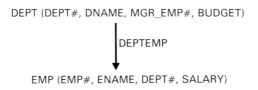

in which the field EMP.DEPT# has been reinstated? Here, DEPT and EMP are essential (as a matter of fact, they are identical to their counterparts in the relational version), but DEPTEMP is now *in*essential—there is no information that can be derived from the database that cannot be derived from DEPT and EMP alone.

It is now possible to pin down the principal difference between a relational database, on the one hand, and a network database, on the other. *A network database must contain at least one essential link*. For if it does not, then it is not a network database at all, but a relational database that happens to have certain physical access paths exposed (and there is no requirement that the user use those access paths, and the question arises as to why they should be exposed anyway when others are not). And it is the essential links that lead to much (not all) of the additional complexity of a network database.

In passing, let me point out that even inessential links will need to be subject to the security mechanism (etc.), even if they are generally not used as navigation paths. An inessential data object is still a data object, and it still carries information. Thus it is not only essential links that are the source of the additional complexity referred to above.

In conclusion, let me stress that there really is a difference between the relational and (essential) link versions of the EMP/DEPT database. Network advocates will sometimes claim that values of the field DEPT# in the EMP record (relational version) are nothing more than pointers that point to the corresponding DEPT records, and that such pointers are just the "parent pointers" typically found in a network link. Not so! Department number values are not pointers; they are simply data values. Data values differ from pointers in at least two ways:

1. They have no directionality. In the example, a "parent pointer" would point *from* the EMP record *to* the DEPT record. In the relational version, by contrast, we can equally well think of each EMP record as designating its corresponding DEPT record, or of each DEPT record as designating its corresponding EMP records, or both.

2. They are "multi-way associative." Each DEPT# value in the database, no matter what record it appears in—a DEPT record or an EMP record or any other record that includes a DEPT# field—is logically associated with *every* record in the database that contains that same DEPT# value. If a new record containing that DEPT# value is added to the database, it is *instantaneously* connected to every one of those existing records (logically speaking, of course); there is no need to issue any kind of explicit CONNECT operation to make any of those connexions.

MYTH NUMBER 18: *Relational databases involve a lot of redundancy.*

This myth is related to Myth No. 9. It stems, like so many others, from a confusion between the logical and physical levels. The redundancy in question is what may loosely be referred to as *"all those keys."* For example, in the EMP/DEPT database, a given department number will appear once in the DEPT record for the department in question (of course), and also once in each EMP record for an employee in that department. The same department number therefore appears multiple times, and it is true that this is redundancy of a kind—at the logical level. But, as already explained under Myth No. 7 (on hierarchic clustering), there is no need to reflect that redundancy at the physical level—though it is true at the time of writing that most systems in fact do.

Actually, the redundancy would not hurt at the logical level either, *if* the system provided the necessary foreign key support—if, for example, changing the value of the DEPT# field in a DEPT record automatically caused that same change to be propagated to all corresponding EMP records. It is only because systems typically do not propagate updates in this fashion today that the redundancy can be regarded as in any way harmful.

There is another rather different point to be made here, however. Consider the following database:

```
COURSE    ( COURSE#, TITLE )
          PRIMARY KEY ( COURSE# )
OFFERING ( COURSE#, OFF#, DATE, LOCATION )
          PRIMARY KEY ( COURSE#, OFF# )
ENROLL    ( COURSE#, OFF#, EMP#, GRADE )
          PRIMARY KEY ( COURSE#, OFF#, EMP# )
```

(primary keys as indicated; I assume for the sake of the example that the same employee can attend multiple offerings of the same course). This example involves an arguably different kind of redundancy. To be specific, if (for example) offering number 3 of course 86 has 20 students enrolled in it, then the fact that course 86 *has* an offering 3 appears 21 times (once in an OFFERING record and 20 times in an ENROLL record). It might be better to introduce a new, noncomposite key—CO#, say—for OFFERING, and then to use CO# in the ENROLL record, as follows:

```
COURSE    ( COURSE#, TITLE )
OFFERING ( CO#, COURSE#, OFF#, DATE, LOCATION )
ENROLL    ( CO#, EMP#, GRADE )
```

This technique reduces redundancy in much the same kind of way that pointers do in a network system—except that CO# values are *not* pointers, as explained in the discussion under Myth No. 17 above.

MYTH NUMBER 19: *The relational model is "just theory."*

Many commentators have attacked the relational model as being somehow "too academic," and not relevant to "the real world." For example: "It is difficult for this author to see a practical application [of the relational model] for operational systems at this time" (from a book published in 1981 [22]). And: ". . . many academics and researchers with no practical experience of data processing could work [i.e., with the relational model, and thus] make contributions, this lack of experience explaining, perhaps, the rather uncritical acceptance of the basic model" [23]. And again: "Much of this work [on the theory of normalization] would seem to be of very doubtful practical value and is perhaps a consequence of a lack of experience and understanding by the research workers involved of how ordinary DP systems analysis and design and practical database design are actually carried out" (from reference [23] again).

Now, the relational model obviously *is* theoretical, but that is hardly a weakpoint; on the contrary, it is precisely the sound theoretical underpinning that makes the relational approach so attractive (see reference [17] for an elaboration of this argument). The objectors' position seems to be (see [7]) that if something is theoretical, it cannot be practical!—equivalently, that only theoreticians are capable of understanding, or need to understand, something that is based on theory. My own position is exactly the opposite: Systems that do not have some solid theoretical base are usually very difficult for *anyone* to understand. It would be superfluous to name any specific examples—readers may supply their own all too readily.

A related criticism (perhaps just another way of expressing the same point) is that the relational model is too *mathematical*: "You need to be a mathematician to use or understand a relational system." This criticism reflects a confusion between function and syntax. Many papers on the relational model—in particular, papers on database design and database query languages, both aspects that very definitely affect the user—do tend to use rather mathematical nomenclature, quite often mathematical symbols too. But such usage is only appropriate, given the intended readership of those papers. It does not follow that user interfaces to commercial products need or should be expressed in those same mathematical terms. There is a world of difference (at the *syntax* level only, of course) between (1)

```
{ x.EMP#, x.SALARY : x memberof EMP
                   & exists y
                   ( y memberof DEPT
                   & x.DEPT# = y.DEPT#
                   & y.BUDGET > 1000000 ) }
```

and (2)

```
SELECT EMP#, SALARY
FROM   EMP
WHERE  DEPT# IN
     ( SELECT DEPT#
       FROM   DEPT
       WHERE  BUDGET > 1000000 ) ;
```

Expression (1) is a predicate calculus formulation of the query "Get employee numbers and salaries for employees whose department has a budget in excess of $1M." Expression (2) is a SQL formulation of the same query, and is probably much easier to understand for many people.

Here is what is for many users an even friendlier representation (Query-By-Example):

```
EMP ¦ EMP# ¦ DEPT# ¦ SALARY ¦      DEPT ¦ DEPT# ¦  BUDGET  ¦
----¦------¦-------¦--------¦      -----¦-------¦----------¦
    ¦  P.  ¦  _DX  ¦   P.   ¦           ¦  _DX  ¦ >1000000 ¦
```

The Query-By-Example language is essentially nothing more than a particularly elegant syntax for applying predicate calculus to relational databases.

Incidentally, I certainly do not mean to imply by the foregoing remarks that I am not in favor of using predicate calculus as the basis for query languages; indeed, the opposite is the case [18]. My comments refer to the syntax of such languages, nothing more.

MYTH NUMBER 20: *Relational databases require "third normal form."*

The relations of the relational model are always "normalized": That is, every field is single-valued—repeating groups are not allowed. Another, equivalent statement is: All relations are in *first normal form* (abbrev. 1NF). In other words, "normalized" and "first normal form" mean exactly the same thing, strictly speaking. (However, "normalized" is frequently, if sloppily, used in the more demanding sense of [at least] *third* normal form. See below.)

The reason first normal form is called "first" is that it is possible to define other, higher levels of normalization: second normal form (abbrev. 2NF), third normal form (3NF), and so on. Briefly, a relation is in 2NF if it is in 1NF and also satisfies a certain additional constraint (which will not be discussed in detail here); it is in 3NF if it is in 2NF and satisfies yet another additional constraint; and so on. Generally speaking, therefore, each level is more restrictive (in a certain specific sense) than the levels below it. Each level is generally also more *desirable* than the levels below it, in the sense that the database designer should generally aim for relations in the higher normal forms. This point is discussed in more detail later. The important point to be made at this juncture is the following:

- *Relational systems do not require any level of normalization other than first.*

Specifically, the operators of the relational algebra require only that the objects they work on be normalized relations, in the strict sense of that term defined in the first paragraph above. The higher levels of normalization are important for users (in particular, for the database designer), rather than for the system—they make the database easier to understand and easier to use—but the system will still function perfectly well if relations are only in (say) second normal form. Suggestions to the contrary, which certainly are sometimes heard, are absolutely *false*.

Despite all of the foregoing, however, it *is* usually a good idea to design the database so that relations are in (at least) third normal form. Here is an informal definition of 3NF (taken from [21]):

- A relation is in 3NF if every fact is a fact about the key, the whole key, and nothing but the key.

  For example, the relation

  ```
  EMP ( EMP#, ENAME, DEPT#, SALARY )
  ```

is in 3NF, because each record consists of (a) a primary key value (employee number) which identifies some particular employee, plus (b) three additional "facts" (name, department, and salary) that describe precisely that employee and nothing else.

It is not the intent of this paper to define the higher normal forms in detail or to describe the "further normalization" process (i.e., the process by which a relation not in one of the higher forms can be converted into equivalent relations that are); those topics are adequately covered in many other places (see, e.g., [11]). But another misconception that seems to have grown up in some circles is that 3NF is somehow "difficult." Nothing could be further from the truth, as the EMP example above surely demonstrates.

This notion (that 3NF is difficult) is probably another aspect of the "function vs. syntax" confusion referred to in the discussion of Myth No. 19. 3NF is really glorified common sense. In fact, the main practical advantage of normalization theory is that *it bolsters up your intuition* ("you" here are the database designer): It tells you that what you would naturally tend to do is in fact a good idea, and it tells you why. It also tells you that full normalization is always possible—that is, 3NF is always attainable (which is *not* intuitively obvious). It is true that the theory itself does tend to be somewhat "difficult," but the designer doesn't have to know how to prove the theorems, or even to understand the proofs—he or she only has to know the results of those theorems and how to apply them. (In fact, this whole area provides a good example of the practical benefits to be obtained from the existence of an underlying mathematical theory. See the comments on this point under Myth No. 19 earlier.)

For further discussion of this topic, see Myth No. 25.

MYTH NUMBER 21: *The primary key concept is unnecessary.*

A criticism that is sometimes leveled at the relational model is that its insistence on primary keys is a burden for the user. Examples are quoted of data for which no "natural" primary key exists: the daily temperature readings at some vacation resort, or the recorded items in someone's phonograph record collection, or the birthdates for the employees in some given department, etc. Any of these collections may very naturally include duplicate values; why is it necessary to invent "artificial" primary keys for them, just to make them "artificially" unique?

To respond to this criticism, it is necessary to delve into "the relational philosophy" once again (see Myth No. 17). The basic point here is that, given any two entities—say two temperature readings—those two entities *must* be distinguishable; for if they are not, then there cannot be two, there must be only one (this is an axiom!). In the temperature readings example, the readings are distinguishable by virtue of the fact that they were taken on different dates. Similar distinguishing features exist in each of the other examples quoted above, and (I would argue) in any other conceivable example.

Given that entities are distinguishable—i.e., that they have an *identity*—the question is: How should that identity be represented in the database? In the relational model, the answer must be "by the value of some field," since that is the *only* mechanism available in the relational model for representing any information at all. And the identifying field is of course the primary key. In the temperature readings example, we would typically use DATE as the primary key:

```
READINGS ( DATE, TEMPERATURE )
         PRIMARY KEY ( DATE )
```

And similarly for the other examples above.

It follows from the foregoing that primary keys are *absolutely fundamental*. They are certainly crucial in the process of database design. *They are also crucial to the relational model as such, because they provide the only record-level addressing mechanism in that model.* That is, the *only* reliable, guaranteed method of identifying an individual record in the relational model is via the combination (R,k), where R is the name of the containing relation and k is the primary key value for the record concerned. Of course, users are not restricted to *accessing* records by their primary key; on the contrary, they can access records by any desired combination of their fields; but it is only if they access by primary key that they are guaranteed to be addressing (at most) a single record.

Despite the foregoing, however, most relational systems currently do not support primary keys. This situation is (presumably) a consequence of a failure on the part of the implementers of those systems to recognize the importance of the primary key concept; in fact, it is (in my opinion) a *DBMS design error*. It is (or should be) incumbent on any would-be implementer of a relational system to understand what the relational model is and why it is the way it is. (Indeed, if this requirement had been met for today's systems, then several of the problems encountered with those systems might never have arisen.)

The situation in most systems today is that those systems typically provide mechanisms that allow users to apply the primary key discipline for themselves (if they so choose), but *the systems do not understand the semantics associated with that discipline*. In DB2, for example, the user can use the combination of a UNIQUE index and the NOT NULL integrity constraint [1] to specify that employee numbers (say) are unique and may not be null (see the discussion of Integrity Rule 1 under Myth No. 13)— but DB2 does not understand what it is the user has done via those specifications. As a result, DB2 support for certain other functions is either deficient or lacking entirely. Here is one trivial example:

- Consider a table T for which no UNIQUE index has been created. That table may contain duplicate rows (so it is *not* a relation). Suppose it does in fact contain two rows that are duplicates of each other. How can those two rows be told apart? By definition, it cannot be by value; so it must be by position, i.e., by *address*. (Of course, if the answer is that they cannot be told apart, then there are not two rows but only one and the problem is defined out of existence. I ignore that possibility.)

   In other words, it is no longer the case that *everything* is represented by values of fields. The fundamental data object in DB2, the SQL table, is thus not a relation at all but a set of ordered pairs of the form $<a,r>$, where a is an address and r is a record. As a result, all of the relational operators—select, project, join, etc.—must be redefined in SQL to work on those different objects. (I do not intend to pick on SQL specifically here, by the way: Similar criticisms apply to almost every system with which I am currently familiar.)

Aside: When I say that the rows of a SQL table are distinguished by address, I do not of course mean that the user is (or should be) able to issue queries of the form "retrieve the *n*th record" or "retrieve the record stored at address *a*." I mean merely that the only way to distinguish between two otherwise identical records is by their relative position (for example, if the records in question are displayed on a screen, then by their relative position on the screen).

The foregoing considerations do lead to some genuine practical problems. Consider, for example, a user performing (interactive) data entry into table T. If that user inadvertently enters the same record twice (all too easily done), then *there is now no way for that user to delete just one of the two copies*: Any WHERE clause that might be specified to identify one of the two in a DELETE operation *must* identify them both. It is thus only possible to delete both and then start over. In other words, in a table that permits duplicates, INSERT and DELETE are not inverses of each other.

Other consequences of the lack of primary key support, far more significant than the one just outlined, are explained in detail in reference [18].

To sum up, the basic message of this section of the paper is as follows: (a) Primary keys are important for database design; (b) they are also important for DBMS implementation; (c) designers and implementers who ignore the primary key discipline do so at their own peril.

MYTH NUMBER 22: *The relational model is only suitable for simple data (e.g., numbers and character strings).*

Most relational databases today support only a very limited range of data types: character strings, numbers (various kinds), dates and times in some cases, and a few others. And the contention is that these are the only data types that the relational model *can* handle. In particular, the fact that data values are not allowed to be nonatomic can be irksome. Consider the following example of a part serial number:

```
2381P7V4
```

It may well be that this serial number not only identifies the part in question, but also indicates that the part is a subassembly of a product with serial number 2381, it was manufactured by plant P7, and it is version 4 of that part. (I have argued elsewhere [13] that such "field overloading" is not a good idea, in general, but the fact is that people will do it.) So the part number is fundamentally not atomic. How should it be handled in a relational system? If it is broken down into its atomic constituents—

```
PART ( PRODUCT#, PLANT#, VERSION#, PART_DESCRIPTION , ... )
     PRIMARY KEY ( PRODUCT#, PLANT#, VERSION# )
```

—then requests for a particular part are very awkward:

```
SELECT *
FROM    PART
WHERE   PRODUCT# = '2381'
AND     PLANT#   = 'P7'
AND     VERSION# = 'V4' ;
```

(instead of just WHERE PART# = '2381P7V4'). Furthermore, any foreign keys matching this primary key will have to be broken down in the same way, and joins become clumsy too:

```
SELECT WAREHOUSE.*
FROM    WAREHOUSE, PART
WHERE   PART_DESCRIPTION = ...
AND     PART.PRODUCT#    = WAREHOUSE.PRODUCT#
AND     PART.PLANT#      = WAREHOUSE.PLANT#
AND     PART.VERSION#    = WAREHOUSE.VERSION# ;
```

And so on.

If on the other hand the part number is not broken down into its atomic constituents but treated as a single field, then (a) in some systems, at any rate, it may not be possible to access those constituents individually, and anyway (b) isn't this violating the "philosophy" of the relational model?

There are a number of separate issues that need to be carefully distinguished here:

1. First, the reason that current systems are preoccupied with character strings and numbers is, of course, that those are the data types that are most widespread in commercial data processing. It is not a fundamental limitation. There is no question that other familiar data types—for example, bit strings—can and will be added in the future (as well as some possibly less familiar ones).

2. In fact, there is no need to consider base data types (such as *string* or *integer*) part of the model as such at all. In the relational model, relations are defined over a collection of *simple domains* of data elements [4]. Those domains could have *any* associated simple (i.e., atomic) data type. Of course, an appropriate set of comparison operators—e.g., =, <, etc.— must be defined for that data type, in order that restrictions, joins, etc. may be meaningful.

3. "Atomic" in the previous paragraph means "atomic so far as the *model* is concerned." It would be possible, for example, to have a domain of part numbers, where those part numbers have an internal structure as sketched in the example above. The DBMS would not have any knowledge of that internal structure, *but the user would*, and could exploit that knowledge in

a variety of ways—at the very least, in interpreting query results and reports, and probably in other ways as well, if the system provided any operators for manipulating substrings. In SQL, for example, there is a LIKE operator for testing whether a given string conforms to a certain pattern, specified as a sequence of substrings (possibly including various "wild card" characters). Note that the fact that the system may provide such substring operators does not mean that the system has to understand the internal structure of a part number, only that it has to recognize that a character string can be regarded as being made up of substrings.

I do not intend by the foregoing to suggest that such attempts to subvert the system should be encouraged, incidentally. I am just trying to dispel a misconception as to what "atomic" means in the relational context. My preferred solution to the part number problem is as indicated in the next paragraph.

4. The relational model also permits *compound* (or composite) domains [4]. For example, the compound domain PART# could be defined as the combination (actually the Cartesian product) of the simple domains PRODUCT#, PLANT#, and VERSION#. The comparison operators = and ~= (not equals) would apply to values from this domain, whereas the comparison operators <, <= (etc.) probably would not. A system that supported this concept would then allow something like the following (to invent some syntax on the fly):

Data definition:

```
DECLARE 1 PART ,
         2 PART# ... PRIMARY KEY ,
           3 PRODUCT# ... ,
           3 PLANT# ... ,
           3 VERSION# ... ,
         2 PART_DESCRIPTION ... ;
```

Request for a particular part:

```
SELECT *
FROM    PART
WHERE   PART# = '2381P7V4' ;
```

Request for all parts from plant P7:

```
SELECT *
FROM    PART
WHERE   PLANT# = 'P7' ;
```

Join example:

```
SELECT WAREHOUSE.*
FROM    WAREHOUSE, PART
WHERE   PART_DESCRIPTION = ...
AND     PART.PART# = WAREHOUSE.PART# ;
```

And so on. But of course the problem is that few products if any currently support these ideas. Let us hope that such facilities will be added to those products as soon as possible.

5. Even "simple" data types (in the sense of paragraph 2) may have an internal structure that is known to the system in some cases. Complex numbers are a case in point; they may be regarded as atomic values in some contexts but composite values in others. Functions can be provided to manipulate the real and imaginary parts of a complex number independently.

6. There is a need in some applications to deal with a vector or array data type also. Time series data provides an obvious example. However, such vectors and arrays must be of fixed bounds; for otherwise they would in fact be repeating groups, which are definitely *not* part of the model.

Some of these points are touched on again under Myth No. 26, later.

The remaining myths differ in kind from those discussed previously. My general objective in this paper so far has been to show that relational systems are (or soon will be) able to do things that critics have suggested they cannot. By contrast, my objective in the remainder of the paper is to show that there are some things they cannot do, despite possible claims to the contrary by some overzealous relational advocate.

MYTH NUMBER 23: *SQL (or QUEL or . . .) is a panacea.*

This statement is obviously a myth, in the sense that SQL (and QUEL and . . .) provide database functions only. From the perspective of the programming user, all of the conventional programming language functions—control structures, subroutine calls, screen I/O facilities, etc.—are clearly also needed. SQL, in particular, relies on conventional programming languages to provide these functions. (So too does QUEL—with the significant difference that embedded QUEL does include some very high-level facilities ("EQUEL/FORMS") for screen I/O, so that users do not need to hand-craft those functions for themselves.) The basic point here is: Most applications involve more than just database operations, and the relational model is concerned only with the database.

Turning to the interactive user: From that user's perspective, numerous other facilities are also needed—report writing, business graphics, statistical operations, maybe text editing functions—depending on the class of user. So again it is obviously the case that SQL (or other relational language) alone is not sufficient.

Even considering database access alone, it is still true that languages such as SQL are not a panacea. The use of such languages still requires a certain degree of programming expertise, and users who are not DP professionals may well prefer some more user-friendly style of interaction, such as is found in the "forms-based" components of INGRES, for example [3]. Other users may prefer a natural language interface such as INTELLECT [1]. However, it is true that relational languages do provide a common core of function that is needed by all such higher-level interfaces; thus, they should provide an appropriate target into which such higher languages can be translated. But note even then that there are some database functions that SQL (etc.) do *not* yet provide, or at least not very elegantly: for example, the "outer join" operation [15], or the ability to compute the transitive closure of a relation [5].

Finally, SQL in particular is very far from ideal as a relational language; but that is a topic that is beyond the scope of this paper. See reference [18].

MYTH NUMBER 24: *Database design is unnecessary in a relational system.*

This is a very common one. It is sometimes encountered in the extreme form: "No data structure is needed at all"! Needless to say, it *is* a myth. It presumably stems from the undoubted facts that (a) the structure of an individual relation is extremely simple, and (b) the logical structure of an entire relational database is also frequently quite simple, at least by comparison with that of an equivalent network database—so much so, that users might perhaps be forgiven for thinking that the relational database is "structure-free." But the fact remains that there certainly is a structure, and that structure certainly does have to be designed.

First, let us distinguish between logical and physical design. I mentioned earlier in this paper (under Myth No. 1) that these two can be decoupled in a relational system, at least to a greater extent than was possible in older systems (though I have also indicated that the degree of decoupling achievable in current products is still not as great as I would like). Design is required at both levels, of course, with logical preceding physical, so I will address them in that order.

At the logical level, the designer's task tends to be easier than in a nonrelational system, for the following reasons:

- First, of course, the logical design *is* decoupled from physical considerations.

- Second, the logical data structure is simpler in a relational system.

- The theory of normalization exists. Note: Normalization is relevant to nonrelational databases also, but not to the same extent.

- The design does not all have to be done at once. It is possible to design and build part of the database and then to start using it at once for productive work, and later to extend the design in a piecemeal yet non-disruptive fashion.

- The design does not have to be 100 percent correct the first time. It is possible to remedy early design errors in a painless or almost painless manner (thanks to data independence).

- Likewise, if requirements change, the design can change too, again in a comparatively painless manner.

- The design process is trivial — in fact, completely intuitive—if the database is fairly simple. This statement *must* be true, incidentally, or databases on microcomputers would not be a feasible proposition; it is significant to note that, of the legion of microDBMS products now available, all but one or two (so far as I am aware) are relational.

However, there is no question that the logical design task can still be complex if the database itself is complex.

Turning now to the physical level, the designer is faced here with many of the same vexing questions that arise at the physical level in a nonrelational system, because of course the physical data structures are essentially the same. However:

- At present most relational systems actually provide fewer options at the physical level than nonrelational systems, so that there are actually fewer decisions to be made. But this state of affairs will not obtain for long.

- It is not so critical to get the physical design right, because the data independence provided in relational systems means that the physical structure can be changed without affecting the logic of existing applications. Thus, a "build now, tune later" approach becomes feasible.

I have suggested elsewhere [12] that a physical database design aid would be an extremely desirable addition to the range of auxiliary products provided with relational systems (much more desirable, in my opinion, than a logical design aid, though the latter might be useful too in complex situations). Note that a physical design aid would need to be more ambitious than the analogous tool in a nonrelational system, because it would need to take account of the system's optimization algorithms (at the same time—in all probability—hiding that information from the human designer). See reference [12] for further discussion.

MYTH NUMBER 25: *Third normal form is a panacea.*

Granted that database design is still necessary in a relational system (see Myth No. 24), it is frequently suggested that "third normal form is all there is to it." Now, it is certainly true that every database designer should be thoroughly conversant with 3NF (and related notions), but there is far more to database design than just the simple concept of 3NF. In fact, I would argue that, in most cases, breaking relations down into 3NF is not even a particularly major part of the design process. For a justification of this position, the reader is referred to the design methodology described in [17].

The foregoing paragraph should not be construed as saying that I think 3NF is unimportant. On the contrary, I have already stated (under Myth No. 17) that third normal form is a good idea, in the sense that the database designer should generally aim for a design in which all relations are 3NF. But it is still not a panacea: In other words, it is not *always* a good idea. To explain this point, let me first give another intuitive definition of 3NF (taken from [11]):

- A relation is in 3NF if it satisfies the objective: "One fact in one place"—loosely speaking, if it involves no redundancy.

The point that needs to be understood here is the following:

(a) 3NF is a good idea because database designs that are based on it are easy to understand and tend to be stable (i.e., resilient to growth), but

(b) designs that are based on 3NF tend to involve a lot of small tables (small, in the sense that they have comparatively few fields each), and

(c) in most current systems, where each table typically maps to a single stored file, such a design can have undesirable performance implications.

In a sense, the 3NF discipline *optimizes for update at the expense of retrieval*: It eliminates certain "update anomalies" [11], but it can lead to the need for lots of joins on retrieval. Sometimes, therefore, it may make sense *not* to have "one fact in one place," but to have one fact in multiple places, or multiple facts in one place—in other words, to live with certain forms of (controlled) redundancy. (Note that redundancy is not necessarily always bad; it is only *uncontrolled* redundancy that is bad.) For example, the following (non3NF) design may improve the efficiency of queries such as "Who is Joe's manager?":

```
EMP ( EMP#, ENAME, DEPT#, MGR_EMP#, SALARY )
```

MGR_EMP# represents the employee number of the manager of the department identified by DEPT#. The redundancy here is that the fact that employee *m* is the manager of department *d* is stated once for every employee *e* belonging to *d*. Such a design is valid enough, but the designer should clearly recognize and understand—and document—the tradeoffs involved in designing the database this way.

The reader may observe, quite rightly, that the foregoing discussion violates the principle of separation between the logical and physical levels that I have referred to so often in this paper. Let me therefore explain my position on this question. It is my opinion that, in an ideal system, the logical design should *always* be based on (at least) 3NF; any redundancy that is introduced for performance reasons should be introduced at the physical level, not the logical level. But today's systems are unfortunately *not* ideal; they do not as yet provide sufficient differentiation between the two levels to make this "ideal" approach a practical proposition in all cases. Specifically, any redundancy that exists at the physical level in today's systems will usually show through to the logical level also. Again, let us hope that those systems will be suitably enhanced at some future time.

MYTH NUMBER 26: *The relational approach is a panacea.*

The relational approach provides a methodology for dealing with certain real-world problems. Now, I venture to suggest that, given *any* methodology, it is possible to find some problem which that methodology cannot handle, or at best can handle only rather awkwardly. And the relational approach is certainly no exception to this general rule. Some examples have already been mentioned under Myths Nos. 22 and 23: the lack of composite field support, in systems if not in the model (which makes dealing with composite data rather clumsy); the lack of an outer join operator (which makes a certain class of problem very awkward, though not impossible); and the lack of a transitive closure operator (which makes another class of problem completely impossible). Here is another example:

- Refer back to the COURSE–OFFERING–ENROLL database (see Myth No. 18):

```
COURSE    ( COURSE#, TITLE )
          PRIMARY KEY ( COURSE# )
OFFERING  ( COURSE#, OFF#, DATE, LOCATION )
          PRIMARY KEY ( COURSE#, OFF# )
ENROLL    ( COURSE#, OFF#, EMP#, GRADE )
          PRIMARY KEY ( COURSE#, OFF#, EMP# )
```

Suppose that employee E1 is enrolled in course C1, but the relevant offering is as yet unknown. Then it is impossible to represent this enrollment in the ENROLL relation, because OFF# is part of the primary key of that relation, and no component of the primary key may be null. (I am of course assuming here that the system is enforcing "Integrity Rule 1." See the discussion of this integrity rule under Myth No. 13, earlier.)

When faced with difficulties such as these, there are basically two things we can do:

1. We can find a way around the problem within the existing methodology (if possible), and live with any slight awkwardness that solution may cause.
2. We can extend the methodology appropriately.

If the extension is of general usefulness, as in the case of composite fields and outer join and transitive closure, the second of these is clearly the right thing to do (albeit in the long-term—it might not provide a solution to the immediate problem, of course). But what should *not* be done is to extend the model in a special-case way to solve a special-case problem. For example, modifying Integrity Rule 1 to allow primary key values to be *partially* but not wholly null (to solve the COURSE–OFFERING–ENROLL problem above) drags a lot of other problems along in its wake. The penalty for solving one user's problem in this way would be increased complexity for *all* users, which hardly seems reasonable.

Having said that, perhaps the most general rule of all is the following: "You can break any rule you like, provided you are prepared to take responsibility for the consequences of your actions." In other words, you can do anything you want (assuming the system will let you!), but think what you're doing before you do it. In the case of the particular set of rules that make up the relational model, you should think especially carefully: Some of those rules have been the subject of extensive study (by mathematicians) for over 100 years. Are you sure that you have thought through all the ramifications of whatever rule it is that you are about to break? If not, then don't break it.

In conclusion, I should like to point out that the foregoing strictures apply to DBMS implementers at least as much as they do to users. The least attractive aspects of current relational systems are found at precisely the points at which those systems have strayed from the prescriptions of the underlying model. As a single example, I can point to the treatment of view updating: No current product (so far as I am aware) handles this problem in anything other than a totally ad hoc manner; and the reason for this state of affairs is that no current product supports primary and foreign keys properly [18]. Thus, systems could certainly be improved in a variety of ways. But even if a product were built that was totally faithful to the model, it would still be the case that there would be some problems that would be difficult or awkward to solve with that product. The relational model is a tremendous contribution, but it is not a panacea, because there are no panaceas.

CONCLUSION

I have discussed a large number of relational "myths" and misconceptions. There are so many such myths around, and some of them are so widespread, that a great deal needs to be said in order to set matters straight. (That fact of course accounts for the length of the paper.) My purpose has been to perform some of that necessary setting straight, in the hope that some at least of the many misconceptions may at last be laid to rest.

ACKNOWLEDGMENTS

I am grateful to Ted Codd and Sharon Weinberg for their many helpful comments on an earlier draft of this paper.

REFERENCES

1. Information on DB2, SQL/DS, QMF, and INTELLECT is available from IBM Corporation, Armonk, New York.

2. Information on ORACLE is available from Oracle Corporation, Menlo Park, California.

3. Information on INGRES and the INGRES forms-based products is available from Relational Technology Inc., Alameda, California.

4. E. F. Codd, "Relational Completeness of Data Base Sublanguages." In *Data Base Systems*: Courant Computer Science Symposia Series, Vol. 6. (Englewood Cliffs, NJ: Prentice-Hall, 1972).

5. E. F. Codd, "Extending the Relational Database Model to Capture More Meaning," *ACM Transactions on Database Systems* 4, No. 4 (December 1979).

6. E. F. Codd, "Data Models in Database Management," *Proc. Workshop on Data Abstraction, Databases, and Conceptual Modelling, Pingree Park, Colorado (June 1980). ACM SIGMOD Record* 11, No. 2 (February 1981).

7. E. F. Codd, "Relational Database: A Practical Foundation for Productivity" (the 1981 ACM Turing Award Lecture). *Communications of the ACM* 25, No. 2 (February 1982).

8. E. F. Codd and C. J. Date, "Interactive Support for Non-Programmers: The Relational and Network Approaches" (in this volume).

9. E. F. Codd and C. J. Date, Readers Platform: Response to a *Computerworld* In Depth article entitled "What Price Relational?" by William H. Inmon (see reference [20]). *Computerworld* (February 6, 1984).

10. C. J. Date, "An Introduction to the Unified Database Language (UDL)" (in this volume).

11. C. J. Date, *An Introduction to Database Systems: Volume I,* 4th edition (Reading, MA: Addison-Wesley, 1985).

12. C. J. Date, "Relational Database: Some Topics for Investigation," *Proc. GUIDE* 54, Anaheim, California (May 1982).

13. C. J. Date, "A Practical Approach to Database Design" (in this volume).

14. C. J. Date, *An Introduction to Database Systems: Volume II* (Reading MA: Addison-Wesley, 1983).

15. C. J. Date, "The Outer Join" (in this volume).

16. C. J. Date, "On the Performance of Relational Database Systems" (in this volume).

17. C. J. Date, *A Guide to DB2* (Reading, MA: Addison-Wesley, 1984).

18. C. J. Date, "A Critique of the SQL Database Language" (in this volume).

19. D. J. DeWitt, "Benchmarking Database Systems: A Systematic Approach," *Proc. 9th International Conference on Very Large Data Bases, Florence, Italy* (November 1983).

20. William H. Inmon, "What Price Relational?" In Depth article, *Computerworld* (November 28, 1983).

21. W. Kent, "A Simple Guide to Five Normal Forms in Relational Database Theory," *CACM* 26, No. 2 (February 1983).

22. Judy M. King, *Evaluating Data Base Management Systems* (New York: Van Nostrand, 1981).

23. P. J. H. King, "Relational Databases—Where Are They Going?" In *DBMSs— A Technical Comparison* (ed., P. J. H. King): Pergamon Infotech State of the Art Report 11:5 (1983).

24. X3H2 (American National Standards Database Committee), Draft Proposed Network Database Language. Document X3H2-84-1 (January 1984).

25. X3H2 (American National Standards Database Committee), Draft Proposed Relational Database Language. Document X3H2-84-2 (January 1984).

7

A Formal Definition of the Relational Model

ABSTRACT

The relational model of data, originally introduced by Codd in [1], has three components: (1) a set of objects (relations, domains, etc.); (2) a set of operators (union, project, etc.); (3) a set of general integrity rules. The purpose of this paper is to provide a formal definition of each of these three components.

COMMENTS ON REPUBLICATION

Once again I have taken the opportunity of making a large number of minor improvements in this republished version. Most of the changes are of course purely editorial in nature, but a few are more substantive. However, the treatment of data integrity, which (as I noted even in the original version of the paper) I believe to be inadequate as it stands, has been very little

---

This paper consists largely of material from *An Introduction to Database Systems: Volume II,* by C. J. Date, copyright 1983, Addison-Wesley, Reading, Massachusetts. Reprinted with permission. The same material originally appeared in *ACM SIGMOD Record* 13, No. 1 (September 1982). Reprinted with permission.

changed from the original. This is because a fully adequate treatment of the subject would have required too many major changes (it seemed to smack too much of rewriting history), and also because a more complete account of this aspect of the model has already been given in the paper "Referential Integrity," reprinted earlier in this part of the book.

INTRODUCTION

The relational model of data, first introduced by Codd in 1970 [1], has undergone a certain amount of revision and refinement since its original formulation. It is true, and indeed significant, that the changes have been evolutionary, not revolutionary, in nature; nevertheless, the situation is now that (to this writer's knowledge) there does not exist any particularly *formal* definition of the relational model as it currently stands. It therefore seems worthwhile to attempt such a definition, to provide a convenient source of reference for the material and to pave the way for an understanding of some of the more recent work on extending the model to incorporate additional meaning [2]. (Note: Reference [2] does include a definition of the "basic" relational model as well as of numerous extensions thereto, but that definition is considerably less formal than the one given in the present paper.)

The relational model, like any other data model, consists of three components [3]:

1. a set of objects;
2. a set of operators;
3. a set of general integrity rules.

The paper examines each of these components in turn, under the headings "Relational Database," "Relational Operations," and "Relational Rules," respectively. It provides definitions for the following concepts, among others:

Relational database
- domain
- relation
  (i.e., relation variable)
- real relation
  (i.e., base relation)
- virtual relation
  (i.e., view)
- degree
- attribute
- tuple
- candidate key
- primary key
- alternate key
- named relation
- unnamed relation

Relational operations

- union
- difference
- product (i.e., extended Cartesian product)
- theta-selection

- projection
- theta-join
- equijoin
- natural join
- relational assignment

Relational rules

- entity integrity

- referential integrity

As already stated, this paper is concerned with *formal* definitions of these concepts; it does not generally discuss their intended interpretation (the reader is assumed to be familiar with such informal aspects already; see, e.g., reference [5] for a tutorial treatment). Also, it should be stressed at the outset that the precise scope of "the relational model" as defined herein reflects to some extent a personal choice on the part of the writer. Other definitions are possible, and may either include additional concepts or exclude some concepts that are included here. Thus, for example, I choose to exclude the operators introduced in [2] for dealing with null values, for reasons given in [7].

I begin with the notion of *relational-system*. (Note: Throughout this paper certain typographical conventions will be followed whenever it is necessary to be formal. First, all terms to be formally defined will be hyphenated, if necessary, to exclude any intervening blanks. Second, terms defined by means of the production rules of Figs. 7.1 and 7.2, such as <relational-database>, will additionally be enclosed in angle brackets.) A relational-system is a database system constructed in accordance with the prescriptions of the relational model. More formally, a relational system consists of three components: a <relational-database>, a collection of <relational-operation>s, and two <relational-rule>s.

RELATIONAL DATABASE

As already indicated, it is convenient to summarize the structure of a <relational-database> by means of a set of production rules (Fig. 7.1). Please note that Fig. 7.1 is *not* a proposal for a concrete syntax for relational database declarations; rather, it is an *abstract* syntax, whose function is merely to indicate the abstract structure of the various objects being defined. Observe in particular that the syntax does not include any mention of the parentheses or other separators that would be needed in practice to avoid ambiguity.

In presenting the syntax, the paper makes use of the following convenient shorthand. Let <xyz> be an arbitrary syntactic category. Then the

```
 1.  <relational-database>
       ::=  <domain-set> <relation-set>

 2.  <domain>
       ::=  <domain-name> <domain-value-set> <ordering-indicator>

 3.  <domain-name>
       ::=  <name>

 4.  <domain-value>
       ::=  <atom>

 5.  <ordering-indicator>
       ::=  YES ¦ NO

 6.  <relation>
       ::=  <named-relation> ¦ <unnamed-relation>

 7.  <named-relation>
       ::=  <real-relation> ¦ <virtual-relation>

 8.  <real-relation>
       ::=  <relation-name> <attribute-set> <primary-key>
                             <alternate-key-set> <tuple-set>

 9.  <relation-name>
       ::=  <name>

10.  <attribute>
       ::=  <attribute-name> <domain-name>

11.  <attribute-name>
       ::=  <name>

12.  <primary-key>
       ::=  <candidate-key>

13.  <candidate-key>
       ::=  <attribute-name-set>

14.  <alternate-key>
       ::=  <candidate-key>

15.  <tuple>
       ::=  <attribute-value-set>

16.  <attribute-value>
       ::=  <attribute-name> <domain-value>

17.  <virtual-relation>
       ::=  <relation-name> <relational-expression>

18.  <unnamed-relation>
       ::=  <relational-expression>
```

Figure 7.1   The structure of a relational-system (Part 1 of 3):
the <relational-database>

expression <xyz-set> is also a syntactic category, representing an unordered, possibly empty set of objects of type <xyz>.

Let us now discuss the constructs of Fig. 7.1 in detail. The following paragraphs are numbered to correspond to the production rules of the figure.

1. A <relational-database> consists of a set of <domain>s and a set of <relation>s. Two points arise immediately.

■ First, note that I am using the term<relational-database> to mean, specifically, a *variable*, in the programming language sense; the value of that variable is assumed to change with time. Similar remarks apply to <relation>, but not to <domain>; a <domain> is *not* a variable, and its value does not change with time.

■ Second, the definition of relational-system is still rather static, the previous point notwithstanding; that is, the <relational-operation>s (defined in Fig. 7.2, later) make no provision for adding new <named-relation>s to the database, nor for destroying existing <named-relation>s, nor for any other changes to the database declaration. Extension of the definitions to handle such aspects is beyond the scope of this paper.

2. A <domain> consists of a <domain-name>, a (fixed, nonempty) set of <domain-value>s, and an <ordering-indicator>.

3. A <domain-name> is simply a <name>—a terminal category with respect to this syntax—representing the name of the <domain> concerned. Every <domain> in a given <relational-database>must have a <domain-name> that is unique with respect to all such names.

4. A <domain-value> is an <atom>—a terminal category with respect to this syntax—representing a value that is nondecomposable so far as the relational-system is concerned. All <domain-value>s for a given <domain>must be of the same data type. The notion of data type is not formalized in this paper.

Note: I assume for the present that <domain>s may include null values—i.e., that the null value is a legal <atom>. However, null values are not considered in this paper in any real depth. In particular, the paper ignores the special treatment required by null values in the definition of <relational-operation>s such as <union>. See [7] for such a discussion.

5. The <ordering-indicator> indicates whether the <domain> concerned is ordered—i.e., whether the operator "greater than" is applicable between pairs of <atom>s from the <domain>. The values YES and NO have the obvious interpretations.

6. A <relation> is either a <named-relation> or an <unnamed-relation>.

7. A <named-relation> is either a <real-relation> or a <virtual-relation>.

8. A <real-relation consists of a <relation-name>, a nonempty set of <attribute>s, a <primary-key>, a (possibly empty) set of <alternate-key>s, and a (time-varying, possibly empty) set of <tuple>s.

Note: In fact, *all* <relation>s (not just <real-relation>s, but also <virtual-relation>s and <unnamed-relation>s) possess an <attribute-set>. For reasons to be explained, however, the formalism of this paper shows <attribute-set> as an explicit component of <real-relation>s only. Similar remarks apply to <primary-key>, <alternate-key-set>, and <tuple-set>; see paragraphs 12-16, later.

The number of <attribute>s in the <attribute-set> of a given <relation> is the *degree* of the <relation> concerned.

9. A <relation-name> is a <name> (it is the name of the <named-relation> concerned). Every <named-relation> in a given <relational-database> must have a <relation-name> that is unique with respect to all such names.

10. An <attribute> consists of an <attribute-name> and a <domain-name>. The <domain> identified by <domain-name> is said to *correspond to* the <attribute> identified by <attribute-name> (see paragraph 11 below); equivalently, the <attribute> identified by <attribute-name> is said to be *defined on* the <domain> identified by <domain-name>.

11. An <attribute-name> is a <name> (it is the name of the <attribute> concerned). Every <attribute> of a given <relation> must have an <attribute-name> that is unique with respect to all such names.

12. A <primary-key> is a <candidate-key> (see paragraph 13 below). Every <relation> has exactly one <primary-key>.

13. A <candidate-key> is a nonempty set of <attribute-name>s. Every <attribute-name> appearing in a given <candidate-key> must be the <attribute-name> for some <attribute> of the <relation> concerned. Every <candidate-key> of a relation R satisfies the following two properties:

- Uniqueness property
  At any given time, no two <tuple>s of the current <tuple-set> of R have the same combination of <attribute-value>s for the set of <attribute>s designated by the <attribute-name-set> of the <candidate-key>.

- Minimality property
  No <attribute-name> can be discarded from the <attribute-name-

set> of the <candidate-key> without destroying the uniqueness property.

Conversely, any subset of the total <attribute-name-set> for a given <relation> that possesses these two properties is a <candidate-key> for that <relation>.

For a given <relation>, exactly one <candidate-key> is (arbitrarily) designated as the <primary-key> for that <relation>, and all other <candidate-key>s (if any) are designated as <alternate-key>s for that <relation>. Note: The distinction between <primary-key> and <alternate-key> is significant in practice only for <real-relation>s.

14. An <alternate-key> is a <candidate-key>. Every <relation> has zero or more <alternate-key>s. See paragraph 13.

15. A <tuple> is a set of <attribute-value>s. The <tuple-set> of a given <relation> represents, informally, the *value* of that <relation>. Let R be a <relation> and let T be the <tuple-set> within R at some particular time. Then every <tuple> of T *conforms to* the <attribute-set> of R; that is, it contains exactly one <attribute-value> for each distinct <attribute> of R, and the <attribute-name> within that <attribute-value> is the name of that <attribute> (see paragraph 16 below).

16. An <attribute-value> consists of an <attribute-name> and a <domain-value>. The <domain-value> is an <atom> from the (unique) <domain> corresponding to the <attribute> identified by <attribute-name>. Note: Informally, it is common to regard the <domain-value> alone as the "attribute-value," ignoring the <attribute-name> component.

17. A <virtual-relation> consists of a <relation-name> and a <relational-expression>. The <relational-expression> is an expression of the relational algebra, whose function is to specify the definition of the <virtual-relation> in terms of other <named-relation>s in the <relational-database> (see Fig. 7.2). The <virtual-relation>, like a <real-relation>, possesses both <attribute>s and a <tuple-set>; however, the <attribute>s and <tuple-set> are derived, in a manner to be explained later, from the <relational-expression>, and are therefore not shown as separate syntactic components. Likewise, a <virtual-relation> also possesses a <primary-key> and an <alternate-key-set>; however, those concepts, while applicable, are not particularly significant in this context, and they are therefore omitted from the formalism.

Note: If V is a <virtual-relation>, then the <relational-expression> defining V must not include, either directly or indirectly, any reference to V itself.

18. An <unnamed-relation> consists of a <relational-expression>. Informally, the <unnamed-relation> represents the result of evaluating that <relational-expression>. The remarks in paragraph 17 concerning <attribute>s, <tuple-set>, <primary-key>, and <alternate-key-set> apply to <unnamed-relation>s also, mutatis mutandis.

RELATIONAL OPERATIONS

The operations of the relational algebra are an integral component of the relational model. A particular relational implementation may support the operators of the algebra directly, or it may provide some alternative set of constructs, such as those of the relational calculus (tuple version or domain version [4,9]). This paper concerns itself only with the algebraic operators, since they are in a sense the most fundamental. Again the definitions are presented in terms of a set of production rules (Fig. 7.2); again that syntax should not be construed as a proposal for a concrete language.

The <relational-operation>s of Fig. 7.2 also include a <relational-assignment> operator (not part of the relational algebra per se). The function of this operator is to assign the result of evaluating some specified <relational-expression> to some specified <real-relation>.

Before explaining Fig.7.2 in detail, it is convenient to introduce the following notation:

- The expression R(A1:D1,...,An:Dn) denotes a <relation> named R, of degree n, with <attribute-set> (A1:D1,...,An:Dn)—i.e., with <attribute>s A1,...,An, defined on <domain>s D1,...,Dn, respectively. When the <domain>s are irrelevant to the purpose at hand, the expression will be abbreviated to just R(A1,...,An). If the <attribute>s are also irrelevant, the expression will be further abbreviated to simply R.

- Similarly, the expression (A1:a1,...,An:an) will be used to denote a <tuple> of R(A1,...,An). Here a1,...,an are values of <attribute>s A1,...,An, respectively (and are therefore drawn from<domain>s D1,...,Dn, respectively).

The following notion of *union-compatibility* is also needed:

- Two <relation>s of degree n, say R(A1,...,An) and S(B1,...,Bn), are said to be *union-compatible with respect to a <correspondence>* C if and only if C is a set of exactly n ordered pairs of <attribute-name>s (Ai,Bj) (i,j = 1,...,n), and the following three conditions hold:

  (a) Each <attribute-name> for R is some Ai (i = 1,...,n);
  (b) Each <attribute-name> for S is some Bj (j = 1,...,n);

```
19. <relational-operation>
      ::=  <relational-algebra-operation>
        |  <relational-assignment>

20. <relational-algebra-operation>
      ::=  <union>
        |  <difference>
        |  <product>
        |  <theta-selection>
        |  <projection>

21. <union>
      ::=  UNION <relation-name> <relation-name>
                                       <correspondence>

22. <correspondence>
      ::=  <attribute-name-pair-set>

23. <attribute-name-pair>
      ::=  <attribute-name> <attribute-name>

24. <difference>
      ::=  DIFFERENCE <relation-name> <relation-name>
                                       <correspondence>

25. <product>
      ::=  PRODUCT <relation-name> <relation-name>

26. <theta-selection>
      ::=  THETA_SELECT <relation-name> <theta-comparison>

27. <theta-comparison>
      ::=  <attribute-name> <theta> <comparand>

28. <theta>
      ::=  =  |  ~=  |  <  |  <=  |  >  |  >=

29. <comparand>
      ::=  <atom>  |  <attribute-name>

30. <projection>
      ::=  PROJECT <relation-name> <attribute-name-set>

31. <relational-assignment>
      ::=  ASSIGN <relation-name> <relational-expression>
                                       <correspondence>

32. <relational-expression>
      ::=  <relation-name>
        |  <relational-algebra-operation>
        |  <relation-literal>

33. <relation-literal>
      ::=  <attribute-set> <tuple-set>
```

Figure 7.2 The structure of a relational-system (Part 2 of 3):
the < relational-operation >s

(c) Within each pair (Ai,Bj) of the set, the <attribute>s designated by Ai and Bj have the same corresponding <domain>.

Note that, for given R and S, there may exist more than one such C— i.e., more than one <correspondence> satisfying (a), (b), and (c).

To continue with the detailed explanations:

19. A <relational-operation> is either a <relational-algebra-operation> or a <relational-assignment>.

20. A <relational-algebra-operation> is a <union>, a <difference>, a <product>, a <theta-selection>, or a <projection>. The result of evaluating a <relational-algebra-operation> is an <unnamed-relation>. As explained earlier (paragraph 18), that <unnamed-relation> possesses both an <attribute-set> and a <tuple-set>; moreover, each <tuple> in that <tuple-set> conforms to that <attribute-set>, in the sense of paragraph 15. The rules for generating the <attribute-set> and <tuple-set> are explained in paragraphs 21–30 below.

21. The <union> operator is defined as follows. Let R(A1:D1, . . ., An:Dn) and S(B1:D1, . . ., Bn:Dn) be two <named-relation>s that are union-compatible with respect to the <correspondence> C = ((A1,B1), . . ., (An,Bn)). The <union> of R and S over this particular <correspondence>, denoted UNION(R,S,C), is an <unnamed-relation> in which:

(a) The <attribute-set> is (arbitrarily) taken to be identical to that of R— i.e., it is the set (A1:D1, . . ., An:Dn);

(b) The <tuple-set> is defined as follows: The <tuple> (A1:a1, . . ., An:an) appears in the <tuple-set> of the <union> if and only if the <tuple> (A1:a1, . . ., An:an) appears in the <tuple-set> of R or the <tuple> (B1:a1, . . ., Bn:an) appears in the <tuple-set> of S (or both).

22. See the definition of union-compatibility, earlier.

23. See the definition of union-compatibility, earlier.

24. The <difference> operator is defined as follows. Let R(A1:D1, . . ., An:Dn) and S(B1:D1, . . ., Bn:Dn) be two <named-relation>s that are union-compatible with respect to the <correspondence> C = ((A1,B1), . . ., (An,Bn)). The <difference> of R and S (in that order) over this particular <correspondence>, denoted DIFFERENCE(R,S,C), is an <unnamed-relation> in which:

(a) The <attribute-set> is identical to that of R—i.e., it is the set (A1:D1, . . ., An:Dn);

(b) The <tuple-set> is defined as follows: The <tuple> (A1:a1, . . ., An:an) appears in the <tuple-set> of the <difference> if and only if the <tuple> (A1:a1, . . ., An:an) appears in the <tuple-set> of R and the <tuple> (B1:a1, . . ., Bn:an) does not appear in the <tuple-set> of S.

Note that the expressions DIFFERENCE(R,S,C) and DIFFERENCE (S,R,C) are not equivalent.

25. The <product> of two *differently-named* <named-relation>s R(A1:D1, . . ., Am:Dm) and S(B1:E1, . . ., Bn:En), denoted PRODUCT (R,S), is an <unnamed-relation> in which:

(a) The <attribute-set> is (RA1:D1, . . ., RAm:Dm,SB1:E1, . . ., SBn:En) —note the attribute renaming, which guarantees that <attribute-name>s in the <attribute-set> of the <product> are unique with respect to all such names;

(b) The <tuple-set> is defined as follows: The <tuple> (RA1:a1, . . ., RAm:am,SB1:b1, . . ., SBn:bn) appears in the <tuple-set> of the <product> if and only if the <tuple> (A1:a1, . . ., Am:am) appears in the <tuple-set> of R and the <tuple> (B1:b1, . . ., Bn:bn) appears in the <tuple-set> of S.

Note 1: The <product> as defined above represents what is sometimes called the *extended Cartesian product*.

Note 2: It is necessary to assume the existence of an *aliasing* operator, which permits the introduction of a new <relation-name> for a given <named-relation>. Such an operator is discussed informally in reference [5]. If it is desired to form the <product> of some <named-relation> R with itself, the aliasing operator can be used to create an alias, say S, for R, so that the <product> can still be expressed in terms of two different <relation-names>s.

26. The <theta-selection> operator is defined as follows. Let R(A1:D1, . . ., An:Dn) be a <named-relation>. Let *theta* denote any one of the comparison operators =, ~ =, <, < =, >, and > =. Let *theta-comparison* denote any comparison of the form "Ai *theta* vi," where vi is either a <domain-value> from Di or is another <attribute-name> Aj of R also defined on Di (i,j = 1, . . ., n), and where *theta* is applicable to Di. The <theta-selection> of R with respect to this particular *theta-comparison*, denoted THETA_SELECT(R,Ai,*theta*,vi), is an <unnamed-relation> in which:

(a) The <attribute-set> is identical to that of R—i.e., it is the set (A1:D1, . . ., An:Dn);

(b) The <tuple-set> is defined as follows: The <tuple> (Al:al, . . ., An:an) appears in the <tuple-set> of the <theta-selection> if and only if the <tuple> (Al:al, . . ., An:an) appears in the <tuple-set> of R and the comparison "ai *theta* vi" evaluates to *true* for that <tuple>.

27. See paragraph 26.

28. See paragraph 26.

29. See paragraph 26.

30. The <projection> operator is defined as follows. Let R(A1:D1, . . ., An:Dn) be a <named-relation>, and let (Ai, . . . Aj) be a subset of the <attribute-name>s specified in the <attribute-set> of R. The <projection> of R with respect to this subset, denoted PROJECT(R,(Ai, . . ., Aj)), is an <unnamed-relation> in which:

(a) The <attribute-set> is (Ai:Di, . . ., Aj:Dj), where each Dk is the Dk corresponding to Ak in the <attribute-set> of R (k = i, . . ., j);

(b) The <tuple-set> is defined as follows: The <tuple> (Ai:ai, . . ., Aj:aj) appears in the <tuple-set> of the <projection> if and only if a <tuple> (A1:al, . . ., An:an) appears in the <tuple-set> of R having ai as its Ai-value, ..., and aj as its Aj-value.

31. The <relational-assignment> operator is defined as follows. The <relation-name> must be the <name> of a <real-relation>, R say. Let R have <attribute>s A1, . . ., An. Let X be a <relational-expression> and let C be a <correspondence>. The <relational-assignment> of X to R in accordance with C, denoted ASSIGN(R,X,C), causes the existing <tuple-set> of R to be replaced by a new <tuple-set>, as follows:

(a) X is evaluated (see paragraph 32) to yield an <unnamed-relation>, S say, with <attribute>s B1, . . ., Bn, say.

(b) R and S must be union-compatible with respect to C. Let corresponding <attribute>s of R and S under C be (A1,B1), . . ., (An,Bn).

(c) The <tuple> (A1:al, . . ., An:an) appears in the new <tuple-set> of R if and only if the <tuple> (B1:al, . . ., Bn:an) appears in the <tuple-set> of S.

Note that the <relational-assignment> will fail if the would-be new <tuple-set> of R violates any integrity constraints that apply to R.

32. A <relational-expression> is a <relation-name>, a <relational-algebra-operation>, or a <relation-literal>. The result of evaluating a <relational-expression> is an <unnamed-relation>, as explained earlier.

In the case of a <relation-name>, the <unnamed-relation> has an <attribute-set> and a <tuple-set> identical to those of the designated <named-relation>. In the case of a <relational-algebra-operation>, it has an <attribute-set> and a <tuple-set> that are derived in accordance with paragraphs 21-30 above. In the case of a <relation-literal>, it has an <attribute-set> and a <tuple-set> identical to those of the designated <relation-literal> (see paragraph 33).

33. A <relation-literal> consists of an <attribute-set> and a <tuple-set>. Each <tuple> in the <tuple-set> must conform to the <attribute-set>. Intuitively, <relation-literal>s permit the insertion of new <tuple>s into the <relational-database> (via a <union> operation), and the deletion of existing <tuple>s from the <relational-database> (via a <difference> operation).

RELATIONAL ALGEBRA: ADDITIONAL OPERATORS

The formal definitions given so far have deliberately restricted themselves to a very primitive (but relationally complete [4]) set of operations. In practice, a relational *implementation* should provide various refinements on that primitive set, for both usability and efficiency reasons. Some examples of such refinements are considered briefly (and informally) below.

- Intersection, join, division

The relational algebra as usually defined includes not only the operators defined above, but also the operators *intersection, join,* and *division* [2]. These operators were excluded from the formalism because they are not true primitives—each can be defined in terms of the other operators, as shown in reference [5]. However, the *join* operator is so important in practice that it is worth including a definition of it here, for purposes of reference. (Actually, the term "join" is used generically to refer to several related but distinct operators, as will be seen.)

Let relations $R(A1, \ldots, Ai:D, \ldots, Am)$ and $S(B1, \ldots, Bj:D, \ldots, Bn)$ be such that attributes Ai and Bj are defined on the same domain D. Let *theta* be a comparison operator that applies to domain D. Then the *theta-join* of R on Ai with S on Bj, denoted THETA_JOIN $(R,Ai,theta,S,Bj)$, is an unnamed-relation with attribute-set as for PRODUCT(R,S). The tuple-set for this relation consists of all tuples

$$(RA1:a1, \ldots, RAi:ai, \ldots, RAm:am, SB1:b1, \ldots, SBj:bj, \ldots, SBn:bn)$$

such that the tuple $(A1:a1, \ldots, Ai:ai, \ldots, Am:am)$ appears in the current tuple-set of R, the tuple $(B1:b1, \ldots, Bj:bj, \ldots, Bn:bn)$ appears in the current tuple-set of S, and the comparison "ai *theta* bj" evaluates to *true*. In other words, the theta-join of R and S is obtained by taking the product of R and S and then applying an appropriate theta-selection to it.

If *theta* is equality, the theta-join is said to be an *equijoin*. In the case of the equijoin, each tuple necessarily has identical values for attributes RAi and SBj. Let C be the set of all attributes of the equijoin except for RAi (or except for SBj). The projection of the equijoin on C is called the *natural* join of R and S (on Ai and Bj).

- Extended and combined operations

It is desirable to provide shorthand equivalents for commonly occurring sequences of the primitive operations, also certain straightforward extensions to those operations. Some candidates are as follows:

- Allow the operands of the relational-algebra-operations to be specified as arbitrary relational-expressions (enclosed in parentheses if necessary in order to avoid ambiguity), instead of only as relation-names;

- Introduce an extended "selection" operator, in which the selection condition consists of an arbitrary Boolean combination of simple theta-comparisons;

- Introduce an analogously extended "join" operator;

- Extend the set of legal "theta" comparison operators to include (e.g.) substring search;

- Extend the set of legal comparands in a "theta-comparison" to include (e.g.) arithmetic expressions;

- Introduce an extended "projection" operator, in which the "attributes" over which the projection is taken can be specified as (e.g.) arithmetic expressions;

- Allow the target for a relational-assignment operation to be a virtual-relation as well as a real-relation (for "updatable" virtual-relations);

- Introduce explicit "insert," "delete," and "modify" operations, instead of relying purely on relational-assignment and appropriate use of the union and difference operators.

- Operators to handle null values

The relational algebra as defined by Codd in reference [2] includes certain additional operators for dealing with null values—for example, a "maybe" version of THETA_SELECT that selects tuples for which the theta-comparison evaluates to *unknown* instead of to *true*. As indicated earlier, all detailed discussion of null values—their effect on the relational algebra, in particular—was omitted from this paper deliberately. See reference [7].

RELATIONAL RULES

As mentioned in the introduction, the basic relational model includes two general integrity rules. (A specific relational-system will typically include a number of specific "local" integrity rules in addition, of course.) The two general rules are defined in Fig. 7.3. The definitions are in the spirit of reference [2]; regarding Rule 2 ("referential integrity"), however, it has been suggested that the formalism of [2] is not entirely satisfactory as it stands [6,8]. The basic point is that Rule 2 does not of itself constitute a complete control on the referential integrity problem; loosely speaking, it is "necessary but not sufficient" (that is, a database could conform to the requirements of Rule 2 and yet still be in violation of some referential constraint). Reference [6] contains a detailed discussion of this topic and presents a more general proposal for expressing referential constraints—a proposal, incidentally, that (unlike Rule 2 as defined here) does not require the notion of "primary domain" at all.

Note that the two rules refer to < real-relation > s only, not to < virtual-relation > s and not to < unnamed-relation > s.

Integrity Rule 1 (entity integrity)

   * Let ⟨attribute⟩ A of ⟨real-relation⟩ R be a component of the ⟨primary-key⟩ of R. Then ⟨attribute⟩ A cannot accept null values. That is, no ⟨tuple⟩ of R can include an ⟨attribute-value⟩ in which the ⟨attribute-name⟩ is A and the ⟨domain-value⟩ is null.

Integrity Rule 2 (referential integrity)

   * Let ⟨domain⟩ D be such that there exists a ⟨real-relation⟩ with (single-attribute) ⟨primary-key⟩ defined on D. Then D may optionally be designated as a *primary* ⟨domain⟩.

   * Now let R(...,A:D,...) be a ⟨real-relation⟩ with ⟨attribute⟩ A defined on primary ⟨domain⟩ D. Then every ⟨tuple⟩ of R must satisfy the constraint that the ⟨domain-value⟩ corresponding to ⟨attribute⟩ A within that ⟨tuple⟩ must be either (a) null, or (b) equal to k, say, where k is the ⟨domain-value⟩ corresponding to the ⟨primary-key⟩ within some ⟨tuple⟩ of some ⟨real-relation⟩ S with ⟨primary-key⟩ defined on D. R and S need not be distinct. The ⟨attribute⟩ A is said to be a *foreign key*.

Figure 7.3   The structure of a relational-system (Part 3 of 3):
        the < relational-rule > s

CONCLUDING REMARKS

I conclude by showing informally how the definitions given earlier lead to certain well-known and important relational properties.

- Within a given relation, no two tuples are identical (at any given time). This follows from the fact that the tuples within the relation at any given time are a *set*, and sets by definition do not contain duplicate elements.

- As a consequence of the previous point, the requirement that relations—in particular, real relations—always have a primary key is a reasonable (i.e., consistent) one. This follows from the fact that at least the combination of *all* attributes has the uniqueness property, and hence that at least one candidate key (the set of all attributes, if necessary) always exists.

- Within a given relation (more accurately, within the tuple-set of a given relation), tuples are unordered. This also follows from the fact that the tuples are a set—sets by definition have no ordering.

- Within a given relation, attributes are unordered. This follows from the fact that the collection of attributes of the relation is also defined as a set.

- All attribute-values are atomic; in other words, all relations are *normalized*. Equivalently, all relations are in (at least) *first normal form*. This level of normalization is required by the relational algebra. Higher levels, such as 4NF [10], are useful for database design purposes but are not an intrinsic part of the relational model per se.

ACKNOWLEDGMENTS

I am grateful to my colleagues Ted Codd, Bill Kent, and Phil Shaw for numerous constructive comments on earlier drafts.

REFERENCES

1. E. F. Codd, "A Relational Model of Data for Large Shared Data Banks," CACM 13, No. 6 (June 1970).

2. E. F. Codd, "Extending the Database Relational Model to Capture More Meaning," ACM TODS 4, No. 4 (December 1979).

3. E. F. Codd, "Data Models in Database Management," ACM SIGMOD Record 11, No. 2 (February 1981).

4. E. F. Codd, "Relational Completeness of Data Base Sublanguages." In *Data Base Systems*: Courant Computer Science Symposia Series, Vol. 6. (Englewood Cliffs, NJ: Prentice-Hall, 1972).

5. C. J. Date, *An Introduction to Database Systems*: *Volume I*, 4th edition (Reading, MA: Addison-Wesley, 1985).

6. C. J. Date, "Referential Integrity" (in this volume).

7. C. J. Date, "Null Values in Database Management" (in this volume).

8. W. Kent, *private communication* (May 1981).

9. M. Lacroix and A. Pirotte, "Domain-Oriented Relational Languages," *Proc. 3rd International Conference on Very Large Data Bases* (October 1977).

10. R. Fagin, "Normal Forms and Relational Database Operators," *Proc. 1979 ACM SIGMOD International Conference on Management of Data* (May 1979).

8

The Relational Model
and Its Interpretation

ABSTRACT

This paper is not intended as yet another tutorial on the relational model. Rather, it is a discussion of what the model *means*; i.e, it is a discussion of the intended interpretation of the model in the real world. An understanding of that interpretation is prerequisite to intelligent use of the model. Lack of such understanding—unfortunately not uncommon—leads to a number of confusions, some of which are sketched briefly in the paper.

Although the paper is of course primarily concerned with the relational model per se, many of the remarks are of a quite general nature and apply to any data model. The reader is assumed to be familiar with the basic concepts of the relational model.

INTRODUCTION

The concept of "data model," first formulated by E. F. Codd in the context of the *relational* model, is by now reasonably familiar to many people. Here

Previously unpublished.

143

is a definition, based loosely on the one given by Codd in his paper "Data Models in Database Management" (reference [1]). A data model consists of a combination of three components:

1. A collection of data object types, which form the basic building blocks for any data base that conforms to the model
2. A collection of general integrity rules, which constrain the set of instances of those object types that can legally appear in any such database
3. A collection of operators, which can be applied to such object instances for retrieval and other purposes

For example, in the case of the relational model, there are basically two types of data object, viz. domains and *n*-ary relations; there are also two general integrity rules, viz. the Entity and Referential Integrity rules; and finally there is a corresponding set of operators, viz. the operators of the *n*-ary relational algebra plus the relational assignment operator. A thorough tutorial treatment of all three of these components can be found in reference [2] and elsewhere.

What are data models for? In the paper referenced earlier [1], Codd goes on to suggest that a data model can be used in any of the following ways (paraphrasing considerably):

1. As a tool for expressing the specific integrity constraints that apply to a specific database
2. As a basis for developing a variety of general database design methodologies
3. As a basis for minimizing the impact of database changes on existing application programs and interactive procedures
4. As a basis for the development of families of very high level database languages
5. As a focus for the design and construction of database management systems
6. As a vehicle for research into the behavioral properties of data and database systems

Needless to say, this list is not intended to be exhaustive.

Underlying all these suggestions, however, there is a tacit but important assumption—an assumption that can be a rich source of confusion, if it is not properly understood and appreciated. That assumption, which I will refer to as *the interpretation principle,* is as follows:

■   *The data model in question must have a commonly accepted (and useful) INTERPRETATION; that is, its objects, integrity rules, and operators must have some generally accepted correspondence to phenomena in the real world.*

For if not, then the model will be merely an academic exercise, of little practical relevance. And of course data models in general, and the relational model in particular, were intended first and foremost to be *useful*—and by "useful" here I definitely mean "useful to database practitioners."

THE ARGUMENT

The remainder of this short paper is an attempt to explain and justify the foregoing claims. I shall present the argument a step at a time, using the relational model (where applicable) as the basis for examples and illustrations. The argument goes as follows.

1. A data model is *a formal system*. A formal system is a system in which a set of precisely defined objects can be manipulated in accordance with (and only in accordance with) a set of precisely defined rules, without any regard for the "meaning" or real-world interpretation of those objects and rules. Any programming language—for example, PL/I—can serve as a familiar example of such a system.

> *Aside:* In fact, it is axiomatic that any computer system, at any level of abstraction, is a formal system. For example, any implementation of PL/I (i.e., any "PL/I machine") is necessarily a formal system.

2. The real world is *not* a formal system—or at least, if it is, then it is one of immense complexity, beyond our ability to formalize at the time of writing, and likely to remain so for the foreseeable future.

> *Aside:* The belief that the real world *is* a formal system, albeit an extremely complex one, and hence totally mechanizable (at least in principle), is the underlying article of faith in what has come to be known in the artificial intelligence community as the *strong AI* position. It is not my purpose to argue either for or against that position in this paper.

3. Thus, part of the trick in defining a data model is to try and find a formal system whose formal behavior mimics the *in*formal behavior of certain aspects of the real world—namely, those aspects of the real world that happen to be of interest in some particular context. Note carefully that the phrase "aspects of the real world" is intended to include both static and dynamic aspects.

4. We obviously therefore need to be able to specify the mapping or correspondence between that formal system—i.e., the data model—on the one hand, and the real world on the other. In other words, we need to be able to specify the *interpretation* of the model. Note, however, that any such interpretation must necessarily be *in*formal, since it involves an informal component (a mapping between two systems can be defined *formally* only if both systems are in turn formal themselves.)

5. It is clearly desirable to find a formal system (and associated interpretation) that can be useful in a very wide class of applications (not necessarily every conceivable application, of course).

6. Before we can talk sensibly about a mapping between some formal system and the real world, we need to have some (informal) notion of what it is that constitutes the real world, so that we can specify what it is in the real world that any given component of the formal system corresponds to.

7. One commonly accepted (informal) notion is that the real world is made up of *entities*—furthermore, that entities have *properties,* and that there are *relationships* of various kinds that connect entities together. It is also usual to assume that such inter-entity relationships are entities too and can have properties of their own and participate in further relationships (and so on, ad infinitum). *Note:* Henceforth I will use the term "primitive entity" to refer to an entity that is not a relationship.

8. It is impossible to pin down the notion of "entity" in any very precise manner (that is, it is impossible to state unequivocally that some object x is an entity and some object y is not); such questions depend to some extent on individual perceptions of the real world. However, one thing that can and must be agreed upon is that entities are *mutually distinguishable.* In other words, one property that must necessarily be possessed by every entity is some kind of unique *id*entity. For if two entities cannot be told apart in any way whatsoever, then there are not two entities but only one! This is the axiom of "identity of indiscernibles."

9. Turning now to the relational model specifically: The relational model is useful precisely because (among other things) it meets the requirements stated in paragraphs 3–5 above admirably. In other words, it does satisfy the interpretation principle, in that it does possess a "commonly accepted and useful" (but—of course—informal) interpretation. That interpretation is sketched in paragraphs 10–22 below.

10. Any entity in the real world, primitive or otherwise, can be represented by an *n*-ary relation. (I am using "entity" here to mean "entity *type*" specifically.) Likewise, the properties of any such entity can be represented by the attributes of such a relation. Conversely, any relation (with its attributes) can be interpreted as an entity (with its properties).

11. In particular, the primary key attribute of a relation corresponds to the identity property of an entity.

12. Before we go any further, it is necessary to distinguish between base and derived relations. A derived relation is a relation that is defined in terms of one or more other relations—i.e., a relation whose value at all times is derived from one or more other relations by evaluating some specified expression of the relational algebra. A base relation is a relation that is not derived. Thus, base relations are *autonomous*.

13. Base relations must necessarily be named. Derived relations may or may not be named. Views (and snapshots) are named derived relations; query results and the like are unnamed derived relations.

14. In deciding how to represent (some portion of) the real world in a database, the database designer must decide which entities are important enough to require explicit representation. Details of how that decision is to be made are outside the purview of the interpretation principle per se; clearly they will depend on the intended use of the database, even to some extent on the whim of the designer (for precisely the reason that the real world is not a formal system). However, all such "important" entities will be represented by base relations. All other entities (by exclusion) will be represented *im*plicitly; such entities will (of course) be represented by derived relations.

15. The two relational integrity rules (the Entity and Referential Integrity rules) constrain base relation values to just those values that "make sense," intuitively speaking. The point is, the universe of all possible values for base relations (and collections of base relations) includes some configurations of values that do not correspond to any feasible configuration of entities in the real world and thus do not have any sensible interpretation. An example of an infeasible configuration is one in which some employee *e* is shown as belonging to some nonexistent department *d*. The intent of the two integrity rules is to exclude such infeasible configurations from consideration.

> *Aside*: The specific integrity rules that apply to some specific database serve to constrain values for the base relations in that particular database still further. Their purpose is to make that particular database act as a representation that is still more faithful to the real world, within its own limited sphere.

16. Note that the two general integrity rules apply specifically to *base* relations. The Entity Integrity rule, for example, states that primary key values in base relations must not be null, either in whole or in part. This rule corresponds to the intuitive fact that if an entity is important enough in the real world to require explicit representation in the database, then that entity must be definitely and unambiguously identifiable (for otherwise it would be impossible even to talk about it in any sensible manner).

Aside: Note carefully that the Entity Integrity rule does not prohibit null values in primary keys in *derived* relations. For if it did, a query such as "List all employee salaries" would be inadmissible if any Employee Salary value currently happened to be unknown (i.e., null). Confusion on this point is not uncommon; for example, remarks such as "The projection of relation Employee on the Salary attribute is not a valid relation" are heard quite frequently. (It may not be a valid *base* relation, but it certainly is a valid *relation*.) Such misconceptions can be attributed to a failure to understand the interpretation principle, as it applies to the relational model.

Note too that if some employee salary does in fact happen to be unknown, it necessarily follows that the query "How many distinct employee salaries are there?" should also return the answer "Unknown." Relational systems today are not always terribly consistent on this point.

17. A foreign key attribute (in a base relation) serves to identify an entity that participates in an (explicitly represented) relationship. As an example, consider the "Works In" relationship, which is represented by the combination of Employee Number (primary key) and Department Number (foreign key) in the Employee base relation:

```
Employee     ( Employee Number, Department Number )
Department   ( Department Number, Location )
```

For a given employee, the Department Number value in the Employee tuple (record) representing that employee identifies the particular department the employee works in (by means of the primary key value for the Department tuple representing the department concerned).

18. The Referential Integrity rule states that each foreign key value in a base relation must be either (a) wholly null or (b) equal to the primary key value somewhere within the base relation representing the relevant participant entity. This rule corresponds to the intuitive fact that if a specific entity is identified as participating in some specific relationship, then that entity must exist (for otherwise the real world would not be consistent). Note, however, that some foreign keys must be allowed to accept null values. Suppose, for example, that in a given company it is legal for an employee to be currently assigned to no department at all. For such an employee, the Department Number attribute would clearly have to be null in the Employee tuple (record) representing that employee in the database.

Aside: Note that the Referential Integrity rule requires the foreign key to match, not just some candidate key, but very specifically the primary key, of the referenced relation. Again, confusion on this point is not uncommon. Arguments and counterarguments can be found in reference [3].

19. Foreign-to-primary key matches are actually just an important special case of a more general mechanism for representing relationships—namely,

the general attribute-comparison mechanism. In fact, *every* possible comparison operation among attributes in the database corresponds to some relationship in the real world. The relational concept of *domains* constrains such comparisons, of course, inasmuch as comparable attributes should normally be defined on the same domain (i.e., they should be of the same semantic data type).

20. The fundamental purpose of a database is to supply answers to questions—in other words, to support the derivation of information. And "derivation of information" means, precisely, *constructing a relation*. That is, the answer to *any* question can be regarded as a relation, a relation that is derived in some way from the original base relations. The relational operators (union, join, etc.) are provided for performing such derivations. Thus, the interpretation of those operations in the real world is as *question answerers;* their function can be characterized as one of materializing (i.e., constructing explicit representations of) entities and relationships that are otherwise represented only implicitly in the original base relations.

21. Following on from the previous point: The relational algebra not only allows certain questions to be answered from the database, *it also defines precisely the set of questions that can be formulated in the first place.* Loose statements such as "If the information is in the database, then it should be possible to retrieve it" are commonly heard. The relational model allows such vague statements to be replaced by others that are 100 percent precise (and of course formal). The two notions of "information being in the database" and "being able to retrieve it" correspond to the expressive capabilities of the structural and manipulative parts of the model, respectively. Thus the relational model, with its associated interpretation, provides an invaluable basis for thinking clearly and precisely about practical database problems.

22. A good illustration of *lack* of such clear thinking—arising presumably from an inadequate understanding of the relational model and its interpretation—is provided by what is sometimes referred to as "semantic disintegrity." Here is an example, taken from a book by James Martin (reference [4]). Consider once again the two relations:

```
Employee    ( Employee Number, Department Number )
Department  ( Department Number, Location )
```

Assume that a given department can have multiple locations. Now consider the relation

```
Result  ( Employee Number, Department Number, Location )
```

obtained by taking the natural join of Employee and Department on Department Number. Martin states that this join is invalid, because if employee *e* works in department *d* and department *d* has locations *x* and *y*, it certainly does not follow that *e* is located in both *x* and *y*. The assumption seems to be that relation Result states otherwise. But of course it does not; it merely states what we already know, namely that *e* works in *d* and *d* has locations *x* and *y*. Relation Result does represent the answer to a certain query, but that query is *not* "Find employee locations." Thus it is definitely wrong to say that the join is invalid (though it may be legitimate to warn against incorrect interpretation of that join).

> *Aside:* Another (related) area in which such considerations are manifestly important is that of *nonloss decomposition,* which provides the basis for the well-known theory of further normalization (beyond the scope of this short paper).

CONCLUSION

From the arguments presented above, I claim the following: *Everyone professionally involved in database management should be thoroughly conversant, not only with the relational model per se* (in this day and age that should go without saying), *but also with its interpretation.* The material is certainly not difficult, but it is fundamental.

REFERENCES

1. E. F. Codd, "Data Models in Database Management," *Proc. Workshop on Data Abstraction, Databases, and Conceptual Modelling,* Michael L. Brodie and Stephen N. Zilles, eds., Pingree Park, Colorado, June 23–26, 1980, pp. 112–114: *ACM SIGART Newsletter* No. 74 (January 1981); *ACM SIGMOD Record* 11, No. 2 (February 1981); *ACM SIGPLAN Notices* 16, No. 1 (January 1981).

2. C. J. Date, *An Introduction to Database Systems: Volume I,* 4th edition (Reading, MA: Addison-Wesley, 1985).

3. C. J. Date, "Why Every Relation Should Have Exactly one Primary Key" (in this volume).

4. James Martin, *Computer Data-Base Organization,* 2nd edition (Englewood Cliffs, NJ: Prentice-Hall, 1977).

## PART II

RELATIONAL VS. NONRELATIONAL SYSTEMS

9

Interactive Support for Nonprogrammers: The Relational and Network Approaches

ABSTRACT

The objectives and strategies of the relational and network approaches are compared. The status of support for nonprogramming users is examined. General purpose support for such users entails provision of an augmented relationally complete retrieval capability without branching, explicit iteration, or cursors. It is clear how this capability can be realized with the relational approach—whether with a formal or informal language interface. It is not at all clear how the network approach can reach this goal, so long as the principal schema includes owner-coupled sets "bearing information essentially." A relational discipline is suggested as a way out for DBTG users.

Originally published in *Proc. 1974 ACM SIGMOD Workshop on Data Description, Access, and Control, Vol. II, "Data Models: Data-Structure-Set versus Relational"* (May 1974). Reprinted with permission.

COMMENTS ON REPUBLICATION

This paper was presented at the 1974 ACM SIGMOD Workshop as part of the "great debate" between proponents of the relational and network approaches. The principal speakers in the debate were E. F. Codd for the relational approach and C. W. Bachman for the network approach. In the debate proceedings the paper is shown as being a joint production by Codd and myself, but in fact it was wholly written by Ted Codd (the companion paper, also attributed to both of us, on application programming considerations—the next paper in this collection—was written by me). I am grateful to Ted for allowing me to share the limelight with him in this fashion, and also for his permission to include both papers in the present volume.

The paper introduces the important concept of *essentiality*, a concept that is crucial to an understanding of data models in general and of relations vs. networks in particular. *The critical difference between a network database and a relational database is that the network database must contain at least one owner-coupled set that bears information essentially.* For if it does not, then it degenerates to a relational database in which certain access paths happen to be exposed, and the question arises as to why those access paths are exposed when others are not (especially as there is no obligation on the user to use them).

The paper also poses a large number of highly pertinent questions regarding the suitability of network structures as a component of the principal (i.e., conceptual) schema—questions that, so far as I am aware, have never been answered in the open literature.

As usual, I have made a number of minor corrections to the republished version, mostly of an editorial nature. The footnotes are new.

INTRODUCTION

Our objective in this paper is to explore the similarities and differences between the relational and network approaches to database management, with special emphasis on the topic of online interaction by nonprogrammers. To explain the marked differences between these two approaches and to prepare for the complementary papers by Date and Codd [1] and Whitney [2], we must raise the key question:

- Do owner-coupled sets (see definition below) really belong in the principal schema; and, if so, what is their role?

The CODASYL DBTG proposal [3,4] is used as an example of the network approach, because it has been widely publicized and because several implementations are being developed. However, we do not wish to dwell on the already well-known (and as yet, in the literature, unanswered) short-comings of DBTG in the matter of data dependence and overly implicit cursor-controlled storage and retrieval [5]. We agree with these criticisms as far as they go, but feel we must probe further in the interest of better understanding of both the relational and network approaches.

In the section "Status of Support for Nonprogrammers" we note the strong lead of the relational approach in development of techniques for nonprogrammer interaction; a possible explanation is suggested in the subsequent section. We then go on to suggest a discipline which, if imposed on DBTG use, might enable the DBTG implementations to take advantage of all the nonprogrammer-oriented developments associated with the relational approach. Our concluding remarks indicate some additional questions that merit investigation.

THE TWO APPROACHES

To be precise about these approaches, we introduce some definitions. We then discuss objectives and strategies, because it is not enough to take note of where these approaches stand today—we must also be clear about where they are going.

Definitions

The concepts of owner-coupled set occurrence and owner-coupled set defined below correspond closely to the inappropriately named concepts of *set occurrence* and *set* in DBTG.

- An *owner-coupled set occurrence* on record types R, S is an ordered pair, the first component of which is a record of type R (the owner record), and the second component of which is an ordered set of records of type S (the member records).

- An *owner-coupled set* on record types R, S is an unordered collection of owner-coupled set occurrences on R, S (one such occurrence for each occurrence of the owner record type R), such that no two owner-coupled set occurrences have any member records in common.

Actually, the DBTG set concept is more complicated than this, since it provides various kinds of access path (owner to member, member to member, and member to owner), it does not require all member records to be of a single record type, and it prohibits the special (and rather important) case in which R = S. The context will make it clear when we wish to consider these other features. It is important to note that an owner-coupled set occurrence is not a set (see the section "Questions Concerning Owner-Coupled Sets" for a discussion of the union problem).

We proceed to discuss the topic of essentiality of declarations in a database schema.

■   A data structure declaration D is *essential* (from an information standpoint) in a schema U if there is an instantaneous database B conforming to U such that removal from B of the structure specified by D causes loss of information from B (i.e., some relation is no longer derivable).

Examples

1. Schema U1:

```
DOMAIN A, B
RELATION R(A,B) ORDERED ON A
```

Declarations of domains A, B and of relation R are essential, while the declaration of the ordering on A is inessential in U1.

2. Schema U2:

```
DOMAIN A, B, C, D
RELATION R(A,B) KEY A
         S(C,D,A) KEY C
OCSET T (R OWNER, S MEMBER) USING COMMON VALUE FOR A
```

Declarations of domains A, B, C, D and of relations R, S are essential. The declaration of owner-coupled set T is, however, inessential in U2.

3. Schema U3:

```
DOMAIN A, B, C, D
RELATION R(A,B) KEY A
         S(C,D) KEY C
OCSET T (R OWNER, S MEMBER)
```

All declarations in schema U3 (including the owner-coupled set) are essential in U3.

Data Structure Types in the Principal Schema

We shall ignore atomic data types (such as character strings, dates, integers, etc.) and concentrate on data aggregates or compound structures.

Both the relational and network approaches entail at least three interface levels to provide logical and physical data independence [6,7,20]: the physical or storage-oriented schema; the principal schema; the user or problem-oriented schema. Corresponding to a single principal schema, a database system would be expected in either approach to support a variety of alternative physical schemas (only one of which is in force at any instant, and its selection is based on the current traffic), and a variety of user schemas (many of which may be in force concurrently, and their selection is determined by the problems currently being solved).

It is in the principal schema that we find one of the important distinctions between the relational and network approaches.

- In the relational approach the principal schema employs only one type of data aggregate to represent the entire information content of the database—namely, the nonhierarchic, *n*-ary relation. Ordering may be used, but only *inessentially* (as defined above).

It should be noted that there is nothing in the relational approach that prohibits a user from employing graph or network structures for display or problem-solving purposes. Such structures would, however, appear in a specialized user schema, not in the principal schema.

- In the network approach there is at least one owner-coupled set in the principal schema bearing information *essentially.*

DBTG permits the following types of data aggregate in the principal schema:

1. COBOL record type
2. repeating group
3. owner-coupled set
4. system-owned set (effectively ownerless)
5. ordering
6. area

Any or all of these types of structure may bear information essentially. Since the system-owned set has a fixed owner that is independent of the information content of the database, it may be treated for most purposes as an ownerless set. This kind of set has very different retrieval properties from the owner-coupled set.

Providing the repeating group were disallowed, the COBOL record type would correspond to the typical tuple of an *n*-ary relation in the relational model. Providing the ownerless set were constrained to consist of records of a single type (again with no repeating groups), such a set would correspond to a relation of the relational model.[1]

---

[1] Actually this paragraph is oversimplified, but complete details of the distinctions are irrelevant for the purpose at hand.

The reader is cautioned to avoid comparing the two approaches *solely* on the basis of differences in data types. An adequate appreciation of the differences between these approaches must entail consideration of the types of operators also.

Operator Types

In the relational approach there are three clearly distinguishable levels of operators (all applicable on the principal schema):

1. The element-by-element level, with operators such as GET NEXT TU-PLE (within relation), GET TUPLE WITH PRIMARY KEY VALUE [12];

2. The algebraic level, with operators such as union, intersection, difference, projection, join, selection, division [10,14];

3. The calculus level, involving expressions of the relational calculus [13].

As far as the authors are aware, in the network approach there is at present just one level of operators applicable on the principal schema (via a subschema). This is the element-by-element (or record-at-a-time) level and includes operators such as GET NEXT RECORD (within owner-coupled set occurrence, ownerless set, or area), GET OWNER (of an owner-coupled set occurrence), GET RECORD DIRECT, SELECT GROUP BY SUB-SCRIPT (within a repeating group).

The absence in the network approach of operators at the algebraic or calculus level is noteworthy, since such operators play a vital role in supporting nonprogrammer interaction, other than specialized parametric use of the database.

Objectives

The two approaches under discussion have many objectives in common. Perhaps the most important of these is the goal of providing a means whereby many application programs can operate concurrently (whenever necessary) on a common database in a device-independent and data-independent manner with adequate safeguards against unintended interaction of programs, unauthorized access, and integrity-damaging activities in general.

The following objectives of the relational approach are cited in [16]:

1. Provide a high degree of data independence;

2. Provide a community view of the data of spartan simplicity, so that a wide variety of users in an enterprise (ranging from the most computer-naive to the most computer-sophisticated) can interact with a *common*

model (while not prohibiting superimposed user views for specialized purposes);

3. Simplify the potentially formidable job of the database administrator;

4. Introduce a theoretical foundation (albeit modest) into database management (a field sadly lacking in solid principles and guidelines);

5. Merge the fact retrieval and file management fields in preparation for the addition at a later time of inferential services in the commercial world;

6. Lift data-based application programming to a new level—a level in which sets (and more specifically relations) are treated as operands instead of being processed element by element.

Now, consider the following statements by C. W. Bachman in [8]:

1. "The Integrated Data Store (IDS) system and all other systems based on its concepts consider their basic contribution to the programmer to be the capability to associate records into data structure sets [i.e., owner-coupled sets] and the capability to use these sets as retrieval paths. All the COBOL DBTG systems fall into this class."

2. "My proposition today is that it is time for the application programmer to abandon the memory-centered view, and to accept the challenge and opportunity of navigation within an *n*-dimensional data space."

3. At the end of his paper Bachman specifically proposes to "provide the [application] programmer with effective tools for navigation."

From these statements together with the significant role of owner-coupled sets in the DBTG data manipulation language, one can conclude that the network approach as exemplified by DBTG is primarily concerned with the provision of tools for *programmers* and, in particular, tools to enable programmers to do their own *navigating* or *searching* in the database. This objective is in sharp contrast to that of the relational approach.

The absence from the DBTG proposal of any specific objectives for the support of nonprogrammer interaction is especially noteworthy.

Strategies

The relational strategy has four main components:

1. Simplify to the greatest practical extent the types of data structure employed in the principal schema (or community view);

2. Introduce powerful operators to enable both programmers and nonprogrammers to store and retrieve target data *without having to "navigate" to the target*;

3. Introduce natural language (e.g., English) with dialog support to permit effective interaction by casual (and possibly computer-naive) users;

4. Express authorization and integrity constraints separately from the data structure (because they are liable to change).

Discussions on the relational approach often become riveted on the first component to the neglect of the other three (see, for example, [19]). To do justice to this approach, all four components must be considered as a package.

The network strategy has two main components:

1. Provide a rich set of alternative types of data structure in the principal schema;

2. Provide numerous alternative tools for accessing and traversing these structures using a "level of procedurality . . . about equal to that of COBOL."

As yet, there is no published strategy for DBTG (and more generally, the network approach) to support online interaction by professional nonprogrammers or casual users. There is merely the statement in both DBTG '69 and '71 that this problem is deferred, and the claim that DBTG "provides a solid foundation for such selfcontained capabilities."

We summarize in Fig. 9.1 the alternative paths for future development of database management.

TYPES OF DATABASE USER AND USAGE

We shall limit our discussion to online nonprogramming users (i.e., we defer the DBA and application programmer to [1]). Three major categories are:

1. Parametric users whose interactions with the database are an integral part of their job and very routine and stylized in nature with quite predictable scope;

2. Analysts, auditors, and researchers whose interactions are also an integral part of their job, but who have quite unpredictable needs (they are quite likely to require access to any and every part of the database);

3. Casual users whose interactions are not motivated by their job or social role, but whose interactions may be just as unpredictable as those of the analysts and researchers.

Within the next decade we can expect a very rapid growth in parametric use. However, since both approaches can support this type of use with no special problems, we shall not discuss this case further.

Growth in online interaction by analysts and researchers will be much

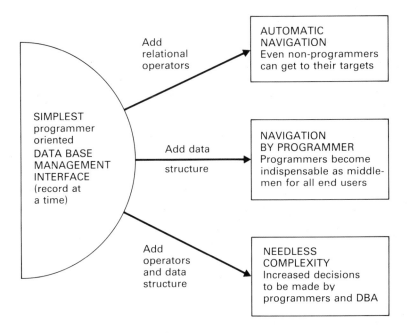

Figure 9.1 Whither database management?

less spectacular, but nevertheless such interaction will be of vital importance to large institutions. Having a job incentive, we can assume that these users are willing to learn a precise language for database interaction. Such a language may range from a formal logic to a restricted natural language such as English, but in any event should not involve branching, explicit iteration, or control of cursors.

Growth in online interaction by casual users can be expected to exceed that for all other types by a large factor—as soon as the technology is proven. Except in the special case where the interaction is known to be of an extremely simple nature, casual users must be provided with at least the illusion of free use of their native language, so that they can express their requirements in an informal way. Such users clearly need a simple logical notion of the data organization in order to frame their queries or modifications in a simple way. These users are even less able and less willing to cope with branching, iteration, and cursors than the analysts and researchers mentioned previously.

In Fig. 9.2 we show the trends we expect to see in database interaction within the next two decades. The majority of online job-trained users (column 3 in Fig. 9.2) are concerned with parametric interaction only. In this paper we are therefore concerned primarily with columns 4 and 5.

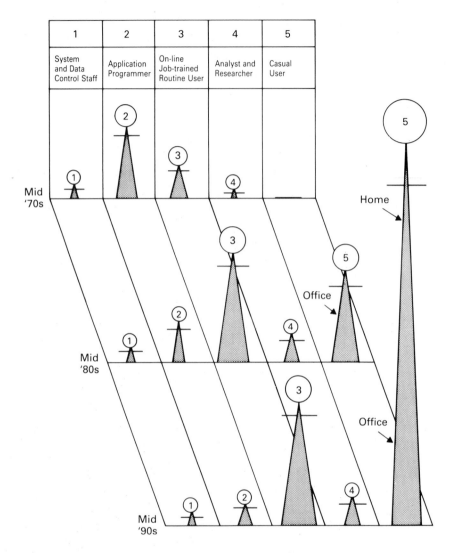

Figure 9.2   Anticipated use of large integrated databases

STATUS OF SUPPORT FOR NONPROGRAMMERS

Associated with the relational approach is the concept of a *relationally complete data sublanguage.* Such a language has at least the retrieval power of a first order predicate calculus when applied to a collection of nonhierarchic relations of assorted degrees [14]. For users with interactions of unpredictable scope and complexity, such a capability is a basic one and should be augmented by a library of functions. For example, the functions COUNT, TOTAL, AVERAGE, MAXIMUM, MINIMUM, would be needed in almost any application environment, while functions that entail data-conditioned termination of iterated joins of a relation with itself are needed in product structure or family tree applications.

■ For nonprogrammers (abbreviated NP) it is essential that such an augmented, relationally complete, retrieval capability (abbreviated ARC) be provided *without* branching, explicit iteration, and cursors. When this condition is fulfilled, we refer to the retrieval capability as NP/ARC. A language will be said to have the NP/ARC capability if it not only provides relational completeness without branching, explicit iteration, and cursors, but includes provision for function invocation to condition the selection of data and to transform the data selected from the database.

Examples of NP/ARC languages are ALPHA [13], the relational algebra [14,10], and SQUARE [17]. Examples of data sublanguages that do *not* possess the NP/ARC capability are GAMMA ZERO [12] and the DBTG data manipulation language.

The effectiveness of this capability is illustrated by an example (given at the end of this paper), where we recode in ALPHA a sample database and application that were originally coded in COBOL-DBTG by Frank and Sibley [9]. The recoding in ALPHA results in the elimination of all GO TO statements (15 of them), all PERFORM UNTIL statements (one of them), and all currency indicators (10 of them).[2] We do not claim that the NP/ARC capability will always yield reductions of this magnitude. A payroll procedure, for example, might not be reduced at all by expressing it in an NP/ARC language. We can, however, expect the NP/ARC capability:

1. To put many applications within the nonprogrammer's reach, where programmers were previously a necessity;

2. To increase the productivity of programmers on many, but not all, database applications.

Figure 9.3 is an outline of an architecture (being implemented at the IBM Research Laboratory in San Jose) by which both professional users (analysts and researchers) and casual users may be supported using the relational approach. The structured English query language SEQUEL [11] is intended for the more professional nonprogramming users and protects such

---

[2]It also eliminates at least two currency errors.

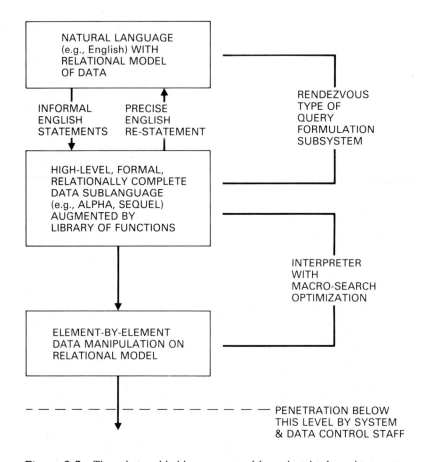

Figure 9.3   The relational ladder: support of formal and informal interaction

users from some of the complications (e.g., quantifiers) inherent in the use of ALPHA. The RENDEZVOUS subsystem [15], on the other hand, is intended for the more casual nonprogramming users. It permits them free use of English except, temporarily, when the subsystem is unable to extract a viable quantum of information from the input statement.

The architecture of RENDEZVOUS itself (Fig. 9.4) is based on the assumption that casual users will frequently misformulate their queries. Accordingly, the subsystem is designed to engage the user in clarification dialog about the query. At appropriate times, it can restate in precise system English what it currently understands the user's query to be.

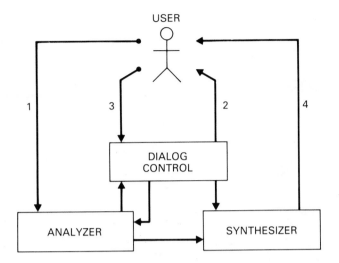

1. User makes initial statement of his query (unrestricted English)
2. System interrogates user *about* his query (to obtain information which is missing or hidden in language the system does not understand, and to resolve ambiguities)
3. User responds to system interrogation
4. System provides a re-statement of user's query in system English (in a very precise way, based on the n-ary relational calculus)

Figure 9.4   RENDEZVOUS subsystem

1. User makes initial statement of the query (unrestricted English)

2. System interrogates user *about* the query (to obtain information that is missing or hidden in language the system does not understand, and to resolve ambiguities)

3. User responds to system interrogation

4. System provides a restatement of user's query in system English (in a very precise way, based on the *n*-ary relational calculus)

An interesting possible application of the RENDEZVOUS subsystem is that of helping the inexpert COBOL-ALPHA or COBOL-SEQUEL programmer determine via informal dialog what ALPHA or SEQUEL statements to include into the program in order to put into effect desired transactions.

Figure 9.5 indicates some of the current activity on various combinations of languages and data structures. The authors have been unable to discover in the literature any reports of research or development in the shaded region of the chart. It seems appropriate to look for a technical explanation of this gap.

Data Sublanguage / Data Structure		Trees	Nets	Relations	
				Degrees 1 & 2 Only	Assorted Degrees (n > 1)
Low	minimal selection capability		IDS Codasyl TOTAL		
Low	restricted selection expressions			RAM HDB	XRAM GAMMA ZERO
Low	boolean selection expressions	GIS UL/1	IMS		ADABAS
Intermediate	attribute −object −value			LEAP TRAMP	
Intermediate	algebra oriented				STDMS MACAIMS IS/1 BETA RDMS
High Formal	calculus oriented	TDMS SYS 2000			COLARD ALPHA
High Formal	mapping oriented				SQUARE SEQUEL
High Natural	one-way restricted English			REL	CONVERSE LSNLIS
High Natural	two-way English with clarification dialog				RENDEZVOUS

Figure 9.5 Languages and data structures

QUESTIONS CONCERNING OWNER-COUPLED SETS

Logical Questions

In the relational model the union, intersection, or difference of any two union-compatible relations is a relation; every projection and every subset of a relation is a relation; every join of two relations is a relation. These closure properties are important in realizing the NP/ARC capability. When part of the information in a database is carried in an essential way by owner-coupled sets, these closure properties do not apply to this part. For example, how do you define a union operation for owner-coupled set occurrences that retains ownership information for each member record *and* yields a result that is an owner-coupled set occurrence?

- Can the NP/ARC capability be supported while retaining the owner-coupled set as an essential information-bearing data type in the principal schema?

If the owner-coupled set has to be relegated to the role of bearing information *inessentially,* what is its intended role in the principal schema? If its role is to act as an interrelation cross-index in order to provide better performance, why is it not treated like other indexes and hidden from both programmers and nonprogrammers, so that their programs and interactions can become more data independent?

Fidelity Questions

Claims have been made in [18] that the network approach and, in particular, the owner-coupled set permit more natural or faithful modeling of the real world than the relational model. Such claims are not easy to support or refute, because our present knowledge of what constitutes a good data structure for solving a given class of problems is highly intuitive and unsystematic.

However, we can observe that many different kinds of geometry, topology, and graphs (or networks) are in use today for solving "real world" problems. Relations tend to be neutral toward these problem-solving representations and yet very adaptable to supporting any of them. This has been demonstrated rather clearly in applications of relations in various kinds of graphics packages.

On the other hand, the owner-coupled set gives rise to a specific kind of network, and is accordingly very convenient in some contexts and very awkward in others. It is convenient when the application involves collections of sets, each of which has both a descriptor and a simple total ordering of its elements. It is awkward when the application involves partial orderings (e.g., PERT charts), loops (e.g., transportation routes), values associated with network links (e.g., utility networks), many-to-many binary relations, relations of degree greater than two, and variable-depth, homogeneous trees (e.g., organization charts).

These considerations give rise to what we call the *separation question:*

- Should we continue to enrich the variety of data types available for use in the principal schema so that it may model the real world more faithfully *or* should we make available only those data types that contribute to ease of control by the database administrator and by the system itself, together with ease of use by the majority of users who have only trivial interactions?

The latter choice implies that the burden for providing support for specialized problem-solving representations is shifted from the principal schema to the user schemas and, hence, falls on specialized packages for the pertinent problem classes.

- Such a clean separation of responsibilities is precisely what is needed to arrive at a practical and expandable network of database machines and data processing machines.

Psychological Questions

In DBTG if the principal schema includes owner-coupled sets that bear information essentially, any application program that needs to use this particular information must include the corresponding owner-coupled set(s) in its subschema. This suggests examination of the following questions for casual, nonprogramming users:

- Can such users reliably retrieve information using the network model? Can they update information using this model?

A DISCIPLINE

If the following rules are adopted in use of DBTG, there is reason to believe that it might be possible for DBTG users to take advantage of the nonprogrammer-oriented developments associated with the relational approach:

1. Exclude from the principal schema all owner-coupled sets that bear information essentially and all repeating groups;
2. For every distinct COBOL record type, declare a system-owned set having this type of record as its only permissible member type; for each of these system-owned sets declare SEARCH KEY IS K and DUPLICATES NOT ALLOWED, where K is the primary key (atomic or compound) of the pertinent record type;

3. For each inessential owner-coupled set that is declared, specify only one type of member record and specify its membership as MANDATORY AUTOMATIC;

4. Exclude from the principal schema any declaration of an ordering that bears information essentially;

5. Exclude exploitation of the AREA construct for the purpose of bearing information essentially by prohibiting the use of two or more area names in a single WITHIN clause.

Some words of caution are perhaps appropriate here. First, this discipline does little to reduce the programming complexities associated with DBTG [1]. Second, attempts to impose a discipline on the use of a software package are likely to be ineffective unless the package itself provides automatic enforcement of this discipline. Third, if the package was not originally designed to operate with this discipline as a normal mode, it may need some tuning to obtain the desired performance. In particular, some extra interrelation indexing may be needed "beneath the covers" to compensate for owner-coupled sets that are dropped altogether from the principal schema. Finally, to support the NP/ARC capability interactively, the system must be capable of dynamically allocating and deallocating an arbitrary (i.e., not predetermined) amount of storage space. Such a feature is, at present, available in very few systems indeed.

If desired, owner-coupled sets can be eliminated altogether from a given schema U as follows:

Case 1: Owner-coupled set T is inessential in U

Drop T from U

Case 2: Owner-coupled set T (*OWNER* R, *MEMBER* S) is essential in U

    a. R has atomic primary key (say R#)

        Incorporate R# as additional attribute
            into declaration of S
        Drop T from U

    b. R has compound primary key

        Introduce new atomic primary key (say R#)
            into declaration of R
        Incorporate R# as additional attribute
            into declaration of S
        Drop T from U

Example of Case 2b (due to C. P. Earnest [19])

Before elimination of owner-coupled set:

```
RELATION PACK(ENGINE#,TRANSMISSION#)
         KEY (ENGINE#,TRANSMISSION#)
         AUTO(MODEL#,DESCRIPTION)
         KEY MODEL#
OCSET    T(OWNER PACK, MEMBER AUTO)
```

After elimination of owner-coupled set:

```
RELATION PACK'(PACK#,ENGINE#,TRANSMISSION#)
         KEY PACK#
         AUTO'(MODEL#,DESCRIPTION,PACK#)
         KEY MODEL#
```

Clearly, adoption of this relational discipline does not immediately yield the full relational approach. It merely places DBTG implementations on the bottom rung of the relational ladder (see Fig. 9.3), with the potential handicap of concurrency controls, integrity controls, and logical-to-physical mapping designed more for the network than the relational context.

CONCLUSION

In the past, many designers of software systems and languages have confused two quite distinct notions: enrichment of features on the one hand, and generality of application on the other. A crucial issue in database management systems is that of the richness (i.e., variety) of data structure types that should be supported in the principal schema. In the event that enrichment of these data structure types beyond the minimum one is proposed, we ask the following questions.

As far as the *system* is concerned, are not more retrieval operators or commands needed? Are not the concurrency and authorization controls more complicated? Hence, is not the implementation more complicated and therefore less reliable?

As far as the *programmers* and *nonprogramming users* are concerned, are they not subjected to an increased burden in deciding which structures to access and which operators or commands to apply? Is there not an increased probability of error and, when errors are discovered, is there not an increased variety of remedial actions to consider?

As far as the *database administrator* is concerned, are there not too many structural choices with few, if any, dependable guidelines for making those choices? Are not the mappings between the logical and physical levels more complicated to define and maintain? Are not security and privacy constraints more complicated to specify?

HISTORICAL NOTE

The relational approach was developed as a response to the following requirements, which were considered to be relatively novel in 1968:

1. data independence
2. integration of files into databases
3. multiple user types
4. many online users at terminals
5. increased dynamic sharing of data
6. networks of mutually remote databases

This approach was *not* developed as a response to the DBTG proposal. As evidence for this, note that one of the early reports on the relational approach as it is currently understood appeared in August 1969 (see [21]), some two months prior to publication of the first DBTG report [3]. In addition, public lectures on the *n*-ary relational model and algebra were presented by Codd in Europe and the USA during October and November 1969.

ACKNOWLEDGMENT

The authors are grateful to Sjir Nijssen of Control Data Corporation in Brussels, Belgium and to Bodo Douque and Johan Schenk of Philips Electrologica in Apeldoorn, Netherlands for helpful discussions concerning the application of the relational discipline to DBTG.

REFERENCES

1. C. J. Date and E. F. Codd, "The Relational and Network Approaches: Comparison of the Application Programming Interfaces" (in this volume).

2. V. K. M. Whitney, "Relational Data Management Implementation Techniques," *Proc. 1974 ACM SIGMOD Workshop on Data Description, Access, and Control,* Vol. II (May 1974).

3. CODASYL, *Data Base Task Group Report.* ACM, New York (October 1969).

4. CODASYL, *Data Base Task Group Report.* ACM, New York (April 1971).

5. R. W. Engles, "An Analysis of the April 1971 Data Base Task Group Report," *Proc. 1971 ACM SIGFIDET Workshop on Data Description, Access, and Control* (November 1971).

6. C. J. Date and P. Hopewell, "File Definition and Logical Data Independence," *Proc. 1971 ACM SIGFIDET Workshop on Data Description, Access, and Control* (November 1971).

7. C. J. Date and P. Hopewell, "Storage Structure and Physical Data Independence," *Proc. 1971 ACM SIGFIDET Workshop on Data Description, Access, and Control* (November 1971).

8. C. W. Bachman, "The Programmer as Navigator," *CACM* 16, No. 11 (November 1973).

9. R. L. Frank and E. H. Sibley, "The Data Base Task Group Report: An Illustrative Example," ISDOS Working Paper No. 71: US National Technical Information Service Document AD-759-267 (February 1973).

10. M. G. Notley, "The Peterlee IS/1 System," IBM UK Scientific Centre Report UKSC-0018 (March 1972).

11. D. D. Chamberlin and R. F. Boyce, "SEQUEL: A Structured English Query Language," *Proc. 1974 ACM SIGMOD Workshop on Data Description, Access, and Control* (May 1974).

12. D. Bjørner, E. F. Codd, K. L. Deckert, and I. L. Traiger, "The Gamma Zero *n*-ary Relational Data Base Interface: Specifications of Objects and Operations," IBM Research Report RJ1200 (April 1973).

13. E. F. Codd, "A Data Base Sublanguage Founded on the Relational Calculus," *Proc. 1971 ACM SIGFIDET Workshop on Data Description, Access, and Control* (November 1971).

14. E. F. Codd, "Relational Completeness of Data Base Sublanguages." In *Data Base Systems*: Courant Computer Science Symposia Series, Vol. 6 (Englewood Cliffs, NJ: Prentice-Hall, 1972).

15. E. F. Codd, "Seven Steps to Rendezvous with the Casual User," *Proc. IFIP TC-2 Working Conference Data Base Management Systems* (eds., Klimbie and Koffeman): North-Holland (April 1974).

16. E. F. Codd, "Recent Investigations in Relational Data Base Systems," *Proc. IFIP* 74: North-Holland (1974).

17. R. F. Boyce, D. D. Chamberlin, W. F. King III, and M. M. Hammer, "Specifying Queries as Relational Expressions: SQUARE," *Proc. ACM SIGPLAN-SIGIR Interface Meeting* (November 1973).

18. *Proc. SHARE Working Conference on Data Base Management Systems,* Montreal, Canada. North-Holland (1973).

19. C. P. Earnest, "A Comparison of the Network and Relational Data Structure Models," *Computer Sciences Corporation Report,* El Segundo, California (April 1974).

20. E. F. Codd, "Normalized Data Base Structure: A Brief Tutorial," *Proc. 1971 ACM SIGFIDET Workshop on Data Description, Access, and Control* (November 1971).

21. E. F. Codd, "Derivability, Redundancy, and Consistency of Relations Stored in Large Data Banks," IBM Research Report RJ599 (August 1969).

APPENDIX: A COMPARATIVE EXAMPLE

In [9] Frank and Sibley selected an example to illustrate the application of the DBTG proposal. The sample database includes information about persons (an identification number, name, birthdate, and salary), medical histories (identification number of person, absent-from-date, absent-to-date, disease, and comment), education (identification number of person, degree, name of university, start date at university, stop date at university), jobs (job number, identification number of person who did the job, actual start date, actual stop date, and performance rating), machines (machine number, machine type), schedules (job number, identification number of person assigned, scheduled start date, scheduled stop date), skills (skill number, skill description), the possession of skills by persons (identification number of person, skill number), the alternative skills needed to operate machines (machine number, skill number).

Except for one or two very minor omissions (e.g., the calculation of age from birth date, privacy locks and keys), the following code sets up a relational schema for the sample database:

```
DOMAIN    P#           PIC 9(6)
          P_NAME       PIC A(20)
          DATE         PIC 99X99X99
          SALARY       PIC 99999V99
          DISEASE      PIC A(30)
          NOTE         PIC A(VAR)
          DEGREE       PIC AA
          UNIV         PIC A(20)
          JOB#         PIC X(4)
          P_RATING     PIC 99V9
          MACH#        PIC 9(5)
          MACH_TYPE    PIC 999
          SKILL#       PIC 999
          SKILL_DES    PIC A(20)

RELATION  PERSON(P#,P_NAME,BIRTH_DATE,SALARY) KEY P#
          MED(P#,ABS_FROM_DATE,ABS_TO_DATE,DISEASE,NOTE)
              KEY(P#,ABS_FROM_DATE,ABS_TO_DATE)
          EDUC(P#,DEGREE,START_DATE,STOP_DATE,UNIV) KEY(P#,DEGREE)
          JOB(JOB#,P#,START_DATE,STOP_DATE,P_RATING) KEY JOB#
          MACHINE(MACH#,MACH_TYPE) KEY MACH#
          SCHED(JOB#,P#,MACH#,SCHED_START_DATE,SCHED_STOP_DATE)
              KEY JOB#
          SKILLS(SKILL#,SKILL_DES) KEY SKILL#
          PERSON_SKILL(P#,SKILL#) KEY(P#,SKILL#)
          MACH_SKILL(MACH#,SKILL#) KEY(MACH#,SKILL#)
```

The sample application can be stated as follows: Given machine X, a job number Y, the desired start date A for the job, and the desired stop date B, find the identification number of a person who has a skill appropriate for the operation of machine X, and who is not scheduled at all between date A and date B; schedule this person, if one is located.

The ALPHA program for the sample application consists of three statements:

```
GET (into workspace) W (at most) (1) PERSON_SKILL.P#: (such that)
    EXIST MACH_SKILL (with
          MACH_SKILL.MACH# = X
          & MACH_SKILL.SKILL# = PERSON_SKILL.SKILL#
          & NOT EXIST SCHED (with
               SCHED.P# = PERSON_SKILL.P#
               & SCHED.SCHED_START_DATE < B
               & SCHED.SCHED_STOP_DATE > A))

MOVE W INTO SCHED_RECORD       (host language)

PUT SCHED_RECORD (into) SCHED
```

A copy of the DBTG schema and application program appears on subsequent pages. Some comparative statistics may be of interest:

	DBTG	ALPHA
GO TO	15	0
PERFORM UNTIL	1	0
currency indicators	10	0
IF	12	0
FIND	9	0
GET	4	1
MOVE	13	1
STORE	2	1

These statistics should not be interpreted as a criticism of Frank and Sibley. Their objective was to provide a tutorial on the application of DBTG, and in this respect they succeeded rather well. The important thing to note is the elimination (in the ALPHA code) of branching, explicit iteration, and cursor control—an essential step toward providing general support for the nonprogramming user, and a desirable step toward removing a large burden of irrelevant decision-making by the programmer.

DBTG Schema for Sample Database

```
SCHEMA NAME IS EMPLOYEE-BASE;
    PRIVACY LOCK IS SCHED-SCHEMA
        OR PROCEDURE SECURE-SCHEDULE;
    AREA NAME IS PANDJ-AREA.
    AREA MED-AREA;
    PRIVACY FOR UPDATE IS PROCEDURE MED-DEPT.
    AREA SECRET; ON OPEN CALL SECURE-PROC;
    ON CLOSE CALL LOCK-PROC.
    AREA REST; PRIVACY IS PROCEDURE SCHED-DEPT
        OR PROCEDURE SECURE-PROC.
    AREA XP; AREA IS TEMPORARY; PRIVACY TEMP-AREA.
```

```
RECORD NAME IS PERSON;
   LOCATION MODE IS CALC EMP-HASH USING
       IDENTIFICATION-NUM DUPLICATES ARE NOT ALLOWED;
   WITHIN PANDJ-AREA;
   ON DELETE CALL MICROFILM-RECORDER;
   PRIVACY LOCK FOR DELETE ONLY IS PROCEDURE EMP-LEFT.
       NAME; PICTURE IS "A(20)".
       IDENTIFICATION-NUM; PICTURE IS "9(6)".
       DATE-OF-BIRTH; PICTURE IS "99X99X99".
   1 AGE; PICTURE "99V9"; IS VIRTUAL RESULT OF
       AGE-CALC USING DATE-OF-BIRTH, TODAYS-DATE.
   1 SALARY; TYPE IS FIXED 7,2; CHECK IS RANGE OF
       8000.00 THRU 75000.00.
   1 EDUCATION; TYPE FIXED 2.
   1 EDUCATION-INFO; OCCURS EDUCATION TIMES.
       2 DEGREE; PICTURE "AA".
       2 START-DATE; PICTURE "99X99X99".
       2 COMPLETION-DATE; PICTURE "99X99X99", CHECK
         NOT-BEFORE USING EDUC-OK, START-DATE.
       2 DEGREE-RECEIVED-FROM PIC "A(20)".
RECORD NAME JOB;
   LOCATION IS VIA JOBSET SET;
   WITHIN PANDJ-AREA.
   1 JOB-CODE; PIC "X(4)".
   1 START-DATE; PIC "99X99X99".
   1 FINISH-DATE; PIC "99X99X99".
   1 PERFORMANCE-RATING; PIC "99V9".
RECORD IS MEDICAL;
   LOCATION MODE CALC USING DISEASE DUPLICATES
       ARE ALLOWED;
   WITHIN MED-AREA.
   1 ABSENCE-DATES; PICTURE "99X99X99X99X99X99".
   1 DISEASE; PICTURE IS "A(30)".
   1 NOTE-PAGES; TYPE IS REAL FIXED DECIMAL 2.
   1 NOTES; OCCURS NOTE-PAGES TIMES.
       2 NOTE-PAGE; PICTURE "A(500)".
RECORD NAME IS MACHINE; LOCATION MODE IS CALC
       MACH-HASH USING MACH-NUMBER
       DUPLICATES NOT ALLOWED;
   WITHIN REST, SECRET AREA-ID MACH-LOCATOR;
   PRIVACY LOCK PROCEDURE IS-IT-SECURE.
   1 MACH-TYPE; PICTURE "999".
   1 MACH-NUMBER; PICTURE "9(5)".
   1 SCHEDULE; PICTURE "99".
   1 SCHEDULED-USE; OCCURS SCHEDULE TIMES.
       2 JOB-CODE; PICTURE "9(8)".
       2 SCHEDULE-COMPLETION; TYPE IS DATE.
       /* NOTE IMPLEMENTOR-TYPE DATE. */
       2 SCHEDULE-START; TYPE IS DATE.
       2 WORKER-IDENTIFICATION; PICTURE "9(6)".
   /* NOTE THERE WOULD BE OTHER ELEMENTS,
       BUT IRRELEVANT TO THIS EXAMPLE */
RECORD SKILL-LINK; LOCATION MODE IS CALC
       USING SKILL-CODE, DUPLICATES ALLOWED;
   WITHIN REST.
   1 SKILL-CODE; PICTURE "999".
   1 SK-SALARY;
       VIRTUAL SOURCE IS SALARY OF OWNER OF HAS-SKILL.
   1 JOB-RATE; PICTURE "9(2)V9(2)";
       IS VIRTUAL RESULT OF AVERAGE-RATE
       USING SK-SALARY.
```

```
      1 MACH-SK; VIRTUAL SOURCE IS MACH-TYPE
          OF OWNER OF NEEDS-SKILL.
RECORD NAME IS CHECK-PERSON;
   LOCATION MODE IS CALC USING CHECK-PERSON-ITEM
       DUPLICATES NOT ALLOWED;
   WITHIN XP.
   /* NOTE: THIS IS THE TEMPORARY AREA. */
   01 CHECK-PERSON-ITEM;
       TYPE IS DATABASE-KEY.
   /* NOTE: THIS ASSUMES THAT A CALC-KEY
       CAN BE A DATABASE-KEY. */
RECORD NAME IS CHECK-MACHINE;
   LOCATION MODE IS CALC USING CHECK-PERSON-ITEM;
       DUPLICATES NOT ALLOWED;
   WITHIN XP.
   01 CHECK-MACHINE-ITEM;
       TYPE IS DATABASE-KEY.
SET NAME IS JOBSET;
   ORDER IS NEXT;
   OWNER IS PERSON.
   MEMBER IS JOB, MANDATORY, AUTOMATIC;
   SET OCCURRENCE SELECTION IS THRU CURRENT OF SET.
SET NAME IS MEDSET;
   ORDER IS LAST;
   OWNER IS PERSON.
   MEMBER IS MEDICAL, OPTIONAL, AUTOMATIC,
   SET OCCURRENCE SELECTION IS THRU CURRENT OF SET.
SET NEEDS-SKILL;
   ORDER IS SORTED DUPLICATES ARE ALLOWED;
   OWNER IS MACHINE.
   MEMBER IS SKILL-LINK OPTIONAL MANUAL
       LINKED TO OWNER;
   DESCENDING KEY SKILL-CODE;
   SET SELECTION THRU CURRENT OF SET.
SET NAME IS HAS-SKILL;
   ORDER IS SORTED DUPLICATES ARE FIRST;
   OWNER IS PERSON.
   MEMBER IS SKILL-LINK OPTIONAL MANUAL
       LINKED TO OWNER;
   ASCENDING KEY SKILL-CODE;
   SELECTION IS LOCATION MODE OF OWNER.
SET NAME IS WORKING-ON;
   ORDER LAST;
   OWNER IS PERSON.
   MEMBER IS MACHINE OPTIONAL MANUAL LINKED TO OWNER
   DUPLICATES NOT ALLOWED FOR SCHEDULE-START;
   SEARCH KEY IS SCHEDULE-START, MACH-NUMBER USING INDEX
       NAME IS MACH-WORK-INDEX DUPLICATES ARE NOT ALLOWED;
   SET OCCURRENCE SELECTION IS THRU
       LOCATION MODE OF OWNER.
   /* NOTE THIS IS CALC. */
SET SYS-MACHINE;
   ORDER IS SORTED INDEXED NAME IS MACHINE-INDEX
   DUPLICATES ARE NOT ALLOWED;
   ON REMOVE CALL SINKING-FUND;
   PRIVACY LOCK FOR REMOVE IS PROCEDURE MACH-AWAY;
   OWNER IS SYSTEM.
   MEMBER IS MACHINE OPTIONAL AUTOMATIC;
   ASCENDING KEY IS MACH-NUMBER.
   /* NOTE NO SELECTION CLAUSE FOR SINGULAR SETS. */
```

COBOL-DBTG Application Program

```
IDENTIFICATION DIVISION.
    PROGRAM-ID. SCHEDULE-PERSON-TO-MACHINE.
    PRIVACY KEY FOR COMPILE IS 'START-SCHEMA';
    PRIVACY KEY OF REST AREA IS PROCEDURE 'DEPT-SCHED'.
    AUTHOR. R.L.FRANK AND E.H.SIBLEY.
    DATE-WRITTEN. JANUARY 1973.
ENVIRONMENT DIVISION.
DATA DIVISION.
SCHEMA SECTION.
    INVOKE SUB-SCHEMA
        SCHEDULE-ID OF SCHEMA EMPLOYEE-BASE.
FILE SECTION.

WORKING-STORAGE-SECTION.

PROCEDURE DIVISION.
    OPEN PANDJ-AREA, WITH-HOLD, REST.
    OPEN nonDBTG files.
FIND-MACHINE.
    OPEN XP.
    MOVE MACHINE-NUMBER TO MACH-NUMBER.
    FIND MACHINE RECORD VIA SYS-MACHINE USING
        MACH-NUMBER.
    IF ERROR-STATUS = 326 GO TO
        NOT-IN-DATA-BASE.

FOUND-REC.
    MOVE CURRENCY STATUS FOR MACHINE RECORD TO
        SAVE-MACHINE.
GET-NEXT-SKILL.
    FIND NEXT SKILL-LINK RECORD OF NEEDS-SKILL SET.
    IF ERROR-STATUS = 326 OR = 307 GO TO NO-ONE-AVAILABLE.
    FIND OWNER IN HAS-SKILL OF CURRENT OF SKILL-LINK RECORD.
    IF ERROR-STATUS = 322 THEN GO TO GET-NEXT-SKILL.
    MOVE CURRENCY STATUS FOR PERSON RECORD
        TO SAVE-PERSON.
    MOVE CURRENCY STATUS FOR
        PERSON RECORD TO CHECK-PERSON-ITEM.
    STORE CHECK-PERSON.
    IF ERROR-STATUS = 1205
        GO TO GET-NEXT-SKILL.

CHECK-PERSONS-SCHEDULE.
    FIND NEXT SKILL-LINK RECORD OF HAS-SKILL SET;
        SUPPRESS NEEDS-SKILL CURRENCY UPDATES.
    IF ERROR-STATUS = 307 GO TO PERSON-IS-FREE.
    FIND OWNER IN NEEDS-SKILL OF CURRENT OF SKILL-LINK RECORD;
        SUPPRESS NEEDS-SKILL CURRENCY UPDATES.
    IF ERROR-STATUS = 322
        GO TO CHECK-PERSONS-SCHEDULE.
    MOVE CURRENCY STATUS FOR MACHINE RECORD TO CHECK-MACHINE-ITEM.
    STORE CHECK-MACHINE.
    IF ERROR-STATUS = 1205 GO TO CHECK-PERSONS-SCHEDULE.
    GET MACHINE.
    MOVE 1 TO AVAILABLE.
    PERFORM SEE-IF-SCHEDULED THRU SEE-EXIT VARYING
        SCHEDULE-COUNT FROM 1 BY 1 UNTIL SCHEDULE-COUNT
        IS GREATER THAN SCHEDULE.
```

```
        IF AVAILABLE = 0 GO TO GET-NEXT-SKILL.
        GO TO CHECK-PERSONS-SCHEDULE.

    SEE-IF-SCHEDULED.
        /* NOTE: HERE WE WILL MARK AS NOT BEING AVAILABLE
           ANYONE WHO IS SCHEDULED FOR THAT TIME. */
        IF SCHEDULE-DATE-START IS GREATER THAN SCHEDULE-START
           IN MACHINE (SCHEDULE-COUNT) AND LESS THAN
           SCHEDULE-COMPLETION IN MACHINE (SCHEDULE-COUNT)
           GO TO PERSON-NOT-AVAILABLE.
        IF SCHEDULE-DATE-END IS GREATER THAN SCHEDULE-START
           IN MACHINE (SCHEDULE-COUNT) AND LESS THAN
           SCHEDULE-COMPLETION IN MACHINE (SCHEDULE-COUNT)
           GO TO PERSON-NOT-AVAILABLE.
        GO TO SEE-EXIT.
    PERSON-NOT-AVAILABLE.
        FIND PERSON USING SAVE-PERSON,
           SUPPRESS ALL CURRENCY UPDATES.
        GET PERSON.
        IF IDENTIFICATION-NUM IN PERSON IS EQUAL
           WORKER-IDENTIFICATION IN MACHINE
           (SCHEDULE-COUNT) MOVE 0 TO AVAILABLE,
           GO TO SEE-EXIT.
        MOVE WORKER-IDENTIFICATION IN MACHINE
           (SCHEDULE-COUNT) TO IDENTIFICATION-NUM IN PERSON.
        FIND PERSON RECORD, SUPPRESS HAS-SKILL
           CURRENCY UPDATES.
        MOVE CURRENCY STATUS FOR PERSON RECORD
           TO CHECK-PERSON-ITEM.
        STORE CHECK-PERSON.
    SEE-EXIT. EXIT.

    PERSON-IS-FREE.
        /* NOTE: HERE WE GET THE MACHINE WE WANTED TO SCHEDULE. */
        FIND MACHINE USING SAVE-MACHINE.
        GET MACHINE.
        FIND PERSON USING SAVE-PERSON.
        GET PERSON.
        ADD 1 TO SCHEDULE IN MACHINE.
        MOVE IDENTIFICATION-NUM IN PERSON TO WORKER-IDENTIFICATION
           IN MACHINE (SCHEDULE IN MACHINE).
        MOVE SCHEDULE-DATE-START TO SCHEDULE-START IN MACHINE
           (SCHEDULE IN MACHINE).
        MOVE SCHEDULE-DATE-END TO SCHEDULE-COMPLETION IN MACHINE
           (SCHEDULE IN MACHINE).
        MOVE SCHEDULE-TASK TO JOB-CODE IN MACHINE (SCHEDULE IN
           MACHINE).
        MODIFY MACHINE.
        IF ERROR-STATUS = 803
           GO TO PERSON-IS-FREE.
        CLOSE XP.
        GO TO GET-NEW-MACHINE.
```

10

The Relational and Network Approaches: Comparison of the Application Programming Interfaces

ABSTRACT

For some time now there has been considerable debate in the field of database systems over the fundamental question of the underlying design philosophy of such a system. The controversy has centered on the structure of the programmer interface, though of course the design chosen for this interface has repercussions throughout the rest of the system. Two approaches to this problem have received particular attention: the network approach, which is typified by the proposals of the CODASYL Data Base

Originally published in *Proc. 1974 ACM SIGMOD Workshop on Data Description, Access, and Control, Vol. II, "Data Models: Data-Structure-Set versus Relational"* (May 1974). Reprinted with permission.

Task Group (DBTG), and the relational approach, which is advocated by the present authors (among others). The purpose of this paper is to give some comparisons between these two approaches (primarily from the application programming viewpoint), and to show what the authors believe to be the advantages of the relational approach. The reader is assumed to have a basic familiarity with the two approaches.

COMMENTS ON REPUBLICATION

This paper, like its predecessor in the present collection, was also presented at the 1974 ACM SIGMOD Workshop as part of the debate on the relative merits of the relational and network approaches. I have edited it considerably for republication, though not in such a way as to change any part of its fundamental message; the changes are limited for the most part to improvements in terminology (e.g., to stress the distinction between domains and attributes), clarifications (e.g., to clarify the subway example in the "Data Independence" section), and minor corrections (e.g., to bring the example at the end of the "Uniformity" section into line with the current version of the SEQUEL language). I have also omitted some minor portions (duly noted in the text).

One point seems worth mentioning here: By the criteria of the preceding paper, the DBTG database used as the basis for examples in this paper (see Fig. 10.6) is not in fact a network database at all!—it does not include any essential owner-coupled sets. However, this omission was due to a deliberate decision on my part. The fact is, DBTG coding is complex enough even in the "inessential" case; it is much worse (particularly on update) in the "essential" case,[1] and I did not want to complicate the examples any further.

INTRODUCTION

It is commonly accepted that application programs in a database system should not be written in terms of the data as stored but rather in terms of a logical view of that data. The programmer's interface to the database thus consists of such a logical view, together with a language that allows that view to be manipulated. For some time now there has been considerable debate over the precise form that view and the associated language should take. In particular the Data Base Task Group (DBTG) of the CODASYL Programming Language Committee has proposed a *network* view, together

---

[1]For evidence in support of this claim, see *An Introduction to Database Systems: Volume I*, 4th edition, by C. J. Date (Addison-Wesley, 1985).

with a corresponding network-handling language [2], whereas E. F. Codd and others have proposed a *relational* view and language [5-10,15]. It is the aim of this paper to compare these two approaches and to show what the authors believe to be (some of) the advantages of the relational approach.

The reader is assumed to be reasonably familiar with these two approaches (see [11] for a tutorial on both).

[*At this point the original paper introduced a few basic concepts—schema, subschema, data sublanguage, etc.—and defined the appropriate terminology in each case. This preliminary material is omitted here.*]

We now present a discussion of what we consider to be the relative advantages of the relational approach, under the following headings:

1. Simplicity

2. Uniformity

3. Completeness

4. Data independence

5. Integrity and security

To be candid, it is not always clear which heading a particular point should come under, but this list represents an attempt to impose some structure on the argument.

One further introductory remark: All DBTG examples are based on the April 1971 proposals [2]; the revisions of [3] and [4], though defining a number of changes in syntax, do not materially affect the discussion.

SIMPLICITY

To a large extent, simplicity may be considered *the* justification for the relational approach. Most of the other arguments in its favor may be viewed as aspects or corollaries of this fundamental point. However, there are some points that deserve specific mention under this heading.

Data Structure

First let us consider an example. Figure 10.1 shows an example of a relational database (suppliers-and-parts); Figure 10.2 shows the corresponding schema (data structure definition). Figure 10.3 shows the same data in network form. To represent such a network using the facilities of DBTG we require two owner-coupled sets, S-SP (owned by record S) and P-SP (owned by record P), with a "linking" record SP as member in both; this structure

S	S#	SNAME	STATUS	CITY
	S1	SMITH	20	LONDON
	S2	JONES	10	PARIS
	S3	BLAKE	30	PARIS
	S4	CLARK	20	LONDON
	S5	ADAMS	30	ATHENS

SP	S#	P#	QTY
	S1	P1	3
	S1	P2	2
	S1	P3	4
	S1	P4	2
	S1	P5	1
	S1	P6	1
	S2	P1	3
	S2	P2	4
	S3	P3	4
	S3	P5	2
	S4	P2	2
	S4	P4	3
	S4	P5	4
	S5	P5	5

P	P#	PNAME	COLOR	WEIGHT
	P1	NUT	RED	12
	P2	BOLT	GREEN	17
	P3	SCREW	BLUE	17
	P4	SCREW	RED	14
	P5	CAM	BLUE	12
	P6	COG	RED	19

Figure 10.1 The suppliers-and-parts database (relational version)

```
DOMAIN      S#      CHARACTER (5)
            P#      CHARACTER (6)
            QTY     NUMERIC   (5)
            SNAME   CHARACTER(20)
            STATUS  NUMERIC   (3)
            CITY    CHARACTER(15)
            PNAME   CHARACTER(20)
            COLOR   CHARACTER (6)
            WEIGHT  NUMERIC   (4)

RELATION    S    (S#,SNAME,STATUS,CITY)
                 KEY (S#)
            P    (P#,PNAME,COLOR,WEIGHT)
                 KEY (P#)
            SP   (S#,P#,QTY)
                 KEY (S#,P#)
```

Figure 10.2 The suppliers-and-parts schema (relational version)

is illustrated in the form of a Bachman diagram in Fig. 10.4. The actual DBTG structure (part only, for reasons of space) is shown in Fig. 10.5, and the corresponding DBTG schema is given in Fig. 10.6. The comparative simplicity of both the database itself and its definition in the relational approach should be apparent from this example. We make the following specific points.

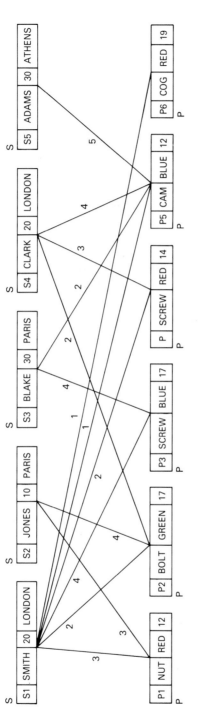

Figure 10.3 The suppliers-and-parts database (network version)

183

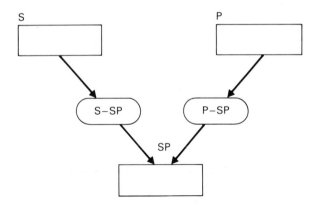

Figure 10.4   Suppliers-and-parts data structure diagram

In the relational approach the only type of structure the programmer has to understand is the table—a table, moreover, in which each column is· self-identifying and in which row order is completely immaterial. In DBTG, by contrast, programmers must understand areas (to some extent), records—which may or may not be normalized [5]—and owner-coupled sets. They must also understand the concept of ordering within such a set (and there are several different types of ordering); they may have to employ several such sets, all defined over the same records, simply to obtain several distinct orderings (a confusion between the mathematical notion of a set as a collection of objects and the concept of an access path to data). They also have to be aware of numerous rules and restrictions concerning owner-coupled sets, such as the meaning of OPTIONAL, AUTOMATIC, and so on, and the fact that the same type of record cannot be both owner and member of the same type of owner-coupled set.

It may be argued, in fact, that the relational model represents data in terms of its natural structure only—it includes absolutely no consideration of storage/access details (pointers, physical ordering, indexing or similar access techniques, etc.); in a word, no "representation clutter" [5]. In the network approach, inasmuch as some owner-coupled sets are defined purely to provide particular orderings (and because of the nature of the data manipulation language), programmers do have to be aware of certain storage/access details. In DBTG in particular, they also have to know the significance of LOCATION MODE IS CALC (an access technique that very definitely affects the way programs must be coded); they have to be familiar with two distinct methods of representing a hierarchic relationship (either as an owner-coupled set or as an unnormalized record); and they are involved with some aspects of areas and of database-keys.

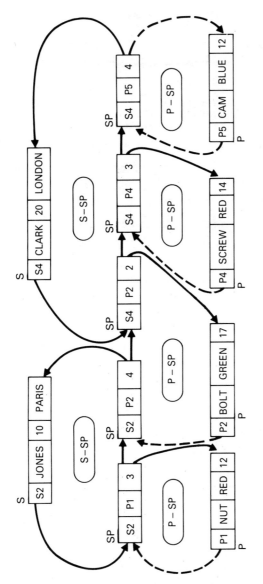

Figure 10.5 The suppliers-and-parts database: DBTG version (part only)

185

```
 1   SCHEMA NAME IS SUPPLIERS-AND-PARTS.
 2
 3   AREA NAME IS BASIC-DATA-AREA.
 4   AREA NAME IS LINK-DATA-AREA.
 5
 6   RECORD NAME IS S;
 7      LOCATION MODE IS CALC HASH-SNO USING SNO IN S
 8                          DUPLICATES ARE NOT ALLOWED;
 9      WITHIN BASIC-DATA-AREA.
10   02 SNO      ; TYPE IS CHARACTER 5.
11   02 SNAME    ; TYPE IS CHARACTER 20.
12   02 STATUS   ; TYPE IS FIXED DECIMAL 3.
13   02 CITY     ; TYPE IS CHARACTER 15.
14
15   RECORD NAME IS P;
16      LOCATION MODE IS CALC HASH-PNO USING PNO IN P
17                          DUPLICATES ARE NOT ALLOWED;
18      WITHIN BASIC-DATA-AREA.
19   02 PNO      ; TYPE IS CHARACTER 6.
20   02 PNAME    ; TYPE IS CHARACTER 20.
21   02 COLOR    ; TYPE IS CHARACTER 6.
22   02 WEIGHT   ; TYPE IS FIXED DECIMAL 4.
23
24   RECORD NAME IS SP;
25      WITHIN LINK-DATA-AREA.
26   02 SNO      ; TYPE IS CHARACTER 5.
27   02 PNO      ; TYPE IS CHARACTER 6.
28   02 QTY      ; TYPE IS FIXED DECIMAL 5.
29
30   SET NAME IS S-SP;
31      MODE IS CHAIN;
32      ORDER IS SORTED;
33      OWNER IS S.
34      MEMBER IS SP
35             OPTIONAL AUTOMATIC;
36             ASCENDING KEY IS PNO IN SP
37                      DUPLICATES ARE NOT ALLOWED;
38             SET OCCURRENCE SELECTION IS THRU
39                      LOCATION MODE OF OWNER.
40
41   SET NAME IS P-SP;
42      MODE IS CHAIN;
43      ORDER IS SORTED;
44      OWNER IS P.
45      MEMBER IS SP
46             OPTIONAL AUTOMATIC;
47             ASCENDING KEY IS SNO IN SP
48                      DUPLICATES ARE NOT ALLOWED;
49             SET OCCURRENCE SELECTION IS THRU
50                      LOCATION MODE OF OWNER.
```

Figure 10.6   The suppliers-and-parts schema (DBTG version)

The relational data structure is particularly suitable for the truly casual user (i.e., a nontechnical person who merely wishes to interrogate the database, for example someone who wants to make enquiries about this week's best buys at the supermarket). In the not too distant future the *majority* of computer users will probably be at this level. The system must therefore be capable of supporting such a view at the casual user level—and this fact in itself is a strong argument for providing the same view at the programmer level also, since any operation at the casual user level must be implementable at the programmer level too.

One other point that may be made with respect to the simplicity of the relational structure is its closeness to traditional "flat files"—i.e., to the enormous number of files that currently exist and are organized sequentially, especially on tape. The incorporation of such files into a relational database system should thus be a comparatively painless process. Contrast the difficulty of converting those same files into an equivalent network structure—probably a much more disruptive process.

The Data Manipulation Language

Again we first consider some examples. For reasons of space we restrict ourselves to examples of retrieval only. Figures 10.7–10.10 show four sample queries against the suppliers-and-parts database as they might appear (a) in the relational language ALPHA, (b) in the DML of DBTG. Notice in the fourth example (Fig. 10.10) that it is necessary to introduce a "singular" (system-owned) set P-SET linking all P occurrences together, in order that we may process all P occurrences one by one. Similar considerations may cause us to introduce such a singular set for each type of record in the

```
Relational DML (ALPHA)          |    Network DML (DBTG)
                                |
GET INTO W (SP.P#)              |        MOVE 'S4' TO SNO IN S.
     WHERE (SP.S# = 'S4')       |        FIND S RECORD.
                                |        IF S-SP SET EMPTY
------------------------------- |           GO TO NONE-SUPPLIED.
                                | NXT. FIND NEXT SP RECORD
Answer:        P#               |        OF S-SP SET.
               --               |        IF ERROR-STATUS = 0307
               P2               |           GO TO ALL-FOUND.
               P4               |        GET SP; PNO.
               P5               |        (add PNO to result)
                                |        GO TO NXT.
```

Query is of form S# = 'S4', P# = ?, QTY = don't care

Figure 10.7   Find part numbers for parts supplied by supplier S4

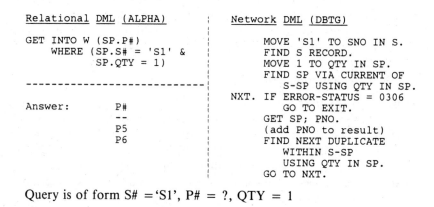

```
Relational DML (ALPHA)          |   Network DML (DBTG)

GET INTO W (SP.QTY)             |      MOVE 'S4' TO SNO IN S.
   WHERE (SP.S# = 'S4' &        |      FIND S RECORD.
          SP.P# = 'P5')         |      MOVE 'P5' TO PNO IN SP.
                                |      FIND SP VIA CURRENT OF
-----------------------------   |         S-SP USING PNO IN SP.
                                |      IF ERROR-STATUS = 0326
Answer:       QTY               |         GO TO NOT-SUPPLIED.
              ---               |      GET SP; QTY.
               4                |
```

Query is of form S# = 'S4', P# = 'P5', QTY = ?

Figure 10.8   Find quantity of part P5 supplied by supplier S4

```
Relational DML (ALPHA)          |   Network DML (DBTG)

GET INTO W (SP.P#)              |      MOVE 'S1' TO SNO IN S.
   WHERE (SP.S# = 'S1' &        |      FIND S RECORD.
          SP.QTY = 1)           |      MOVE 1 TO QTY IN SP.
                                |      FIND SP VIA CURRENT OF
-----------------------------   |         S-SP USING QTY IN SP.
                                | NXT. IF ERROR-STATUS = 0306
Answer:       P#                |         GO TO EXIT.
              --                |      GET SP; PNO.
              P5                |      (add PNO to result)
              P6                |      FIND NEXT DUPLICATE
                                |         WITHIN S-SP
                                |         USING QTY IN SP.
                                |      GO TO NXT.
```

Query is of form S# = 'S1', P# = ?, QTY = 1

Figure 10.9   Find part numbers for parts supplied by supplier S1
           in a quantity of 1

database, in the extreme case. The comparative simplicity of the relational
approach is immediately apparent in these examples.

The relational DML is close to natural language. This is particularly
true for retrieval; a case can be made out for the update operations also,
although of course these are not illustrated in Figs. 10.7–10.10. Apart from
the obvious advantage to the casual user, this is a good argument for giving
the programmer such a language as well: It may be viewed as another step
in the general historical trend toward programming languages of ever higher
level. All the usual arguments apply: reduction in the number of decisions
the programmer has to make, reduced scope for errors, reduced maintenance, increased productivity, and so on.

```
Relational DML (ALPHA)          |   Network DML (DBTG)

GET INTO W (P.PNAME,S.CITY)     |       MOVE 0 TO NTH.
    WHERE EXISTS SP             |   NXP. ADD 1 TO NTH.
          (SP.S# = S.S# &       |       FIND NTH RECORD
           SP.P# = P.P#)        |          OF P-SET SET.
                                |       IF ERROR-STATUS = 0307
----------------------------    |          GO TO EXIT.
                                |       IF P-SP SET EMPTY
Answer:    PNAME     CITY       |          GO TO NXP.
           -----     ------     |       GET P; PNAME.
           NUT       LONDON     |   NXX. FIND NEXT SP RECORD
           NUT       PARIS      |          OF P-SP SET.
           BOLT      LONDON     |       IF ERROR-STATUS = 0307
           BOLT      PARIS      |          GO TO NXX.
           SCREW     LONDON     |       FIND OWNER RECORD
              .        .        |          OF S-SP SET.
              .        .        |       GET S; CITY.
                                |       (add PNAME/CITY pair to
(note duplicate elimination)    |        result unless already
                                |        present)
                                |       GO TO NXX.
```

Figure 10.10   For each shipment, find part name and supplier city

It can be claimed, in fact, that generally speaking the complexity of any given ALPHA statement is in direct proportion to the complexity of the operation it represents. It is certainly true that "simple" operations are genuinely simple to perform—see Fig. 10.7, for example. This is in sharp contrast to the situation in DBTG, where complexity is often introduced by the nature of the schema and DML even when it is not intrinsic to the operation to be performed.

The relational DML is highly nonprocedural. This has the effect of removing the burden of arbitrary and error-prone decisions from the programmer's shoulders. The network DML, by contrast, forces programs to be extremely procedural. The DBTG notion of currency in particular has many consequences on programs in this area. For example, to INSERT (i.e., connect) a record occurrence R into an owner-coupled set occurrence S, the programmer must (a) find the set occurrence S, then (b) find the record occurrence R, and then (c) issue an INSERT to link the latter into the former. The point here is that, although steps (a) and (b) are quite unrelated to each other, they *must* be performed in the sequence stated (because INSERT operates on the current of run-unit).

Last, the relational DML operates in terms of *sets* (mathematical sets, not the DBTG construct); that is, the programmer simply states a definition of the set—actually the relation—to be accessed, and leaves all details of how the accessing is done to the system. This has two significant corollaries.

First, optimization is possible. Since the access strategy is not embedded in the program, the system has a chance to make dynamic decisions as to the best way of actually performing the operation, based upon considerations such as the current storage structure and current distributions of data values. Some interesting work has been done on this problem by Palermo [17] and by Rothnie [21]. In the network approach, of course, many of the details of access strategy are firmly embedded in the logic of the application program.

The second corollary of the orientation toward set handling in the relational DML is that it will lead to more effective use of communications lines if the database is distributed. Basically this is because the system receives one request for each (mathematical) set of records required, rather than one for each individual record. Again this is not the case in the network approach, where programs operate entirely in a one-record-at-a-time mode.

Further specific criticisms may be made of the DBTG DML under the heading of simplicity (or rather lack of it). In particular the concept of currency and the associated notion of selective currency suppression contribute greatly to the complexity of the DML. There are of course no comparable concepts in ALPHA. Another complicating factor is the number of different FIND statements that seem to be required.

UNIFORMITY

Data Structure

The relational model provides a uniform view of data, in the sense that no distinction is made between "entities" (such as suppliers or parts) and "relationships" (such as supplier-part links); both are represented in the same way, namely as *tuples*. In other words, there is one and only one way of representing an entity (on the understanding that a "relationship" is merely a particular type of entity)—namely, as an entity identifier (the primary key value) together with a set of associated descriptive properties. A corollary of this fact is that a significantly smaller set of operations is required in a relational DML.

The network model, by contrast, does make a distinction between "entities" and "relationships." Roughly speaking, "entities" are represented as records in the traditional way, whereas "relationships" are represented by (owner-coupled) set membership and (owner-coupled) set ordering. At first sight this distinction may appear fairly natural and indeed attractive—but in fact it is the source of additional complexity, both in the model and the language, and may lead to disruptive growth. We shall return to this latter point in the section on data independence, later.

The Data Manipulation Language

We have already mentioned that in the relational DML a very small set of operations is sufficient. This is certainly not the case with the network approach. Consider what is involved in DBTG, for example, in retrieving information about an "entity"—say supplier S4—as opposed to retrieving information about a "relationship"—say that between supplier S4 and part P5. (See Fig. 10.8. A GET after the second statement would suffice for the first of these retrievals; the entire procedure is required for the second.) Consider, too, the differences between creating an "entity" (which involves a STORE) and creating a "relationship" (which requires a STORE and an INSERT, at least conceptually).

The uniformity of the relational data structure permits *symmetric exploitation* in the relational DML [5]. This means that we can access a relation by specifying values for any combination of its attributes (and the form of the access statement is essentially the same in all cases). For example, see Figs. 10.8 and 10.9, in both of which we are accessing relation SP with values specified for two attributes and retrieving corresponding values for the third. Notice that the corresponding DBTG formulations are certainly not symmetric.

For practical purposes, except when the operation is extremely complicated, there is effectively one and only one way of expressing any given operation in a relational DML. This follows from the fact that the programmer writes a *definition* of the set to be accessed. Sometimes it is possible to write such a definition in a number of different ways, but the differences are only superficial. Figure 10.11 shows three superficially distinct ALPHA GET statements that are in fact all equivalent to each other.

```
GET INTO W (S.SNAME) WHERE

(a) EXISTS SP (SP.S# = S.S# & EXISTS P (P.P# = SP.P# &
                                        P.COLOR = 'RED'))

(b) EXISTS P (P.COLOR = 'RED' & EXISTS SP (SP.P# = P.P# &
                                           SP.S# = S.S#))

(c) EXISTS P EXISTS SP (P.COLOR = 'RED' & SP.P# = P.P# &
                                          SP.S# = S.S#)
```

Figure 10.11   Find names of suppliers who supply at least one red part

Once again, then, the effect is to reduce the number of decisions that have to be made by the programmer.

In the network approach, of course, there are many quite distinct ways of performing any given operation. As a simple example, consider Fig. 10.8; the procedure there starts at the supplier (S4), but it could equally well have started at the part (P5). Once again this puts an added burden on the programmer. Incidentally, these two alternative procedures, though both eventually accessing the same SP occurrence, have different side effects, inasmuch as different currency indicators are set in the two cases—which represents an additional and very serious problem. To reach any specific target data, the network normally requires the programmer to choose between many paths, and sometimes between different *types* of path. In making this choice, the programmer must also try to anticipate how the various currency indicators will be affected.

This is probably a good point at which to note that not all relational DMLs need involve the "strange symbolism" of predicate calculus. SEQUEL [22] is an example of one that does not. The query of Fig. 10.11 might appear in SEQUEL as follows:

```
SELECT SNAME FROM S
WHERE  S# IN
       (SELECT S# FROM SP
        WHERE  P# IN
               (SELECT P# FROM P
                WHERE  COLOR = 'RED'))
```

Even in ALPHA it would clearly be possible to introduce a default mechanism so that the existential quantifier need never be written explicitly.

COMPLETENESS

Data Structure

The relational model is *complete* in the sense that, as shown in [6], all data structures commonly employed in database systems can easily be cast into relational form. Hence relations are at least adequate—there are no restrictions on what can be represented.

Moreover, the design discipline of "third normal form" [8,16,18] allows the data representation to be *nonredundant* in the following (somewhat intuitive) sense: Each fact is represented once and once only (i.e., in precisely one place). "Fact" here refers to the association between an entity and one of its properties, e.g., the fact that supplier S4 is located in London. Hence relations are not only adequate, they are also *not too rich*. (These remarks should not be taken to mean that *all possible* redundancy is automatically eliminated by third normal form. For example, unnormalized records may be considered less redundant than a normalized relation in some circumstances.)

Thus relations provide the ability to construct an accurate model of the real world, which consists of a number of entities (of various types), together with their properties, and *nothing else*. Notice, however, that we require the concept of *primary key* to build such a model (a concept that is absent from DBTG). It may indeed be argued that a given third normal form structure is a *canonical representation* of the data concerned, in that it contains all the intrinsic properties of the data and nothing besides.

Turning now to the network model, it too is complete in the above sense. However, it is no *more* complete, despite its far greater complexity (i.e., there is nothing that can be represented in network form and not in relational form). Moreover, networks frequently do contain redundant information (with the aim of simplifying retrieval, at the expense of complicating maintenance)—for example, the fact that supplier S4 supplies part P5 is represented twice in the network of Fig. 10.5, once by the appearance of 'S4' within a particular occurrence of record SP and once by the appearance of that SP occurrence within a particular occurrence of owner-coupled set S-SP.

Moreover, despite the fact that networks do permit completeness of representation, it is usually the case that the network does not contain a *direct* representation of everything (specifically, of every *relationship*), simply because it would be extremely complex if it did. As an example, suppose that in the suppliers-and-parts database (Fig. 10.1) we have an additional piece of information for each part, namely CITY, representing the city where the part is stored. (For the sake of the example we assume that each part is stored in one and only one city.) In the relational case this addition corresponds to the addition of a new attribute to relation P; for example, see Fig. 10.12.

```
      --    -----   -----   ------  ------
P     P#    PNAME   COLOR   WEIGHT  CITY
      --    -----   -----   ------  ------
      P1    NUT     RED         12  LONDON
      P2    BOLT    GREEN       17  OSLO
      P3    SCREW   BLUE        17  PARIS
      P4    SCREW   RED         14  NICE
      P5    CAM     BLUE        12  PARIS
      P6    COG     RED         19  PARIS
```

Figure 10.12   Relation P extended to include attribute CITY

An analogous change is made to the network database (i.e., a new data item CITY is added to record type P). Now consider the query "Find all suppliers and parts that are colocated, i.e., have the same value for CITY." See Fig. 10.13.

Notice, incidentally, that in the network case we now need a singular set of suppliers (S-SET) as well as one of parts (P-SET). The point about this example is that the network chosen does not *directly* represent the relationship that connects suppliers and parts with the same CITY value. (By contrast, it does directly represent the relationship connecting S's and SP's with the same supplier number, also the relationship connecting P's and SP's with the same part number.) Of course it is possible to represent this relationship "directly," by introducing appropriate owner-coupled sets. However, the authors contend that it is unreasonable to represent *all* such relationships directly, because of the tremendous complexity this would introduce into the structure. Thus the programmer has to be aware of which relationships are represented directly and which not, since it very directly affects the code that has to be written. (Note, too, that we have only considered cases in which the basic comparison operator defining the relationship is equality. The problem is greatly magnified if we consider other operators as well.) Another corollary is that the database designer has to be able to anticipate the various uses to which the data is to be put in order to provide the appropriate structures.

```
Relational DML (ALPHA)              Network DML (DBTG)

GET INTO W (S.S#,P.P#)                   MOVE 0 TO NTH.
     WHERE (S.CITY = P.CITY)        NXS. ADD 1 TO NTH.
                                         FIND NTH RECORD
-----------------------------              OF S-SET SET.
                                         IF ERROR-STATUS = 0307
Answer:      S#      P#                      GO TO EXIT.
             --      --                   GET S.
             S1      P1                   MOVE CITY IN S
             S2      P3                      TO CITY IN P.
             S2      P5                   FIND P VIA CURRENT
             S2      P6                      OF P-SET
             S3      P3                      USING CITY IN P.
             S3      P5              NXP. IF ERROR-STATUS = 0326
             S3      P6                      GO TO NXS.
                                         GET P.
(note duplicate elimination)             (add SNO/PNO pair to
                                          result)
                                         FIND NEXT DUPLICATE
                                            WITHIN P-SET
                                            USING CITY IN P.
                                         GO TO NXP.
```

Figure 10.13   Find all suppliers and parts that are colocated

In the relational approach, of course, the relationship is "directly" supported, in the sense that it is specified via a predicate in the GET statement. In other words, the connexion between suppliers and parts with the same CITY value is expressed in exactly the same sort of way as the connexion between S's and SP's with the same supplier number.

The Data Manipulation Language

The ALPHA language is based on predicate calculus. We therefore *know* that any relation definable in terms of the given relations by means of a predicate in the relational calculus can be retrieved in a single GET statement. In the network approach, of course, for all but the very simplest cases it is necessary to write a (multistatement) procedure. For examples, see Figs. 10.7–10.10 and Fig. 10.13. Once again this difference is highly significant from the point of view of programmer productivity.

It is not really suggested that the programmer actually express very complex queries in the form of a single GET; of course it is always possible to break such queries down into a sequence of simpler ones. (Nevertheless, the power of the language is such that even "simple" queries may actually be quite complex.) More important, however, the relational completeness of ALPHA makes it an extremely suitable candidate as a target for higher-level language translators—where by "higher-level language" we mean a language suitable for casual users, not a functionally equivalent alternative to ALPHA such as SEQUEL [22]. Since all the basic retrieval power any such language may need is embodied in ALPHA, we can implement this basic retrieval capability once instead of many times. If instead a network language is used as such a target language, there will be much duplication of function (e.g., in generation of access strategies) in the corresponding higher-level language translators.

DATA INDEPENDENCE

It is generally agreed that data independence should be a goal of database systems. However, different people have different ideas as to what this expression means. We mean:

(a) Program immunity to change in the storage structure (sometimes referred to as physical data independence [12]); also

(b) Program immunity to growth in the database schema (sometimes referred to as logical data independence [13]).

We want storage structure independence to allow the storage structure to be tuned to optimize overall performance, to implement new standards in the storage structure, to take advantage of new hardware technology as it is developed, and for many other reasons. We want growth independence to allow the addition of new types of entity and/or the addition of new facts about existing types of entity; in particular this kind of independence is essential to the *gradual* introduction of a database system into an organization.

Storage Structure Independence

As far as the relational approach is concerned, it is obvious that neither the model nor the ALPHA language contain any reference to storage constructs of any type, nor to any corresponding access techniques; they are both solely concerned with the *information* in the database. Specifically, there is absolutely no mention of the stored form of relations or domains or to pointer chains, indexes, hashing algorithms, or any other access mechanism. Hence the implementation is free to choose any one of a very large class of possible storage structures and corresponding access techniques, as is shown in [12]. As an example, MacAIMS [15] actually provides an open-ended set of *different* storage structures all within the same system; each structure has an associated "relational strategy module" whose function is to manage that structure and to make it look like the "pure" (tabular) structure to the rest of the system. Incidentally, the lack of fact redundancy in the logical relational representation does not necessarily force "zero redundancy" in the physical storage structure; the implementation may certainly introduce redundancy at this level if required, say for performance reasons.

By way of contrast, it is the very essence of the network approach that the programmer is involved in tracing access paths; i.e., access strategy is embedded in the application program. (It is usual to talk in terms of "pointers" and "chains," though as Bachman [1] has indicated, these "chains" need not be implemented as actual stored chains of pointers. However, the programmer may always think of these "chains" as physically existing, even if they are represented by some alternative method, because of the chain-traversing nature of the data manipulation language.) It follows that the implementation must provide exactly the "chains" the programmer sees; for if programs depend on a "chain" that is not there they will not work, and there is no point in providing any extra "chains" because programs by definition will not use them. This requirement very severely limits the degree of variation possible in the storage structure.

In DBTG in particular there are a number of additional considerations that constrain matters still further. These include programmer dependence on LOCATION MODE and SET OCCURRENCE SELECTION (especially

LOCATION MODE IS CALC), also the visibility of areas and of database-keys. See Engles [14].

Growth Independence

Growth can be very clearly defined in relational terms. Adding a new type of entity corresponds to adding a new relation; adding a new fact about an existing type of entity corresponds to adding a new attribute to an existing relation. Neither of these two types of change will have any effect on any existing program, because no existing program will contain any explicit reference to the new attribute or new relation. Inspection of the examples earlier in this paper will show this to be so for retrieval; as for the update operations, UPDATE and DELETE operations will be unaffected, PUT operations will create tuples that are extended by the system to include null values in positions corresponding to new (unspecified) attributes.

In most cases growth can also be satisfactorily accommodated in the network approach, *provided* that the network is designed on what may be called "third normal form principles." Specifically, there must exist a one-to-one correspondence between the tuples of a third normal form relational representation and the record occurrences of the network representation; and in the case of a linking relation (i.e., one with a multi-component primary key), the corresponding record must be a linking record that participates as a member in N owner-coupled sets, where N is the number of components in the primary key. (Of course, the foregoing remarks are very imprecise; they can be tightened up if necessary.)

Even if these principles are adhered to, however, there is an important situation in which growth causes problems in the network approach. This is the case of adding a new fact about an existing type of entity, where the entity concerned is represented by *owner-coupled set ordering*. For example, suppose two adjacent member record occurrences represent two adjacent stations on a subway line, and it is required to introduce a new item, namely the distance between the two stations. This item can be placed in one of the two member records—but which one? Whichever is chosen, the effect will be that the logic involved in manipulating the "relationship" will be radically different depending on the direction of processing (the algorithm for "traveling the line" between two stations A and B, for example, will depend on whether A precedes or follows B on the line).

The subway example illustrates a number of other points in addition to the one just mentioned. The essence of the problem is that, despite the fact that a subway network is a "natural" candidate for a network structure, casting it into network form gives rise to several problems that are not present in the relational equivalent. For example, the "obvious" network representation involves an owner-coupled set for each line, having as members the appropriate station records in the appropriate order. However, this structure does not accurately model the case of a circular or closed-loop line—the fact that the "first" and "last" stations on the line are adjacent has to be dealt with as a special case. A suitable relational structure for this problem is a relation

```
R (LINE,LINE_SEGMENT,UP,DOWN,DIST)
```

where UP and DOWN represent two adjacent stations on LINE, connected by LINE_SEGMENT, and DIST is the distance between them. Note that this relation may be viewed as representing the line in both the UP and DOWN directions, whereas the "obvious" network representation is unidirectional. Moreover, this single relation can accommodate circular lines, even if it is not known at the outset that such lines might be built.

INTEGRITY AND SECURITY

In addition to creating the schema, the database designer is also responsible for the specification of various integrity and security constraints. By *security constraints* we mean, for example, checks that must be applied to ensure that the programmer is authorized to perform the operation being attempted. By *integrity constraints* we mean checks that must be applied when the programmer attempts to change the database to ensure that the change is a valid one. Note that constraints of either type may be arbitrarily complex. The database management system is of course responsible for implementing the constraints as specified; in addition, it must include some means of handling the data sharing problem (concurrent access), another aspect of integrity. In this section we consider the two approaches from the standpoint of integrity and security.

A major advantage of a third normal form relational structure is that a clean separation is achieved between the underlying data and any constraints one may wish to impose on top of it. In the network approach, such a separation could be achieved if all constraints were expressed by database procedures. However, it is normally the case that certain constraints are deliberately built into the data structure itself—indeed, this is one of the main reasons given for the existence of the owner-coupled set construct. Thus, to achieve the separation referred to above, the database designer is faced with the problem of disentangling the security and integrity requirements from the complexities of the data structure. In the relational approach, by contrast, the designer has only one type of structure to consider, and a very simple coordinate system (identification of relations and columns by name, and rows by content) by which to refer to any individual item or portion of that structure.

As an example of how constraints may be independently superimposed in the case of the relational model, consider the suppliers-and-parts database, in which for consistency it would probably be required that any S# value appearing in relation SP must also exist in relation S. This integrity constraint can be simply expressed in the schema as follows:

<u>CONSTRAINT</u> { SP.S# } <u>CONTAINED IN</u> { S.S# }

(i.e., the [mathematical] set of S# values from relation SP is a subset of the [mathematical] set of S# values from relation S). This implies checks on PUT operations for relation SP and DELETE operations for relation S (among other things).

As an example of the interweaving of constraints and structure in the network model, consider the owner-coupled set structure of Fig. 10.14.

For each department we have a set of employees, for each employee a salary history, i.e., a set of salaries. With this structure how can we specify the security constraint that a particular user (a) can see EMP occurrences, (b) can see DEPT/SAL combinations, but (c) cannot see EMP/SAL combinations? The answer is that another owner-coupled set DEPTSAL (owner DEPT, member SAL) must be introduced, and the user granted access to DEPTEMP and DEPTSAL but not EMPSAL. Observe how the data structure is dictated by the constraint requirement.

Another point to consider in connexion with security in the network model is the following: The very fact that a particular record (occurrence)

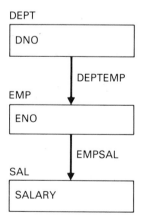

Figure 10.14 The owner-coupled sets DEPTEMP and EMPSAL

is a member of a particular owner-coupled set (occurrence) may itself be sensitive (consider the case of a set of employees in which the qualification for membership is that the employee's salary exceeds some specified value). Thus it may not be adequate to provide checks against record retrieval only —constraints may also have to be applied at the owner-coupled set level too. This is another corollary of the fact that there are several structurally distinct ways of representing information in the network approach.

[*The remainder of this section was concerned with problems arising from the need to support concurrent access to the database. The original DBTG proposals included a scheme based on the concept of* warning: *The system was supposed to inform the program if some concurrent program had accessed data which the first program had indicated it was interested in. This scheme suffered from a number of flaws and was subsequently abandoned.*]

SUMMARY

By way of summary we list again the major headings under which we have presented our argument:

1. Simplicity—of both the data structure and the language;
2. Uniformity—likewise;
3. Completeness—likewise;
4. Data independence—with respect to both storage structure and growth;
5. Integrity and security.

In conclusion it is only fair to mention the major *disadvantage* of the relational approach, which is this: At the time of writing no fullscale implementations exist (though a number of prototype systems incorporating relational ideas have been built at universities and elsewhere, and investigations are continuing within General Motors Research [25] and IBM Research [22–24], to name just two). It is thus not yet possible to state what the performance of such a system will be like, either in terms of space utilization or response time. However, some interesting work has been done in this area, and there is good reason to be hopeful about the outcome.

ACKNOWLEDGMENT

The authors would like to thank numerous colleagues at IBM San Jose Research Laboratory, especially R. F. Boyce, D. D. Chamberlin, W. F. King, and I. L. Traiger, for reading an early draft of this paper and for their many helpful suggestions.

REFERENCES

1. C. W. Bachman, "Implementation Techniques for Data Structure Sets," *Proc. SHARE Workshop on Data Base Management Systems,* Montreal (July 1973).

2. CODASYL Data Base Task Group, *Report* (April 1971).

3. CODASYL Data Base Language Task Group, *Proposal* (February 1973).

4. CODASYL Data Description Language Committee, *Journal of Development* (June 1973).

5. E. F. Codd, "A Relational Model of Data for Large Shared Data Banks," *CACM* 13, No. 6 (June 1970).

6. E. F. Codd, "Normalized Data Base Structure: A Brief Tutorial," *Proc. 1971 ACM SIGFIDET Workshop on Data Description, Access, and Control* (November 1971).

7. E. F. Codd, "A Data Base Sublanguage Founded on the Relational Calculus," *Proc. 1971 ACM SIGFIDET Workshop on Data Description, Access, and Control* (November 1971).

8. E. F. Codd, "Further Normalization of the Data Base Relational Model." In *Data Base Systems*: Courant Computer Science Symposia Series, Vol. 6 (Englewood Cliffs, NJ: Prentice-Hall, 1972).

9. E. F. Codd, "Relational Completeness of Data Base Sublanguages." In *Data Base Systems*: Courant Computer Science Symposia Series, Vol. 6 (Englewood Cliffs, NJ: Prentice-Hall, 1972).

10. E. F. Codd, "Access Control for Relational Data Base Systems." Presented at BCS Symposium on Relational Database Concepts, London (April 1973).

11. C. J. Date, "Relational Database Systems: A Tutorial," *Proc. 4th International Symposium on Computer and Information Science, Miami Beach* (New York: Plenum Press, 1972).

12. C. J. Date and P. Hopewell, "Storage Structure and Physical Data Independence," *Proc. 1971 ACM SIGFIDET Workshop on Data Description, Access, and Control* (November 1971).

13. C. J. Date and P. Hopewell, "File Definition and Logical Data Independence," *Proc. 1971 ACM SIGFIDET Workshop on Data Description, Access, and Control* (November 1971).

14. R. W. Engles, "An Analysis of the April 1971 DBTG Report," *Proc. 1971 ACM SIGFIDET Workshop on Data Description, Access, and Control* (November 1971).

15. R. C. Goldstein and A. J. Strnad, "The MacAIMS Data Management System," *Proc. 1970 ACM SIGFIDET Workshop on Data Description and Access* (November 1970).

16. I. J. Heath, "Unacceptable File Operations in a Relational Database," *Proc. 1971 ACM SIGFIDET Workshop on Data Description, Access, and Control* (November 1971).

17. F. P. Palermo, "A Data Base Search Problem," *Proc. 4th International Symposium on Computer and Information Science, Miami Beach* (New York: Plenum Press, 1972).

18. P. H. Prowse, "The Relational Model as a System Analysis Tool." Presented at BCS Symposium on Relational Database Concepts, London (April 1973).

19. C. W. Bachman, "Data Structure Diagrams," *Data Base* 1, No. 2 (Summer 1969).

20. C. W. Bachman, "The Programmer as Navigator" (1973 Turing Award Lecture), *CACM* 16, No. 11 (November 1973).

21. J. B. Rothnie, "The Design of Generalized Data Management Systems," Ph.D. Dissertation, Dept. of Civil Engineering, MIT (September 1972).

22. D. D. Chamberlin and R. F. Boyce, "SEQUEL: A Structured English Query Language," *Proc. 1974 ACM SIGMOD Workshop on Data Description, Access, and Control* (May 1974).

23. R. F. Boyce and D. D. Chamberlin, "Using a Structured English Query Language as a Data Definition Facility," IBM Research Report RJ1318.

24. D. D. Chamberlin, R. F. Boyce, and I. L. Traiger, "A Deadlock-Free Scheme for Resource Locking in a Database Environment," *Proc. 1974 IFIP Congress.* North-Holland (1974).

25. V. K. M. Whitney, "Fourth Generation Data Management Systems," *Proc. 1973 National Computer Conference,* New York.

11

An Introduction to the
Unified Database Language
(UDL)

ABSTRACT

UDL consists of a set of database extensions for programming languages such as COBOL and PL/I. The first description of UDL was given in [1], and detailed specifications were published in [2–6]. The present paper provides an informal introduction to the concepts and facilities of UDL as currently defined [3,4], and thus forms a replacement for the original paper [1].

UDL per se is not dependent on any particular host programming language; its constructs and functions, or some suitable subset of them, can be mapped into the concrete syntax of a variety of such languages. For

Copyright 1980 IEEE. Reprinted, with permission, from *Proc. 6th International Conference on Very Large Data Bases* (Montreal, Canada, October 1–3), pp. 15–32. Some additional material has been incorporated into the version printed here, taken from *An Introduction to Database Systems: Volume I* (3rd edition, portions of Chapter 27 and Section 15.4), by C. J. Date, copyright 1981, Addison-Wesley, Reading, Massachusetts. Reprinted with permission.

definiteness, however, this paper uses one specific language, namely PL/I, as the basis for all examples.

COMMENTS ON REPUBLICATION

A significant portion of my IBM career was devoted to the design of the language described in this paper. At that time, of course, I had hopes of it becoming the basis of a commercial product; the idea was that, given that all three database approaches (relational, hierarchic, network) seemed certain to have to coexist for some considerable time to come, it would be nice if that coexistence could be as amicable as possible. Thus, the idea of using a single, well-structured language as a common interface to a variety of disparate systems seemed a very attractive one: It could greatly simplify problems of communication between users of different systems, it could ease education problems, and it could assist with the migration of programs and programmers from one system to another (including, in particular, migration from a nonrelational system to a relational one). For example, if the relational portions of UDL were implemented as an interface to DB2 and the hierarchic portions as an interface to IMS, then the migration path from IMS to DB2 would be considerably simplified (see the discussion of this topic in the next paper in this collection).

Of course, there is now virtually no chance of any kind of UDL product ever appearing. Nevertheless, I still feel that the language itself is worthy of attention, if only as a teaching vehicle, thanks to its consistent treatment of the three approaches: It provides a sound basis for treating the essential similarities and essential differences among those approaches, without getting sidetracked by the quirks and idiosyncrasies of specific implemented systems. In addition, of course, it provides further evidence in support of the arguments of the two preceding papers in this collection.

I have included a certain amount of new material in the paper as printed here, most of it material that originally appeared in the 3rd edition of *An Introduction to Database Systems: Volume I* but had to be excluded from the 4th edition for a variety of reasons. Specifically, I have added:

- Set-level hierarchic and network versions of the enrollment example (Figs. 11.14 and 11.15);
- A new appendix (Appendix B) showing a CODASYL DBTG solution to the enrollment problem and giving some comparative statistics;
- Another new appendix (Appendix C) discussing some performance aspects.

Regarding the last of these, it is worth mentioning that a number of actual performance tests were made on an (undocumented) prototype UDL implementation. The results of those tests were in broad agreement with the theoretical analysis given in that appendix.

INTRODUCTION

A proposal for a set of high-level language database extensions was originally outlined in [1]. Those extensions were subsequently christened the Unified Database Language, or UDL, since a major objective was to deal with the three well-known database structures—relations, hierarchies, networks—in a unified and consistent manner. Despite the name, however, UDL is not a standalone language; rather, it is a set of database facilities that can be incorporated, with suitable syntactic modifications, into a variety of host languages.[1] The general approach to the design of UDL was to define, in a host-independent way, the various types of data structure to be supported, together with appropriate operators on those structures, and the detailed problem of mapping those structures and operators into the syntax of specific languages was tackled as a follow-on activity [3,4].

Some more detailed objectives for UDL (taken from [3,4]) are listed below. First, *any* language extension, no matter what function it is providing, should satisfy at least the following criteria.

1. It should be designed from the user's point of view rather than the system's (i.e., design should proceed from the outside in).
2. It should fit well with the base language. Wherever possible, it should exploit existing language features rather than introducing new ones.
3. It should transcend and outlive all features of the underlying hardware and software that are specific to those systems.
4. It should provide access to as much function of the underlying systems as possible without compromising on the other objectives.

The following objectives are specific to UDL per se.

1. It should establish a stable long-range design that can be gracefully subset for short-range implementation.
2. It should support each of the three well-known database structures (relations, hierarchies, networks).
3. Both record-at-a-time and set-at-a-time operations should be available for each of these structures.

---

[1]Of course, there is no reason why a standalone, and indeed interactive, version of UDL could not be constructed if desired.

4. The support for the three structures should consist of a single integrated set of facilities, not three discrete sets (insofar as possible).

5. A wide range of navigational operations should be provided at the record level.

6. A wide range of derivational expressions should be provided at the set level.

7. A program should be able to hold any number of positions in a database simultaneously.

8. Holding positions should be by explicit, not implicit, program command.

9. A flexible and comprehensive locking scheme should be provided, with simple and foolproof defaults.

10. The language should be efficiently implementable.

AN INTRODUCTORY EXAMPLE

It is convenient to begin by presenting an introductory example in order to convey the overall flavor of the language. The example is intended to be broadly self-explanatory. The sample database, which is hierarchic in structure, is shown in Fig. 11.1; a UDL declaration for that database is given in Fig. 11.2; and a UDL procedure that produces a report from that database is given in Fig. 11.3.

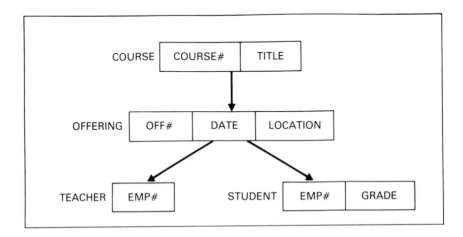

Figure. 11.1 Database for the introductory example

```
DCL EDUC DATABASE
  BASESETS (
    CSET RECTYPE (1 COURSE BASED(C),
                  2 COURSE# CHAR(3) ...),
    OSET RECTYPE (1 OFFERING BASED(O),
                  2 OFF# ...),
    TSET RECTYPE (1 TEACHER BASED(T),
                  2 EMP# ...),
    SSET RECTYPE (1 STUDENT BASED(S),
                  2 EMP# ...)           )
  FANSETS (
    RECORD (OFFERING) UNDER (COURSE),
    RECORD (TEACHER)  UNDER (OFFERING),
    RECORD (STUDENT)  UNDER (OFFERING)    );
```

Figure 11.2   UDL declaration for the sample database

```
GET LIST (GIVEN.EMP#);

DO STUDENT WHERE STUDENT.EMP# = GIVEN.EMP#;
  FIND UNIQUE (OFFERING OVER STUDENT);
  FIND UNIQUE (COURSE OVER OFFERING);
  DO TEACHER UNDER OFFERING;
    PUT SKIP LIST (COURSE#, DATE, LOCATION,
                   TEACHER.EMP#, GRADE);
  END;
END;
```

Figure 11.3   UDL procedure to print a report

DIRECT REFERENCE

Throughout this paper we are concerned with databases *as they are perceived by the programmer*. To use the terminology of the ANSI/X3/SPARC Study Group on Database Systems, we are interested in the "external view" of a database (described by an external schema)—and not the underlying "conceptual" view (described by the conceptual schema), nor the stored data itself (described by the internal schema). From here on we will use the term "database" to refer exclusively to an external view.

From the programmer's point of view the significant features of a database are that it is *persistent* and *shared*. By "persistent" we mean, broadly speaking, that the data already exists when the program starts to execute, and that it continues to exist after the program has terminated; by "shared" we mean that the program may have to be aware of the fact that the database is subject to reference and update by other concurrently running programs. But in other respects, a database can be considered as just a new kind of data aggregate. The question arises, how should such an aggregate be presented to the programmer?

Of course this is basically just a syntactic question. There are obviously several ways of representing a database in terms of concrete syntax. However, since it is axiomatic that the entire syntax will be crucially dependent on the particular representation chosen, and since the syntax of [3,4] uses a slightly unobvious approach, we choose to discuss the issue briefly here. In this syntax a database is represented, not as some new kind of input/output file, but instead as part of the program's directly addressable storage area—rather like an array, a queue, or any other "in-core" aggregate—and the programmer is allowed to operate on database data in situ ("direct reference"). Explicit I/O operations are specifically *not* required. (There is an obvious analogy here with virtual storage systems.) Some reasons for adopting such an approach are listed below.

- The basic point is simply that data in a database is *in the system*, and from the programmer's point of view it should not be necessary to move it from one place to another in order to process it—it should be possible to access it directly, just as it is with ordinary (nonpersistent, nonshared) or "local" data. A comparative uniformity of reference for local and global data is a great simplifying factor for the user.

- Direct reference automatically provides a great deal of function within existing language. For example, in PL/I, the existing power of operational expressions is immediately available for database data. Thus the database language extensions can be kept to a comparatively manageable size—it is not necessary to have one set of language constructs for database data and one for ordinary data. Retrieval, for example, can be handled by means of an ordinary assignment statement in which the source is a variable in the database.

- As an extension of the previous point, direct reference allows operations of the form

  ```
  ASSIGN Y TO X;
  ```

  where X and Y are both references to objects in the database. Such an operation would require two steps if READ and REWRITE statements were involved. (For reasons not discussed here UDL uses a keyword form of the assignment statement instead of the more familiar "target = expression;" form.)

- A more specific example:

  ```
  ASSIGN (EMPLOYEE.SALARY + 500) TO EMPLOYEE.SALARY;
  ```

  EMPLOYEE here is a reference to some database record, SALARY is a field in that record (see below). This example shows how the "update

but not see'' function—sometimes stated as a security requirement—
could be handled in UDL.

- The foregoing example also shows that field-level access (a major requirement) can be incorporated very naturally into the direct reference
language.

- There is an important semantic distinction between assignment operations and READ/WRITE operations, at least as they apply to source/
sink devices, which has been obscured in the past by the fact that
READ/WRITE operations have also been used for storage devices such
as disks. Typically, once a piece of data has been accessed by means of
an input operation, it cannot be accessed again (think of a message
from a terminal). An assignment operation, on the other hand, can be
repeated indefinitely and will normally produce the same result every
time (unless of course it modifies its own source variables). A database
retrieval operation will also normally produce the same result every
time. Similar remarks apply to output; in particular, once a piece of
data—say an output message—has been transmitted, it is generally not
possible to access it again, whereas it generally is possible to reaccess
a piece of data after it has been placed in the database. The direct reference proposal is in line with these semantic distinctions. (As a corollary, I/O statements, not direct reference, should be used for source/
sink access. Of course, this remark should not be construed to mean
that a program's source/sink data cannot be held on a storage or
"database" device.)

- UDL also introduces "local basesets"—i.e., sets of records similar to
those found in a database, but local to the program. A local baseset
may be used, for example, to contain a set of records that are derived
in some way from records in the database. It seems undesirable to have
to use READ/WRITE statements to access an aggregate that is purely
local to the program. At the same time it seems desirable to be able to
access basesets uniformly regardless of whether they are local or global
(i.e., in a database).

The programmer, then, perceives a database as a storage area containing data in the form of records. The records are partitioned into sets called
basesets (a baseset is the collection of all records of one type). Records form
a new kind of aggregate data-item (a new kind of structure in PL/I); fields
within a record in turn form a new kind of scalar or elementary data-item.
To operate on a specific record, the programmer must normally obtain
"addressability" to that record by executing an appropriate FIND statement—for example:

```
FIND UNIQUE (EMPLOYEE WHERE EMPLOYEE.EMP# = '562170') SET(E);
```

This FIND statement locates a particular EMPLOYEE record and sets the *cursor* E to point to it. A cursor is a "database pointer." After the FIND above, the value of cursor E—conceptually—is the address of the EMPLOYEE record in the database (*not* the address of a copy of that record in a buffer). That record, and fields within it, can now be referenced by means of *cursor-qualified references* (analogous to pointer-qualified references in existing PL/I)—for example:

```
PUT SKIP LIST (E->EMPLOYEE);
ASSIGN (E->EMPLOYEE.SALARY + 500) TO E->EMPLOYEE.SALARY;
```

The first of these two statements prints the EMPLOYEE record pointed to by E; the second adds 500 to the SALARY field in that record. In each of the two statements E is being used as a cursor qualifier; "E→ EMPLOYEE" is a cursor-qualified *record* reference, "E→EMPLOYEE. SALARY" is a cursor-qualified *field* reference. Cursor qualification, like pointer qualification, may frequently be implicit, as subsequent examples will show.

One very important feature of cursors is that cursor values are changed only by explicit program action—with the minor exception that a cursor may occasionally be switched into the "preselecting" state as a side-effect of operations such as DISCONNECT (see the section "Cursors and Cursor States," later).

THE APPROACH TO COMMONALITY

As explained earlier, one of the most important of the original objectives for UDL was to support all three of the well-known data structures (relations, hierarchies, networks). This objective was subsequently extended to include "linear" data structures as well. It was also a major objective to provide as much commonality of language as possible across the different structures. The approach taken to achieving that commonality is based on the realization that, in essence,

(a) a hierarchy is merely a special case of a network—one in which each child record has exactly one parent;

(b) a linear structure is a special case of a hierarchy—one consisting of a root only; and

(c) a relation is a special case of a linear structure—one in which no record is allowed to be a duplicate of any other.

However, this intuitive statement is far too vague to be useful other than as a broad indication of direction; let us immediately make it more precise by considering each of the data structures in turn and defining the data constructs that are involved in each case.

- In the relational case the only data construct is the relation itself. Relations can be perceived as having an ordering but such ordering cannot be used to carry information "essentially" [10]. (A construct is "essential" if it carries information that would be lost if the construct were removed. Thus, for example, ordering based on field values is "inessential"—no information is actually lost if the records are shuffled into a different sequence—whereas ordering based on, say, time of arrival is "essential.") Relations are represented in UDL by a constrained form of baseset.

- In the linear case, the baseset is again the primary data construct, but now basesets can contain duplicate records and can have "essential" ordering (based on time of arrival or controlled by program).

- In the network case, there are basically two data constructs, the record type and the fanset (analogous to the DBTG "set type" [7]). Fansets are usually thought of as coming in two varieties, "singular" and "multiple"; in actuality, however, the two constructs behave very differently; in UDL the term "fanset" is reserved for the "multiple" case, and another construct, the *sequence*, is introduced to handle the "singular" case. Space precludes detailed discussion of sequences in this paper.

   Both record types and fansets can be used to carry information essentially. In fact, "record type" in this context is just another way of saying "baseset"; that is, a network structure *includes* certain linear structures (possibly relations). Fansets are used to represent certain relationships between record types (basesets), relationships that in the relational case would be represented by means of fields (actually foreign keys) in the record types concerned. For example, see Fig. 11.4.

   It must be emphasized, however, that in general not all such relationships will be represented by fansets. For example, in Fig. 11.4(b), all employees having the same department are associated via the fanset DEPTEMP; but all employees having the same salary are associated, not via a fanset, but via equality of SALARY values in the EMPLOYEE record type. This latter method of representing relationships is the only method available in the relational case. It follows that a network language has to be capable of exploiting both methods of representing relationships, whereas a relational language need only be capable of handling the second method.

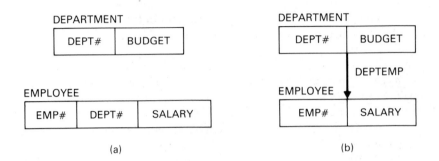

Figure 11.4   (a) Relational representation, and
(b) Network representation,
of a department-employee structure

- A hierarchy is merely a special case of a network in which each record type except one (the "root") is a child in exactly one fanset; the root is not a child in any fanset; and there is a unique path (sequence of fansets) connecting the root to each nonroot. Fansets in a hierarchy are conventionally unnamed, since no ambiguity can result.

The definitions just given, while capturing the most significant aspects of the different structures, do not cater for certain minor features of the hierarchies of IMS [12] or the networks of DBTG [7]. The features in question are ones that it is widely felt have no place in a controlled database environment [8,10,11,13], though it must be admitted that there is a certain amount of contention on this point. Space does not permit the arguments and counter-arguments to be repeated here. For reference, however, the characteristics of hierarchic and network structures as described above that distinguish them from the corresponding constructs of IMS and DBTG are summarized below.

- Records cannot contain repeating groups.
- Fansets cannot contain more than one type of child.
- No ordering is defined across records of different types.

(Any of these constraints could be dropped if sufficient cause were shown, but only at the cost in each case of a considerable amount of additional language.)

To return to the main argument: If the definitions given earlier are accepted, it can be seen that—as stated at the beginning of this section—a relation is a special case of a linear structure, a linear structure is a special case of a hierarchy, and a hierarchy is a special case of a network. This observation permits us to define a single set of language constructs encompassing all four structures. To be more specific:

- The language needed to *declare* a relational structure is a subset of that needed for linear structures, which is in turn a subset of that needed for hierarchies, which is in turn a subset of that needed for networks;

- The operators needed to *manipulate* a relational structure are a subset of those needed for linear structures, which are in turn a subset of those needed for hierarchies, which are in turn a subset of those needed for networks;

- (For a given operator, as applicable) the *operands* (parameters) needed for relations are a subset of those needed for linear structures, which are in turn a subset of those needed for hierarchies, which are in turn a subset of those needed for networks.

The entire UDL language thus has an "onion-layer" structure, as illustrated in Fig. 11.5.

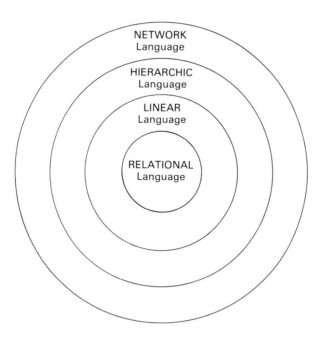

Figure 11.5   The onion-layer language

DECLARATIVE LANGUAGE

The declarative features of UDL provide for a *programming language* declaration of a database—not to be confused with the "system" declaration, i.e., the description known to the underlying DBMS. Of course, the two declarations must not be in conflict; at some point the UDL declaration must be bound to the system declaration, but details of that process fall outside the UDL framework as such. (The situation is analogous to that found today with conventional files: The programming language declaration of the file must be bound to the "system declaration" of the corresponding data set; the data set declaration consists, typically, of entries in a system catalog, and the necessary connexion between the two declarations is established by job control statements.) Note, however, that in some situations it may be possible to use the system declaration to generate the UDL declaration automatically. Whether this is done or not, UDL programmers will *not* normally have to write UDL declarations themselves (at the very least, it should be possible to COPY or INCLUDE those declarations from some source library). But conceptually the UDL declaration is part of the source program; it is used by the compiler in compiling UDL manipulative statements, it will appear in the program listing, and it must be understood by the UDL programmer.

The basic purpose of a UDL declaration is to define the programmer's view of the database. To achieve this aim, the declarative language should permit the specification of as many of the programmer's assumptions about the database as possible. Such specifications will in turn allow a number of system checks to be applied, many of them at compilation time, and will generally help to prevent programs from executing under false assumptions and hence from producing incorrect results. In the design of the declarative language, therefore, the ground rule was: Be as explicit as possible.

Example (an extended version of the introductory example)

An education database contains information about an in-house company training scheme. For each training course the database contains details of all prerequisite courses for that course and all offerings of that course; and for each offering it contains details of all teachers and all students for that offering. The database also contains information about employees. A relational structure for this information is shown in Fig. 11.6; Figs. 11.7 and 11.8 show, respectively, a hierarchic and a network structure for the same information. Note that two hierarchies (one of them "root-only") are required in Fig. 11.7 if redundancy is to be avoided. All fansets are deliberately chosen to be "essential." We do not present a linear (as opposed to

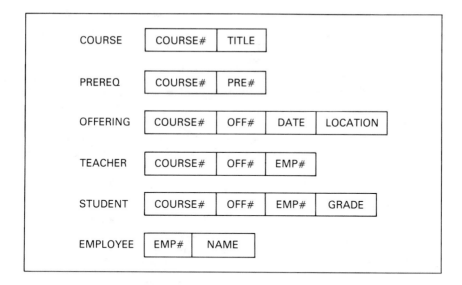

Figure 11.6 Relational structure for the education database

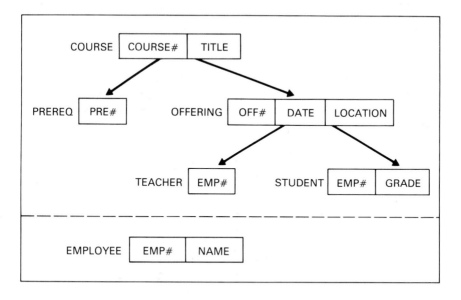

Figure 11.7 Hierarchic structure for the education database

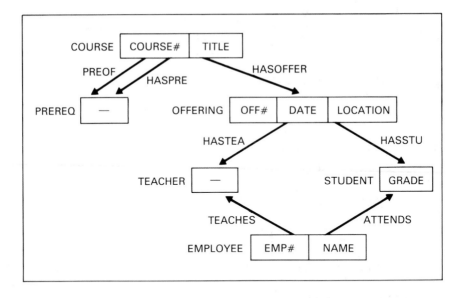

Figure 11.8   Network structure for the education database

relational) version of the example, since the differences between the linear and relational structures are more subtle than those between the relational and hierarchic/network structures.

The UDL declarations corresponding to Figs. 11.6–11.8 define a *database* containing various *basesets* and *fansets*. We discuss the basesets first. (For the sake of the example the basesets have all been named, although in practice names can be omitted if they are never referenced elsewhere in the program.)

```
DCL EDUC DATABASE
   BASESETS (
      CSET RECTYPE (1 COURSE BASED(C),
                    2 COURSE# CHAR(3),
                    2 TITLE CHAR(33))
                   UNIQUE (COURSE#),
      PSET RECTYPE (1 PREREQ BASED(P),
**                  2 COURSE# CHAR(3),
*                   2 PRE# CHAR(3))
**                 UNIQUE,
      OSET RECTYPE (1 OFFERING BASED(O),
**                  2 COURSE# CHAR(3),
                    2 OFF# CHAR(3),
                    2 DATE CHAR(6),
                    2 LOCATION CHAR(12),
                    2 DURATION FIXED BIN(15))
**                 UNIQUE ((COURSE#,OFF#)),
```

```
         TSET RECTYPE (1 TEACHER BASED(T),
**                    2 COURSE# CHAR(3),
**                    2 OFF# CHAR(3),
*                     2 EMP# CHAR(6))
**                UNIQUE,
         SSET RECTYPE (1 STUDENT BASED(S),
**                    2 COURSE# CHAR(3),
**                    2 OFF# CHAR(3),
*                     2 EMP# CHAR(6),
                      2 GRADE CHAR(1))
**                UNIQUE ((COURSE#,EMP#)),
         ESET RECTYPE (1 EMPLOYEE BASED(T),
                      2 EMP# CHAR(6),
                      2 NAME CHAR(18),
                      2 JOB CHAR(12))
                  UNIQUE (EMP#)                 )
```

Lines marked with a single asterisk are omitted for the network case (Fig. 11.8); lines marked with a double asterisk are omitted for both hierarchic and network cases (Figs. 11.7 and 11.8). (Such omissions will of course entail minor adjustments in the surrounding punctuation.) The omissions are possible because the relevant information is carried by the hierarchic/network structuring, instead of by field values as in the relational case. (It would be possible not to omit these fields in the hierarchic and network versions, but then the fansets would become inessential. See reference [10].) In the network case the omissions cause the record types PREREQ and TEACHER to contain no data fields at all (but of course the record types still exist, and corresponding occurrences still appear in the database).

Each record type has a cursor associated with it (specified in the BASED clause). C, for example, is a cursor that will be used to point to individual COURSEs (only). Also, C serves as the *default* cursor for implicitly qualified references to COURSE in the processing part of the program. Further cursors can be defined for a record type by means of explicit cursor declarations. For example:

```
DCL C1 CURSOR RECTYPE (COURSE);
```

Every individual cursor is constrained to a single record type.

In the relational case, each baseset has a UNIQUE clause, specifying that each record in the baseset has a unique value for the indicated field or field combination (at any given time). Omitting the field-name specification from a UNIQUE clause is equivalent to specifying the combination of all fields in the record type concerned (see, e.g., PREREQ). In the hierarchic and network cases, UNIQUE is specified for COURSE and EMPLOYEE only—the other four basesets are not relations in these structures.

Any or all of the six basesets could be defined to have an *ordering*. For example, we could specify ORDER(UP COURSE#) for courses (and such an entry would imply UNIQUE(COURSE#) unless NONUNIQUE were specified in the ORDER entry). For the relational case, the only valid orderings are value-controlled and system-defined, for the other structures additional types of ordering can be specified. For simplicity, we have assumed default (system-defined) ordering in every case.

To impose a hierarchic or network structure on the database, the declaration must include a FANSETS specification as well as the BASESETS specification already shown. For the hierarchic structure of Fig. 11.7 the FANSETS specification would be:

```
FANSETS (
  RECORD (PREREQ)   UNDER (COURSE)   UNIQUE,
  RECORD (OFFERING) UNDER (COURSE)   UNIQUE (OFF#),
  RECORD (TEACHER)  UNDER (OFFERING) UNIQUE,
  RECORD (STUDENT)  UNDER (OFFERING) UNIQUE (EMP#)      )
```

The syntax here has been chosen to emphasize the fact that the important thing about a fanset is the children, rather than the children plus the parent (speaking very loosely). For example, the scope of a DO-loop—see later—is typically the set of children in some fan, not the entire fan (children plus parent). The four fansets shown above are unnamed, though there is no reason why they should not be given names if desired. The UNIQUE entries refer to uniqueness within each fan of the applicable fanset (e.g., each offering under a given course has a unique offering number). It is also possible to specify an ORDER for the children of each fan; again default (system-defined) ordering has been chosen for simplicity.

For the network structure of Fig. 11.8 the FANSETS entry could be as follows. This time the fansets have been named, although there is no reason why they should not remain unnamed if no name is required. Notice, however, that the first two fansets *must* be named, since otherwise there would be no way to distinguish between them (they both consist of PREREQs under COURSEs).

```
FANSETS (
  PREOF    RECORD (PREREQ)   UNDER (COURSE),
  HASPRE   RECORD (PREREQ)   UNDER (COURSE),
  HASOFFER RECORD (OFFERING) UNDER (COURSE)   UNIQUE (OFF#),
  HASTEA   RECORD (TEACHER)  UNDER (OFFERING),
  HASSTU   RECORD (STUDENT)  UNDER (OFFERING),
  TEACHES  RECORD (TEACHER)  UNDER (EMPLOYEE),
  ATTENDS  RECORD (STUDENT)  UNDER (EMPLOYEE)              )
```

The fanset entries as shown are still not complete. For any given fanset, in general, the child record type may be (a) AUTOMATIC or MANUAL, and (b) FIXED, MANDATORY, or OPTIONAL, with respect to that fanset. (For a hierarchy only AUTOMATIC and FIXED are valid, and these are the defaults.) The meanings of these terms are as for DBTG [7]. Each fanset declaration should include a specification of the programmer's assumptions with respect to AUTOMATIC, FIXED, etc., so that appropriate compile- and bind-time checks can be made.

In the hierarchic and network cases, it would be possible to include additional UNIQUE specifications (for both basesets and fansets), to indicate that, for example, no two STUDENTs under a given OFFERING have the same parent EMPLOYEE. We do not discuss this possibility in detail for reasons of space.

CURSORS AND CURSOR STATES

A cursor is an object whose primary function is to provide addressability to some record by means of that record's *record identifier* (RID). Each record has a unique RID that identifies it and distinguishes it from all others within that record's baseset. The format of an RID is implementer-defined.

A cursor C is set to select some record R by means of an operation (typically FIND) that selects R from within some set S that contains it, according (usually) to some ordering O for that set. After C has been set to select R it includes, not only the RID for R, but also an identification of the set S and the corresponding ordering O (if O was used in the selection process; otherwise the implementation will arbitrarily choose an ordering). Note that C may be associated with different sets and orderings at different times. These ideas can be amplified as follows.

The set S must be one of the following:

(a) a baseset;

(b) the set of records in a sequence;

(c) the set of children in a single fan of a fanset.

When a cursor C is set to select some record that record must be chosen from a set of one of these three types. Suppose, then, that the program requests C to be set to select a record from within some set, and suppose also that the request is independent of C's current value—i.e., it is an *absolute* request. For example:

```
FIND FIRST (COURSE WHERE condition) SET(C);
```

or

```
FIND UNIQUE (COURSE WHERE condition) SET(C);
```

(both of which are requests to set C to some specific COURSE record from the COURSE baseset (CSET) without regard to C's current value). The specific COURSE required is the first (or only) record, according to some ordering, that satisfies the WHERE condition. In the example the ordering is that defined for the baseset CSET (i.e., system default ordering); alternatively, the programmer could have specified an explicit ORDER in the FIND itself. When the selection is performed, an association is established between C and the pair $<S,O>$, where S is the set and O the ordering used in the selection process.

Suppose now that the program requests C to be set to select a record from within some set S in such a way that the request does depend on C's current value—i.e., it is a *relative* request. For example:

```
FIND FIRST (COURSE AFTER C) SET(C);
```

(which is a request to set C to the next COURSE record after C's current position within the COURSE baseset (CSET), according to the ordering currently associated with C). C must currently identify a position within CSET, otherwise an error occurs. After this selection, the association between C and the pair $<S,O>$ remains unchanged.

More details are given below.

The combination of a set S and an ordering O for that set is known as an *ordered record set* (ORS). A given record can participate in any number of ordered record sets simultaneously. An ORS can be modeled as a linear directed list (see Fig. 11.9). The list has a beginning position (P-begin) and an end position (P-end). It is convenient to consider the list as always containing at least one object, namely a dummy RID "RID-end," located at position P-end and identifying a dummy "end-record." At any given time, then, the list contains a set of $n+1$ objects (n greater than or equal to zero), located at $n+1$ discrete positions P1, P2, P3, ..., Pn, P-end. These $n+1$ positions are such that, with respect to the list direction, P-begin precedes P1, P1 precedes P2, P2 precedes P3, ..., and Pn precedes P-end. The object at Pi $(0<i<n+1)$ is the RID of the record that is ith in the ORS being modeled.

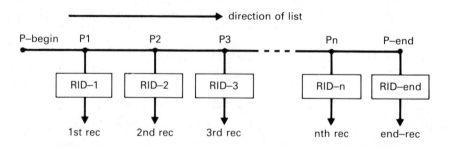

Figure 11.9   An ordered record set

Now let C be a cursor for record type R. Conceptually C can be thought of as an ordered triple:

$$< state,RID,ordset >$$

"State" takes one of the values *null, begin, end, selecting, preselecting*. A cursor in the *null* state is not selecting a record and is not positioned anywhere. A cursor in the *begin* or *end* state is positioned before the first record (for *begin*), or on the dummy end-record (for *end*), in every ORS containing type R records. A cursor in the *selecting* state is selecting the record identified by the RID component of the cursor and is positioned on that record, and the "ordset" component identifies the applicable ORS. Finally, a cursor in the *preselecting* state is positioned before the record identified by the RID component, and again the "ordset" component identifies the applicable ORS. The preselecting case arises when a cursor is positioned on a record and that record is removed from the ORS associated with that cursor (e.g., the record is DISCONNECTed—see later). In such a case, the cursor is automatically advanced to preselect the successor of the now removed record. If the programmer attempts to step the cursor along to the next record via a FIND statement, the cursor will not actually move but will simply switch from the preselecting to the selecting state.

BOUND CURSORS

The importance of the ordered record set construct should be clear from the previous section. The language must allow the programmer to write expressions to denote such sets—not only predeclared ones, such as the set of all EMPLOYEE records, but also dynamically generated ones, such as that subset of EMPLOYEE records where the job is 'PROGRAMMER'. In UDL such an expression can be written:

```
E->EMPLOYEE WHERE E->EMPLOYEE.JOB = 'PROGRAMMER'
```

—or, if E is the default cursor for EMPLOYEE, and if the unqualified name JOB is unambiguous:

```
EMPLOYEE WHERE JOB = 'PROGRAMMER'
```

(a more intuitive form). Either way, the programmer can think of this expression as being evaluated as follows: Cursor E is used to run through the entire baseset of EMPLOYEEs, one record at a time, in some sequence, and records not satisfying the predicate (the condition following the WHERE) are eliminated. However, cursor E itself is not really used—a system-supplied cursor is used instead. In fact, the current value of cursor

E is irrelevant and is not changed; the symbol "E" is merely being used as a syntactic device to link field references in the predicate to specific instances of the record type concerned. E here is an example of a *bound cursor*.

As another example, the expression:

```
E->EMPLOYEE WHERE E->EMPLOYEE.JOB = F->EMPLOYEE.JOB
```

is a reference to the set of employees having the same job as the employee selected by cursor F. Cursor F here is performing its normal selection function; cursor E, by contrast, is a bound cursor.

MANIPULATIVE LANGUAGE

This section discusses some of the major features of the manipulative language, primarily by means of examples. The most important statement is FIND—syntax:

```
FIND record-reference SET(cursor);
```

Example (using the relational structure of Fig. 11.6):

```
FIND FIRST (PREREQ WHERE PREREQ.PRE# = '322') SET(P);
```

In this example, "PREREQ WHERE ..." is a *set reference*, i.e., an expression denoting an ordered record set (actually a subset of the PREREQ baseset, with an ordering inherited from that baseset), and FIRST is a "builtin reference" that selects the first record in that ordered record set. Cursor P is set to point to that record. Note that P is also acting as the (implicit) bound cursor in the references to PREREQ (because P is the cursor named in the BASED specification for PREREQ). The phrase SET(P) could have been omitted; if no SET option appears in a given FIND statement the appropriate default cursor is assumed.

It is now possible to refer to the selected PREREQ record, and to fields within it, using P as a (possibly implicit) cursor qualifier.

Examples:

```
ASSIGN P->PREREQ.COURSE# TO X;          /* field retrieval  */
ASSIGN X TO P->PREREQ.COURSE#;          /* field update     */
ASSIGN PREREQ TO STRUC;                 /* record retrieval */
ASSIGN STRUC TO PREREQ;                 /* record update    */
IF PREREQ.COURSE# = '860' THEN
    PUT SKIP LIST (PREREQ);             /* etc., etc., etc. */
```

The FIND statement may optionally include a FOUND/NOTFOUND clause (analogous to THEN/ELSE in IF).

Example (following the previous FIND statement):

```
FIND NEXT (PREREQ WHERE PREREQ.PRE# = '322')
FOUND found-unit
NOTFOUND notfound-unit
```

This statement will step P along to the next PREREQ with PRE# equal to 322. ("Next" here refers to the ordering of the PREREQ baseset.) If such a PREREQ is found the found-unit will be executed; otherwise the notfound-unit will be executed. If FIND fails to find a record and NOT-FOUND is not specified, an error condition is raised (the NOTFOUND ON-condition in PL/I).

To loop through all PREREQs with PRE# = '322':

```
DO PREREQ WHERE PREREQ.PRE# = '322' SET(P);
    [ body of loop ]
END;
```

This extended form of the familiar PL/I DO statement is defined to be semantically equivalent to a sequence of FIND statements, with appropriate checking for the NOTFOUND condition. Again the SET option can be omitted, as for FIND.

Now for a more complete example, which illustrates a number of additional features. The input consists of a structure called GIVEN, containing a COURSE#, an OFF#, and an EMP#; the significance of this input is that the given employee wishes to enroll in the given offering of the given course. The following code performs the requested enrollment, if and only if the employee has attended all immediate prerequisites of the given course. We show a relational procedure (Fig. 11.10), a hierarchic procedure (Fig. 11.11), and a network procedure (Fig. 11.12) for this problem.

```
APPLICATION_OK = '1'B;
DO PREREQ WHERE PREREQ.COURSE# = GIVEN.COURSE#
            WHILE (APPLICATION_OK);
    IF EXISTS (STUDENT WHERE STUDENT.EMP# = GIVEN.EMP#
                        & STUDENT.COURSE# = PREREQ.PRE#)
    THEN ;  /* employee has attended this prereq */
    ELSE APPLICATION_OK = '0'B;
END;
IF APPLICATION_OK THEN
    ALLOCATE STUDENT INITIAL (GIVEN, ' ');
```

Figure 11.10   The enrollment procedure (relational version)

```
APPLICATION_OK = '1'B;
FIND UNIQUE (COURSE WHERE COURSE.COURSE# = GIVEN.COURSE#);
DO PREREQ UNDER COURSE
         WHILE (APPLICATION_OK);
   IF EXISTS (STUDENT WHERE STUDENT.EMP# = GIVEN.EMP#
              & UNIQUE (COURSE.COURSE# OVER STUDENT)
                                       = PREREQ.PRE#)
   THEN ;  /* employee has attended this prereq */
   ELSE APPLICATION_OK = '0'B;
END;
IF APPLICATION_OK THEN
   DO;
      FIND UNIQUE (OFFERING UNDER COURSE
                   WHERE OFFERING.OFF# = GIVEN.OFF#);
      ALLOCATE STUDENT INITIAL (GIVEN.EMP#, ' ')
                      CONNECT (UNDER OFFERING);
   END;
```

Figure 11.11   The enrollment procedure (hierarchic version)

```
APPLICATION_OK = '1'B;
FIND UNIQUE (COURSE WHERE COURSE.COURSE# = GIVEN.COURSE#);
DO PREREQ UNDER COURSE VIA HASPRE
         WHILE (APPLICATION_OK);
   IF EXISTS (STUDENT WHERE
                      UNIQUE (EMPLOYEE.EMP# OVER STUDENT)
                                       = GIVEN.EMP#
              & UNIQUE (COURSE.COURSE# OVER STUDENT)
                                       =
              UNIQUE (COURSE.COURSE# OVER PREREQ
                                          VIA PREOF)
   THEN ;  /* employee has attended this prereq */
   ELSE APPLICATION_OK = '0'B;
END;
IF APPLICATION_OK THEN
   DO;
      FIND UNIQUE (OFFERING UNDER COURSE
                   WHERE OFFERING.OFF# = GIVEN.OFF#);
      FIND UNIQUE (EMPLOYEE
                   WHERE EMPLOYEE.EMP# = GIVEN.EMP#);
      ALLOCATE STUDENT INITIAL (' ')
                      CONNECT (UNDER OFFERING,
                               UNDER EMPLOYEE);
   END;
```

Figure 11.12   The enrollment procedure (network version)

The example illustrates the following additional features:

(a) The builtin function EXISTS, which returns the value *true* ('1'B) if its argument set is nonempty, the value *false* ('0'B) otherwise;

(b) ALLOCATE, which is used (in the PL/I version of UDL) to create a

new record, with field values for that record as specified by the INI-
TIAL clause;

(c) UNDER, which is used in hierarchies and networks to refer to child
records of a given parent (via a given fanset);

(d) OVER, which is used in hierarchies and networks to refer to an ancestor
record of a given child record (via a given path of fansets);

(e) CONNECT, which is used in hierarchies and networks to connect a
given child record to a given parent record (via a given fanset);

(f) VIA, which is used in networks to specify a (path of) fanset(s) when
there is more than one such linking two specified record types; and

(g) the multiple CONNECT, which is used in networks as a shorthand for
a set of single CONNECTs.

By way of illustration we also give "set-level" solutions to the enrollment problem (Figs. 11.13–11.15). We place "set-level" in quotes because
actually the boundary between set- and record-levels is somewhat arbitrary.
Note that the set-level solutions each consist of a single statement, and that
there is thus presumably a single trip across the interface to the DBMS. The
solutions involve no explicit loop, no cursors, and no flag to define, set,

```
IF EXISTS (PREREQ WHERE PREREQ.COURSE# = GIVEN.COURSE#
          &  ~ EXISTS (STUDENT WHERE
                       STUDENT.EMP# = GIVEN.EMP#
                       & STUDENT.COURSE# = PREREQ.PRE#))
THEN ;  /* employee does not have some prereq */
ELSE ALLOCATE STUDENT INITIAL (GIVEN, ' ');
```

Figure 11.13   The enrollment procedure (relational, set-level)

```
IF EXISTS (PREREQ UNDER
   UNIQUE (COURSE WHERE COURSE.COURSE# = GIVEN.COURSE#)
   WHERE  ~ EXISTS (STUDENT WHERE
                    STUDENT.EMP# = GIVEN.EMP#
                  & UNIQUE (COURSE.COURSE# OVER STUDENT)
                           = PREREQ.PRE#))
THEN ;  /* employee does not have some prereq */
ELSE
     ALLOCATE STUDENT INITIAL (GIVEN.EMP#, ' ')
     CONNECT (UNDER UNIQUE (OFFERING UNDER
                   UNIQUE (COURSE WHERE
                           COURSE.COURSE# = GIVEN.COURSE#)
                   WHERE OFFERING.OFF# = GIVEN.OFF#));
```

Figure 11.14   The enrollment procedure (hierarchic, set-level)

```
IF EXISTS (PREREQ UNDER
   UNIQUE (COURSE WHERE COURSE.COURSE# = GIVEN.COURSE#)
                                             VIA HASPRE
      WHERE ‾ EXISTS (STUDENT WHERE
                       UNIQUE(EMPLOYEE.EMP# OVER STUDENT)
                                   = GIVEN.EMP#
                     & UNIQUE (COURSE.COURSE# OVER STUDENT)
                                   =
                       UNIQUE (COURSE.COURSE# OVER PREREQ
                                              VIA PREOF)))
   THEN ;   /* employee does not have some prereq */
   ELSE
      ALLOCATE STUDENT INITIAL (' ')
      CONNECT (UNDER UNIQUE (OFFERING UNDER
                     UNIQUE (COURSE WHERE
                             COURSE.COURSE# = GIVEN.COURSE#)
                     WHERE OFFERING.OFF# = GIVEN.OFF#),
                UNDER UNIQUE (EMPLOYEE
                     WHERE EMPLOYEE.EMP# = GIVEN.EMP#));
```

Figure 11.15   The enrollment procedure (network, set-level)

or test. Observe once again that the relational language features are a subset of the hierarchic features, which are in turn a subset of the network features.

To complete the discussion of the manipulative language, here is a brief survey of its remaining features.

FREE

Just as ALLOCATE is used to create new records (in PL/I), so FREE is used to destroy them.

Fanset Operations

CONNECT, DISCONNECT, and RECONNECT statements are provided to create, destroy, and modify the link between a given child record and a given parent record (via a given fanset). Note: These operators can also be used to CONNECT/DISCONNECT records to/from sequences and to reposition (RECONNECT) records within sets having program-controlled ordering.

Transaction Handling

A COMMIT statement is provided to commit database updates. A ROLLBACK statement is provided to back out uncommitted updates. Extensive locking and recovery features are provided (see reference [15]).

Exception Handling

Several exceptional conditions are defined in the language. In the PL/I version these are handled by means of various ON-conditions: NOTFOUND, NONUNIQUE, ADDREX (addressing exception—raised if, e.g., the cursor in a cursor-qualified reference is not in the selecting state), and DB-ERROR (a catchall). Associated debugging functions, such as ONREC-TYPE, are also provided. System action for DBERROR is to raise ERROR. System action for the other conditions is to raise DBERROR. Thus the programmer is able to trap exceptions at a variety of different levels.

Builtin Functions

In addition to EXISTS, the debugging functions (ONRECTYPE, etc.), and the "builtin references" such as FIRST, UDL provides functions to count the number of records in a set, to find the greatest value in a set, and so on.

SUMMARY

We have presented some major features of the UDL database language. The highlights of the language can be summarized as follows.

- Several different data structures are supported.
- Both record- and set-level operations are provided.
- The database is represented as an extension of the program's directly addressable storage area.
- The programmer can retain multiple explicit positions in the database simultaneously (via multiple cursors).
- Record references permit a wide variety of "navigational" operations (UNIQUE, FIRST, NEXT, plus others not discussed in this paper).
- Set expressions have the generality and "completeness" [9] of predicate calculus.
- The language includes a flexible and comprehensive locking scheme, with safe and simple defaults [15].

We conclude with a word on why we believe a language such as UDL is important. The two principal objectives of UDL are to support several distinct data structures and to provide both record- and set-level functions. On the first count, it seems virtually certain that the various different data structures are going to coexist for many years to come; granted this premise, then a language that provides as much commonality among those structures as possible seems an attractive proposition. Such a language could ease problems of program portability and migration from one system to another, and likewise could make it easier for *programmers* to move from system to system. On the second count, the set level is desirable for reasons of productivity and ease of programming, in general—but the record level is important too, partly because it serves as a bridge to existing function in the host language, and partly also because there are some problems for which the record level simply seems more suitable.

ACKNOWLEDGMENTS

I am pleased to acknowledge useful discussions and communications with a large number of colleagues, especially David Beech, Bob Engles, Don Haderle, Chris Paradine, John Roskell, Ming Shan, Phil Shaw, and Russ Williams. Thanks are also due to the Future Database Language Project of GUIDE International, which was party to the design of several aspects of UDL, and to the DBMS Language Task Force of SHARE [16], which provided additional valuable input. Mention should also be made of Rita Summers, Charlie Coleman, and Eduardo Fernandez, who independently developed language extensions very similar to the relational portions of the present proposal [14].

REFERENCES

1. C. J. Date, "An Architecture for High-Level Language Database Extensions," *Proc. ACM International Conference on Management of Data* (June 1976).

2. C. J. Date, "An Architecture for High-Level Language Database Extensions: PL/I Version. Part I: Record-at-a-Time Operations," *Proc. SEAS Anniversary Meeting* (September 1977).

3. C. J. Date, "An Architecture for High-Level Language Database Extensions (Unified Database Language—UDL): PL/I Version." A major revision of [2]. *IBM Technical Report TR 03.099* (June 1980).

4. C. J. Date, "An Architecture for High-Level Language Database Extensions (Unified Database Language—UDL): COBOL Version," Internal IBM report (December 1978).

5. C. J. Date, Relational subset of [3]. Internal IBM report (April 1979).

6. C. J. Date, Relational subset of [4]. Internal IBM report (April 1979).

7. Data Base Task Group of CODASYL Programming Language Committee: Final Report (April 1971).

8. *Proc. IFIP TC-2 Special Working Conference: A Technical In-Depth Evaluation of the DDL* (Namur, Belgium, 13-17 January 1975). North-Holland (1975).

9. E. F. Codd, "Relational Completeness of Data Base Sublanguages." In *Data Base Systems:* Courant Computer Science Symposia Series, Vol. 6. (Englewood Cliffs, NJ: Prentice-Hall 1972).

10. E. F. Codd and C. J. Date, "Interactive Support for Nonprogrammers: The Relational and Network Approaches" (in this volume).

11. R. W. Engles, "An Analysis of the April 1971 DBTG Report," *Proc. 1971 ACM SIGFIDET Workshop on Data Description, Access, and Control* (November 1971).

12. IBM Corporation, *Information Management System/ Virtual Storage General Information Manual,* IBM Form No. GH20–1260.

13. G. M. Nijssen, "Data Structuring in DDL and Relational Data Model." In *Data Base Management Systems* (eds., Klimbie and Koffeman), *Proc. IFIP TC-2 Working Conference,* Cargese, Corsica (April 1974). North-Holland (1974).

14. R. C. Summers, C. D. Coleman, and E. B. Fernandez, "A Programming Language Extension for Access to a Shared Data Base," *Proc. ACM Pacific Conference,* San Francisco, California (April 1975).

15. C. J. Date, "Locking and Recovery in a Shared Database System: An Application Programming Tutorial," *Proc. 5th International Conference on Very Large Data Bases* (October 1979).*

16. SHARE DBMS Language Task Force, "An Evaluation of Three COBOL Data Base Languages—UDL, SQL, and CODASYL," *Proc. SHARE 53* (August 1979).

APPENDIX A: PL/I-UDL SYNTAX (SIMPLIFIED)

```
database-declaration
   ::=  database-name DATABASE
            BASESETS (baseset-spec-commalist)
          [ SEQUENCES (sequence-spec-commalist) ]
          [ FANSETS (fanset-spec-commalist) ]

baseset-spec
   ::=  [ baseset-name ] baseset-defn

baseset-defn
   ::=  rectype-spec [ uniqueness ] [ ordering ]

rectype-spec
   ::=  RECTYPE ( 1 record-name BASED (cursor-reference)
                    [, field-defn-commalist ] )

uniqueness
   ::=  UNIQUE [ (uniqueness-spec-commalist) ]

uniqueness-spec
   ::=  field-spec ¦ (field-spec-commalist)
```

---

*This reference has since been superseded by the chapter on concurrency control in *An Introduction to Database Systems: Volume II*, by C. J. Date (Addison-Wesley 1982).

```
field-spec
   ::= dot-qualified-field-name ¦ ancestor-field-spec

ancestor-field-spec
   ::= dot-qualified-field-name OVER record-name
         [ VIA { fanset-name ¦ (fanset-name-commalist) } ]

ordering
   ::= ORDER ( { value-ordering ¦
                 FIRST ¦ LAST ¦ HERE ¦ SYSTEM } )

value-ordering
   ::= value-ordering-spec-commalist
         [ NONUNIQUE [ ( { FIRST ¦ LAST ¦ HERE } ) ] ] ]

value-ordering-spec
   ::= { UP ¦ DOWN } { field-spec ¦ (field-spec-commalist) }

sequence-spec
   ::= sequence-name sequence-defn

sequence-defn
   ::= RECORD (record-name) [ uniqueness ] [ ordering ]
         [ AUTOMATIC ¦ MANUAL ] [ FIXED ¦ MANDATORY ¦ OPTIONAL ]

fanset-spec
   ::= [ fanset-name ] fanset-defn

fanset-defn
   ::= RECORD (record-name) UNDER (record-name)
         [ uniqueness ] [ ordering ]
         [ AUTOMATIC ¦ MANUAL ] [ FIXED ¦ MANDATORY ¦ OPTIONAL ]

baseset-declaration
   ::= baseset-name BASESET (baseset-defn)

cursor-declaration
   ::= cursor-name [ dimension ] CURSOR RECTYPE (record-name)

find-statement
   ::= FIND record-reference [ set-option ] [ assignto-option ]
         { ; ¦ FOUND executable-unit
               NOTFOUND executable-unit }

set-option
   ::= SET (cursor-reference)

assignto-option
   ::= ASSIGNTO (structure-reference)

record-reference
   ::= cursor-qualified-record-reference
         ¦ { UNIQUE ¦ FIRST ¦ LAST ¦ NEXT ¦ PRIOR }
                                      (set-reference) }

cursor-qualified-record-reference
   ::= [ cursor-reference -> ] record-name

set-reference
   ::= bound-record defining-property-list
```

```
bound-record
   ::=  [ cursor-name -> ] record-name

defining-property
   ::=  in-option
        | under-option
        | over-option
        | order-option
        | after-option
        | before-option
        | matching-option
        | where-option

in-option
   ::=  IN { baseset-name | sequence-name | fanset-name }

under-option
   ::=  UNDER record-reference [ via-option ]

via-option
   ::=  VIA { fanset-name | (fanset-name-commalist) }

over-option
   ::=  OVER record-reference [ via-option ]

order-option
   ::=  ORDER ( { value-ordering | ANY } )

after-option
   ::=  AFTER cursor-expression

before-option
   ::=  BEFORE cursor-expression

cursor-expression
   ::=  cursor-reference | NULL | BEGIN | END |
                                  (cursor-expression)

matching-option
   ::=  MATCHING structure-reference [ ON field-name-commalist ]

where-option
   ::=  WHERE element-expression

field-reference
   ::=  cursor-qualified-field-reference
        | { UNIQUE | FIRST | LAST | NEXT | PRIOR }
                            (sliced-set-reference)

cursor-qualified-field-reference
   ::=  [ cursor-reference -> ] dot-qualified-field-name

sliced-set-reference
   ::=  slice-spec defining-property-list

slice-spec
   ::=  bound-field | (bound-field-commalist)

bound-field
   ::=  [ cursor-name -> ] dot-qualified-field-name
```

```
do-statement
   ::=  DO set-reference [ set-option ]
           [ WHILE (element-expression) ]
           [ UNTIL (element-expression) ] ;
        ¦ DO set-expression NOSET assignto-option ;

set-expression
   ::=  set-reference
        ¦ sliced-set-reference
        ¦ constructed-set-expression
        ¦ DISTINCT (set-expression)
        ¦ (set-expression)

constructed-set-expression
   ::=  ( cse-component, cse-component-commalist
                                  [ order-option ] )

cse-component
   ::=  { bound-record ¦ slice-spec } [ defining-property-list ]

assign-statement
   ::=  ASSIGN { assignment ¦ (assignment-commalist) } ;

assignment
   ::=  single-assignment ¦ iterated-assignment

single-assignment
   ::=  expression TO reference

iterated-assignment
   ::=  ( single-assignment-commalist
              DO set-reference [ set-option ] )

allocate-statement
   ::=  ALLOCATE allocation-commalist ;

allocation
   ::=  record-name [ initial-option ]
                   [ set-option ¦ NOSET ]
                   [ connect-option ]

initial-option
   ::=  INITIAL (expression-commalist)

connect-option
   ::=  CONNECT (connexion-commalist)

connexion
   ::=  [ in-option ¦ under-option ]
                   [ after-option ¦ before-option ]

free-statement
   ::=  FREE record-reference-commalist ;

connect-statement
   ::=  CONNECT record-reference connexion-commalist ;

disconnect-statement
   ::=  DISCONNECT record-reference disconnexion-commalist ;
```

```
disconnexion
   ::=  FROM { sequence-name ¦ fanset-name
                              ¦ record-name [ via-option ] } }

reconnect-statement
   ::=  RECONNECT record-reference connexion-commalist ;

commit-statement
   ::=  COMMIT ;

rollback-statement
   ::=  ROLLBACK ;

database-condition
   ::=  NOTFOUND ¦ NONUNIQUE ¦ ADDREX ¦ DBERROR

database-condbif
   ::=  ONRECTYPE ¦ ONBASESET ¦ ONSEQUENCE ¦ ONFANSET
                  ¦ ONCURSOR ¦ DBSTATUS ¦ DBCODE

exists-bif
   ::=  EXISTS (set-expression)

aggregate-bif
   ::=  { SETCOUNT ¦ SETMAX ¦ SETMIN ¦ SETSUM ¦ SETAVG }
          ( set-expression [, constant ] )

connected-bif
   ::=  CONNECTED ( record-reference,
                    { sequence-name ¦ fanset-name } )
```

APPENDIX B: A CODASYL VERSION OF THE ENROLLMENT PROBLEM

For interest we show a CODASYL DBTG solution to the enrollment problem from the body of the paper. For this procedure we assume that SET SELECTION for both ATTENDS and HASSTU is BY APPLICATION.

```
    DECLARATIVES.
    USE FOR DB-EXCEPTION ON '0502100'.
EOF-PROC.
    MOVE 'YES' TO EOF.
    .....
    END DECLARATIVES.

    MOVE 'YES' TO APPLICATION-OK
    MOVE COURSENO OF GIVEN TO COURSENO IN COURSE
    FIND ANY COURSE USING COURSENO IN COURSE
    MOVE EMPNO OF GIVEN TO EMPNO IN EMPLOYEE
    FIND ANY EMPLOYEE USING EMPNO IN EMPLOYEE
    MOVE 'NO' TO EOF
    PERFORM UNTIL EOF = 'YES'
              OR APPLICATION-OK = 'NO'
       FIND NEXT PREREQ WITHIN HASPRE
       IF EOF = 'NO'
```

```
     FIND OWNER WITHIN PREOF
          RETAINING HASPRE, RECORD CURRENCY
     GET COURSENO IN COURSE
     MOVE COURSENO IN COURSE TO TEMP
     MOVE 'NO' TO APPLICATION-OK
     FIND CURRENT EMPLOYEE
     PERFORM UNTIL EOF = 'YES'
        FIND NEXT STUDENT WITHIN ATTENDS
        IF EOF = 'NO'
           FIND OWNER WITHIN HASSTU
           FIND OWNER WITHIN HASOFFER
                 RETAINING HASPRE, RECORD CURRENCY
           GET COURSENO IN COURSE
           IF COURSENO IN COURSE = TEMP
              MOVE 'YES' TO APPLICATION-OK
              MOVE 'YES' TO EOF
           END-IF
        END-IF
     END-PERFORM
     MOVE 'NO' TO EOF
  END-IF
END-PERFORM
IF APPLICATION-OK = 'YES'
   FIND CURRENT COURSE
   MOVE OFFNO OF GIVEN TO OFFNO IN OFFERING
   FIND OFFERING WITHIN HASOFFER CURRENT
                 USING OFFNO IN OFFERING
   FIND CURRENT EMPLOYEE
   MOVE SPACES TO GRADE IN STUDENT
   STORE STUDENT
END-IF
```

It is interesting to compare this solution with the UDL solution of Fig. 11.12, since of course they both represent record-at-a-time network procedures for the same problem. Admittedly, Fig. 11.12 uses PL/I whereas the DBTG solution uses COBOL, but that fact alone does not account for the differences between them. Those differences, and also the differences among the various UDL (record-at-a-time) solutions, are summarized in the table opposite. (In order to be as fair as possible all figures are based on COBOL solutions, though actually the UDL figures are almost independent of whether PL/I or COBOL is the host language. Note, however, that the definition of "token" is a little arbitrary, so that the token counts should be construed only as rough measures of relative procedure size, not as absolute figures of merit. The DBTG count does not include USE procedures for other exceptions, which are required but are not shown in the DBTG code above.)

Incidentally, one of the primary reasons for the complexity of the DBTG solution is that the programmer has to handle the central existence test by means of procedural code. Note that there are at least two strategies for performing that test: (a) Check all student records for the given employee to see if any of them is for the current prerequisite course; (b) check all

	Relational	Hierarchic	Network	DBTG
Database as seen by user	6 basesets	6 basesets + 4 fansets	6 basesets + 7 fansets (2 names nec.)	6 record types + 7 (named) "sets"
Number of tokens in procedure (Note 1)	48	71	102	189
Manipulative language contructs (Note 2)	FIND WHERE	FIND WHERE FIND UNDER FIND OVER	FIND WHERE FIND UNDER [VIA] FIND OVER [VIA]	FIND ANY FIND NEXT WITHIN FIND OWNER WITHIN FIND CURRENT FIND WITHIN USING –SET SELECTION GET RETAIN CURRENCY
	ALLOCATE	ALLOCATE [CONNECT]	ALLOCATE [CONNECT [VIA]]	STORE –SET SELECTION

Note 1. A token is a "lexical" unit in the source program; e.g., "MOVE 'NO' TO EOF" consists of four tokens. All figures are based on COBOL.

Note 2. DO (PERFORM in COBOL) is equivalent to a sequence of FIND WHERE operators.

student records for the current prerequisite course to see if any of them is for the given employee. Which strategy is more efficient will depend on many parameters, including in particular the average number of students per course and the average number of courses attended per employee. The choice of strategy is left to the system in UDL but must be made by the programmer in DBTG. (For further discussion of this efficiency question, see Appendix C to this paper.)

The reader's attention is also drawn to the complexities caused by the notion of currency in the DBTG procedure. Note in particular the necessity for the two RETAINING phrases ("RETAINING HASPRE, RECORD CURRENCY" means "do not update the currency indicators for the HASPRE fanset or for the record type that is to be found"). It is instructive to work through the entire procedure in detail. Finally, note that matters would be considerably worse if STUDENTs were to be maintained in course number order within the ATTENDS fanset and in employee number order within the HASSTU fanset; these (reasonable) requirements can be specified declaratively and taken care of by the system in UDL, but must be dealt with procedurally in DBTG.

APPENDIX C: A NOTE ON PERFORMANCE

In this appendix we use UDL as the basis for a brief discussion of certain performance aspects of the three database approaches. The discussion is presented in the form of an exercise-and-answer dialog, all of it based on the three (record-level) solutions given in the body of the paper for the enrollment problem.

Exercise 1: For each approach, design a storage structure to represent the database, mapping each record to a single stored record but using indexes, pointer chains, etc., as you feel appropriate.

Answer 1:

(a) Relational:
The obvious approach is to map each record directly into an isomorphic stored record, and to add an index on the primary key for each record type. In fact, since PREREQs and TEACHERs are both "all key," the index alone would be sufficient in those two cases—no data records would be needed at all; however, we assume here that data records do exist in all cases.

(b) Hierarchic:
Map each fanset into a stored fanset. Each parent record has a pointer to the first child. Each child record has a pointer to the next child (if such a next child exists), together with a pointer to the parent. Also, index COURSEs and EMPLOYEEs on their primary keys.

(c) Network:
Same approach as for the hierarchic case.

Exercise 2: Derive expressions representing the amount of storage space required by each of your solutions to Exercise 1. State any assumptions you make.

Answer 2:
Let:
c = the number of COURSEs,
e = the number of EMPLOYEEs,

p = the average number of PREREQs per COURSE,
x = the average number of OFFERINGs per COURSE,
y = the average number of STUDENTs per OFFERING, and
z = the average number of TEACHERs per OFFERING.

(Note that the average number of STUDENTs per EMPLOYEE will then be cxy/e.)

Assume 4-byte pointers; assume also for simplicity that an index consists solely of a set of entries, one for each indexed record, and that each entry consists of just a field value and a pointer (i.e., ignore index levels above the lowest, also the fact that indexes may be compressed). Then storage space requirements are as follows.

(a) Relational:

COURSEs	$c(36 + (3 + 4))$	$= 43c$
PREREQs	$cp(6 + (6 + 4))$	$= 16cp$
OFFERINGs	$cx(24 + (6 + 4))$	$= 34cx$
STUDENTs	$cxy(13 + (9 + 4))$	$= 26cxy$
TEACHERs	$cxz(12 + (12 + 4))$	$= 28cxz$
EMPLOYEEs	$e(24 + (6 + 4))$	$= 34e$

Total $= c(2x(13y + 14z + 17) + 16p + 43) + 34e$ bytes.

(If PREREQs and TEACHERs are subsumed by the corresponding indexes, this total reduces by $6c(p + 2xz)$ bytes.)

(b) Hierarchic:

COURSEs	$c(36 + 4 + 4 + (3 + 4))$	$= 51c$
PREREQs	$cp(3 + 4 + 4)$	$= 11cp$
OFFERINGs	$cx(21 + 4 + 4 + 4 + 4)$	$= 37cx$
STUDENTs	$cxy(7 + 4 + 4)$	$= 15cxy$
TEACHERs	$cxz(6 + 4 + 4)$	$= 14cxz$
EMPLOYEEs	$e(24 + (6 + 4))$	$= 34e$

Total $= c(x(15y + 14z + 37) + 11p + 51) + 34e$ bytes.

(c) Network:

COURSEs	$c(36 + 4 + 4 + 4 + (3 + 4))$	$= 55c$
PREREQs	$cp(4 + 4 + 4 + 4)$	$= 16cp$
OFFERINGs	$cx(21 + 4 + 4 + 4 + 4)$	$= 37cx$
STUDENTs	$cxy(1 + 4 + 4 + 4 + 4)$	$= 17cxy$
TEACHERs	$cxz(4 + 4 + 4 + 4)$	$= 16cxz$
EMPLOYEEs	$e(24 + 4 + 4 + (6 + 4))$	$= 42e$

Total $= c(x(17y + 16z + 37) + 16p + 55) + 42e$ bytes.

As an illustration, suppose $c = 100$, $e = 1000$, $p = 3$, $x = 8$, $y = 16$, and $z = 1.5$. Then the three expressions evaluate as follows.

Relational:	436,700 bytes
Hierarchic:	280,800 bytes
Network:	318,700 bytes

Exercise 3:   Derive expressions representing the number of stored records (both data records and index records) accessed in executing the three enrollment procedures. Again, state any assumptions you make.

Answer 3:

Consider just the loop portion of the procedure, which is executed p times (assuming that the given employee has in fact attended all relevant prerequisite courses). In all three cases each iteration of the loop involves two calls to the DBMS, one to move to the next PREREQ and one to check for existence of a STUDENT. Thus the total number of calls is $2p$ in every case. However, the calls themselves get progressively more complex, and the DBMS has to do correspondingly more work, as we move from relations to hierarchies to networks. The expressions derived below give some indication of this increase in complexity. The reader is cautioned, however, not to take these figures as any absolute measure of performance or relative merit.

(a) Relational:

We assume that it is possible to locate a given index entry in a single access, a reasonable assumption if the relevant higher-level portion of the index is already in main storage. (In fact, it is quite likely that all index entries for PREREQs of the given COURSE will be on a single physical page, and all STUDENT index entries for the given COURSE will also be on a single page, but we do not make any such assumptions in the simple analysis we are presenting here.) In the case of PREREQs, therefore, there will be p accesses to the PREREQ index. Note, however, that no access is needed to the corresponding PREREQ data records—all the necessary data values are available from the index itself. Thus, each PREREQ will involve just one (index) record access. Turning now to the EXISTS test, note that the test is for a STUDENT having a given primary key value, and that therefore the result of the test can be determined from the index alone—again no access is needed to the data itself. Hence the final expression for the total number of records accessed in the loop is simply $2p$ (p for the PREREQ index and p for the STUDENT index).

(b) Hierarchic:

Since the given COURSE points to its first PREREQ and each of its PREREQs in turn points to the next, we again assume that each PREREQ involves only one access (a data record access this time, not an index record access). The EXISTS test is more complicated, however. Assuming that the implementation will search down from the top of the hierarchy, we have:

> one access to the COURSE index on the basis of PREREQ.PRE#
> one access to the corresponding COURSE
> scan half the x corresponding OFFERINGs (on average)
> for each—
> > one access to OFFERING
> > scan all y corresponding STUDENTs
> > for each—
> > > one access to STUDENT

So the final expression is

$$p(1 + 1 + 1 + (x/2)(1 + y)) = ((xy/2) + (x/2) + 3)p.$$

(c) Network:

Assume once again that each PREREQ involves a single access. However, there are now two strategies for the EXISTS test, one searching down from the prerequisite COURSE and one searching down from the given EMPLOYEE. For the first of these we have:

> one access to COURSE via PREOF parent pointer
> scan half the x corresponding OFFERINGs (on average)
> for each—
> > one access to OFFERING
> > scan all y corresponding STUDENTs
> > for each—
> > > one access to STUDENT
> > > one access to EMPLOYEE via ATTENDS parent pointer

So the first possibility is

$$p(1 + 1 + (x/2)(1 + y(1 + 1))) = (xy + (x/2) + 2)p.$$

For the second strategy we have:

> scan half the cxy/e STUDENTs for the given EMPLOYEE
> for each—
> > one access to STUDENT
> > one access to OFFERING via HASSTU parent pointer
> > one access to COURSE via HASOFFER parent pointer

So the second possibility is

$$p(1 + (cxy/2e)(1 + 1 + 1)) = ((3cxy/2e) + 1)p.$$

Note that both the network expressions would be much worse in the absence of parent pointers.

Taking the same values for c, e, p, x, y, and z as before, these expressions evaluate as follows:

Relational: 6
Hierarchic: 213
Network: 402 (1st possibility)
               61 2nd possibility)

Why Is It So Difficult to Provide a Relational Interface to IMS?

ABSTRACT

Several commercial DBMSs—but not however IMS—now claim to provide an interface by which users can obtain relational access to existing (i.e., nonrelational) data. This paper shows that there are certain inherent (and possibly insuperable) difficulties in trying to provide such an interface. It illustrates those difficulties by considering the specific case of attempting to provide a SQL interface to IMS.

COMMENTS ON REPUBLICATION

Given that users of a nonrelational DBMS may wish to migrate to a relational system, the question arises: How is that migration to be achieved?

Originally published in *InfoIMS 4,* No. 4 (4th Quarter 1984). Reprinted with permission.

An ideal solution to this problem, or one that would be close to ideal, would be to migrate the old data to the new relational system but to continue to support old-style nonrelational operations on that data, so that new relational applications could be developed while existing applications continue to operate unchanged. A second solution, not ideal but still attractive, would be to support the new relational operations on the old (unmigrated) data, so that at least new relational applications could be developed to operate against existing data. I wrote this paper to show why it is unlikely that either of those solutions will be easy to achieve in practice, advertising claims to the contrary notwithstanding.

INTRODUCTION

Support for the relational model is now commonly regarded as a sine qua non for modern database systems. One indicator of the widespread acceptance of relational ideas is provided by the extensive list of nonrelational systems—IDMS, DATACOM/DB, ADABAS, MODEL 204, System 2000, TIS, and others—that now claim to be relational, or at least to support a relational interface. But among this list of "born again" relational systems, IMS is conspicuous by its absence. Why is this?

Of course, a relational interface to IMS (if such a thing were possible) would be a very attractive proposition. It would mean, among other things, that an installation that was currently committed to IMS could reap the benefits of the relational approach—or at least some of those benefits—without having to migrate any existing data and (more important) without having to rewrite any existing programs. Unfortunately, however, there is good evidence to suggest that a true relational interface to IMS will never be anything more than a pipedream. The purpose of this paper is to explain why this is so—and, by extension, why a true relational interface to *any* nonrelational system may be a difficult thing to achieve.

Note: There is of course an obvious converse question: Would it be possible to provide a DL/I interface to a relational system such as DB2? Such an interface would arguably be an even more attractive proposition: An IMS installation would be able to migrate to that relational system, and thereby obtain *all* of the advantages of the relational approach—at least for new applications—and still not have to rewrite any programs. I will consider this converse question toward the end of this paper.

One final introductory remark: In order to focus the discussion, it is convenient to make a number of simplifying assumptions:

(a) First, I assume (where it makes any difference) that the relational interface we would like IMS to support is, specifically, the "Structured

Query Language" SQL (usually pronounced "sequel"), as implemented by DB2. However, most of the points made in what follows apply with little change to any relational interface, not just to SQL. Furthermore, they also apply—as suggested earlier—to other nonrelational systems (at least in some cases), not just to IMS.

(b) Second, I also assume that "IMS support for SQL" means, specifically, that SQL operations are to be implemented by translating them into standard DL/I calls. I discount the alternative possibility of bypassing DL/I entirely and translating SQL statements directly into I/O operations against the stored data, for reasons that I will explain later.

(c) Finally, for most of the paper I choose to ignore IMS Main Storage databases. Main Storage databases are really a very special case in IMS; their behavior is significantly different from that of other kinds of database (for example, they support different data types). However, one aspect of their behavior is mentioned explicitly at the end of the next section.

SOME FUNDAMENTAL INCOMPATIBILITIES

The aim of this part of the paper is to show that there exist some very basic incompatibilities between IMS and SQL. The principal (though not the only) source of those incompatibilities is the comparative lack of discipline imposed in IMS; the user in IMS is given more freedom than is perhaps consistent with the general database objectives of control, stability, data independence, and so forth. As a result, there are many situations in IMS in which the meaning of the data is at least partly hidden in procedural code, instead of being made explicit in some IMS data definition. And, needless to say, it is often impossible to expose such hidden meaning through a disciplined relational interface, which requires *all* of the information in the database to be represented by explicit field values.

1. The basic data aggregate is different in the two systems—in IMS it is the segment, in SQL it is the record (or row). An IMS segment is just a byte string; a SQL record, by contrast, is a collection of named, typed values. Thus, all of the following are possible in IMS, and not in SQL:

(a) *Anonymous or undefined fields*: For example, segment type S might be defined to be 100 bytes long, with bytes 1–10 defined as field A, bytes 91–100 defined as field Z, and bytes 11–90 undefined. Perhaps more realistically, anonymous fields can be used (and indeed are used) as a means of allowing multiple different segment types to occupy the same position in the hierarchy. For example, segment type S (100 bytes) might be defined with just one named field SEGTYPE (bytes 1–4, say); the user program can test that field (e.g., "if SEGTYPE = '0001' this is a type 1 segment, if SEGTYPE = '0002' it is a type 2 segment"), and can then map the segment internally to a set of appropriate program variables.

(b) *Arbitrarily overlapping fields*: For example, bytes 1–10 of some segment might be defined as field A and bytes 6–13 as field B. This facility might very well be used in conjunction with the technique mentioned under (a) above for allowing different segment types to appear at the same hierarchic position, but of course it is not restricted to such a context. A more reasonable example of its use is in subdividing composite fields—for example, bytes 12–17 might be defined as a DATE field, with bytes 12–13, 14–15, and 16–17 redefined as YEAR, MONTH, and DAY fields respectively. Now, it is certainly true that composite field support is sorely needed in relational languages such as SQL; however, allowing arbitrarily overlapping byte string fields is not the best solution to that problem.

(c) *Different data types for the "same" field*: For example, bytes 1–10 of some segment might be defined as type P (packed decimal) and bytes 6–13 as type X (hexadecimal). As the example suggests, this facility might again be used in conjunction with the technique mentioned under (a) for allowing multiple segment types to share the same position, but again it is not restricted to such a context.

Each of (a), (b), (c) above means that, in general, an IMS segment cannot simply be equated to a SQL record.

2. Even if the IMS segment in question is "well behaved," in the sense that none of (a), (b), (c) under subsection 1 above applies, the basic data types are different in the two systems. The IMS data types are as follows:

C (character)	: corresponds to SQL data type CHAR
X (hexadecimal)	: no SQL equivalent
P (packed decimal)	: no SQL equivalent

Note in particular that IMS type P does *not* correspond to SQL type DECIMAL. IMS type P and SQL DECIMAL differ from each other in at least the following two ways:

- First, data types are not (usually) checked in IMS. Thus there is no guarantee that a type P field does actually contain a valid packed decimal number. If it does not, of course, then user programs may fail at run time.

- Second, all comparisons in IMS are (usually) performed bit by bit from left to right, regardless of data type. Thus in IMS packed decimal " – 1" will probably be considered greater than packed decimal " + 1" (for example); likewise, two values that are equal under the System/370 rules of packed decimal representation will not actually be considered as equal if they happen to have different sign codes. It follows that, if an IMS segment is to masquerade as a SQL record, a new SQL data type corresponding to IMS type P will have to be invented (e.g., "IMS DECIMAL"?), with its own (bizarre) comparison rules. Analogous remarks apply to type X also, of course. Alternatively, it might be possible to restrict comparisons to "equals" and "not equals" only, in which case there would be a better chance—though still no guarantee—that values might compare in accordance with intuition.

In addition, of course, SQL DECIMAL is capable of representing noninteger values, though that fact is not relevant to the present discussion.

Note: It might appear from the foregoing discussion that IMS types C, P, and X are in fact all the same—they are all just byte strings, and they could all map to SQL type CHAR. Such is not the case, however; there are some subtle differences among the three, though the details are beyond the scope of this short paper. See the discussion of variable-length segments in the next subsection for one example of those differences.

3. IMS segments can be variable-length. So of course can SQL records—but with the following critical difference:

(a) Basically, a SQL record is variable-length if and only if it includes one or more variable-length fields—i.e., fields that are explicitly defined to the system to be variable-length. (Actually there are certain additional circumstances under which a SQL record may also be considered to be variable-length, at least in DB2, but those circumstances are of no concern to the ordinary SQL user.)

(b) In IMS, by contrast, there is no notion of variable-length fields. Instead, a variable-length segment is defined as a byte string of a certain (fixed) *maximum* length, made up of a set of fields of certain (fixed) lengths. If a particular occurrence of the segment is less than the maximum length, then fields at the right hand end are simply considered to be missing, either in total or in part.

For example, suppose segment type S (maximum length 100 bytes) is defined to consist of fields A, B, C, and D, in that order, and each of A, B, C, and D is 25 bytes; and suppose a particular occurrence of S is only 65 bytes long. Then the last 10 bytes of field C and the whole of field D are considered as missing from that occurrence.

If the user is "sensitive" to a missing or partly missing field (i.e., if that field has been named in a SENFLD statement in the PCB), then on retrieval that field will be filled in the user's I/O area with blank characters (for type C) or binary zeros (for type X) or packed decimal zeros (for type P). Note that "missing" in IMS is thus not the same as "null" in SQL. However, a search against a missing field will always return "not found," regardless of the specified search condition.

Each occurrence of a variable-length segment of course includes a length field that specifies the actual length of that particular occurrence. Furthermore, if field sensitivity is not in effect (i.e., if the PCB does not include any SENFLD statements for the segment in question), then that length field is exposed to the user (on both retrieval and update operations). In particular, the user is responsible for specifying a value for that field when an occurrence of the segment is stored. As for retrieval, the length field can be (and has been) used as the basis for distinguishing between different segment types that have been allowed to occupy the same position in the hierarchy (see the remarks on this topic under subsection 1 above); for example, "if length = 52 this is a type X segment, if length = 86 it is a type Y segment." This trick might obviate the need for a separate SEGTYPE field.

4. The collection of all segments of a given type is ordered in IMS, whereas the collection of all records of a given type (i.e., a table) is unordered in SQL. In SQL, a given set of records is guaranteed to be returned to the user in a specific order only if the retrieval request includes an appropriate ORDER BY clause. This fact suggests that, if IMS segments are surfaced through a relational interface as SQL records, then all SQL SELECTs against those records *must* include an ORDER BY clause that specifies the ordering that IMS will in fact use (ignoring for the moment the point that not all IMS orderings can in fact be specified in SQL terms anyway—see subsection 5 below). For otherwise SQL programs that operated on IMS data (if such a thing were possible) would very likely contain some unpleasant (and hidden) data dependencies.

Given the foregoing, incidentally, it is unfortunate that SQL does not currently permit a program that retrieves data via SELECT . . . ORDER BY to update that data, at least not directly.

5. In fact, as suggested under 4. above, not all IMS orderings are expressible in SQL anyway. In fact, the *only* form of ordering in IMS that has an exact SQL equivalent is ordering via a "unique sequence field" (more precisely, ordering via a unique "fully concatenated key"; for brevity I will continue to use the more usual IMS term). Segments in IMS that do not possess a unique sequence field are ordered in one of the following ways:

(a) If the segments have no sequence field at all, then the possibilities are FIRST, LAST, and HERE.

(b) If the segments do have a sequence field but it is not unique, then that sequence field serves as the major ordering item, but the set of duplicates with respect to a given sequence field value are ordered (again) FIRST, LAST, or HERE within that major sequence.

FIRST and LAST mean that the ordering is controlled by time of arrival—FIRST means a new segment is stored in front of existing segments, LAST means a new segment is stored after existing segments. HERE means that the ordering is controlled by the user program—a new segment is stored at a position specified procedurally by user program code. And the fact that a particular segment is stored "here" and not "there" of course carries meaning—meaning that is embedded in the logic of the program and cannot be surfaced through a pure relational interface.

FIRST, LAST, and HERE are all examples of what is called "essential ordering." An ordering is essential if and only if information would be lost if that ordering were destroyed. Note that ordering by a unique sequence field is *in*essential by this definition, because it would still be possible to find, e.g., the employee with the fourth highest serial number, even if employees were not originally ordered by serial number in the database. Relational systems—in particular, SQL—deliberately do not support any form of essential ordering. For a justification for this position, see "Interactive Support for Nonprogrammers: The Relational and Network Approaches," by E. F. Codd and C. J. Date, published in *Data Models: Data-Structure-Set vs. Relational* (Vol. II of *Proc. ACM SIGMOD Workshop on Data Description, Access, and Control;* May 1-3, 1974).[1]

6. One final (comparatively minor) incompatibility: In the case of Main Storage databases (only), IMS update operations have unconventional semantics. Specifically, if a transaction T updates a segment S and then retrieves that segment S again, it will not see the effect of its own update. The reason is that IMS does not actually apply the update to the database until (successful) end-of-transaction, and unfortunately this fact is exposed to the user.

DEFINING A FLAT RECORD VIEW OF IMS DATA

Despite everything said in this paper so far, it nevertheless would be possible, given some collection of IMS data, to construct a variety of "flat

---

[1]Reprinted elsewhere in the present book.

record views" over that data. Of course, such a flat record view would not be the same thing as a SQL relation, for all the reasons outlined in the previous section. (Though it might be close, if the IMS data is "well behaved" and does not involve any anonymous fields, essential orderings, or similar nonrelational constructs; however, experience suggests that IMS databases rarely are "well behaved" in this sense.)

The definition of such a flat view would involve a variety of IMS operations (both definitional and manipulative) that traverse various predefined hierarchic paths. Let us consider an example. Here is an IMS representation of (a simplified version of) the familiar suppliers-and-parts database (actually it involves two physical databases in IMS):

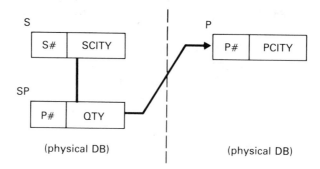

Segment type S (supplier) has two fields:

- S# (supplier number): unique sequence field
- SCITY (supplier city)

Likewise, segment type P (part) also has two fields:

- P# (part number): unique sequence field
- PCITY (part city)

Finally, segment type SP (shipment) also has two fields:

- P# (part number): unique sequence field (see below)
- QTY (quantity)

At any given time, at most one shipment can exist for a given supplier/part combination; thus, field SP.P# is "unique within parent," where "parent" means "supplier." In fact, segment type S is the *physical* parent of segment type SP, and segment type P is the *logical* parent. (Equivalently, SP is a physical child of S and a logical child of P.) The pointer from segment type SP to segment type P is a logical parent pointer (it is concealed from the user, of course). In general, IMS would permit field SP.P# to be virtual, but we wish to use it as the sequence field for segment type SP, which means that it must be physical, not virtual. The SP segments for a given S segment are thus sequenced in P# order.

Note, incidentally, that both of these IMS databases are "well behaved."

Given these two physical databases, it is possible to define the following logical database:

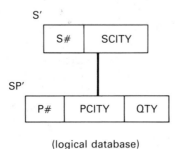

(logical database)

Note: For reasons that need not concern us here, the SP′ segment would actually consist of *four* fields, namely P#, QTY, P# (again), and PCITY, in that order. I ignore such details.

Finally, it is possible to flatten this logical hierarchy by means of appropriate DL/I calls (probably path calls) and present it to a "relational" user in the form

SP″

S#	SCITY	P#	PCITY	QTY

A number of points should be made before we go any further:

1. Observe first that the definition of this flat record view requires both (a) a lot of *pre*definition of physical access paths on the disk and (b) considerable IMS professional expertise in constructing the view. "Relational" users would thus certainly not be able to define new flat record views for themselves dynamically as the need arose.

2. In fact, I have omitted one of the definitional steps—namely, the step of defining a Program Communication Block (PCB) for the logical hierarchy. For simplicity, I assume that the PCB defines a hierarchy that is identical to that shown as the logical database above.

3. It should be pointed out that the term "logical database" is something of a misnomer anyway, because "logical" databases are really rather physical in IMS. (Certainly they involve all kinds of physical access paths on the disk, just as physical databases do.)

4. What I have suggested is that some IMS expert (the database administrator?) would be responsible for writing flat record view definitions—in particular for writing a (simple) set of DL/I calls to be invoked as part of the SQL-to-DL/I translation process. In the case at hand, it might be desirable to extend that definition process to screen out fields SCITY and PCITY from the flat record view (since SP″ as shown above is not in third normal form). For generality, however, I will continue to assume that those fields are indeed visible in the view.

Let us therefore now consider which SQL operations could be supported on the flat record view SP″. By "supported" here, of course, I mean (as stated earlier in this paper) "supported via an automatic translation to an appropriate set of DL/I calls"; obviously, *anything* (or almost anything) can be supported if someone is prepared to handcode a program to do it, but that is not the point at issue here. For similar reasons I discount the possibility that a flat record view might be defined that did not depend on predefined hierarchic paths.

First, retrieval (SELECT operations):

- SELECT clause:
  The only legal operands are the fieldnames S#, SCITY, P#, PCITY, and QTY. Arithmetic expressions such as QTY + 150, simple constants, and builtin functions such as AVG (QTY) cannot be supported. Also (most significant) DISTINCT cannot be supported—unless (just conceivably) the SELECT clause includes both S# and P#, in which case DISTINCT would be a no-op anyway.

- FROM clause:
  Almost certainly, only a single tablename (SP″ in the case at hand) would be allowed; i.e., that table cannot be joined to any other table. (The problem with join is that it generates a new table that is completely different from any existing table, in general. If IMS needed to materialize such a new table, it would first need to create a data definition for it, and unfortunately new IMS definitions cannot be created dynamically.)

  Note: The foregoing may be too extreme. It may in fact be possible to support joins that correspond to *predefined hierarchic paths*, if such joins have not already been factored into the view definition. For example, suppose view SP″ is replaced by the following two views:

  ```
  S''' ( S#, SCITY )
  SP'''( S#, P#, PCITY, QTY )
  ```

  (corresponding, more or less, to the segments S′ and SP′ in the logical hierarchy shown earlier). Then the SQL join

```
SELECT ...
FROM    S''', SP''
WHERE   S'''.S# = SP'''.S#
```

can obviously be implemented by traversing the hierarchic path between S′ and SP′ in that logical hierarchy. In view SP″, by contrast, the join has been built into the view definition itself.

- WHERE clause:
  Basically, only restriction predicates can be supported. (A restriction predicate is a predicate that involves only constants and/or fields of the record in question; it can be evaluated as true or false for a given record by examining just that record in isolation.) Furthermore, not all such predicates will be legal:

  - The predicate *must* (at its most complex) be of the form "(*p1*) AND (*p2*)," where *p1* is a restriction predicate on the S′ segment and *p2* is a restriction predicate on the SP′ segment (however, either *p1* or *p2* could be omitted). The reason for this rule is that S′ and SP′ are at different levels of the (logical database) hierarchy, and IMS cannot handle predicates that involve an OR between hierarchic levels.

  - For reasons explained earlier in this paper, comparison operators other than "equals" and "not equals" may be disallowed in some cases.

  - Comparisons of the form "fieldname comparison-operator fieldname" are not allowed.

  - Comparands cannot be represented as arithmetic expressions (such as QTY + 150).

  - LIKE comparisons cannot be supported (except for trivial cases).

  - IS NULL comparisons cannot be supported.

  Since only restriction predicates are supportable, the following SQL constructs are also not allowed:

  - IN with a subquery

  - EXISTS

  - Scalar comparison operator (e.g., "equals" or "greater than") with a subquery

- GROUP BY clause:
  Cannot be supported.

- HAVING clause:
  Cannot be supported.

- ORDER BY clause:
  Cannot be supported, other than as described earlier in this paper.

Finally, UNION also cannot be supported.

Now the update operations. First, of course, limitations similar to those described above for WHERE (etc.) apply to these operations also, in general. Note, too, that (as mentioned previously) view SP″ is not in third normal form (in fact, it is not even in second normal form); as a result, strange update behavior is only to be expected. But the situation is worse than it would be in a "pure" relational system in a number of ways, as will soon be seen. Consider first the UPDATE operation itself:

- Field QTY is updatable (no surprises).

- Field SCITY is also updatable, but with side-effects, owing to the fact that the information that a certain supplier is located in a certain city appears not once but many times in the view. Of course, that same information is represented only once on the disk; as a result, changing a supplier's city in one SP″ record causes the same change to occur instantaneously in all other SP″ records for that supplier. Of course, it can very reasonably be argued that this side-effect is desirable, and indeed a good thing; but it does have to be explained to the user, and it does mean that the user's view of the data is more complicated than the simple data structure SP″ (S#,SCITY,P#,PCITY,QTY) alone would suggest.

- Field PCITY may or may not be updatable, depending on the IMS replace rule for segment type P. If it is, then of course considerations analogous to those described above for field SCITY apply.

- *Fields S# and P# cannot be updated at all.* In general, if V is a "relational" view of some IMS database D, and if F is a field in V, then it looks as if F will not be updatable in V if it is either (a) (a component of) the primary key of V or (b) (a component of) a foreign key in V that corresponds to a parent-child link in D. The second of these two restrictions in particular is extremely unfortunate, since updating foreign keys is perfectly legal and indeed commonplace in a relational system. For example, given the relation

```
EMP ( EMP#, ENAME, DEPT#, SALARY ) ,
```

moving some employee from department D1 to department D2 is accomplished precisely by updating the foreign key field EMP.DEPT# for that employee from D1 to D2.

As for INSERT and DELETE operations:

- DELETE on SP″ is always legal; however, under certain circumstances it may have the side-effect of deleting the corresponding P segment also (depending on the IMS delete rule for that segment).

- INSERT on SP″ will fail if no corresponding S segment exists; it may or may not fail if no corresponding P segment exists (depending on the IMS insert rule for that segment). If it does not fail, then (a) if no corresponding P segment exists, then one may automatically be created; (b) if a corresponding P segment does exist, then either PCITY in that segment will be replaced by PCITY from the new SP″ record, or the other way around. Of course, all of this is dependent (once again) on various IMS rules. What will happen if SCITY in the new SP″ record is different from SCITY in the existing S segment is unclear.

In general, the behavior of INSERT, UPDATE, and DELETE is very difficult to explain in a SQL framework, as the foregoing may serve to illustrate. The situation is somewhat ironic, as a matter of fact:

(a) Whatever the behavior of those operations actually is, it is necessary to expose the IMS rules at the SQL interface in order to explain that behavior;

(b) However, SQL currently has no framework in which to couch any such explanations, because SQL currently does not support foreign keys (of course, this is a well-known SQL deficiency).

(c) On the other hand, the IMS rules are both less and more than the rules that I, at any rate, feel are desirable for a relational system (see *A Guide to DB2*, by C. J. Date, published by Addison-Wesley, 1984).

In addition, of course, if the IMS databases are not "well behaved" —in particular, if they involve any essential ordering—then the behavior of INSERT specifically will be hard to explain at the "relational" interface (in fact, it may be unpredictable).

Finally, note that a "flat record view" mechanism along the lines indicated in this section would require a new catalog to be built on top of the existing IMS "catalog" (i.e., the existing IMS data definitions). The purpose of that new catalog would be to show the flat record views that were available, to serve as a repository for the definitions of those views in terms of IMS data, to indicate what operations were legal against those views and (in the legal cases) what their semantics were, and so on. As a result, the system (or the DBA?) would be faced with all the standard problems of having to keep two catalogs in synch.

WHAT ABOUT BYPASSING DL/I?

I have been assuming up to this point that a SQL interface to IMS would "cascade through DL/I." What about the possibility of bypassing DL/I and translating SQL operations directly into I/O operations against the stored IMS data? In other words, would it be possible to provide a component (which I will call *the SQL data manager*) whose function would be to provide SQL access to stored IMS data in much the same way that the DL/I data manager provides DL/I access to such data in IMS today?

If such an approach were possible, it would certainly overcome some of the objections raised earlier in this paper. For example, such a SQL data manager could support the SQL ORDER BY clause by performing a dynamic sort, instead of having to be constrained by just those orderings that are statically predefined. However:

(a) There would still be difficulties—for example, data that does not conform to its declared data type, anonymous and overlapping fields, missing fields, essential ordering, etc. At the very least it would seem that a separate set of SQL definitions would be required for the stored data, over and above the existing DL/I definitions; and once again there would be the problem of keeping two sets of definitions in synch (not to mention the fact that some of the data may well not even be definable in SQL terms anyway).

(b) It might be possible to deal with some of the difficulties mentioned under (a) by means of exit routines, whose function would be to "clean" the IMS data before exposing it to SQL. But in order to be able to write such routines it would first of all be necessary to understand what the IMS data means—and (as explained earlier) some of that meaning will in general be buried in procedural user code. Thus the person writing the exit routines may have to study many user programs in order to discover that meaning; and can there ever be any guarantee that the process of discovering that meaning is complete?

(c) Perhaps more to the point: Consider what would be involved in constructing such a SQL data manager. It would obviously be at least as difficult a task as the original task of constructing the DL/I data manager of IMS in the first place. In fact, of course, it would be much more difficult, for at least the following two reasons:

  ▪ SQL is a much richer language, functionally speaking, than DL/I.

  ▪ An optimizer would be required, for exactly the same reason that an optimizer is required in DB2 (namely, because performance would almost certainly be intolerable without it).

(d) To pursue the last point in the previous paragraph a little further: Note that such an optimizer would require a considerable amount of original invention. In fact, it looks to me like a research problem: Almost all existing work on relational optimization assumes that the target storage structure is based on indexing or hashing or a combination of the two;

almost nothing has been published (so far as I am aware) on optimizing against IMS-style pointer-based structures.

From all of the above, I conclude that a "SQL data manager" that would operate directly against IMS stored data:

(a) would certainly be a nontrivial undertaking;

(b) would probably require a certain amount of hand-tailoring by the DBA (at the very least, in the way of additional data definition);

(c) may still belong more in the realm of research than in that of commercial products;

(d) may not even be technically feasible;

(e) may not solve all of the problems even if it is; and

(f) may not be cost-effective even if it does.

CONCLUDING REMARKS

In this paper, I have sketched some of the difficulties involved in attempting to provide relational (specifically SQL) access to existing IMS data. I have shown that, in general, a genuine relational interface is an impossibility; however, I have also shown that, in some cases at least, a "flat record view" interface might be a possibility. But note clearly that such an interface would almost certainly support:

(a) predefined views only,

(b) using predefined hierarchic paths only,

(c) and possibly retrieval operations only (because of the complexity and apparent arbitrariness of update operations).

Note, moreover, that those retrieval operations would be limited, in relational terms, to "projection" (in quotes because there would be no possibility of duplicate elimination) and certain forms of restriction only. Join would not be supported (except possibly for the case of a join that traverses a predefined hierarchic path), and restriction would be subject to a series of complex and apparently arbitrary constraints. Furthermore, if the IMS data is not "well behaved," the flat record views will not be "well behaved" either. Please note that I do not claim that such an interface might not serve some useful practical purpose; however, I do claim that it would not be relational.

Of course, all of our discussions have been in terms of IMS specifically. Now, it may well be the case that, considered as a target for a relational interface, IMS is more complex than other nonrelational systems; nevertheless, the reader should realize that, as pointed out near the beginning of this paper, problems analogous to those we have discussed—though possibly less severe—are quite likely to arise with other systems also. Thus, if you are considering investing in a nonrelational system that claims to support a relational interface, you are advised to make sure you understand exactly what that interface really involves before you commit yourself. "Look before you leap" is the watchword.

I conclude this paper (as promised) with a brief note on the converse question—namely, is it possible to support a DL/I interface to a relational system such as DB2? The short answer (as the reader will probably have guessed) is no, it is not:

- First, of course, all of the points raised in the section "Some Fundamental Incompatibilities" apply equally in the opposite direction. For example, it does not seem possible to simulate the behavior of HERE-style ordering or IMS-style variable-length segments on top of SQL records.

- Second, support for the DL/I update operations would require SQL support for foreign keys (and more besides). Furthermore, as indicated earlier in this paper, it is not even clear that equivalents of all of the IMS update rules are even desirable in a relational system (I would argue that they are not all desirable).

- Third, there are problems even with retrieval operations (even if the IMS data is completely "well behaved," though the problems are considerably worse if it is not). For example, DL/I operations are crucially dependent on various notions of "current position" (current segment, current parent, etc.). The notion of "current parent" may break down because (again) SQL does not enforce foreign key constraints; a given "child" might not in fact have any "parent" in the SQL database. (I am not necessarily suggesting that this state of affairs is desirable, merely explaining what that state of affairs is.) As for the notion of "current segment," it is not even all that well defined; in particular, "current segment" after a "not found" condition in DL/I seems to depend on the underlying IMS access method (HISAM, HIDAM, etc.).

In addition to all the above, of course, there is the point that an implementation of DL/I on a relational system—if such a thing were possible at all—would almost certainly perform exceedingly poorly, because it would involve the simulation of a record-level (or rather segment-level) language on top of a set-level interface. Note that it *would* necessarily be on top of a set-level interface; true relational systems deliberately do not provide any lower-level interface to the data, in order to prevent the possibility of users bypassing the relational controls and thereby subverting the system in a variety of ways. In fact, this last point can be seen as yet another distinction between genuine relational systems on the one hand and "born again" relational systems on the other—in the latter case, there is always the possibility that a user can get in under the covers and perform some operation that undermines the system in some way. A true relational system does not permit such subversive activity.

ACKNOWLEDGMENTS

I am grateful to Ted Codd for encouraging me to write this paper in the first place. I am also grateful to Colin White for his numerous helpful comments on an earlier draft, and to Doug Hembry for assistance with some technical questions regarding the behavior of variable-length segments in IMS.

THE SQL
LANGUAGE

13

Some Principles of Good Language Design

(WITH ESPECIAL REFERENCE TO THE DESIGN OF DATABASE LANGUAGES)

ABSTRACT

The purpose of this note is to try to pull together a list of language design principles that will serve as a reference for database language designers and any others who might be interested. The list is not taken from any one place but rather is culled from a variety of sources, including computer science folklore and "conventional wisdom."

COMMENTS ON REPUBLICATION

This paper was originally written primarily to provide a reference for the next paper in this collection, "A Critique of the SQL Database Language."

Originally published in *ACM SIGMOD Record* 14, No. 3 (November 1984). Reprinted with permission.

However, I feel it is worth preserving in its own right as a convenient single source for the material.

INTRODUCTION

First a position statement. It is my opinion that:

1. Database languages ("query languages") are nothing but special-purpose *programming* languages.
2. Therefore, the same design principles apply.
3. There are well-established (though not well-documented) principles for the design of programming languages.
4. There is little evidence that current database languages have been designed in accordance with any such principles.

The purpose of this note is as stated in the Abstract: namely, to try to pull together a list of such principles that will serve as a reference for database language designers and any others who might be interested. The list is (obviously) not taken from any one place but rather is culled from a variety of sources, including computer science folklore and "conventional wisdom." One general point that is worth stating at the outset is the following (paraphrased from [2]):

> "Most languages are too big and intellectually unmanageable. The problems arise in part because the language is too restrictive; the number of rules needed to define a language increases when a general rule has additional rules attached to constrain its use in certain cases. (Ironically, these additional rules usually make the language *less* powerful.) . . . *Power through simplicity, simplicity through generality, should be the guiding principle.*"

ORTHOGONALITY

The "guiding principle" espoused in the foregoing quote is frequently referred to in language design circles as the *principle of orthogonality*. The term "orthogonality" refers to what might better be called "concept independence": *Distinct concepts should always be cleanly separated, never bundled together*. To amplify:

- An example of orthogonality is provided by the PL/I rule that allows any scalar-valued expression to appear wherever a scalar value is required, instead of insisting on (e.g.) a simple identifier in certain specific contexts. The effect of this rule is to allow scalar expressions to be arbitrarily nested; for example, the subscript in a subscripted variable reference can itself consist of a subscripted variable.

- The prize example of *lack* of orthogonality is provided by the fanset construct of DBTG. (I deliberately use the term "fanset" [1] in preference to the unfortunate term "set" that is used in official DBTG literature.) The fanset construct bundles together at least three concepts and arguably as many as six, viz: (a) a relationship between an owner record and a set of member records; (b) a relationship among a set of member records; (c) certain integrity rules; (d) a set of access paths; (e) a scope for concurrency control purposes; and (f) a scope for authorization purposes. As a result, it may be impossible to drop a fanset that was originally introduced purely for integrity reasons but is no longer needed for that purpose, because some program may now be using it as an access path. This is only one example of the kind of problem that lack of orthogonality can lead to.

The advantage of orthogonality is that it leads to a coherent language. A coherent language is one that possesses a simple, clean, and consistent structure (both syntactic and semantic), a structure that is easy for the user to grasp. If the language is coherent, users are able (perhaps without realizing the fact) to build a simple mental model of its behavior, from which they can make extrapolations and predictions with confidence. There should be no exceptions or unpleasant surprises. In a nutshell, the manuals are thinner, and the training courses are shorter. As reference [5] puts it: "Orthogonal design maximizes expressive power while avoiding deleterious superfluities." (Slightly paraphrased.)

A number of related points arise from the notion of orthogonality:

1. The number of concepts should be small (though not necessarily minimal), in order that the language may be easy to describe, learn, implement, and use. An example of the distinction between "small" and "minimal" is provided by the operations of ordinary arithmetic: Given the operators "infix plus" and "prefix minus," the operators "infix minus," "times," and "divide by" are all strictly speaking unnecessary—but we would not think much of a language that excluded them. As another example, more directly relevant to database languages per se, consider the natural join operator of relational algebra. Natural join is not a primitive operator of the algebra (it is equivalent to a projection of a restriction of a product), and so it may be excluded from a *minimal* set of relational operators (and is in

fact so excluded from many relational languages, including in particular the "Structured Query Language" SQL); however, it is of such overwhelming practical utility that a good case can be made for supporting it directly.

2. A given syntactic construct should have the same meaning everywhere it appears. Counterexample: Consider the two DBTG FIND statements below.

```
FIND EMP WITHIN DEPT-EMP USING SALARY

FIND DUPLICATE EMP USING SALARY
```

In the first of these, "USING SALARY" refers to the SALARY field in the User Work Area; in the second, it refers to the SALARY field in the current EMP record. Error potential is high.

3. A given semantic construct should have the same syntax everywhere it appears. Counterexamples: (a) In SQL, the SALARY field of the EMP table is referred to as EMP.SALARY in some contexts, as SALARY FROM EMP in others, and as EMP(SALARY) in still others; (b) in SQL again, rows of tables are designated as "*" in SELECT and COUNT but as blank in INSERT and DELETE (e.g., why is the syntax not DELETE * FROM T ?).

4. Statement atomicity: Statements should be either executed or not executed—there should be no halfway house. It should not be possible for a statement to fail in the middle and leave the database (or other variables) in an undefined state. Counterexamples: In SQL (at least as implemented in the IBM product SQL/DS), the set-level INSERT, UPDATE, and DELETE statements are not atomic.

5. Symmetry: To quote Polya [3] (writing in a different context): "Try to treat symmetrically what is symmetrical, and do not destroy wantonly any natural symmetry." Counterexamples: In SQL, (a) a GRANT of UPDATE authority can be field-specific, but the corresponding REVOKE cannot, and neither can a GRANT of SELECT authority; (b) in a table that permits duplicate rows, the INSERT and DELETE operations are not inverses of each other.

The following rule is another aspect of symmetry: Default assumptions should always be explicitly specifiable. Counterexample: In SQL, "nulls not allowed" can be explicitly specified (via the NOT NULL clause), but "nulls allowed" (the default) cannot. It is difficult even to talk about a construct if there is no explicit syntax for it.

6. No arbitrary restrictions: While of course it is understood that the implementer may have to impose local restrictions for a variety of pragmatic reasons, such restrictions should not be built into the fabric of the language. Counterexamples: The keyword DISTINCT can appear at most once in a SQL SELECT statement; DL/I supports exactly ten distinct "lock classes" A, B, . . ., J; DBTG does not allow a fanset to have the same record-type for both owner and member.

7. No side-effects: No amplification necessary. Major counterexample: Currency indicators in DBTG (which incidentally constitute the absolute linchpin of the DBTG data manipulation language!).

8. Recursively defined expressions: This does not mean that the language should necessarily support recursion per se—merely that it should not have artificial restrictions on the nesting of expressions. (This point was touched on earlier.) Counterexamples: In SQL, (a) the argument to a function-reference cannot itself be another function-reference, so that (for example) it is impossible in a single statement to compute the sum of a set of averages; (b) a subquery cannot involve a union (and that fact has numerous repercussions, beyond the scope of this short note). See the further discussion of expressions later.

LANGUAGE DEFINITION

The language should possess a rigorous (formal) definition that is independent of any particular implementation. The purposes of that definition are:

1. To provide precise, definitive answers to technical questions and hence to act as the arbiter in any disputes;

2. To (attempt to) prevent the possibility of divergent and incompatible implementations;

3. Generally to serve as *the* reference source for users, manual writers, teachers, implementers, and anyone else who is concerned with the details of the language at any time.

Counterexamples: Just about every database language in wide usage today. SQL is superior to most in this regard, in that it does (now) possess a formal definition [6], but unfortunately that definition was not produced until after the initial implementation (and that implementation in turn formed the basis of many of the current commercial implementations). Many of the problems with SQL today might well have been avoided if the definition had been produced first.

EXPRESSIONS

In general, the classes of data object supported by a given language fall into a natural hierarchy (or set of hierarchies). For example, relational languages support tables, columns, rows, and scalars, and these object classes can be partially ordered as indicated in the following diagram:

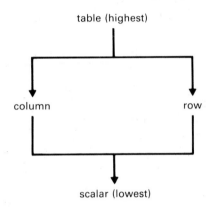

table (highest)

column   row

scalar (lowest)

(columns are neither higher nor lower than rows with respect to this hierarchic ordering). Now, completeness dictates that for each class of object it supports, a language should provide at least all of the following:

- A constructor function, i.e., a means for constructing an object of the class from literal (constant) values and/or variables of lower classes (e.g., it should be possible in a relational language to construct a table from a set of arguments represented as row-expressions);

- A means for comparing two objects of the class, at least for equality and possibly also for comparative rank according to some defined ordering;

- A means for assigning the value of one object in the class to another;

- A selector function, i.e., a means for extracting component objects of lower classes from an object of the given class (e.g., it should be possible in a relational language to extract an individual column from a table);

- A general, recursively defined syntax for expressions representing objects of the given class that exploits to the full any closure properties the object class may possess (e.g., if A + B is a valid scalar-expression, then it should be possible to specify the operands A and B as arbitrary scalar-expressions—it should not be necessary to restrict them to be just simple variable-names).

It is instructive to examine a language such as SQL to see to what extent it meets this "expression completeness" requirement.

MISCELLANEOUS POINTS

I conclude this short note by listing some additional design principles and objectives, taken from a variety of sources (as indicated), without however offering any additional comments.

From the definition of Algol 68 [5]:

- Security

    "Most syntactical and many other errors [should be easily detectable] before they lead to calamitous results. Furthermore, the opportunities for making such errors [should be] greatly reduced."

- Efficiency
  This point includes:
  - Static type checking
  - Type-independent parsing
  - Independent compilation
  - Loop optimization
  - Representation (support for multiple character sets)

From an evaluation of a number of proposals for incorporating database functions into COBOL [4]: [Any COBOL database language should:]

- Be a natural extension of COBOL
- Be easy to learn
- Conform to a standard
- Support relations, hierarchies, and networks
- Promote quality programming
- Be usable as a query language
- Provide set-level access
- Have a stable definition
- Increase programmer productivity
- Be data independent
- Reflect user input in its design

From a proposal of my own for extending the conventional high-level ("host") languages to include database functions [1]:

- [The language] should be designed from the user's point of view rather than the system's (i.e., design should proceed from the outside in).

- It should fit well with the host language. Wherever possible it should exploit existing language features rather than introducing new ones.

- It should transcend and outlive all features of the underlying hardware and software that are specific to those systems.

- It should provide access to as much of the function of the underlying systems as possible without compromising on the first three objectives.

- It should establish a stable long-range design that can be gracefully subset for short-range implementation.

- It should be efficiently implementable.

REFERENCES

1. C. J. Date, "An Introduction to the Unified Database Language (UDL)" (in this volume).

2. R. Morrison, *S-Algol Reference Manual,* Internal Report CSR-80-81, Dept. of Computer Science, University of Edinburgh (February 1981).

3. G. Polya, *How To Solve It,* 2nd edition (Princeton, NJ: Princeton University Press 1971).

4. SHARE DBMS Language Task Force, "An Evaluation of Three COBOL Data Base Languages—UDL, SQL, and CODASYL," *Proc. SHARE* 53 (August 1979).

5. A. van WijnGaarden et al. (eds.), *Revised Report on the Algorithmic Language Algol 68* (Springer-Verlag, 1976).

6. X3H2 (American National Standards Database Committee), Draft Proposed Relational Database Language, Document X3H2-83-152 (August 1983).

14

A Critique of the SQL
Database Language

ABSTRACT

The ANS Database Committee (X3H2) is currently at work on a proposed standard relational database language (RDL), and has adopted as a basis for that activity a definition of the "Structured Query Language" SQL from IBM [10]. Moreover, numerous hardware and software vendors (in addition to IBM) have already released or at least announced products that are based to a greater or lesser extent on the SQL language as defined by IBM. There can thus be little doubt that the importance of that language will increase significantly over the next few years. Yet the language is very far from perfect. The purpose of this paper is to present a critical analysis of the language's major shortcomings, in the hope that it may be possible to remedy some of the deficiencies before their influence becomes too all-pervasive. The paper's standpoint is primarily that of formal computer languages in general, rather than that of database languages specifically.

Originally published in *ACM SIGMOD Record* 14, No. 3 (November 1984). Reprinted with permission.

COMMENTS ON REPUBLICATION

At the time this paper was first written it appeared that the ANS Database Committee X3H2 was in fact in the process of making a number of improvements to SQL along the lines I was suggesting. However, the version of the language that was eventually proposed as a standard [11] did not include those improvements; in fact, standard SQL is virtually identical to IBM SQL, in all except a few minor respects. The criticisms documented in this paper thus apply almost wholesale to the proposed ANS standard version also.

INTRODUCTION

The relational language SQL (the acronym is usually pronounced "sequel"), pioneered in the IBM prototype System R [1] and subsequently adopted by IBM and others as the basis for numerous commercial implementations, represents a major advance over older database languages such as the DL/I language of IMS and the DML and DDL of the Data Base Task Group (DBTG) of CODASYL. Specifically, SQL is far easier to use than those older languages; as a result, users in a SQL system (both end-users and application programmers) can be far more productive than they used to be in those older systems (improvements of up to 20 times have been reported). Among the strongpoints of SQL that lead to such improvements are the following:

- Simple data structure
- Powerful operators
- Short initial learning period
- Improved data independence
- Integrated data definition and data manipulation
- Double mode of use
- Integrated catalog
- Compilation and optimization

These advantages are elaborated in the appendix to this paper.

The language does have its weak points too, however. In fact, it cannot be denied that SQL in its present form leaves rather a lot to be desired—even that, in some important respects, it fails to realize the full potential of the relational model. The purpose of this paper is to describe and examine some of those weak points, in the hope that such aspects of the language may be improved before their influence becomes too all-pervasive.

Before getting into details, I should like to make one point absolutely clear: *The criticisms that follow should not be construed as criticisms of the original designers and implementers of the SQL language.* The paper is intended solely as a critique of the SQL language as such, and nothing more. Note also that the paper applies specifically to the dialect of SQL implemented by IBM in its products SQL/DS, DB2, and QMF. It is entirely possible that some specific point does not apply to some other implemented dialect. However, most points of the paper do apply to most of the dialects currently implemented, so far as I am aware.

The remainder of the paper is divided into the following sections:

- Lack of orthogonality: expressions
- Lack of orthogonality: builtin functions
- Lack of orthogonality: miscellaneous items
- Formal definition
- Mismatch with host languages
- Missing function
- Mistakes
- Aspects of the relational model not supported
- Summary and conclusions

Reference [3] gives some background material—specifically, a set of principles that apply to the design of programming languages in general and database languages in particular. Many of the criticisms that follow are expressed in terms of those principles. Note: Some of the points apply to interactive SQL only and some to embedded SQL only, but most apply to both. I have not bothered to spell out the distinctions; the context makes it clear in every case. Also, the structure of the paper is a little arbitrary, in the sense that it is not really always clear which heading a particular point belongs under. There is also some repetition (I hope not too much), for essentially the same reason.

LACK OF ORTHOGONALITY: EXPRESSIONS

It is convenient to begin by introducing some nonSQL terms.

- A *table-expression* is a SQL expression that yields a table—for example, the expression

```
SELECT  *
FROM    EMP
WHERE   DEPT# = 'D3'
```

■ A *column-expression* is a SQL expression that yields a single column—for example, the expression

```
SELECT EMP#
FROM   EMP
WHERE  DEPT# = 'D3'
```

A column-expression is a special case of a table-expression.

■ A *row-expression* is a SQL expression that yields a single row—for example, the expression

```
SELECT *
FROM   EMP
WHERE  EMP# = 'E2'
```

A row-expression is a special case of a table-expression.

■ A *scalar-expression* is a SQL expression that yields a single scalar value—for example, the expression

```
SELECT AVG (SALARY)
FROM   EMP
```

or the expression

```
SELECT SALARY
FROM   EMP
WHERE  EMP# = 'E2'
```

A scalar-expression is a special case of a row-expression and a special case of a column-expression.

Note that these four kinds of expression correspond to the four classes of data object (table, column, row, scalar) supported by SQL. Note, too, that (as pointed out in [3]) the four classes of object can be partially ordered as follows:

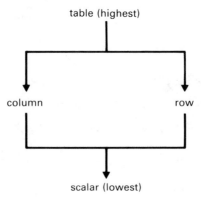

(columns are neither higher nor lower than rows with respect to this ordering).

As explained in [3] (again), a language should provide, for each class of object it supports, at least all of the following:

- A constructor function, i.e., a means for constructing an object of the class from literal (constant) values and/or variables of lower classes;
- A means for comparing two objects of the class;
- A means for assigning the value of one object in the class to another;
- A selector function, i.e., a means for extracting component objects of lower classes from an object of the given class;
- A general, recursively defined syntax for expressions that exploits to the full any closure properties the object class may possess.

The table below shows that SQL does not really measure up to these requirements.

opn obj	constructor	compare	assign	selector	gen expr
table	no	no	only via INSERT – SELECT	yes	no (see below)
column	only as arg to IN (host vbles & consts only)	no	no	yes	no
row	only in INSERT & UPDATE (host vbles & consts only)	no	only to/ from set of host scalars	(yes)	no
scalar	N/A	yes	only to/ from host scalar	(yes)	no

Let us consider table-expressions in more detail. The SELECT statement, which, since it yields a table, may be regarded as a table-expression (possibly of a degenerate form, e.g., as a column-expression), currently has the following structure:

```
SELECT scalar-expression-commalist
FROM   table-name-commalist
WHERE  predicate
```

(ignoring numerous minor details). Notice that it is just *table-names* that appear in the FROM clause. Completeness suggests that it should be *table-expressions* (as Gray puts it [8], "anything in computer science that is not recursive is no good"). This is not just an academic consideration, by the way; on the contrary, there are several practical reasons as to why such recursiveness is desirable.

- First, consider the relational algebra. Relational algebra possesses the important property of closure—that is, relations form a closed system under the operations of the algebra, in the sense that the result of applying any of those operations to any relation(s) is itself another relation. As a consequence, the operands of any given operation are not constrained to be real ("base") relations only, but rather can be any algebraic expression. Thus, the relational algebra allows the user to write *nested relational expressions*—and this feature is useful for precisely the same reasons that nested expressions are useful in ordinary arithmetic.

- Now consider SQL. SQL is a language that supports, directly or indirectly, all of the operations of the relational algebra (i.e., SQL is relationally complete). However, the table-expressions of SQL (which are the SQL equivalent of the expressions of the relational algebra) *cannot* be arbitrarily nested. Let us consider the question of exactly which cases SQL does support. Simplifying matters slightly, the expression SELECT–FROM–WHERE is the SQL version of the nested algebraic expression

```
projection ( restriction ( product ( table1, table2, ... ) ) )
```

(the product corresponds to the FROM clause, the restriction to the WHERE clause, and the projection to the SELECT clause; table1, table2, ... are the tables identified in the FROM clause—and note that, as remarked earlier, these are simple table-names, not more complex expressions). Likewise, the expression

```
SELECT ... FROM ... WHERE ...
UNION
SELECT ... FROM ... WHERE ...
    .....
```

is the SQL version of the nested algebraic expression

```
union ( tabexp1, tabexp2, ... )
```

where tabexp1, tabexp2, ... are in turn table-expressions of the form shown earlier (i.e., projections of restrictions of products of named tables). But it is not possible to formulate direct equivalents of any other nested algebraic expressions. Thus, for example, it is not possible to write a direct equivalent in SQL of the nested expression

```
restriction ( projection ( table ) )
```

Instead, the user has to recast the expression into a semantically equivalent (but syntactically different) form in which the restriction is applied before the projection. What this means in practical terms is that the user may have to expend time and effort transforming the "natural" formulation of a given query into some different, and arguably less "natural," representation (see Example below). What is more, the user is therefore also required to understand exactly when such transformations are valid. This may not always be intuitively obvious. For example, is a projection of a union always equivalent to the union of two projections?

Example: Given the two tables

```
NYC ( EMP#, DEPT#, SALARY )
SFO ( EMP#, DEPT#, SALARY )
```

(representing New York and San Francisco employees, respectively), list EMP# for all employees.

"Natural" formulation (projection of a union):

```
SELECT EMP# FROM ( NYC UNION SFO )
```

SQL formulation (union of two projections):

```
SELECT EMP# FROM NYC
UNION
SELECT EMP# FROM SFO
```

Note in passing that allowing both formulations of the query would enable different users to perceive and express the same problem in different ways. (Of course, both formulations should ideally translate to the same internal representation, for otherwise the choice between them would no longer be arbitrary.)

- The foregoing example tacitly makes use of the fact that a simple table-reference (i.e., a table-name) *ought* to be just a special case of a general table-expression. Thus I wrote

```
NYC UNION SFO
```

instead of

```
SELECT * FROM NYC UNION SELECT * FROM SFO    ,
```

which current SQL would require. It would be highly desirable for SQL to allow the expression "SELECT * FROM T" to be replaced by simply "T" wherever it appears, in the style of more conventional languages. In other words, SELECT should be regarded as a *statement* whose function is to retrieve a table (represented by a table-expression). Table-expressions per se—in particular, *nested* table-expressions—should not require the "SELECT * FROM." Among other things this change would improve the usability of the EXISTS builtin function (see later). It would also be clear that INTO and ORDER BY are clauses of the SELECT *statement* and not part of a table- (or column-) expression; the question of whether they can appear in a nested expression would then simply not arise, thus avoiding the need for a rule that looks arbitrary but is in fact not.

- A nested table-expression is permitted—in fact required—in current SQL as the argument to EXISTS (but strangely enough not as the argument to the other builtin functions; this point is discussed in the next section). Nested *column-expressions* ("subqueries") are (a) *required* with the ANY and ALL operators (includes the IN operator, which is just a different spelling for =ANY); and (b) *permitted* with scalar comparison operators ($<$, $>$, $=$, etc.), if and only if the column-expression yields a column having at most one row. Moreover, the nested expression is allowed to include GROUP BY and HAVING in case (a) but not in case (b). More arbitrariness.

- Elsewhere I have proposed some extensions to SQL to support the outer join operation [4]. The details of that proposal do not concern us here; what does concern us is the following. If the user needs to compute an outer join of three or more relations, then (a) that outer join is constructed by performing a sequence of *binary* outer joins (e.g., join relations A and B, then join the result and relation C); and (b) it is essential that the user indicate the sequence in which those binary joins are performed, because different sequences will produce different results, in general. Indicating the required sequence is done, precisely, by writing a suitable nested expression. Thus, nested expressions are *essential* if SQL is to provide direct (i.e., single-statement) support for general outer joins of more than two relations.

- Another example (involving outer join again): Part of the proposal for supporting outer join [4] involves the use of a new clause, the PRESERVE clause, whose function is to preserve rows from the indicated table that would not otherwise participate in the result of the SELECT. Consider the tables

```
COURSE   ( COURSE#, SUBJECT )
OFFERING ( COURSE#, OFF#, LOCATION )
```

and consider the query "List all algebra courses, with their offerings if any." The two SELECT statements following (neither of which is valid in current SQL, of course) represent two attempts to formulate this query:

```
SELECT    ALGEBRA.COURSE#, OFF#, LOCATION
FROM    ( SELECT COURSE#
          FROM    COURSE
          WHERE   SUBJECT = 'Algebra' ) ALGEBRA, OFFERING
WHERE     ALGEBRA.COURSE# = OFFERING.COURSE#
PRESERVE ALGEBRA

SELECT    COURSE.COURSE#, OFF#, LOCATION
FROM      COURSE, OFFERING
WHERE     COURSE.COURSE# = OFFERING.COURSE#
AND       SUBJECT = 'Algebra'
PRESERVE COURSE
```

Each of these statements does list all algebra courses, together with their offerings, for all such courses that do have any offerings. The first also lists algebra courses that do not have any offerings, concatenated with null values in the OFFERING positions; i.e., it preserves information for those courses (note the introduced name ALGEBRA, which is used to refer to the result of evaluating the inner expression). The second, by contrast, preserves information not only for *algebra* courses with no offerings, *but also for all courses for which the subject is not algebra* (regardless of whether those courses have any offerings or not). In other words, the first preserves information for algebra courses only (as required), the second produces a lot of unnecessary output. And note that the first cannot even be formulated (as a single statement) if nested expressions are not supported.

■ In fact, SQL does already support nested expressions in a kind of "under the covers" sense. Consider the following example.

Base table:

```
S ( S#, SNAME, STATUS, CITY )
```

View definition:

```
CREATE VIEW LONDON_SUPPLIERS
    AS SELECT S#, SNAME, STATUS
       FROM   S
       WHERE  CITY = 'London'
```

Query (Q):

```
SELECT *
FROM    LONDON_SUPPLIERS
WHERE   STATUS > 50
```

Resulting SELECT statement (Q'):

```
SELECT  S#, SNAME, STATUS
FROM    S
WHERE   STATUS > 50
AND     CITY = 'London'
```

The SELECT statement Q' is obtained from the original query Q by a process usually described as "merging"—statement Q is "merged" with the SELECT in the view definition to produce statement Q'. To the naive user this looks a little bit like magic. But in fact what is going on is simply that the reference to LONDON_SUPPLIERS in the FROM clause in Q is being replaced by the expression that *defines* LONDON_SUPPLIERS, as follows:

```
SELECT  *
FROM  ( SELECT S#, SNAME, STATUS
        FROM    S
        WHERE   CITY = 'London' )
WHERE   STATUS > 50
```

This explanation, though both accurate and easy to understand, cannot conveniently be used in describing or teaching SQL, precisely because SQL does not support nesting at the external or user's level.

- UNION is not permitted in a subquery, and hence (among other things) cannot be used in the definition of a view (although strangely enough it *can* be used to define the scope for a cursor in embedded SQL). So a view cannot be "any derivable relation," and the relational closure property breaks down. Likewise, INSERT ... SELECT cannot be used to assign the union of two relations to another relation. Yet another consequence of the special treatment given to UNION is that it is not possible to apply a builtin function such as AVG to a union. See the following section.

I conclude this discussion of SQL expressions by noting a few additional (and apparently arbitrary) restrictions.

- The predicate C BETWEEN A AND B is equivalent to the predicate A < = C AND C < = B—*except* that B (but not A or C!) can be a column-expression (subquery) in the second formulation but not in the first.

- The predicate "field comparison (subquery)" must be written in the order shown and not the other way around; i.e., the expression "(subquery) comparison field" is illegal.

- If we regard SELECT, UPDATE, and INSERT all as special kinds of assignment statement—in each case, the value of some expression is being assigned to some variable (a newly created variable, in the case of INSERT)—then source values for those assignments can be specified as scalar-expressions (involving database fields, host variables, constants, and scalar operators) for SELECT and UPDATE, but must be specified as simple host variables or constants for INSERT. Thus, for example, the following is valid:

```
SELECT :X + 1
FROM   T
   ...
```

and so is:

```
UPDATE T
SET    F = :X + 1
   ...
```

but the following is not:

```
INSERT INTO T ( F )
       VALUES ( :X + 1 )
```

- Given the tables

```
S ( S#, SNAME, STATUS, CITY )
P ( P#, PNAME, COLOR, WEIGHT, CITY )
```

the SELECT statement

```
SELECT COLOR
FROM   P
WHERE  CITY =
     ( SELECT CITY
       FROM   P
       WHERE  P# = 'P1' )
```

is legal, but the UPDATE statement

```
UPDATE P
SET    COLOR = 'Blue'
WHERE  CITY =
     ( SELECT CITY
       FROM   P
       WHERE  P# = 'P1' )
```

is not. Worse, neither is the UPDATE statement

```
UPDATE P
SET    CITY =
     ( SELECT CITY
       FROM   S
       WHERE  S# = 'S1' )
WHERE  ...
```

Even worse, given

```
EMP      ( EMP#, SALARY )
BONUSES ( EMP#, BONUS )
```

the following (potentially very useful) UPDATE is also illegal:

```
UPDATE EMP
SET     SALARY = SALARY + ( SELECT BONUS
                            FROM   BONUSES
                            WHERE  EMP# = EMP.EMP# )
```

(Actually there is a slight problem in this last example. Suppose a given employee number, say e, appears in the EMP table but not in the BO-NUSES table. Then the parenthesized expression will evaluate to null for employee e, and the UPDATE will therefore set e's salary to null as well—whereas what is wanted is clearly for e's salary to remain unchanged. To fix this problem, we need to replace the parenthesized expression by (say)

```
ROWMAX ( ( SELECT BONUS ... EMP.EMP# ) , 0 )
```

where ROWMAX is a function that operates by (a) ignoring any of its arguments that evaluate to null and then (b) returning the maximum of those that are left, if any, or null otherwise. Note that ROWMAX is different in kind from the builtin functions currently provided in SQL—it is in fact a scalar-valued function, whose arguments are scalar-expressions.)

LACK OF ORTHOGONALITY: BUILTIN FUNCTIONS

Frankly, there is so much confusion in this area that it is difficult to criticize it coherently. The basic point, however, is that the argument to a function such as SUM is a column of scalar values and the result is a single scalar value; hence, orthogonality dictates that (a) any column-expression should be permitted as the argument, and (b) the function-reference should be permitted in any context in which a scalar can appear. However, (a) the argument is in fact specified in a most unorthodox manner, which means in turn that (b) function references can actually appear only in a rather small set of special-case situations. In particular, function-references cannot appear nested inside other function-references. In addition to this fact, functions are subject to a large number of peculiar and apparently arbitrary restrictions.

Before getting into details, I should point out that SQL in fact supports two distinct categories of function, not however in any uniform syntactic style. The two categories can be referred to, informally, as *column* and *table* functions, respectively. I discuss each in turn.

Column Functions

Column functions are the ones that one usually thinks of whenever functions are mentioned in connexion with SQL. A column function is a function that reduces an entire column of scalar values to a single value. The functions in this category are COUNT [excluding COUNT(*)], SUM, AVG, MAX, and MIN. A functional notation is used to represent these functions; however, as suggested above, the scoping rules for representing the argument are somewhat unconventional. Consider the following database (suppliers and parts):

```
S  ( S#, SNAME, STATUS, CITY )
P  ( P#, PNAME, COLOR, WEIGHT, CITY )
SP ( S#, P#, QTY )
```

and consider also the following query:

```
SELECT SUM (QTY)
FROM   SP
```

The argument to SUM here is in fact the entire column of QTY values in table SP, and a more conventional syntax would accordingly be

```
SUM ( SELECT QTY
      FROM    SP )
```

(though once again the keyword SELECT seems rather obtrusive; QTY FROM SP, or—even better—simply SP.QTY, would be more orthodox). As another example, the query

```
SELECT SUM (QTY)
FROM   SP
WHERE  P# = 'P2'
```

would more conventionally be expressed as

```
SUM ( SELECT QTY
      FROM    SP
      WHERE   P# = 'P2' )
```

or (better) as:

```
SUM ( SP.QTY WHERE SP.P# = 'P2' )
```

As it is, the argument has to be determined by reference to the context. An immediate consequence of this fact is that a query such as "Find parts supplied in a total quantity of more than 1000" cannot be expressed in a natural style. First, the syntax

```
SELECT P#
FROM   SP
WHERE  SUM (QTY) > 1000
```

clearly does not work, either with SQL's rules for argument scope or with any other rules. The most logical formulation (but retaining a SQL-like style) is

```
SELECT DISTINCT SPX.P#
FROM    SP SPX
WHERE   SUM ( SELECT QTY
              FROM   SP SPY
              WHERE  SPY.P# = SPX.P# )
        > 1000
```

(The DISTINCT is required because of SQL's rules concerning duplicate elimination.) However, the normal SQL formulation would be

```
SELECT P#
FROM    SP
GROUP   BY P#
HAVING SUM (QTY) > 1000
```

Note that the user is not really interested in grouping per se in this query; by writing GROUP BY, he or she is in effect telling the system how to *execute* the query, instead of simply stating what the query *is*. In other words, the statement begins to look more like a prescription for solving the problem, rather than a simple description of what the problem is.

More important, it is necessary to introduce the HAVING clause, the justification for which is not immediately apparent to the user ("Why can't I use a WHERE clause?"). *The HAVING clause—and the GROUP BY clause also, come to that (see later)—are needed in SQL ONLY as a consequence of the column-function argument scoping rules.* As a matter of fact, it is possible to produce a SQL formulation of this example that does not use GROUP BY or HAVING at all, and is fairly close to "the most logical formulation" suggested earlier:

```
SELECT DISTINCT P#
FROM    SP SPX
WHERE   1000 <
        ( SELECT SUM (QTY)
          FROM   SP SPY
          WHERE  SPY.P# = SPX.P# )
```

As mentioned earlier, current SQL requires the predicate in the outer WHERE clause to be written as shown (i.e., in the order "constant-comparison-(subquery)," instead of the other way around).

An important consequence of all of the foregoing is that *SQL cannot support arbitrary retrievals on arbitrary views*. Consider the following example.

View definition:

```
CREATE VIEW PQ ( P#, TOTQTY )
     AS SELECT P#, SUM(QTY)
        FROM   SP
        GROUP  BY P#
```

Attempted query:

```
SELECT *
FROM    PQ
WHERE   TOTQTY > 1000
```

This statement is invalid, because the "merging" process described earlier leads to something like the following:

```
SELECT P#, SUM(QTY)
FROM    SP
WHERE   SUM(QTY) > 1000
GROUP   BY P#
```

and this is not a legal SELECT statement. Likewise, the attempted query

```
SELECT AVG (TOTQTY)
FROM    PQ
```

also does not work, for similar reasons.

The following is another striking example of the unobviousness of the scoping rules. Consider the following two queries:

```
SELECT SUM (QTY)           SELECT SUM (QTY)
FROM    SP                 FROM    SP
                           GROUP   BY P#
```

In the first case, the query returns a single value; the argument to the SUM invocation is the entire QTY column. In the second case, the query returns multiple values; the SUM function is invoked multiple times, once for each of the groups created by the GROUP BY clause. Notice how the meaning of the syntactic construct "SUM (QTY)" is dependent on the context. In fact, SQL is moving out of the strict tabular framework of the relational model in this second example and introducing a new kind of data object, viz. *a set of tables* (which is of course not the same thing as a table at all). GROUP BY converts a table into a set of tables. In the example, SUM is then applied to (a column within) each member of that set. A more logical syntax might look something like the following:

```
APPLY ( SUM, SELECT QTY
             FROM ( GROUP SP BY P# ) )
```

where "GROUP SP BY P#" produces the set of tables, "SELECT QTY FROM (...)" extracts a corresponding set of columns, and APPLY applies the function specified as its first argument to each column in the set of columns specified as its second argument, producing a set of scalars—i.e., another column. (I am not suggesting a concrete syntax here, only indicating a possible direction for a systematic development of such a syntax.)

As a matter of fact, GROUP BY would be logically unnecessary in the foregoing example anyway if column function invocations were more systematic:

```
SELECT DISTINCT SPX.P#, SUM ( SELECT QTY
                               FROM   SP SPY
                               WHERE  SPY.P# = SPX.P# )
FROM    SP SPX
```

This formulation also shows, incidentally, that it might be preferable to declare aliases (range variables) such as SPX and SPY by means of separate statements before they are used. As it is, the use of such variables may well precede their definition, possibly by a considerable amount. Although there is nothing logically wrong with this, it does make the statements difficult to read (and write) on occasion.

Yet another consequence of the scoping rules (already touched on a couple of times) is that it is not possible to nest column function references. Extending the earlier example of generating the total quantity per part (i.e., a column of values, each of which is a total quantity), suppose we now wanted to find the *average* total quantity per part—i.e., the average of that column of values. The logical formulation is something like:

```
AVG ( APPLY ( SUM, SELECT QTY
                   FROM ( GROUP SP BY P# ) ) )
```

But (as already stated) existing SQL cannot handle this problem at all in a single expression.

Let us now leave the scoping rules and consider some additional points. Each of SUM, AVG, MAX, and MIN can optionally have its argument qualified by the operator DISTINCT. (COUNT *must* have its argument so qualified, though it would seem that there is no intrinsic justification for this requirement. For MAX and MIN such qualification is legal but has no semantic effect.) If and only if DISTINCT is *not* specified, then the column argument can be a "computed" column, i.e., the result of an arithmetic expression—for example:

```
SELECT AVG ( X + Y )
FROM    T
    ...
```

(X and Y here must be column-names or constants, incidentally, not arbitrary scalar-expressions.) And if and only if DISTINCT is *not* specified (again), the function reference can itself be an operand in an arithmetic expression—for example:

```
SELECT AVG ( X ) * 3
FROM   T
       . . .
```

In current SQL, null values are always eliminated from the argument to a column function, regardless of whether DISTINCT is specified. However, this should be regarded as a property of the existing functions specifically, rather than as a necessary property of all column functions. In fact, it would be better *not* to ignore nulls but to introduce a new function whose effect is to reduce a given column to another in which nulls have been eliminated—and, of course, to allow this new function to be used completely orthogonally.

Table Functions

Table functions are functions that operate on an entire table (not necessarily just on a single column). There are four functions in this category, two that return a scalar value and two that return another table. The two that return a scalar value are COUNT(*) and EXISTS.

- COUNT(*) is basically very similar to the column functions discussed above. Thus, most of the comments made above apply here also. For example, the query:

```
SELECT COUNT(*)
FROM   SP
```

would more logically be expressed as

```
COUNT ( SELECT *
        FROM   SP )
```

or (better) as:

```
COUNT ( SP )
```

COUNT(*) does *not* ignore nulls (i.e., all-null rows) in its argument, unlike the column functions.

- EXISTS, interestingly enough, does use a more logical syntax. For example:

```
SELECT *
FROM   S
WHERE  EXISTS
     ( SELECT *
       FROM   SP
       WHERE  SP.S# = S.S# )
```

—though the EXISTS argument would look better if the "SELECT * FROM" could be elided:

```
SELECT *
FROM   S
WHERE  EXISTS ( SP WHERE SP.S# = S.S# )
```

or (better still):

```
S WHERE EXISTS ( SP WHERE SP.S# = S.S# )
```

EXISTS takes a table as its argument (though that table *must* be expressed as a SELECT-expression, not just as a table-name) and returns the value *true* if that table is nonempty, *false* otherwise. (A table that contains only null values—i.e., all-null rows—is not considered to be empty, incidentally.) Because there is currently no BOOLEAN or BIT data type in SQL, EXISTS can be used only in a WHERE clause, not (e.g.) in a SELECT clause (lack of orthogonality once again).

Now I turn to the functions that return another table, viz. DISTINCT and UNION.

- DISTINCT takes a table and returns another which is a copy of that first table except that redundant duplicate rows have been removed (rows that are entirely null are considered as duplicates of each other in this process—that is, the result will contain at most one all-null row). Once again the syntax is unconventional. For instance:

```
SELECT DISTINCT S#
FROM   SP
```

  instead of:

```
DISTINCT ( SELECT S#
           FROM   SP )
```

  or (better):

```
DISTINCT ( SP.S# )
```

  There is an apparently arbitrary restriction that DISTINCT may appear at most once in any given SELECT statement.
- UNION takes two tables (each of which must be represented by means of a SELECT-expression, not just as a simple table-name) and produces another table that is their union. It is written as an infix operator. Because of the unorthodox syntax, it is not possible (as mentioned before) to apply a column function such as AVG to a union of two columns.

Note: I consider UNION, alone of the operators of the relational algebra, as a function in SQL merely because of the special syntactic treatment it is given. SQL is really a hybrid of the relational algebra and the relational calculus; it is not precisely the same as either, though it does lean somewhat toward the calculus.

LACK OF ORTHOGONALITY: MISCELLANEOUS ITEMS

Indicator Variables

Let F be a database field that can accept null values, and let HF be a corresponding host variable, with associated indicator variable HN. Then:

```
SELECT F
INTO    :HF:HN
   ...
```

is legal, and so are

```
INSERT ...
VALUES ( :HF:HN ... )
```

and

```
UPDATE ...
SET    F = :HF:HN
  ...
```

But the following is not:

```
SELECT ... ( or UPDATE or DELETE )
   ...
WHERE  F = :HF:HN
```

References to Current Data

Let C be a cursor that currently identifies a record of table T. Then it is possible to designate the "CURRENT OF C"—i.e., the record currently identified by C—as the target of an UPDATE or DELETE statement, e.g., as follows:

```
UPDATE T
SET    ...
WHERE  CURRENT OF C
```

Incidentally, a more logical formulation would be

```
UPDATE CURRENT OF C
SET    ...
```

Specifying the table-name T is redundant (this point is recognized in the syntax of FETCH, see later), and in any case "CURRENT OF C" is not the same kind of construct as the more usual WHERE-predicate (e.g., "SALARY > 20000"). Nor is it permitted to combine "CURRENT OF C" with other predicates and write (e.g.) "WHERE CURRENT OF C AND SALARY > 20000." But to return to the main argument: Although the (first) UPDATE statement above is legal, the analogous SELECT statement

```
SELECT ...
FROM    T
WHERE   CURRENT OF C
```

is not. Nor can fields within the "CURRENT OF C" be simply referenced (i.e., even without being retrieved)—e.g., the following is also illegal:

```
SELECT *
FROM    EMP
WHERE   DEPT# =
    ( SELECT DEPT#
      FROM    DEPT
      WHERE   CURRENT OF D )
```

Turning now to the FETCH statement, we have here an example of bundling. "FETCH C INTO ..." is effectively a shorthand for a sequence of two distinct operations—

```
STEP C TO NEXT

SELECT * INTO ... WHERE CURRENT OF C
```

—the first of which (STEP) advances C to the next record in T in accordance with the ordering associated with C, and the second of which (SELECT) then retrieves that record. (Note that that SELECT does not logically require any FROM clause, incidentally.) Replacing the FETCH statement by two more primitive statements in this way would have a number of advantages:

(a) It is clearer;

(b) It is a more logical structure (incidentally, "FETCH C" does not really make intuitive sense—it is not the *cursor* that is being fetched);

(c) It would allow SELECTs of individual fields of the current record (i.e., "SELECT field-name" as well as "SELECT *");

(d) It would allow selective (and repeated) access to that current record (e.g., "SELECT F" followed by "SELECT G," both selecting fields of the same record);

(e) It would be extendable to other kinds of STEP operation—e.g., STEP C TO PREVIOUS (say).

In fact I would go further. First, note that "CURRENT OF C" is an example of a row-expression. Let us therefore introduce a (new) FETCH statement, whose argument is a row-expression (as opposed to SELECT, whose argument is a table-expression), and whose function is to retrieve the row represented by that expression. Next, outlaw SELECT where FETCH is really intended. Next, introduce "(row-expression).field-name"—e.g., (CURRENT OF C).F—as a new form of scalar-expression. Finally, support all of these constructs orthogonally. Thus, for example, all of the following would be legal:

```
FETCH CURRENT OF C INTO ...

FETCH (CURRENT OF C).F INTO ...

SELECT *
FROM    EMP
WHERE   DEPT# = (CURRENT OF D).DEPT#

UPDATE CURRENT OF C
SET    ...

DELETE CURRENT OF C
```

The examples illustrate the point that "CURRENT OF C" is really a very clumsy notation, incidentally, but an improved syntax is beyond the scope of this paper. See [5] for a preferable alternative.

ORDER BY in Cursor Declaration

Specifying ORDER BY in the declaration of cursor C means that the statements UPDATE/DELETE ... CURRENT OF C are illegal (in fact, the declaration of C cannot include a FOR UPDATE clause if ORDER BY is specified). The rationale for this restriction is that ORDER BY may cause the program to operate on a copy instead of on the actual data, and hence that updates and deletes would be meaningless; but the restriction is unfortunate, to say the least. Consider a program that needs to process employees in department number order and needs to update some of them as it goes. The user is forced to code along the following lines:

```
EXEC SQL DECLARE C CURSOR FOR
                SELECT EMP#, DEPT#, ...
                FROM    EMP
                ORDER BY DEPT# ;

EXEC SQL OPEN C ;
DO WHILE more-to-come ;
    EXEC SQL FETCH C INTO :EMP#, :DEPT#, ... ;
    if this record needs updating, then
    EXEC SQL UPDATE EMP
            SET    ...
            WHERE  EMP# = :EMP# /* instead of CURRENT OF C */ ;
END ;
EXEC SQL CLOSE C ;
```

The UPDATE statement here is an "out-of-the-blue" UPDATE, not the CURRENT form. Problems:

(a) The update will be visible through cursor C if and only if C is running through the real data, not a copy.
(b) If cursor C is running through the real data, and if the UPDATE changes the value of DEPT#, the effect on the position of cursor C within the table is apparently undefined.

I cannot help pointing out also that the FOR UPDATE clause is a little mysterious (its real significance is not immediately apparent); it is also logically unnecessary. The whole of this area smacks of a most unfortunate loss of physical data independence.

The NULL Constant

The keyword NULL may be regarded as a "builtin constant," representing the null value. However, it cannot appear in all positions in which a scalar constant can appear. For example, the statement

```
SELECT  F, NULL
FROM    T
```

is illegal. This is unfortunate, since the ability to select NULL is precisely what is required in order to construct an outer join (in the absence of direct system support for such an operation). See [4].

Empty Sets

Let T be a table-expression. If T happens to evaluate to an empty set, then what happens depends on the context in which T appears. For example, consider the expressions

```
SELECT  SALARY              and       SELECT  AVG (SALARY)
FROM    EMP                           FROM    EMP
WHERE   DEPT# = 'D3'                   WHERE   DEPT# = 'D3'
```

and suppose that department D3 currently has no employees. Note that the second of these expressions represents the application of the AVG function to the result of the first; as pointed out earlier, it would more logically be written as

```
AVG (SELECT  SALARY
     FROM    EMP
     WHERE   DEPT# = 'D3')
```

- The statement

```
EXEC SQL SELECT SALARY
         INTO    :S:SN
         FROM    EMP
         WHERE   DEPT# = 'D3' ;
```

gives "not found" (SQLCODE = +100, host variables S and SN unchanged).

- The statement

```
EXEC SQL SELECT AVG (SALARY)
         INTO    :S:SN
         FROM    EMP
         WHERE   DEPT# = 'D3' ;
```

sets host variable SN to an unspecified negative value to indicate that the value of the expression is null. The effect on host variable S is unspecified.

- The statement

```
EXEC SQL SELECT ...
         INTO    :S:SN
         FROM    ...
         WHERE   field IN
                 ( SELECT SALARY
                   FROM    EMP
                   WHERE   DEPT# = 'D3' ) ;
```

gives "not found" (at the *outer* level).

- The statement

```
EXEC SQL SELECT ...
         INTO    :S:SN
         FROM    ...
         WHERE   field =
                 ( SELECT SALARY
                   FROM    EMP
                   WHERE   DEPT# = 'D3' ) ;
```

also gives "not found" at the outer level, though there is a good argument for treating this case as an error, as follows: The parenthesized expression "(SELECT SALARY . . .)" should really be regarded as a shorthand for the expression "*UNIQUE* (SELECT SALARY . . .)," where UNIQUE is a quantifier (analogous to EXISTS) meaning "there exists *exactly one*"—or, in other words, a function whose effect is to return the single element from a singleton set, and to raise an error if that set does not in fact contain exactly one member. Note that an error *would* be raised in the example if the parenthesized expression yielded a set having *more than one* member (which in general, of course, it would).

- The statement

```
EXEC SQL SELECT ...
         INTO   :S:SN
         FROM   ...
         WHERE  field =
              ( SELECT AVG (SALARY)
                FROM   EMP
                WHERE  DEPT# = 'D3' ) ;
```

also gives "not found" at the outer level.

Inconsistent Syntax

Compare the following:

```
SELECT * FROM T ...

UPDATE        T ...

DELETE   FROM T ...

INSERT   INTO T ...

( FETCH C ... )
```

A more consistent approach would be to define "table-expressions" (as suggested earlier in this paper), and then to recognize that SELECT, UPDATE, etc., are each *operators*, one of whose arguments is such a table-expression. (A problem that immediately arises is that a simple table-name is currently *not* a valid table-expression!—i.e., instead of being able to write simply "T," the user has to write "SELECT * FROM T." This point has been mentioned before, and is of course easily remedied.)

Note, too, that the syntax "UPDATE T SET F = . . ." does not extend very nicely to a form of UPDATE in which an entire record is replaced en bloc ("SET * = . . ."?). And this touches on yet another point, viz: SQL currently provides whole-record SELECT (and FETCH) and INSERT operators, but no whole-record UPDATE operator. (DELETE of course *must* be a "whole-record" operation, by definition.)

Long Fields (LONG VARCHAR, or VARCHAR(n) with n > 254)

Long fields are subject to numerous restrictions. Here are some of them (this may or may not be an exhaustive list). A long field:

- Cannot be referenced in a predicate
- Cannot be indexed
- Cannot be referenced in SELECT DISTINCT

- Cannot be referenced in GROUP BY
- Cannot be referenced in ORDER BY
- Cannot be referenced in COUNT, MAX, or MIN (note that SUM and AVG would make no sense anyway)
- Cannot be involved in a UNION
- Cannot be involved in a "subquery" (i.e., column-expression)
- Cannot be INSERTed from a constant or SELECT-expression
- Cannot be UPDATEd from a constant (UPDATE from NULL is legal, however)

UNION Restrictions

Union is not permitted on long fields or in a subquery (in particular, in a view definition). Also, the data types of corresponding items in a UNION must be *exactly* the same:

- If the data type is DECIMAL(p,q), then p must be the same for both items and q must be the same for both items
- If the data type is CHAR(n), then n must be the same for both items
- If the data type is VARCHAR(n), then n must be the same for both items
- If NOT NULL applies to either item, then it must apply to both items

Given these restrictions, it is particularly unfortunate that a character string constant such as 'ABC' is treated as a *varying* string (maximum length 3, in this example).

Note also that UNION always eliminates duplicates. There is no "DISTINCT/ALL" option as there is with a simple SELECT; and if there were, the default would have to be DISTINCT (for compatibility reasons), whereas the default for a simple SELECT is ALL.

GROUP BY Restrictions

GROUP BY:

- Only works to one level (it can construct a "set of tables" but not a "set of sets of tables," etc.)
- Can only have simple fields as arguments (unlike ORDER BY)

The fact is, as indicated earlier in the discussion of functions, an orthogonal treatment of GROUP BY would require a thorough treatment of an entirely new kind of data object, namely the "set of tables"—presumably a major undertaking.

NULL Anomalies

- Null values are implemented by hidden fields in the database. However, it is necessary to expose those fields in the interface to a host language such as PL/I, because PL/I has no notion of null (in the SQL sense, that is). As an example, if F and G are two fields in table T, the UPDATE statement to set F equal to G is:

```
EXEC SQL UPDATE T
        SET     F = G ...
```

—but the UPDATE statement to set F equal to a host variable H (with corresponding null indicator variable HN) is:

```
EXEC SQL UPDATE T
        SET     F = :H:HN ...
```

(assuming in both cases that the source of the assignment might be null).

- Indicator variables are not permitted in all contexts where host variables can appear (as already discussed).

- To test in a WHERE clause whether a field is null, SQL provides the special comparison "field IS NULL." It is not intuitively obvious why the user has to write "field IS NULL" and not "field = NULL"—especially as the syntax "field = NULL" *is* used in the SET clause of the UPDATE statement to update a field to the null value. (In fact, the WHERE clause "WHERE field = NULL" is syntactically illegal.)

- Null values are considered as duplicates of each other for the purposes of UNIQUE and DISTINCT and ORDER BY but not for the purposes of WHERE and GROUP BY. Null values are also considered as greater than all nonnull values for the purposes of ORDER BY but not for the purposes of WHERE.

- Null values are always eliminated from the argument to a builtin function such as SUM or AVG, regardless of whether DISTINCT is specified in the function reference—except for the case of COUNT(*), which counts all rows, including duplicates and including all-null rows. Thus, for example, given:

```
SELECT AVG (STATUS) FROM S    --    Result: x

SELECT SUM (STATUS) FROM S    --    Result: y

SELECT COUNT(*)     FROM S    --    Result: z
```

there is no guarantee that x = y/z.

- Likewise, the function reference SUM(F) is *not* semantically equivalent to the expression

```
f1 + f2 + ... + fn
```

where f1, f2, ..., fn are the values appearing in field F at the time the function is evaluated. Perhaps even more counterintuitively, the expression

```
SUM ( F1 + F2 )
```

is not equivalent to the expression

```
SUM ( F1 ) + SUM ( F2 )      .
```

Host Variables

Host variables are permitted wherever constants are permitted, also in the INTO clause of SELECT and FETCH, but nowhere else. In particular, table-names and field-names cannot be represented by host variables.

Introduced Names

The user can introduce names ("aliases"—actually range variables) for tables—e.g., FROM T TX—but not for scalars. This latter could easily be done via the SELECT clause—e.g., SELECT F FX. Such a facility would be particularly useful when the scalar is in fact represented by an operational expression—e.g., SELECT A + B C, D + E F, ... The names C, F, . . . could be used in WHERE or ORDER BY or GROUP BY or as an inherited name in CREATE VIEW (etc.).

Legal INSERTs/UPDATEs/DELETEs

Certain INSERT, UPDATE, and DELETE statements are not allowed. For example, consider the requirement "Delete all suppliers with a status less than the average." The statement

```
DELETE
FROM    S
WHERE   STATUS <
        ( SELECT AVG (STATUS)
          FROM    S )
```

is illegal: The FROM clause in the subquery is not allowed to refer to the table against which the DELETE is to be done. Likewise, the UPDATE statement

```
UPDATE  S
SET     STATUS = 0
WHERE   STATUS <
        ( SELECT AVG (STATUS)
          FROM   S )
```

is also illegal, for analogous reasons. Third, the statement

```
INSERT INTO T
       SELECT * FROM T
```

(which might be regarded as a perfectly natural way to "double up" on the contents of table T) is also illegal, again for analogous reasons.

FORMAL DEFINITION

As indicated earlier in this paper, it would be misleading to suggest that SQL does not possess a formal definition. However, as was also indicated earlier, that definition [10] was produced "after the fact." In some respects, therefore, it represents a definition of the way implementations actually work rather than the way a "pure" language ought to be (although it must be said that many of the criticisms of the present paper have indeed been addressed in [10]). At the same time, it provides definitive answers to some questions that are not in agreement with the way IBM SQL actually works! Furthermore, there still appear to be some areas where the definition is not yet precise enough. Examples of all of these aspects are given below.

- Cursor positioning

    Let C be a cursor that is currently associated with a set of records of type R. Suppose moreover that the ordering associated with C is defined by values of field R.F. If C is positioned on a record r and r is deleted, C goes into the "before" state—i.e., it is now positioned "before" record r1, where r1 is the immediate successor of r with respect to the ordering associated with C—or, if there is no such successor record, then it goes into the "after" state—i.e., it is "after" the last record in the set. (Note: The "after" state is possible even if the set is empty.)
    Questions:

(a) If C is "before r1" and a new record r is inserted with a value of R.F such that r logically belongs between r1 and r1's predecessor (if any), what happens to C? [Answer: Implementation-defined.]

(b) Does it make a difference if the new record r logically precedes or follows the old record r that C was positioned on before that record was deleted? [Answer: Implementation-defined.]

(c) Does it make a difference if C was actually running through a copy of the real set of records? [Answer: Implementation-defined.]

Note for cases (a)-(c) that it *is* guaranteed that the next "FETCH C" will retrieve record r1 (provided no other DELETEs etc. occur in the interim).

(d) What if the new r is not an INSERTed record but an UPDATEd record? [Answer: Not defined.]

(e) If C is positioned on a record r and the value of field F in that record is updated (not via cursor C, of course), what happens to C? [Answer: Not defined.]

- LOCK statement

Does LOCK SHARED acquire an S lock or an SIX lock [9]? If the answer is S, are updates permitted? When are locks acquired via LOCK TABLE released?

- Name resolution

First, consider the two statements

```
SELECT  S#
FROM    S
WHERE   CITY = 'London'

SELECT  P#
FROM    P
WHERE   CITY = 'London'
```

The meaning of the unqualified name CITY depends on the context—it is taken as S.CITY in the first of these examples and as P.CITY in the second. But now suppose the columns are renamed SCITY and PCITY respectively, so that now the names are globally unique, and consider the query "Find suppliers located in cities in which no parts are stored." The obvious formulation of this query is

```
SELECT  S#
FROM    S
WHERE   NOT EXISTS
        ( SELECT  *
          FROM    P
          WHERE   PCITY = SCITY )
```

However, this statement is invalid. SQL assumes that "SCITY" is shorthand for "P.SCITY," and then complains that no such field exists.

The following statement, by contrast, is perfectly valid:

```
SELECT  S#
FROM    S
WHERE   NOT EXISTS
      ( SELECT *
        FROM    P
        WHERE   PCITY = S.SCITY )
```

So also is:

```
SELECT  S#
FROM    S SX
WHERE   NOT EXISTS
      ( SELECT *
        FROM    P
        WHERE   PCITY = SX.SCITY )
```

Is the following legal? ("Suppliers who supply P1 and P2.")

```
SELECT  *
FROM    S
WHERE   EXISTS ( SELECT *
                 FROM    SP SPX
                 WHERE   SPX.S# = S.S#
                 AND     SPX.P# = 'P1'
                 AND     EXISTS ( SELECT *
                                  FROM    SP SPX
                                  WHERE   SPX.S# = S.S#
                                  AND     SPX.P# = 'P2' ) )
```

What if "FROM SP SPX" is replaced by "FROM SP" (twice) and all other occurrences of "SPX" are replaced by "SP"? And is the following legal?

```
SELECT  *
FROM    S
WHERE   EXISTS ( SELECT *
                 FROM    SP SPX
                 WHERE   SPX.S# = S.S#
                 AND     SPX.P# = 'P1' )
AND     EXISTS ( SELECT *
                 FROM    SP SPX
                 WHERE   SPX.S# = S.S#
                 AND     SPX.P# = 'P2' )
```

(etc.). In other words: What *are* the name scoping rules?

There is another point to be made while on the subject of name resolution, incidentally. Consider the statement

```
SELECT S.S#, P.P#
FROM   S, P
WHERE  S.CITY = P.CITY
```

(reverting to the simple name CITY for each of the two tables). This statement is (conceptually) evaluated as follows:

- Form the product of S and P; call the result TEMP1
- Restrict TEMP1 according to the predicate S.CITY = P.CITY; call the result TEMP2
- Project TEMP2 over the columns S.S# and P.P#

But how can this be done? The predicate "S.CITY = P.CITY" does not refer to any columns of TEMP1 (it refers to columns of S and P, obviously). Similarly, S.S# and P.P# are not columns of TEMP2. In order for these references to be interpreted appropriately, it is necessary to introduce certain *name inheritance rules*, indicating how result tables inherit their column-names from their source tables (which may of course themselves also be [intermediate] result tables, with inherited column-names of their own). Such rules are currently defined only very informally, if at all. Such rules become even more important if SQL is to provide support for nested expressions, as suggested earlier in this paper.

- Base vs. copy data

When exactly does a cursor iterate over the real "base data" and when over a copy?

- Binding of "SELECT *"

When exactly does "*" become bound to a specific set of field-names? [Answer: Implementation-defined—but this seems an unfortunate aspect to leave to the implementer, especially as the binding is likely to be different for different *uses* of the feature (e.g., it may depend on whether the "*" appears in a program or in a view definition).]

MISMATCH WITH HOST LANGUAGES

The general point here is that there are far too many frivolous distinctions between SQL and the host language in which it happens to be embedded; also that in some cases SQL has failed to benefit from lessons learned in the design of those host languages. Generally, orthogonality suggests that what is useful on one side of the interface in the way of data structuring and access for "permanent" (i.e., database) data is likely to be useful on the other side also for "temporary" (i.e., local) data; thus, a distinct sublanguage is the wrong approach, and a two-level store is wrong too (fundamentally so!). Some specific points:

- SQL does not exploit the exception-handling capabilities of the host (e.g., PL/I ON-conditions). This point and (even more so) the following one mean that SQL does not exactly encourage the production of well-structured, quality programs, and that in some respects SQL programming is at a lower level than that of the host.

- SQL does not exploit the control structures of the host (loop constructs in particular). See the previous point.

- SQL objects (tables, cursors, etc.) are not known and cannot be referenced in the host environment.

- Host objects can be referenced in the SQL environment only if:
  - They are specially declared (may not apply to all hosts)
  - They are scalars or certain limited types of structure (in particular, they are not arrays)
  - The references are marked with a colon prefix (admittedly only in some contexts—but in my opinion "some" is worse than "all")
  - The references are constrained to certain limited contexts (e.g., they can appear in a SELECT clause but not a FROM clause)
  - The references are constrained to certain limited formats (e.g., no subscripting, only limited dot qualification, etc.)

  Host procedures cannot be referenced in the SQL environment at all.

- SQL object names and host object names are independent and may clash. SQL names do not follow the scoping rules of the host.

- SQL keywords and host keywords are independent and may clash (e.g., PL/I SELECT vs. SQL SELECT).

- SQL and host may have different name qualification rules (e.g., T.F in SQL vs. F OF T in COBOL; and note that the SQL form must be used even for host object references in the SQL environment).

- SQL and host may have different data type conversion rules.

- SQL and host may have different expression evaluation rules (e.g., SQL division and varying string comparison differ from their PL/I analogs, at least in SQL/DS).

- SQL and host may have different Boolean operators (AND, OR, and NOT in SQL vs. &, |, and ~ in PL/I).

- SQL and host may have different comparison operators (e.g., COBOL has IS NUMERIC, SQL has BETWEEN [and several others]).

- SQL imposes statement ordering restrictions that may be alien to the host.

- SQL DECLARE cannot be abbreviated to DCL, unlike PL/I DECLARE.

- Null is handled differently on the two sides of the interface.
- Function references have different formats on the two sides of the interface.
- SQL name resolution rules are different from those of the host.
- Cursors are a clumsy way of bridging the gap between the database and the program. A much better method would be to associate a query with a conventional *sequential file* in the host program, and then let the program use conventional READ, REWRITE, and DELETE statements to access that file (maybe WRITE statements too).
- The "structure declarations" in CREATE TABLE should use the standard COBOL or PL/I (etc.) syntax. As it is, it is doubtful whether they can be elegantly extended to deal with minor structures (composite fields) or arrays, should such extensions ever prove desirable (they will).
- The SQL parameter mechanism is regressive, clumsy, ad hoc, restrictive, and different from that of the host.

MISSING FUNCTION

The "missing function" here refers primarily to the embedded (programming) version of SQL. Other missing function is discussed later under the heading "Aspects of the Relational Model Not Supported." In any case, the list of desirable extensions for any given language is probably always endless. But the items listed below are particularly obvious omissions from a programmer's standpoint. Note: It is obviously possible to extend the existing language to incorporate most if not all of these features. I include them only for completeness.

- Ability to override WHENEVER NOT FOUND at the level of an individual statement.
- "Whole-record" UPDATE.
- Procedure call instead of GO TO on WHENEVER.
- Cursor stepping other than "next."
- Cursor comparison.
- Cursor assignment.
- Cursor constants.
- Cursor arrays.
- Dynamically created cursors and/or cursor stacks.
- Reusable cursors.

- Ability to access a unique record and keep a cursor on it without having to go through separate DECLARE, OPEN, and FETCH: e.g., "FETCH UNIQUE (EMP WHERE EMP# = 'E2') SET (C) ;".

- Fine control over locking.

MISTAKES

- Null values

I have argued against null values at length elsewhere [6], and I will not repeat those arguments here. In my opinion the null value concept is far more trouble than it is worth. Certainly it has never been properly thought through in the existing SQL implementations (see the discussion under "Lack of Orthogonality: Miscellaneous Items," earlier). For example, the fact that functions such as AVG simply ignore null values in their argument violates what should surely be a fundamental principle, viz: *The system should never produce a (spuriously) precise answer to a query when the data involved in that query is itself imprecise.* At least the system should offer the user the explicit option either to ignore nulls or to treat their presence as an exception.

- Unique indexes

Field uniqueness is a logical property of the data, not a physical property of an access path. It should be specified on CREATE TABLE, not on CREATE INDEX. Specifying it on CREATE INDEX is an unfortunate bundling, and may lead to a loss of data independence (dropping the index puts the integrity of the database at risk).

- FROM clause

The only function of the FROM clause that is not actually redundant is to allow the introduction of range variables, and that function would be better provided in some more elegant manner. (The normal use, as exemplified by the expression SELECT F FROM T, could better be handled by the expression SELECT T.F, especially since this latter expression—with an accompanying but redundant FROM clause—is already legal SQL.)

- Punning

SQL does not make a clear distinction between tables, record types, and range variables. Instead, it allows a single symbol to stand for any one of those objects, and leaves the interpretation to depend on context. Conceptual clarity would dictate that it at least be *possible* always to distinguish among these different constructs (i.e., syntactically), even if there are rules that allow such punning games to be played when intuitively convenient. Otherwise it may be possible that—for example— extendability may suffer, though I have to admit that I cannot at the time of writing point to any concrete problems. (But it shouldn't be *necessary* to have to defend the principle of a one-to-one correspondence between names and objects!)

While on the subject of punning, I might also mention the point that SQL is ambivalent as to the meaning of the term "table." Sometimes "table" means, specifically, a *base* table (as in CREATE TABLE or LOCK); at other times it means "base table or view" (as in GRANT or COMMENT ON). Since the critical point about a view is that it *is* a table (just as the critical point about a subset is that it *is* a set), I would vote for the following changes:

(a) Replace the terms "base table" and "view" by "real table" and "virtual table," respectively;

(b) Use the term "table" generically to mean "real table or virtual table";

(c) In concrete syntax, use the expressions [REAL] TABLE and VIRTUAL TABLE (where it is necessary to distinguish them, as in CREATE), with REAL as the default.

■ "SELECT *"

This is a good example of a situation in which the needs of the end-user and those of the application programmer are at odds. "SELECT *" is fine for the interactive user (it saves keystrokes). I believe it is rather dangerous for the programmer (because the meaning of "*" may change at any time in the life of the program). The use of "ORDER BY n" (where n is an integer instead of a field-name) in conjunction with "SELECT *" could be particularly unfortunate. Similar remarks apply to the use of INSERT without a list of field-names.

Incidentally, I believe that the foregoing are the *only* situations in the entire SQL language in which the user is dependent on the left-to-right ordering of columns within a table. It would be nice to eliminate that dependence entirely (except possibly for "SELECT *," for interactive queries only).

■ =ANY (etc.)

The comparison operators =ANY, >ALL, etc., are totally redundant and in many cases actively misleading (error potential is high). The following example, which is taken from the IBM manual "IBM Database 2 SQL Usage Guide" (IBM Form No. GG24-1583), illustrates the point very nicely:

"Select employees who are younger than any member of department E21" (irrelevant details omitted).

```
SELECT  EMPNO, LASTNAME, WORKDEPT
FROM    TEMPL
WHERE   BRTHDATE >ANY ( SELECT BRTHDATE
                        FROM    TEMPL
                        WHERE   WORKDEPT = 'E21' )
```

This SELECT does *not* find employees who are younger than any employee in E21!—at least in the sense that this requirement would normally be understood in colloquial English. Rather, it finds employees who are younger than *some* employee in E21.

To illustrate the redundancy, consider the query: "Find supplier names for suppliers who supply part P2." This is a very simple problem, yet it is not difficult to find no less than seven formulations for it, all of them at least superficially distinct (see below). Of course, the differences would not be important if all formulations worked equally well, but that is unlikely.

```
1. SELECT  SNAME
   FROM    S
   WHERE   S# IN
           ( SELECT S#
             FROM    SP
             WHERE   P# = 'P2' )

2. SELECT  SNAME
   FROM    S
   WHERE   S# =ANY
           ( SELECT S#
             FROM    SP
             WHERE   P# = 'P2' )

3. SELECT  SNAME
   FROM    S
   WHERE   EXISTS
           ( SELECT *
             FROM    SP
             WHERE   S# = S.S# AND P# = 'P2' )

4. SELECT  DISTINCT SNAME
   FROM    S, SP
   WHERE   S.S# = SP.S# AND SP.P# = 'P2'

5. SELECT  SNAME
   FROM    S
   WHERE   0 <
           ( SELECT COUNT(*)
             FROM    SP
             WHERE   S# = S.S# AND P# = 'P2' )

6. SELECT  SNAME
   FROM    S
   WHERE   'P2' IN
           ( SELECT P#
             FROM    SP
             WHERE   S# = S.S# )
```

```
7. SELECT  SNAME
   FROM    S
   WHERE   'P2' =ANY
         ( SELECT P#
           FROM   SP
           WHERE  S# = S.S# )
```

In general, the WHERE clause

```
WHERE x $ANY ( SELECT y FROM T WHERE p )
```

(where $ is any one of =, >, etc.) is equivalent to the WHERE clause

```
WHERE EXISTS ( SELECT * FROM T WHERE (p) AND x $ T.y )
```

Likewise, the WHERE clause

```
WHERE x $ALL ( SELECT y FROM T WHERE p )
```

is equivalent to the WHERE clause

```
WHERE NOT EXISTS ( SELECT * FROM T WHERE (p)
                             AND NOT ( x $ T.y ) )
```

As a matter of fact, it is not just the comparison operators =ANY (etc.) that are redundant; the entire "IN (subquery)" construct could be removed from SQL with no loss of function at all! (Nested table- and column-expressions, etc., would of course still be required, as argued earlier.) This is ironic, since it was the subquery notion that was the justification for the "Structured" in "Structured Query Language" in the first place.

ASPECTS OF THE RELATIONAL MODEL NOT SUPPORTED

There are several aspects of the full relational model (as defined in, e.g., [2]) that SQL does not currently support. They are listed here in approximate order of importance. Again, of course, most of these features can be added to SQL at some later point—the sooner the better, in most cases. However, their omission now leads to a number of situations in current SQL that are extremely ad hoc and may be difficult to remedy later on, for compatibility reasons.

■   Primary keys

Primary keys provide the sole record-level addressing mechanism within the relational model. That is, the *only* system-guaranteed method of identifying an individual record is via the combination (R,k), where R is the name of the containing relation and k is the primary key value for the record concerned. Every relation (to *be* a relation) is required to have a primary key. Primary keys are (of course) required to be unique; in the case of real (i.e., base) relations, they are also required to be wholly nonnull.

SQL currently provides mechanisms that allow users to apply the primary key discipline for themselves (if they so choose), but does not understand the semantics associated with that discipline. As a result, SQL support for certain other functions is either deficient or lacking entirely, as I now explain.

1. Consider the query

```
SELECT P.P#, P.WEIGHT, AVG (SP.QTY)
FROM   P, SP
WHERE  P.P# = SP.P#
GROUP  BY P.P#, P.WEIGHT
```

The "P.WEIGHT" in the GROUP BY clause is logically redundant, but must be included because SQL does not understand that P.WEIGHT is single-valued per part number (i.e., that parts have only one weight). This may be only a minor annoyance, but it could be puzzling to the user.

2. Primary key support is prerequisite to foreign key support (see the following subsection). This is probably the most significant justification for supporting primary keys in the first place, as a matter of fact.

3. An understanding of primary keys is required in order to support the updating of views correctly. SQL's rules for the updating of views are in fact disgracefully ad hoc. I consider projection, restriction, and join views in some detail here; further discussion of this topic can be found in [7]. Note: I assume in each case that the data underlying the view is itself updatable, of course.

(a) Projections are logically updatable if and only if they preserve the primary key of the underlying relation. However, SQL supports updates, not on projections per se, but on what might be called *column subsets*— where a "column subset" is any subset of the columns of the underlying table for which duplicate elimination is not requested (via DISTINCT)—with a "user beware" if that subset does not in fact include the underlying primary key. (Actually the situation is even worse than this. Even a column subset is not updatable if the FROM clause in the definition of that subset lists multiple tables. Moreover, updates are prohibited if duplicate elimination is requested, even if that request can have no effect because the column subset does include the underlying primary key.)

(b) Any restriction is logically updatable. SQL however does not permit such updates if duplicate elimination is requested (even though such a request can have no effect if the underlying table does have a primary key), nor if the FROM clause lists multiple tables. What is more, even when it does allow updates, SQL does not always check that updated records satisfy the restriction predicate; hence, an updated (or inserted) record may instantaneously vanish from the view, and moreover there are concomitant security exposures (e.g., a user who is restricted to accessing employees with salary less than $40K may nevertheless *create* a salary greater than that value via INSERT or UPDATE). [Note: The CHECK option, which is intended to prevent such abuses, cannot always be specified.] Also, the fact that SQL automatically supplies null values for missing fields in inserted records means that it is *impossible* for such records to satisfy the restriction predicate in some cases (consider, for example, the view "employees in department D3," if the view does not include the DEPT# field). However, these latter deficiencies are nothing to do with SQL's lack of knowledge of primary keys per se.

(c) A join of two tables on their primary keys is logically updatable. So also is a join of one table on its primary key to another on a matching foreign key (though the details are not totally straightforward). However, SQL does not allow *any* join to be updated.

- Foreign keys

Foreign keys provide the principal referencing mechanism within the relational model. Loosely speaking, a foreign key is a field in one table whose values are required to match values of the primary key in another table. For example, field DEPT# of the EMP table is a foreign key matching the primary key (DEPT#) of the DEPT table.

SQL does not currently provide any kind of support for the foreign key concept at all. I regard lack of such support as the major deficiency in relational systems today (SQL is certainly not alone in this regard). Proposals for such support are documented in some detail in [7].

- Domains

SQL currently provides no support for domains at all, except inasmuch as the fundamental data types (INTEGER, FLOAT, etc.) can be regarded as a very primitive kind of domain.

- Relation assignment

A limited form of relation assignment is supported via INSERT ... SELECT, but that operation does not overwrite the previous content of the target table, and the source of the assignment cannot be an arbitrary algebraic expression (or SQL equivalent).

- Explicit JOIN

I mentioned earlier that explicit support for the (natural) join operation was desirable. At that point I was tacitly discussing the *inner* or regular join (specifically, the natural join). The observation is still more applicable to *outer* join. Reference [4] shows how awkward it is to extend the circumlocutory SELECT-style join to handle outer joins. Thus, support for an explicit JOIN operator is likely to become even more desirable in the future than it is already.

- Explicit INTERSECT and DIFFERENCE

These omissions are not particularly serious (equivalent SELECT-expressions exist in each case); however, symmetry would suggest that, since UNION *is* explicitly supported, INTERSECT and DIFFERENCE ought to be explicitly supported too. Some problems are most "naturally" formulated in terms of explicit intersections and differences. On the other hand, as indicated earlier, it is usually not a good idea to provide a multiplicity of equivalent ways of formulating the same problem, unless it can be guaranteed that the implementation will recognize the equivalences and will treat all formulations in the same way, which is probably unlikely.

SUMMARY AND CONCLUSIONS

I have discussed a large number of deficiencies and shortcomings in the SQL language as currently defined. I have also suggested how matters might be improved in many cases. The primary purpose of the paper has been to identify certain problems, and thereby to try to contribute to the solution of those problems, before their influence becomes too irrevocably widespread. As mentioned earlier, many of the shortcomings have in fact already been addressed to some extent in the proposals of the ANS Database Committee X3H2 [10]; the paper may thus also be seen as a rationale and justification for some of the decisions of that committee.[1] I hasten to add, however, that the paper has no official status whatsoever—specifically, it carries no endorsement from ANS or X3H2. Everything in it is entirely my own responsibility.

   Of course, I realize that many of the deficiencies I have been discussing will very likely be dismissed as academic, trivial, or otherwise unimportant by many people, especially as SQL is so clearly superior to older languages such as the DML of DBTG. However, experience shows that "academic" considerations have a nasty habit of becoming horribly practical a few years further down the road. The mistakes we make now will come back to haunt us in the future. Indeed, the language in its present form is already proving difficult to extend in some (desirable) ways because of limitations in its

---

[1]But see the "Comments on Republication."

present structure. A very trivial example is provided by the problem of adding support for composite fields or minor structures.

In conclusion, I should like to emphasize the point that most other database languages today suffer from deficiencies similar to those discussed in this paper; SQL is (as stated before) certainly not the sole offender. But the fact is that SQL is likely to be the most influential of those languages, for reasons adequately discussed earlier; and if it is adopted on a wide scale in its present form, then we will to some degree have missed the relational boat, or at least failed to capitalize to the fullest possible extent on the potential of the relational model. That would be a pity, because we had an opportunity to do it right, and with a little effort we could have done so. The question is whether it is now too late. I sincerely hope not.

ACKNOWLEDGMENTS

I am very pleased to acknowledge the helpful comments and criticisms I received on earlier drafts of this paper from my friends and colleagues Ted Codd, Phil Shaw, and Sharon Weinberg.

REFERENCES

1. M. M. Astrahan et al., "System R: Relational Approach to Database Management," *ACM TODS* 1, No. 2 (June 1976).

2. E. F. Codd, "Extending the Database Relational Model to Capture More Meaning," *ACM TODS* 4, No. 4 (December 1979).

3. C. J. Date, "Some Principles of Good Language Design" (in this volume).

4. C. J. Date, "The Outer Join" (in this volume).

5. C. J. Date, "An Introduction to the Unified Database Language (UDL)" (in this volume).

6. C. J. Date, "Null Values in Database Management" (in this volume).

7. C. J. Date, *A Guide to DB2* (Reading, MA: Addison-Wesley, 1984).

8. J. N. Gray, private communication.

9. J. N. Gray et al., "Granularity of Locks in a Large Shared Data Base," *Proc. 1st International Conference on Very Large Data Bases,* Framingham, MA (September 1975).

10. X3H2 (American National Standards Database Committee), Draft Proposed Relational Database Language, Document X3H2-83-152 (August 1983).

11. X3H2 (American National Standards Database Committee), Draft Proposed American National Standard Database Language SQL, Document X342-85-40 (February 1985).

APPENDIX: SQL STRONGPOINTS

Simple Data Structure

SQL is based on the relational model, and as such supports the simple tabular data structure of that model. It does *not* support any user-visible links between tables.

Powerful Operators

SQL also supports (indirectly) all the operators of the relational algebra, including in particular the operators SELECT (i.e., RESTRICT), PROJECT, and (natural) JOIN (which are the ones required most often in practice). Each of these operators is *very high-level*, in the sense that it treats entire sets of records as single operands.

Short Initial Learning Period

It is very easy to learn enough of the SQL language to "get on the air" and start doing real, useful work; thus, the initial learning period is typically very short indeed—certainly hours rather than days or weeks.

Improved Data Independence

Users are insulated, to a greater degree than with earlier languages, from the physical structure of the database (physical data independence). This fact means that: (a) Users can concentrate on the logic of their application without having to concern themselves with irrelevant physical details; (b) the physical structure of the database can be changed without necessitating any corresponding reprogramming. Users are also insulated to some extent from the *logical* structure of the database (logical data independence); this means that users can concentrate on just that portion of the data that is of interest to them (they may not even be aware of other portions), and it also means that some limited changes can be made to the logical structure of the database without very much reprogramming (probably not without any, however).

Integrated Data Definition and Data Manipulation

SQL imposes comparatively few artificial boundaries between definition functions and manipulation functions. For example, the creation of a view (a definition function) involves essentially the same SELECT operation as does the formulation of a query (a manipulation function). This uniformity, again, makes the language easier to learn and use.

Dual Mode of Use

SQL can be used both interactively (i.e., as a query language) and embedded in a program (i.e., as a database programming language). This capability is desirable for several reasons. First, it improves communication: End-users and application programmers are "speaking the same language." Second, it makes programmers, as well as end-users, more productive—the benefits sketched above (e.g., the provision of high-level operators) apply to programmers too. And third, the interactive interface provides a very convenient programmer debugging facility; that is, application programmers can take the SQL portions of their program and debug them interactively at the terminal.

Integrated Catalog

Since the database catalog is represented just like any other data in the system (i.e., as a collection of tables), it can be interrogated by means of SQL SELECT statements, just like any other data in the system. Users do not have to learn two languages, one for querying the dictionary (for the catalog is in effect exactly that, a rudimentary, online, active dictionary), and one for querying the database.

Compilation and Optimization

SQL is capable of efficient implementation, via the by now well-known compilation/optimization techniques pioneered in the IBM prototype System R. Moreover, the fact that SQL is compiled, and hence that systems such as System R are "early binding" systems, does not compromise the flexibility of those systems. If a change is made to the database (such as the dropping of an index) that invalidates an existing compiled program, then that program—or, more accurately, the SQL statements within that program—will automatically be recompiled and rebound on the next invocation. Thus the system can provide the flexibility of late binding without incurring the interpretation overheads normally associated with such binding.

15

Null Values
in Database Management

ABSTRACT

We examine the question of null values in a database system. We begin by
defining the term "null value" and outlining the problems that null values
are intended to solve. We go on to discuss the properties of null values in
detail, and describe some extensions to the relational model for dealing with
such values. We then discuss some of the difficulties that occur in connexion
with the null value concept. It is our opinion that the problem is generally
not well understood, and that any attempt to incorporate support for null
values into an implemented system should be considered premature at this
time. We sketch an alternative approach based on the concept of *default*
values.

COMMENTS ON REPUBLICATION

There is no question that the problem of missing information is an important one. It is the thesis of this paper, however, that the SQL approach of

Originally published in *Proc. 2nd British National Conference on Databases* (Bristol, England,
July 1982; invited paper). Reprinted with permission. An earlier version of the paper appeared
in somewhat different form in *An Introduction to Database Systems*: *Volume II*, by C. J.
Date, copyright 1983, Addison-Wesley, Reading, Massachusetts. Reprinted with permission.

using a special null value to represent such missing information is not a satisfactory solution to that problem. Indeed, it is my opinion that the SQL null value concept introduces far more problems than it solves. Some of those problems are illustrated in this paper.

The paper is included in this part of the book because it applies very directly to SQL; indeed, it might well have been given the title "A Critique of the SQL Null Value Construct." However, the ideas and criticisms are relevant to any system that attempts to support null values, at least as that term is commonly understood.

I have made the following changes in the version of the paper printed here:

1. I have revised the section on defaults in order to make it a little more concrete.

2. I have removed all discussion of the outer join operator, since that material is treated in more detail in a subsequent paper in this collection.

3. I have added a significant new example illustrating the problems that can arise from taking the sum of an empty set to be null.

4. I have replaced all references to System R by references to (the IBM dialect of) the SQL language.

5. I have made a large number of editorial changes to improve the exposition throughout.

INTRODUCTION

We begin by assuming that, barring explicit constraints to the contrary, every attribute of every relation may potentially accept a null value, denoted by "?". The null value may be thought of as a placeholder for some "real" (nonnull) value in the domain of the attribute concerned. Its interpretation is thus "value at present unknown"; note, however, that other types of null can be defined—for example, a null meaning "property inapplicable." Those other types of null are not considered here.

Why do we need the concept of a null value? The short answer is that real-world information is very frequently incomplete, and we need some way of handling such incompleteness in our formal systems. For example, historical records sometimes include such entries as "Date of birth unknown"; meeting agendas often show a speaker as "To be announced"; and police records frequently include the entry "Present whereabouts unknown." Putting the matter into more specific database terms, null values facilitate the automatic support of situations such as the following (where "automatic support" means "support that does not require any special action on the part of the user"):

1. A new tuple is to be created, but the user is unable to supply values for certain attributes at this time. (The user might not even be aware of the existence of those attributes.) The system can supply null values for the new tuple in the missing positions.

2. A new attribute is to be added to an existing base relation. The value of the new attribute can be set to null in all existing tuples.

3. An aggregate function such as AVG is to be applied to some attribute of some relation. In computing the function, it is desirable for the system to be able to recognize and ignore tuples for which no nonnull value has yet been supplied for the attribute in question. (But note carefully that it is also desirable for users to understand what is going on in such a situation; for otherwise they may be surprised to discover that, e.g., the average is not equal to the sum divided by the count.)

4. An aggregate function such as AVG is to be applied to some attribute of some relation, and that relation happens to be currently empty. Raising an exception condition in such a situation can lead to awkwardness for the user—particularly if the function reference is embedded within a predicate (for example, take the query "Find departments for which the average employee salary is greater than $50,000," and consider what the system should do if it encounters a department that currently has no employees). It seems preferable to define the function in such a way that it will return a null value if its argument set happens to be empty.

Let F be a field (attribute) that can accept null values. To represent a null value of F in the database, it is necessary to find a bit configuration that is different from all legal bit configurations for F (i.e., those configurations that represent all possible nonnull values of F). For example, if the data type of F is packed decimal, then any bit configuration in which the sign code (rightmost four bits) is invalid could be used to represent the null value. If no such illegal bit configuration exists—i.e., if all possible bit configurations represent some legal nonnull value—then it is necessary to introduce a *hidden field* for F. In this case, every instance of F in the database will have an associated instance of the hidden field—call it H—whose value indicates to the system whether the corresponding F-value is to be ignored or not (is null or not). Theoretically H need be no more than a single bit wide, though for pragmatic reasons it may be more convenient to let it occupy an entire byte.

Note incidentally that, whatever representation scheme is chosen, the possibility that F may be null is likely to impose significant computational overhead on all manipulative operations involving F.

A SCHEME FOR HANDLING NULLS

As stated at the beginning of the paper, it is our feeling that nulls should not be supported. To justify this position, however, it is first necessary to indicate exactly what such support would consist of. This section therefore presents a detailed scheme for dealing with nulls. Note: The development that follows is similar but not identical to that of reference [2]. It can be regarded as an attempt to specify the formal semantics of null values as they appear in SQL [1].

First, let *theta* denote any one of the comparison operators $=$, $\sim =$, $<$, $\sim <$, $>$, and $\sim >$. What is the result of evaluating the comparison "x *theta* y" if x or y, or both, happen to be null? Since by definition null represents an unknown value, we define the result in every case to be *unknown* (i.e., null) also, rather than *true* or *false*. To deal with null values properly, therefore, it is necessary to adopt a 3-valued logic in place of the more usual 2-valued logic. This 3-valued logic is defined by the truth tables shown below. Note that the *unknown* or null truth-value can reasonably be interpreted as "maybe."

AND	T	?	F		OR	T	?	F		NOT	
T	T	?	F		T	T	T	T		T	F
?	?	?	F		?	T	?	?		?	?
F	F	F	F		F	T	?	F		F	T

It is an immediate consequence of the foregoing definition that the comparison "x = y" (taking *theta* as equality) evaluates to null if x or y *or both* happen to be null; i.e., the value of "null = null" is *null*, not *true*. It follows that the comparison "x = x" does not necessarily yield the value *true*—it cannot be *false*, but it may be *unknown*. (Intuitively, it is this fact—that "null = null" does not evaluate to *true*—that lies at the root of most of the problems that arise over null.)

Similarly, let *alpha* denote any one of the arithmetic operators +, -, *, /, and let x and y denote any two numeric values. Then the value of the arithmetic expression "x *alpha* y" is defined to be null if x is null or y is null or both. Unary (prefix) + and - are treated analogously—i.e., if x is null, then +x and -x are also considered to be null.

set membership

Next, consider the question of whether sets are allowed to contain null values. Suppose, for example, that the collection C = {1,2,3,?} is to be permitted as a legal set. Then there are two possibilities:

(a) The particular null value appearing in C is of course unknown, but is known to be distinct from 1 and 2 and 3;

(b) The null value in C is *completely* unknown (i.e., it may in fact stand for one of the values 1, 2, 3), in which case the cardinality of C in turn is unknown (it may be either 3 or 4).

Possibility (a) implies that we must be prepared to deal with a variety of distinct nulls—a null that is known not to be 1, a null that is known not to be 2, a null that is known not to be 1 or 2, and so on. We refer to such nulls as "distinguished nulls." Possibility (b) has effectively the same implication; for example, the best that a COUNT function applied to C can do is return the value "unknown, but known to be either 3 or 4"—which is simply another example of a distinguished null. Distinguished nulls are troublesome from the standpoints of both definition and implementation. Consider, for example, the problem of assigning a truth value to the expression "x = y" if x is known to be 1 or 2 or 3 and y is known to be 2 or 3 or 4. Consider also the difficulty of physically representing a value that is known to be one of some (possibly very large) specified set of values. In this discussion, therefore, we stay with just the one kind of null, namely the one representing "value completely unknown."

To return to the original question: Since possibilities (a) and (b) above both lead to difficulties, we propose the following approach. Sets per se are not allowed to contain any null values at all. Instead, a new construct is introduced, which we will refer to as an *n-set*. An n-set of cardinality r is a collection of r values, in which at most one value is null and no two nonnull values are equal to each other. A set is a special case of an n-set. We permit at most one null value in an n-set to avoid (again) the problems of distinguished nulls; our feeling is that it does not seem wise to tackle such refinements before the simpler problem is fully understood. (But see Lipski [5] for a proposal that does address the more general problem.)

Next, we assign an extended meaning to the term *duplicate*. A duplicate with respect to a given n-set N is defined to be a value v such that some element of N has value equal to v, or, if v happens to be null, some element of N has the null value. (Informally, an attempt to introduce a duplicate into N via an INSERT or UPDATE operation will be rejected.)

We now define the existential and universal quantifiers, as follows. Let N be an n-set containing precisely the values v1, v2, ..., vr (at most one of which can be null); let x be a variable that ranges over N (i.e., a variable whose permitted values are precisely v1, v2, ..., vr); and let p(x) be a predicate in x. The truth value of

```
EXISTS x ( p(x) )
```

is defined to be the same as the truth value of

```
p(v1) OR p(v2) OR ... OR p(vr)
```

The truth value of

```
FORALL x ( p(x) )
```

is defined to be the same as the truth value of

```
p(v1) AND p(v2) AND ... AND p(vr)
```

Now let x be any value (possibly null). We define the membership predicate

```
x memberof N
```

to be equivalent to the expression

```
x = v1 OR x = v2 OR ... OR x = vr
```

In other words, if N contains a nonnull value vi such that "x = vi" is *true*, the membership predicate evaluates to *true*; otherwise, if N contains a value vi, possibly null, such that "x = vi" is *unknown*, the membership predicate evaluates to *unknown*; otherwise the membership predicate evaluates to *false*. Some examples:

```
2 memberof { 2,3,? }    :    true
4 memberof { 2,3,? }    :    unknown
? memberof { 2,3,? }    :    unknown
? memberof { 2,3 }      :    unknown
4 memberof { 2,3 }      :    false
```

Now let N1 and N2 be two n-sets. The subset predicate

```
N1 subsetof N2
```

is defined to be equivalent to the expression

```
COUNT(N1) <= COUNT(N2) AND FORALL x ( EXISTS y ( x = y ) )
```

where x and y range over N1 and N2 respectively, and where the function COUNT applied to an n-set of cardinality r is defined to return the value r. (The requirement "COUNT(N1) < = COUNT(N2)" is included to guarantee that, for example, the n-set {3,4,5} cannot possibly be considered as a subset of the n-set {3,?}. The COUNTs of these two n-sets are 3 and 2, respectively.)

We can now proceed to develop a revised version of the relational algebra in which the fundamental domains are not sets but n-sets. We do not show the complete formal development here. However, the main points are sketched informally below.

- The Cartesian product of a collection of domains (n-sets) D1, D2, . . ., Dn, written D1 X D2 X ... X Dn, is defined as the set of all possible tuples (d1,d2, ...,dn) such that d1 is a duplicate of some value in D1, d2 is a duplicate of some value in D2, ..., and dn is a duplicate of some value in Dn. Note carefully that we are using the term "duplicate" in the special sense defined earlier in this paper. Note too that the Cartesian product is a *set* rather than an n-set.

- It follows from the definition that the Cartesian product D1 X D2 X ... X Dn cannot contain two distinct tuples that are duplicates of each other—where, again, we are using the term "duplicate" in an extended sense:

  Definition: Two tuples (d1,d2, . . .,dn) and (e1,e2, . . .,en) are said to be duplicates of each other if and only if, for all i (i = 1, . . .,n), either di and ei are both nonnull and di = ei, or di and ei are both null. In other words, di and ei are duplicates of each other for all i.

- A *relation* on domains (n-sets) D1, D2, . . ., Dn is defined to be a subset of the Cartesian product D1 X D2 X . . . X Dn. Of course, we are considering only the "tuple-set" component—i.e., the value—of the relation here, to use the terminology of reference [3]. Also, we assume, purely for reasons of simplicity, that the left-to-right ordering of domains (and hence of attributes) within a relation is significant.

- It follows that a relation also can never contain two distinct tuples that are duplicates of each other. In particular, a relation (like a Cartesian product) can contain at most one tuple consisting entirely of null values. The operators of the relational algebra are carefully defined to ensure that these properties are preserved (see the next section).

- Note that tuples in which some or all component values are null are still well-formed tuples (they are not themselves considered as null values). In particular, a tuple consisting entirely of null values is not itself the same thing as a "null tuple"—just as, e.g., the set whose sole member is the empty set is not itself an empty set. We do not use the concept of a "null tuple" at all, in fact.

EFFECT ON THE RELATIONAL ALGEBRA

The effect of the development in the preceding section on the operators of the relational algebra is as follows (in outline). Note: At first glance, the definitions below may appear to be equivalent to the familiar definitions of those operations, in which null values are ignored. However, they are different (although of course they do reduce to the old form in the absence of null values). The differences stem from the extended meaning we have assigned to the term "duplicate tuple."

- Union

The union of two union-compatible relations R and S is the relation consisting of all tuples t such that t is a duplicate of some tuple in R or of some tuple in S (or both). For example, if relations R and S are as follows:

```
    ---  ---         ---  ---
R    A    B      S    A    B
    ---  ---         ---  ---
     a    b           x    y
     a    ?           ?    b
     ?    b           ?    ?
     ?    ?
```

then their union is:

```
    ---  ---
     A    B
    ---  ---
     a    b
     a    ?
     ?    b
     ?    ?
     x    y
```

- Difference

The difference of two union-compatible relations R and S (in that order) is the relation consisting of all tuples t such that t is a duplicate of some tuple in R and not of any tuple in S. For example, if R and S are as under "Union" above, the difference between R and S (in that order) is:

```
    ---  ---
     A    B
    ---  ---
     a    b
     a    ?
```

- Product

The product operation is unchanged.

- Theta-selection

The theta-selection operation is unchanged, but it should be stressed that tuples appear in the result only when the theta-comparison evaluates to *true*, not to *false* and not to *unknown*.

- Projection

The projection of a relation R over the attributes Ai, . . .,Aj is the relation obtained from R by eliminating attributes that are not included in the set Ai,...,Aj and then eliminating redundant duplicate tuples from what remains. For example, if R is as under "union" above, the projection of R on attribute A is:

```
---
A
---
a
?
```

ADDITIONAL OPERATORS

We now introduce some additional operators to assist in dealing with null values. First, it is necessary to define a truth-valued function IS_NULL, whose argument is an arbitrary scalar expression and whose value is *true* if that argument evaluates to null and *false* otherwise. Using this function, we can define two new algebraic operators, MAYBE_SELECT and MAYBE_JOIN. Basically, MAYBE_SELECT selects tuples for which the value of a specified attribute is null, and MAYBE_JOIN joins tuples for which the value of either of the joining attributes is null:

- MAYBE_SELECT (R, A)
     = THETA_SELECT (R, IS_NULL (R.A))

- MAYBE_JOIN (R, S, A, B)
     = THETA_SELECT (PRODUCT (R, S),
                      (IS_NULL (R.A) OR IS_NULL (S.B))

(See reference [3] for definitions of THETA_SELECT and PRODUCT. We are assuming here that THETA_SELECT can accept any relational expression as its first argument and any truth-valued expression as its second argument. The versions of the "maybe operators" shown above represent a refinement of the definitions given in reference [2].)

Here is an example to illustrate the need for MAYBE_SELECT. Suppose we have a relation

```
S ( S#, SNAME, STATUS, CITY )
```

representing information for a set of suppliers, and suppose that certain supplier cities are unknown. The two operations

```
THETA_SELECT ( S, CITY = 'London' )
```

and

```
THETA_SELECT ( S, CITY ˜= 'London' )
```

between them will then *not* select all S tuples. (As a matter of fact, neither will the single operation

```
THETA_SELECT ( S, CITY = CITY )    ,
```

as is clear from the fact that "null = null" does not evaluate to *true*.) To select the remaining S tuples, we need:

```
MAYBE_SELECT ( S, CITY )
```

The justification for MAYBE_JOIN is similar.

[*At this point the original paper included a brief discussion of outer join. That material is omitted here because it duplicates material in the paper "The Outer Join," reprinted later in this collection.*]

CONSEQUENCES OF THE FOREGOING TREATMENT

It is our opinion that the scheme outlined in the previous sections for the treatment of null values is as reasonable as any that has been given in the literature. However, it still suffers from a number of problems, which we now proceed to discuss. Those problems fall into two broad classes: intuitive difficulties and implementation anomalies.

- The intuitive difficulties are inherent. They arise primarily from the counterintuitive nature of 3-valued logic: Human beings, especially "naive end-users," are simply more able to deal with 2-valued rather than 3-valued logic. It is true that the difficulties *can* all be explained away, but that fact does not reduce the likelihood of users becoming confused or making mistakes, and there are so many difficulties that the cumulative effect is (to say the least) to give a strong impression of inelegance.

- The implementation anomalies arise from the fact that system implementers are human too, and are therefore just as liable to get confused as anybody else. Indeed, this observation is part of the overall thesis of this paper: Even if the intuitive difficulties can all be satisfactorily resolved, it is extremely likely that inconsistencies will arise in any specific implementation, precisely because of the subtle and counterintuitive behavior of 3-valued logic.

Intuitive difficulties are discussed below; implementation anomalies are discussed in the next section. Note: In what follows, all values should be considered as nonnull unless explicitly stated otherwise.

- Let R(A,B,C) be a relation satisfying the functional dependency A → B. (Note: We do not assume that attribute A is a candidate key. Of course, if it is not, then R is not in BCNF.) Can attribute A accept null values?

(a) Suppose the answer is yes. In that case, can R contain two tuples (?,b1,c1) and (?,b2,c2), where b1 and b2 are distinct? If so, then the two null values must be distinct (because of the functional dependency A → B), which leads us into the problem of distinguished nulls once more. If not, then the second tuple (i.e., whichever is submitted second) must presumably be rejected on the grounds that it *might* violate the dependency, which leads to further difficulties. Consider, for example, the relation

```
EMP ( SS#, JOB, EMP# )
```

where EMP# is the primary key and SS# stands for social security number. (The attributes have deliberately been ordered left to right to suggest the correspondence A:SS#, B:JOB, C:EMP#.) The rule for social security numbers is that they are unique if nonnull—but they *can* be null. It is not reasonable to reject an EMP tuple having a null SS# value just because such a tuple already exists; thus we are forced into having to admit that we do not have a functional dependency of JOB on SS#. This is unfortunate, since JOB clearly *is* functionally dependent on SS# if we ignore the nulls.

Another, perhaps more serious objection to permitting attribute A to take on null values—regardless of whether tuples (?,b1,c1) and (?,b2,c2) are both allowed to exist—is that the normalization procedure breaks down. For example, a fundamental theorem that is used to support and justify that procedure is the following: If relation R(A,B,C) satisfies the functional dependency A → B, then R can be nonloss-decomposed into its projections R1(A,B) and R2(A,C)—i.e., R can be recovered by taking the natural join of R1 and R2 on A. It is easy to see that the theorem is no longer true if A can accept null values. For example, if R is as follows:

```
      ---   ---   ---
R     A     B     C
      ---   ---   ---
      a1    b1    c1
      ?     b2    c2
```

then the projections R1 and R2 and the corresponding natural join are:

```
      ---   ---              ---   ---              ---   ---   ---
R1    A     B         R2     A     C                A     B     C
      ---   ---              ---   ---              ---   ---   ---
      a1    b1                a1    c1              a1    b1    c1
      ?     b2                ?     c2
```

Incidentally, the maybe join is no help with this problem.

(b) Suppose then that the answer is no (i.e., attribute A cannot accept null values). Then again we have to admit (in the EMP example) that JOB is not functionally dependent on SS#, since SS# can be null. Moreover, another consequence of this decision is that the integrity rule of the relational model concerning inadmissibility of null values [2,3] will now apply to all candidate keys, not just to the primary key.

(c) It is possible to avoid some of the foregoing problems by refining the definition of functional dependence, as follows: Attribute R.B is functionally dependent on attribute R.A if and only if each *nonnull* value of R.A has associated with it exactly one value of R.B (at any one time). This revision would permit any number of tuples of the form (?,b,c), where b and c are arbitrary, to be inserted into R without violating the dependency A → B. (Updating a null A-value to some nonnull value would be subject to the usual checks, of course.) But this "solution" does not address the objection mentioned under (a) above concerning the normalization procedure.

▪ Again, let R(A,B,C) be a relation satisfying the functional dependency A → B. Can attribute B accept null values?

If A is a candidate key the answer must be yes, for otherwise no nonkey attribute would ever be allowed to accept null values. What if A is not a candidate key? If the answer is yes in this case, then R cannot contain two distinct tuples (a1,b1,c1) and (a1,?,c2), because of the dependency; the "?" would have to be equal to b1, contrary to the intuitive interpretation of null as unknown. The system could *set* the null to b1, of course; but then the tuple (a1,?,c2) would or would not be a duplicate of the tuple (a1,b1,c1)—and the INSERT thus would or would not fail —depending on whether c1 and c2 were duplicates. It seems preferable to prohibit null values for B if A is not a candidate key, though admittedly the argument is not very strong.

The reader is referred to [6] for a formal treatment of null values and functional dependencies.

- Consider the following program fragments (expressed in some Algol-like language):

```
1. x := y ;
   if x = y
   then executable-unit

2. if y = y
   then executable-unit
```

In conventional programming, barring side-effects and the like, "executable-unit" would clearly be executed in both cases. If null values are introduced, however, and if y happens to be null, then "executable-unit" will not be executed in either case—an affront to intuition. To obtain the same guarantees as before (that "executable-unit" will in fact be executed in each case) in the face of the possibility that y might be null, the programmer must write:

```
1. x := y ;
   if x = y
   or ( IS_NULL ( x ) and IS_NULL ( y ) )
   then executable-unit

2. if y = y
   or IS_NULL ( y )
   then executable-unit
```

Of course, we do not mean to suggest that users would genuinely write programs like these—only that the mode of thinking underlying the examples is probably quite common, and that it might well lead to some very hard-to-find program bugs.

- The interpretation of nulls is not obvious. We have considered only the "value unknown" null in our treatment so far. However, consider the two binary relations

```
ES ( EMP#, SALARY )
```

and

```
EM ( EMP#, MAIDEN_NAME )   .
```

Let e denote some particular employee that is known to exist. The absence of a tuple for e from ES would typically be construed as "salary unknown," whereas the absence of a tuple for that same employee from

EM would typically be taken to mean *property inapplicable.* Of course, there may be employees represented in ES but not EM, and vice versa. If we perform an outer join of ES and EM on EMP# (see reference [4] for an explanation of outer join), how should we interpret the null values that appear in the result? (Of course, this question is significant only if ''value unknown'' nulls and ''property inapplicable'' nulls behave differently under the operations of the relational algebra.)

- We have already indicated that (for example) ''Suppliers in London'' and ''Suppliers not in London'' together do not in general account for all suppliers. Of course, this state of affairs can be justified: ''Suppliers in London'' really means ''Suppliers *known to the system* to be in London,'' and ''Suppliers not in London'' really means ''Suppliers *known to the system* not to be in London''—but the distinction is a subtle one, and one that is liable to mystify the user.

- We have assigned the *unknown* truth-value to all comparisons involving null and some other (null or nonnull) value. However, if we ask to see *all* tuples in a relation ordered by values of some attribute—say employees in salary order—the tuples having null values for that attribute must appear *somewhere* in that ordering, implying that in this context comparisons such as ''null > v'' (where v is a nonnull value) do have a known truth-value. Moreover, those tuples will probably all appear together, implying also that in this context null values are all equal to each other. Of course, it can be argued that the two operations of (a) imposing a sequence on a set of tuples for the purpose of processing those tuples one by one, and (b) performing comparisons between pairs of tuples of that set to determine the relative values of some attribute, are somehow different in kind—but again it is rather a nice distinction. (In fact, one of the arguments against null values is precisely that there seems to be no ''right'' answer to certain questions. We will return to this point in the next section.)

- We need some additional operations—specifically, the truth-valued function IS_NULL, and the relational operations MAYBE_SELECT and MAYBE_JOIN.

[*At this point the original paper included further discussion of the outer join operator. Again that material is omitted here.*]

- The duplicate elimination rule is difficult to justify intuitively. Specifically, it appears that (again) ''null = null'' has to be regarded as *true* in this context, even though it is *unknown* in others.

IMPLEMENTATION ANOMALIES

We illustrate the scope for anomalies in implementation by describing some aspects of the behavior of null values in one specific system, namely (the IBM dialect of) SQL [1].

- Null values are implemented by hidden fields in the database. However, it is necessary to expose those fields in the interface to a host language such as PL/I, because PL/I has no notion of null. (In the database sense, that is. The PL/I "null string" and "null pointer" are nothing to do with database nulls, of course. On the contrary, each represents a specific *known* value—the null string is really an *empty* string, the null pointer is an explicitly *invalid* pointer.) Thus, given the supplier relation S, with attributes S#, SNAME, STATUS, and CITY, for example, a PL/I programmer might write:

```
EXEC SQL SELECT STATUS
         INTO    :ST:STX
         FROM    S
         WHERE   S# = 'S4' ;
IF STX < 0 THEN /* selected STATUS value was null */ ... ;
```

[handwritten annotations: STX = -1 if null; Host language has to deal with the hidden fields!]

The PL/I "indicator variable" STX corresponds to the hidden field for STATUS. Such variables must be declared and manipulated by the programmer (i.e., tested on retrieval and set on update). It is not clear that the "automatic" handling of null values by the system is really saving the programmer very much work, therefore; moreover, treating null values differently on the two sides of the interface is unnecessarily confusing.

As an example of that difference in treatment, consider the following. Let F and G be two fields in table T. Then the UPDATE statement to set F equal to G is:

```
EXEC SQL UPDATE T
         SET     F = G ...
```

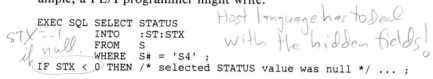

[handwritten annotations: column in table, Note - no indicator like]

—but the UPDATE statement to set F equal to a host variable H (with corresponding null indicator variable HN) is:

```
EXEC SQL UPDATE T
         SET     F = :H:HN ...
```

[handwritten annotations: working storage host variable]

(assuming in both cases that the expression on the right-hand side of the SET clause might evaluate to null).

Note, incidentally, that the hidden field technique is wasteful of storage space in those cases where a special value of the real field (say -1 for an HOURS_WORKED field) could be set aside to serve as the "null" value for that field.

- Indicator variables are not permitted in all contexts where host variables can appear (lack of orthogonality). For example, the following is illegal:

```
EXEC SQL UPDATE  S
        SET     STATUS = 35
        WHERE   CITY = :CT:CTX ;
```

Instead, the programmer must write:

```
IF CTX < 0
THEN EXEC SQL UPDATE S
             SET     STATUS = 35
             WHERE   CITY IS NULL ;
ELSE EXEC SQL UPDATE S
             SET     STATUS = 35
             WHERE   CITY = :CT ;
```

- To test (in a WHERE clause) whether a field is null, SQL provides the special comparison "field IS NULL" (the SQL implementation of IS_NULL(field); see the previous paragraph for an example). It is not intuitively obvious why the user has to write "field IS NULL" and not "field = NULL"—especially as the format "field = NULL" *is* used in the SET clause of the UPDATE statement to assign the null value to a field. (In fact, the WHERE clause "WHERE field = NULL" is illegal.)

- Two null values *are* considered as equals for indexing and duplicate elimination purposes. Thus, for example, (a) a UNIQUE index over a given field X will permit at most one null value for X; (b) "SELECT DISTINCT Y" will return at most one null value for Y (regardless of whether a UNIQUE index exists for Y). Two null values are also considered to be equal to one another (and moreover to be greater than all nonnull values) for the purposes of ordering. However, null values are *not* considered as equals for grouping purposes. Thus, for example, "GROUP BY Z" will generate a distinct group for each null value occurring in field Z.

- Null values are always eliminated from the argument to a builtin function such as SUM or AVG, regardless of whether DISTINCT is specified in the function reference—except for the case of COUNT(*), which counts all rows, including duplicates and including all-null rows. Note, incidentally, that this behavior is certainly not a logical consequence of the scheme for dealing with nulls outlined earlier in this paper. (Recall that expressions of the form "x *alpha* y," where x and y are numeric values and *alpha* is an arithmetic operator, are considered to evaluate to null if x or y or both happen to be null; in particular, "x - x" is null, not zero, if x is null, just as "x = x" is *unknown*, not *true*, in the same situation.)

Indeed, it could be argued that the SQL functions are very mis-leadingly named, even dangerously so. The SUM function, for exam-ple, is not truly a function that sums all the values in its argument; that is, the function reference SUM(F) is *not* semantically equivalent to the expression

```
f1 + f2 + ... + fn
```

where f1, f2, ..., fn are the values appearing in field F at the time the function is evaluated. Perhaps even more counterintuitively, the expression

```
SUM ( F1 + F2 )
```

is not equivalent to the expression

```
SUM ( F1 ) + SUM ( F2 )        .
```

Likewise, given:

```
SELECT AVG (STATUS) FROM S    --    Result: x

SELECT SUM (STATUS) FROM S    --    Result: y

SELECT COUNT(*)     FROM S    --    Result: z
```

there is no guarantee that x = y/z.

- The nulls scheme presented in this paper did not explicitly address the question of what should happen if the argument to a builtin function should happen to be the empty set. In the case of COUNT the result should clearly be zero; but what about the other functions, such as SUM? SQL takes the position that the result should be null in all cases other than COUNT. Here is an example (from real life) of the diffi-culties that this position can lead to. Consider the tables

```
MEMBERS  ( MEMBER#, NAME, ADDRESS, ... )
PAYMENTS ( MEMBER#, DATE, AMOUNT, ... )
```

representing a list of members in a certain association and their annual dues payments, and consider the query "Which members have not paid their dues this year?" Annual dues are $100, but members are allowed to pay in installments, so it is not sufficient simply to look for members for whom no payment exists at all; rather, we must look for members such that the *sum* of their payments is less than $100. Thus a plausible SQL formulation is:

```
SELECT NAME, ADDRESS
FROM   MEMBERS, PAYMENTS
WHERE  DATE = sometime this year
GROUP  BY MEMBER.MEMBER#, NAME, ADDRESS
HAVING SUM (AMOUNT) < 100
```

Missing

(Not particularly obvious syntax, incidentally, but that is not what is at issue here.) The point is, this formulation is not sufficient: It does not find members who have paid nothing at all!—because, for a member who has paid nothing at all, the argument to the SUM reference is the empty set, and the "sum" is therefore null, and null is not less than 100. The correct formulation is much more complicated:

```
SELECT NAME, ADDRESS
FROM   MEMBERS, PAYMENTS
WHERE  DATE = sometime this year
GROUP  BY MEMBER.MEMBER#, NAME, ADDRESS
HAVING SUM (AMOUNT) < 100
UNION
SELECT NAME, ADDRESS
FROM   MEMBERS
WHERE  NOT EXISTS
       ( SELECT *
         FROM    PAYMENTS
         WHERE   PAYMENTS.MEMBER# = MEMBER.MEMBER#
         AND     DATE = sometime this year )
```

The point of the example is that it is all too easy (in the presence of null values) to formulate a query that looks correct but in fact is not—even if the user is in fact quite familiar with the way null values behave. (In the real-life situation on which this example is based, the error was spotted only because the user happened to know that a certain member had paid no dues at all and yet did not appear in the initial output. The user in question was thoroughly familiar with SQL.)

This example bears out the contention made earlier in the paper that there seems to be no "right" answer to certain questions. The example lends support to the view that the sum of an empty set should be zero, not null; yet how could one then distinguish (in the context of SUM) between an empty set and a nonempty set whose elements happened to add up to zero? And what about AVG? Exactly analogous arguments can be used to support the view that the average of an empty set should be zero also; but then the average would certainly not be equal to the sum divided by the count (since as pointed out previously the count of an empty set legitimately is zero, the sum divided by the count would have to be 0/0 or undefined).

DEFAULT VALUES

The original purpose of null values was to help the user, especially the "naive end user." However, it is our claim that they are far more likely to be a hindrance than a help, at least in the form in which they have been implemented in SQL today; and the source of the problem is the lack of a simple and consistent underlying model of the way that nulls are supposed to behave.

By contrast, the concept of default values leads to a less ambitious but more straightforward approach to the question of missing information: less ambitious, in that it requires more effort on the part of the user in certain circumstances, but more straightforward in that it is easy to understand and avoids all the difficulties associated with the null value scheme. In outline the approach works as follows.

Note: The approach is deliberately formulated below in terms of attributes rather than domains, because most relational systems currently do not support domains. Of course it would be a simple matter to reformulate it to take account of domains also, if desired.

- Associated with the declaration of each attribute of each named relation is either a DEFAULT clause designating the default value for that attribute, or else the specification NODEFAULT, meaning that the attribute in question does not have a default value. For example:

```
DECLARE 1 S RELATION,
       2 S#      ... NODEFAULT ,
       2 SNAME   ... DEFAULT ( '    ' ) ,
       2 STATUS  ... DEFAULT ( -1 ) ,
       2 CITY    ... DEFAULT ( '???' ) ,
       PRIMARY KEY ( S# ) ;
```

  NODEFAULT is assumed (and cannot be overridden) for all attributes that participate in a base relation primary key. For other attributes, if no DEFAULT clause is stated explicitly, then it might be possible for the system to assume a "default default"—e.g., blanks for character string attributes, zero for numeric attributes.

- When a new tuple is inserted into a base relation:

(a) The user must supply a value for every attribute that does not have a default value;

(b) For other attributes, the system will supply the applicable default value if the user does not provide a value.

- When a new attribute is added to a base relation:

(a) That new attribute must have an (explicit or implicit) DEFAULT specification (i.e., NODEFAULT cannot be specified);

(b) The value of the new attribute is automatically set to the applicable default value in all existing tuples in the relation.

- The builtin function DEFAULT(R.A), where R is a relation and A is an attribute of that relation, returns the default value applicable to R.A. It is an error if no such default value exists.

- Integrity Rules 1 and 2 of the relational model (see reference [3]) are revised to refer to default values instead of null values. In other words (loosely speaking):

  1. No component of the primary key of a base relation can accept default values;

  2. Every nondefault value of a foreign key must match some primary key value in some base relation.

- In applying an aggregate function such as AVG to a particular attribute, the user must specify an explicit predicate to exclude default values, if that is what is desired. For example:

```
SELECT AVG (SP.QTY)
FROM    SP
WHERE   QTY ~= DEFAULT(SP.QTY) ;
```

Note: It might be desirable to introduce a truth-valued function IS_DEFAULT in addition. The function reference IS_DEFAULT (R.A), where R is a relation and A is an attribute of that relation, would be defined to return the value *true* if its argument R.A evaluated to the applicable default value, the value *false* otherwise. The foregoing SELECT statement could then be reformulated:

```
SELECT AVG (SP.QTY)
FROM    SP
WHERE   ~ IS_DEFAULT(SP.QTY)
```

But it should be stressed that (unlike IS_NULL) IS_DEFAULT would be a mere convenience, *not* a necessity.

Purely as a convenience again, it might also be desirable to introduce some additional functions PSEUDO_SUM, PSEUDO_AVG, etc., analogous to SUM, AVG, etc. but defined to exclude default values from their argument before performing the desired computation (as SUM, AVG, etc. do in SQL today). For example:

```
SELECT PSEUDO_AVG (SP.QTY)
FROM    SP
```

(shorthand for the AVG example—either flavor—shown above).

- Aggregate functions such as AVG (and PSEUDO_AVG) are extended to include an optional second argument, defining the value to be returned if the first argument evaluates to the empty set. For example:

```
SELECT  DEPT#
FROM    DEPT
WHERE   50000 <
    ( SELECT  PSEUDO_AVG(SALARY,0)
      FROM    EMP
      WHERE   EMP.DEPT# = DEPT.DEPT# )
```

If set is null,

If the second argument is omitted, the function returns the value obtained by substituting default values for all attributes mentioned in the first argument. For example, suppose the default value for field F is −1, and suppose the database currently contains no values for field F; then the expression SUM(F) would return the value -1, and the expression SUM(F + 3) would return the value 2. It is an error if the first argument evaluates to the empty set and some attribute mentioned in that argument does not have a default value.

- The MAYBE_SELECT and MAYBE_JOIN operators are no longer needed.

- For some attributes it may be the case that every legal bit configuration is in fact a permissible (nondefault) value of the attribute in question. Such cases must be handled by explicit, user-controlled indicator fields (as with the host side of the interface in SQL).

- Most of the functional dependency problems go away. In particular, the normalization procedure no longer breaks down. (However, we still have to admit in the social security number example that JOB is not functionally dependent on SS#. What is needed is a means of specifying that *nondefault* values of attribute SS# are unique—just as a means is needed of referring to nondefault values of a foreign key in connexion with the revised version of Integrity Rule 2 mentioned above.)

CONCLUSION

The whole point of the default-value approach is that a default value is a normal value and behaves in predictable ways. It is therefore intuitively more satisfactory than the null-value approach. It is true that it requires (or may require) more explicit involvement on the part of the user; nevertheless, we see little reason to be hopeful that further research on null values will lead to any significant breakthroughs, and we feel strongly that default values represent the preferred alternative.

ACKNOWLEDGMENTS

I am grateful to my colleagues Bill Kent and Phil Shaw for numerous constructive comments on earlier drafts, and to Ted Codd, whose ideas on null values in [2] formed the basis for the scheme for handling nulls presented in the first part of this paper.

REFERENCES

1. Information on the IBM dialect of SQL is available from IBM Corporation, Armonk, New York.

2. E. F. Codd, "Extending the Database Relational Model to Capture More Meaning," *ACM TODS* 4, No. 4 (December 1979).

3. C. J. Date, "A Formal Definition of the Relational Model" (in this volume).

4. C. J. Date, "The Outer Join" (in this volume).

5. W. Lipski, Jr., "On Semantic Issues Connected with Incomplete Information Databases," *ACM TODS* 4, No. 3 (September 1979).

6. Y. Vassiliou, "Functional Dependencies and Incomplete Information," *Proc. 6th International Conference on Very Large Data Bases* (October 1980).

The Outer Join

ABSTRACT

We present a discussion of the outer join operation, together with a concrete proposal for supporting that operation in a relational language such as SQL. We also compare our proposal with an earlier proposal due to Chamberlin [2].

COMMENTS ON REPUBLICATION

Outer join is an important problem; it is required in a surprising number of practical applications, and it is relevant to semantic modeling and to many database design methodologies. Yet few systems today provide any kind of direct support for the outer join operation. Furthermore, of those that do provide some such support, no system (so far as I am currently aware) supports it in anything other than a purely ad hoc manner, and no system caters for all possible variants of the operation. This paper gives some indication as to why this is the case. It also suggests a possible approach to the problem. But the reader is warned that outer join in its general

Originally published in *Proc. 2nd International Conference on Databases,* edited by S. M. Deen and P. Hammersley (Cambridge, England, August–September 1983), copyright 1983 by Wiley Heyden Ltd. Reprinted by permission of John Wiley & Sons, Ltd.

form is by no means a simple operation, which of course accounts for the length of the paper.

Incidentally, the notion of outer join is very much interwoven with the notion of null values. However, it should be stressed that support for outer join does not necessarily require support for the rather peculiar kind of null values found in SQL (which were castigated in the previous paper in this collection). Default-style "null values" (again, see the previous paper) would be completely satisfactory. Details of a "default"-style outer join are not spelled out in this paper, however.

In this reprinting I have made a slight change in notation, for reasons of clarity. The symbol "*theta*" is used to designate the comparison operator in the join predicate for a full or symmetric outer join. Likewise, the symbols "*theta" and "theta*" are used for the operators in the corresponding left and right outer joins. If *theta* is equality, the symbols of course become "* = *", "* = ", and " = *", respectively. In an analogous fashion I have used the symbols "*∧*", "*∧", and "∧*" for the full, left, and right outer natural joins.

One final comment: Since first writing this paper, I have become more than ever convinced that adding an explicit (natural, inner/outer) join operator to SQL would be a good idea. The specific proposal to this effect contained in this paper is inadequate as it stands, however, and requires some additional work.

INTRODUCTION

We begin with an informal explanation of what outer join is intended to achieve. (Formal definitions are given in a later section.) First, we assume that the reader is familiar with the regular theta-join and natural join operations of the relational algebra, as defined in (for example) references [3,4,6]. In this paper we refer to those operations generically as *inner* joins. Now, it is well known that under certain circumstances an inner join can "lose information," in the sense that unmatched tuples in the relations to be joined do not participate in the result of the join. In other words, if a tuple in one of the original relations does not match any tuples in the other (under the join-defining predicate), then that tuple will not appear in the join result.

The outer join, by contrast, does not lose such information. An outer join is obtained by appending certain additional tuples to the result of the corresponding inner join. There is one such additional tuple for each unmatched tuple in each of the original relations; it consists of a copy of that unmatched tuple, extended with null values in the other attribute positions.

Examples are given in a subsequent section. (Note: The null value is interpreted as "information missing" or "information unknown.")

The outer join operation was first introduced by Heath [8], and has been formally defined by Lacroix and Pirotte [9] and by Codd [3]. A proposal for supporting it in the language SQL was given by Chamberlin in reference [2]. We shall examine Chamberlin's proposal (and contrast it with our own) toward the end of this paper. We remark that outer join is important in the context of semantic modeling; see, for example, the use made by Codd of outer join operations in his extended relational model RM/T [3].

A NOTE ON NULL VALUES

It is clear from the introductory section that an understanding of the concept of null values is a prerequisite for any discussion of outer join. It is not our aim to give a thorough treatment of null values here (see references [7], [4], or [3] for such a treatment); however, we briefly summarize those aspects that are most directly relevant to the outer join question.

- Let *theta* denote any one of the comparison operators $=$, $\sim =$, $<$, $\sim <$, $>$, and $\sim >$, and let x and y denote any two scalar values that may validly be compared with each other by means of that operator. Then the truth-value of the comparison expression "x *theta* y" is defined to be *null* (unknown), not *true* or *false*, if x is null or y is null or both. (Observe in particular that the comparison "x $=$ y" evaluates to *null*, not *true*, if x and y both happen to be null.) Thus it is necessary to adopt a 3-valued logic, as defined by the following truth tables:

AND	T ? F		OR	T ? F		NOT	
T	T ? F		T	T T T		T	F
?	? ? F		?	T ? ?		?	?
F	F F F		F	T ? F		F	T

(where "?" represents the null value).

- Similarly, let *alpha* denote any one of the arithmetic operators +, -, *, /, and let x and y denote any two numeric values. Then the value of the arithmetic expression "x *alpha* y" is defined to be null if x is null or y is null or both. Unary (prefix) + and - are treated analogously—i.e., if x is null, then +x and -x are also considered to be null.

- Consider the operations of the relational algebra, viz. the SELECT, PROJECT, PRODUCT, UNION, DIFFERENCE, INTERSECTION, (inner) JOIN, and DIVISION operations. Of these, only the first five are truly primitive—the remaining three can be expressed in terms of those five. The definitions of the five primitive operations (and hence of the other three) are extended to take account of null values, as follows:

1. The operations SELECT, DIFFERENCE, and PRODUCT remain unchanged (but note in the case of SELECT that tuples are selected only where the selection predicate evaluates to *true,* not to *false* and not to *null*);

2. As usual, redundant duplicate tuples are eliminated from the result of PROJECT and UNION operations. For this purpose, two tuples (u1,u2, ...,un) and (v1,v2, ...,vn) are considered to be duplicates of each other if and only if, for all i (i = 1, ...,n), either ui and vi are both nonnull and ui = vi, *or ui and vi are both null.*

- We introduce a truth-valued function IS_NULL, whose argument is an arbitrary scalar expression and whose value is *true* if that argument evaluates to null and *false* otherwise.

- Using the IS_NULL function, we define two new algebraic operators, MAYBE_SELECT and MAYBE_JOIN. Informally, MAYBE_SELECT selects tuples for which the value of a specified attribute is null, and MAYBE_JOIN joins tuples for which the value of either of the joining attributes is null. (See [4] or [7] for details. Our versions of the ''maybe operators'' represent a refinement of those given in reference [3].)

Aside: We have argued elsewhere [4,7] that the null value problem is still not adequately understood, and that support for such values in an implemented system should be considered as premature at this time. We have also presented an alternative approach based on the notion of *default* values. For the purposes of the present paper, however, it makes little difference which approach is adopted. To be consistent with other publications in this area, therefore, we frame all our discussions in terms of null values rather than defaults.

DEFINITIONS AND EXAMPLES

Let R(A,B1) and S(B2,C) be two relations with (possibly composite) attributes R.A, R.B1, S.B2, S.C. For simplicity we assume that the left-to-right order of attributes within a relation is significant; it is easy to relax this restriction, at the expense of complicating the definitions somewhat. Assume that R.B1 and S.B2 may validly be compared with each other. Let *theta* denote any one of the operators =, ~ =, <, ~ <, >, ~ > that is applicable to R.B1 and S.B2. Define T to be the (inner) theta-join of R on B1 with S on B2:

```
T  =  R [ B1 theta B2 ] S
```

We assume that the attributes of T inherit their names from the corresponding attributes of R and S; i.e., the attributes of T are A, B1, B2, and C. For simplicity, again, we assume that these names are all distinct. Define R1 as follows:

```
R1  =  R - T [ A, B1 ]
```

Here T[A,B1] is the projection of T on A and B1, and "-" is the set difference operator. R1 is thus the set of tuples of R not appearing in the projection of T on (A,B1)—loosely, the set of "unmatched" tuples of R with respect to the inner join T. Similarly, define S1 as follows:

```
S1  =  S - T [ B2, C ]
```

Then the outer theta-join of R on B1 with S on B2, written

```
R [ B1 *theta* B2 ] S
```

is defined to be equal to the expression

```
T  union  ( R1 X ( ?, ? ) )  union  ( ( ?, ? ) X S1 )
```

where "?" denotes the null value, as before, and "X" denotes the extended Cartesian product. (The *theta* is merely notation, used to distinguish the outer theta-join from the regular or inner theta-join.) As indicated in the introductory section, the purpose of this operation is to preserve information for tuples in one relation having no match in the other according to the joining condition "B1 *theta* B2" (such tuples appear in the result concatenated with null values). See Example 1 below.

We also define the *left* and *right* outer theta-joins. The left outer theta-join of R on B1 with S on B2, denoted

```
R [ B1 *theta B2] S    ,
```

is

```
T  union  ( R1 X ( ?, ? ) )
```

(where T and R1 are as defined above). The left outer theta-join preserves information for the left relation of the pair only (i.e., relation R). Similarly, the right outer theta-join of R on B1 with S on B2, denoted

```
R [ B1 theta* B2] S    ,
```

is

```
( ( ?, ? ) X S1 )  union  T
```

(where S1 and T are as defined above). The right outer theta-join preserves information for the right relation of the pair only (i.e., relation S). The "full" or "symmetric" outer theta-join is the union of the corresponding left and right outer theta-joins. We will reserve the unqualified term "outer theta-join" for the symmetric case, and always qualify by "left" or "right," as appropriate, if the left or right outer theta-join is intended.

If *theta* is equality, the theta-join is referred to as an *equi*join (applies to both inner and outer versions).

Note: It is trivial to extend the definitions to include the case of an arbitrary join predicate, instead of just a single comparison of the form "B1 *theta* B2" as above.

- *Example 1* (suppliers and parts, outer equijoin):

Consider the following database, in which relation S represents suppliers and relation P represents parts.

```
S ( S#, SCITY )
   PRIMARY KEY ( S# )

P ( P#, PCITY )
   PRIMARY KEY ( P# )
```

Sample values:

S	S#	SCITY		P	P#	PCITY
	S1	London			P1	London
	S2	Paris			P2	Oslo
	S3	?			P3	?
	S4	NY			P4	NY
	S5	SFO			P5	LA

The outer equijoin of these two relations on SCITY and PCITY—i.e., the relation

```
S [ SCITY *=* PCITY ] P    ,
```

to use the notation introduced above—is relation XSP:

XSP	S#	SCITY	P#	PCITY
	S1	London	P1	London
	S2	Paris	?	?
	S3	?	?	?
	S4	NY	P4	NY
	S5	SFO	?	?
	?	?	P2	Oslo
	?	?	P3	?
	?	?	P5	LA

The left outer equijoin of S and P over SCITY and PCITY consists of just those tuples of XSP in which S# is nonnull; likewise, the right outer equijoin consists of just those tuples in which P# is nonnull. We remark that relation XSP is not a legal base relation, since its primary key is (obviously) allowed to accept null values, in violation of one of the two fundamental integrity rules of the relational model [3,4,6]. (Of course, this does not mean it is not a legal *relation*.) By contrast, the left and right outer equijoins in this example *are* legal base relations (their primary keys are S# and P#, respectively).

Exercise for the reader: Given data values as shown above, what is the value of the outer greater-than join

```
S [ SCITY *>* PCITY ] P    ?
```

What about the left and right versions?

We also define the outer *natural* join. The outer natural join of R on B1 with S on B2, written

```
R [ B1 *^* B2 ] S    ,
```

is defined to be equal to the expression

```
T  [ A, B1, C ] union  ( R1 X ( ? ) )  union  ( ( ? ) X S1 )
```

(where T, R1, and S1 are as defined earlier, with *theta* taken as equality). The "*∧*" is merely notation.

As with outer theta-join, left and right outer natural joins can also be defined, and the full or symmetric outer natural join is the union of the corresponding left and right versions. We will reserve the unqualified term "outer natural join" for the symmetric case, and always qualify by "left" or "right," as appropriate, if the left or right outer natural join is intended.

Notation: We denote the left and right outer natural joins as

```
R [ B1 *^ B2 ] S
```

and

```
R [ B1 ^* B2 ] S    ,
```

respectively.

- *Example 2* (suppliers and parts, outer natural join):

Given relations S and P as in Example 1, the outer natural join of those two relations over SCITY and PCITY—i.e., the relation

```
S [ SCITY *^* PCITY ] P
```

—is the following relation (let us call it XNSP):

```
          --    ------    --
XNSP  S#    CITY      P#
          --    ------    --
          S1    London    P1
          S2    Paris     ?
          S3    ?         ?
          S4    NY        P4
          S5    SFO       ?
          ?     Oslo      P2
          ?     ?         P3
          ?     LA        P5
```

We show the name of the joining attribute in XNSP as simply CITY, instead of SCITY or PCITY, for reasons of symmetry. The left outer natural join would consist of just those tuples of XNSP in which S# is nonnull; the right outer natural join would consist of just those tuples in which P# is nonnull. Like XSP, XNSP is not a legal base relation.

It is a remarkable fact that the outer natural join is not a projection of the outer equijoin, in general. In particular, relation XNSP of Example 2 is not a projection of relation XSP of Example 1. By contrast, the inner natural join is always a projection of the inner equijoin; indeed, that is how it is defined.

How then *is* the outer natural join related to the corresponding outer equijoin? An examination of relations XNSP and XSP provides the answer. Attribute CITY of relation XNSP represents a *coalescing* of attributes SCITY and PCITY of relation XSP, where that coalescing is defined as follows:

■ Let y be a tuple of relation XSP, and let z be the corresponding tuple of XNSP. (Note that there is necessarily a one-to-one correspondence between tuples of XSP and tuples of XNSP.) Then:

1. If y.SCITY = y.PCITY, then z.CITY is also equal to each of these two values;

2. Otherwise, at least one of y.SCITY and y.PCITY must be null. If they are both null, then z.CITY is also null; otherwise, z.CITY is equal to the nonnull member of the pair.

Aside: Informally, attribute CITY is "almost" the union of attributes SCITY and PCITY—almost, but not quite, because that union will contain at most one null value (follows from the duplicate elimination rule used in the definition of *union*), whereas attribute CITY in the example contains two.

Although it is true in general that, as we have shown, the outer natural join is not a projection of the outer equijoin, it *will* be such a projection if the relations in question satisfy a certain kind of referential constraint

[5] which we will refer to here as a *subset* constraint. Let the two relations whose outer natural join is to be formed be R and S, and let the attributes over which the join is to be taken be R.B1 and S.B2. Relations R and S will be said to satisfy a subset constraint if it is not possible for relation S to contain a value of S.B2 that does not simultaneously exist as a value of R.B1 in relation R. In other words, at all times the set of values appearing in attribute S.B2 is a subset of the set of values appearing in attribute R.B1. Note in particular that the subset constraint will be satisfied if R.B1 is the primary key of R, S.B2 is a corresponding foreign key in S, and S.B2 cannot accept null values. (The last of these conditions is important, by the way. Foreign keys do not necessarily have the "nulls not allowed" property [5,6].)

■ *Example 3* (courses and offerings, outer natural join):

Consider the following database concerning courses and offerings (the FOREIGN KEY clause should be self-explanatory):

```
COURSE    ( COURSE#, SUBJECT )
          PRIMARY KEY ( COURSE# )

OFFERING ( COURSE#, OFF#, LOCATION )
          PRIMARY KEY ( COURSE#, OFF# )
          FOREIGN KEY ( COURSE# IDENTIFIES COURSE
                        NULLS NOT ALLOWED )
```

Sample values:

COURSE	COURSE#	SUBJECT	OFFERING	COURSE#	OFF#	LOCATION
	C1	Algebra		C1	O1	MIT
	C2	Calculus		C1	O2	UCLA

The outer natural join of COURSE and OFFERING over COURSE. COURSE# and OFFERING.COURSE# is relation XNCO:

XNCO	COURSE#	SUBJECT	OFF#	LOCATION
	C1	Algebra	O1	MIT
	C1	Algebra	O2	UCLA
	C2	Calculus	?	?

Here the outer natural join *is* a projection of the corresponding outer equijoin, because relations COURSE and OFFERING satisfy an appropriate subset constraint. To be specific, relation XNCO is identical to the outer equijoin of COURSE and OFFERING over course numbers, except that that outer equijoin includes an additional, identical copy of the COURSE# attribute. Neither of these outer joins is a legal base relation.

DISCUSSION AND FURTHER EXAMPLES

The topic of outer join is surprisingly subtle. It is necessary to examine several examples in order to appreciate all the ramifications of the concept. In this section, therefore, we present some additional examples in order to illustrate some of those ramifications; we also show how the user might formulate queries involving outer joins in the absence of any direct support for outer join in the language at hand. Specifically, we show how the language SQL [1] could be used—where possible—to express the queries of our examples, both those shown in the previous section and some additional ones introduced below. A point of detail: We take one slight liberty with the SQL language as defined in [1], by assuming that it is valid to include the NULL constant in a SELECT-clause. (For some reason SQL does not currently permit such a usage, although it does allow the SELECT-clause to include other constant values.)

- *Example 1* (suppliers and parts, outer equijoin):

```
SELECT  S#, SCITY, P#, PCITY
FROM    S, P
WHERE   SCITY = PCITY

UNION

SELECT  S#, SCITY, NULL, NULL
FROM    S
WHERE   NOT EXISTS
      ( SELECT *
        FROM    P
        WHERE   PCITY = SCITY )

UNION

SELECT  NULL, NULL, P#, PCITY
FROM    P
WHERE   NOT EXISTS
      ( SELECT *
        FROM    S
        WHERE   SCITY = PCITY )
```

Here we have a single SELECT-expression, consisting of three smaller SELECT-expressions that are "UNIONed together." The three smaller expressions correspond directly to the three components of an outer equijoin (see the "Definitions and Examples" section earlier): The first represents the inner equijoin, the second represents the additional tuples needed to preserve information for relation S, and the third represents the additional tuples needed to preserve information for relation P.

- *Example 1A* (suppliers-parts-projects, outer equijoin):

The following database is an extended version of that used in Example 1. Relation J represents projects.

```
S ( S#, SCITY )
  PRIMARY KEY ( S# )

P ( P#, PCITY )
  PRIMARY KEY ( P# )

J ( J#, JCITY )
  PRIMARY KEY ( J# )
```

Sample values:

S	S#	SCITY		P	P#	PCITY		J	J#	JCITY
	S1	London			P1	London			J1	London
	S2	Paris			P2	Oslo			J2	Rome
	S3	?			P3	?			J3	?
	S4	NY			P4	NY			J4	SFO
	S5	SFO			P5	LA			J5	LA

Suppose we wish to form "the outer equijoin of relations S, P, and J over cities." Let us examine this requirement in detail. As we shall see, it will turn out that this "outer join" is not well-defined, and it will be necessary to be more specific in the problem definition. First, let XSP be the outer equijoin of S and P over SCITY and PCITY (as in Example 1):

XSP	S#	SCITY	P#	PCITY
	S1	London	P1	London
	S2	Paris	?	?
	S3	?	?	?
	S4	NY	P4	NY
	S5	SFO	?	?
	?	?	P2	Oslo
	?	?	P3	?
	?	?	P5	LA

Then:

(a) The outer equijoin of XSP and J on SCITY and JCITY is:

XSPJA	S#	SCITY	P#	PCITY	J#	JCITY
	S1	London	P1	London	J1	London
	S2	Paris	?	?	?	?
	S3	?	?	?	?	?
	S4	NY	P4	NY	?	?
	S5	SFO	?	?	J4	SFO
	?	?	P2	Oslo	?	?
	?	?	P3	?	?	?
	?	?	P5	LA	?	?
	?	?	?	?	J2	Rome
	?	?	?	?	J3	?
	?	?	?	?	J5	LA

(b) The outer equijoin of XSP and J on PCITY and JCITY is:

XSPJB	S#	SCITY	P#	PCITY	J#	JCITY
	S1	London	P1	London	J1	London
	S2	Paris	?	?	?	?
	S3	?	?	?	?	?
	S4	NY	P4	NY	?	?
	S5	SFO	?	?	?	?
	?	?	P2	Oslo	?	?
	?	?	P3	?	?	?
	?	?	P5	LA	J5	LA
	?	?	?	?	J2	Rome
	?	?	?	?	J3	?
	?	?	?	?	J4	SFO

Observe that these two results (XSPJA and XSPJB) are different (they differ in the 5th, 8th, and 11th tuples as shown). Hence it is not possible to refer unambiguously to "the outer equijoin of S, P, J on SCITY, PCITY, JCITY"; loosely speaking, the value of the outer equijoin differs depending on whether the join predicate is

```
SCITY = PCITY  AND  SCITY = JCITY
```

or

```
SCITY = PCITY  AND  PCITY = JCITY
```

or indeed

```
SCITY = JCITY  AND  PCITY = JCITY
```

the third possibility (exercise for the reader). This is unfortunate, since these three join predicates are intuitively all equivalent to each other, and indeed are actually so in the absence of null values. As a consequence, any language proposal that supports outer equijoins of more than two relations must allow the user to indicate exactly which of the various possible results is required.

Let us assume, then, that the required result in the example is the relation XSPJA shown above. In other words, we wish to preserve:

- Matching S and P tuples that have no matching J tuple;
- Matching S and J tuples that have no matching P tuple;
- S tuples that have no matching P tuple;
- P tuples that have no matching S tuple;
- J tuples that have no matching S tuple.

The general requirement is thus to be able to preserve information, not just for one or more individual relations, but rather for one or more *matching combinations* of one or more relations each. A suitable SQL expression for the example is as follows:

```
SELECT  S#, SCITY, P#, PCITY, J#, JCITY
FROM    S, P, J
WHERE   SCITY = PCITY
AND     SCITY = JCITY

UNION

SELECT  S#, SCITY, P#, PCITY, NULL, NULL
FROM    S, P
WHERE   SCITY = PCITY
AND     NOT EXISTS
        ( SELECT *
          FROM   J
          WHERE  JCITY = SCITY )

UNION

SELECT  S#, SCITY, NULL, NULL, J#, JCITY
FROM    S, J
WHERE   SCITY = JCITY
AND     NOT EXISTS
        ( SELECT *
          FROM   P
          WHERE  PCITY = SCITY )

UNION

SELECT  S#, SCITY, NULL, NULL, NULL, NULL
FROM    S
WHERE   NOT EXISTS
        ( SELECT *
          FROM   P
          WHERE  PCITY = SCITY )

UNION

SELECT  NULL, NULL, P#, PCITY, NULL, NULL
FROM    P
WHERE   NOT EXISTS
        ( SELECT *
          FROM   S
          WHERE  SCITY = PCITY )

UNION

SELECT  NULL, NULL, NULL, NULL, J#, JCITY
FROM    J
WHERE   NOT EXISTS
        ( SELECT *
          FROM   S
          WHERE  SCITY = JCITY )
```

The six SELECT-expressions that are UNIONed together here correspond, in order, to the inner join and the five distinct relation combinations for which information is to be preserved. This example illustrates very clearly the desirability of some more explicit support for the outer join operation in the user language.

- *Example 2* (suppliers and parts, outer natural join):

```
SELECT  S#, SCITY /* or PCITY */, P#
FROM    S, P
WHERE   SCITY = PCITY

UNION

SELECT  S#, SCITY, NULL
FROM    S
WHERE   NOT EXISTS
      ( SELECT *
        FROM    P
        WHERE   PCITY = SCITY )

UNION

SELECT  NULL, PCITY, P#
FROM    P
WHERE   NOT EXISTS
      ( SELECT *
        FROM    S
        WHERE   SCITY = PCITY )
```

Note that some of the SELECT-expressions that are UNIONed together here have to select supplier cities and some part cities, even though all those cities correspond to the same attribute in the result. A similar remark would apply to any language that is based on the concept of taking projections (as SQL is, and as indeed most relational languages are). The reason is that, as pointed out before, the outer natural join in this example is not a projection of the corresponding outer equijoin.

- *Example 2A* (suppliers-parts-projects, outer natural join):

Suppose now that we wish to form the outer *natural* join of relations S, P, and J over cities. It will turn out that this outer join *is* well-defined; the ambiguities that arose in Example 1A do not appear here. First, let XNSP be the outer natural join of S and P over SCITY and PCITY (as in Example 2):

XNSP	CITY	S#	P#
	London	S1	P1
	Paris	S2	?
	?	S3	?
	NY	S4	P4
	SFO	S5	?
	Oslo	?	P2
	?	?	P3
	LA	?	P5

(we now show the CITY attribute at the left to facilitate comparison with relation XNSPJ below). Then the outer natural join of XNSP and J on CITY and JCITY is:

XNSPJ	CITY	S#	P#	J#
	London	S1	P1	J1
	Paris	S2	?	?
	?	S3	?	?
	NY	S4	P4	?
	SFO	S5	?	J4
	Oslo	?	P2	?
	?	?	P3	?
	LA	?	P5	J5
	Rome	?	?	J2
	?	?	?	J3

It should be clear from the internal symmetry of relation XNSPJ that the result would be the same no matter which two of S, P, J were joined first. Thus, the expression "the outer natural join of relations R1, R2, ..., Rn over attributes R1.A1, R2.A2, ..., Rn.An" is always unambiguous, and can be evaluated by repeatedly replacing pairs of relations in the set by their outer natural join over the applicable pair of attributes, until the entire set has been reduced to a single relation—namely, the result of the original join. In performing this evaluation, pairs of relations to be joined can be selected in a totally arbitrary sequence.

The fact that outer natural join is unambiguous in the foregoing sense can be informally (and imprecisely) but conveniently characterized in either of the following two ways:

(a) Outer natural join is associative (unlike outer equijoin). That is, if A, B, and C are relations and if *∧* represents the outer natural join operator, then A*∧*(B*∧*C) and (A*∧*B)*∧*C can each be unambiguously simplified to A*∧*B*∧*C. (We are not seriously proposing a notation here. The representation *∧* would clearly be inadequate in practice, since it does not identify the attributes over which the join is to be taken.)

(b) Outer natural join produces *all matching combinations* of the input (as well as preserving that part of the input that does not match anything). In relation XNSPJ, for example, we see tuples for:

▪ Matching suppliers, parts, and projects (i.e., suppliers, parts, and projects that all have the same city);

   ▪ Matching suppliers and parts that have no matching project;

   ▪ Matching parts and projects that have no matching supplier;

   ▪ Matching projects and suppliers that have no matching part;

- Suppliers that have no matching part or project;
- Parts that have no matching project or supplier;
- Projects that have no matching supplier or part.

The SQL formulation for this example involves seven SELECT-expressions all UNIONed together. Details are left as an exercise for the reader.

- *Example 3* (courses and offerings, outer natural join):

```
SELECT COURSE.COURSE#, SUBJECT, OFF#, LOCATION
FROM   COURSE, OFFERING
WHERE  COURSE.COURSE# = OFFERING.COURSE#

UNION

SELECT COURSE#, SUBJECT, NULL, NULL
FROM   COURSE
WHERE  NOT EXISTS
     ( SELECT *
       FROM   OFFERING
       WHERE  OFFERING.COURSE# = COURSE.COURSE# )
```

This example is comparatively straightforward in SQL because the outer natural join here *is* a projection of the outer equijoin (the relations satisfy an appropriate subset constraint). But we stress the "comparatively."

- *Example 3A* (courses-offerings-students, outer natural join):

This is an extended version of the database used in Example 3:

```
COURSE   ( COURSE#, SUBJECT )
         PRIMARY KEY ( COURSE# )

OFFERING ( COURSE#, OFF#, LOCATION )
         PRIMARY KEY ( COURSE#, OFF# )
         FOREIGN KEY ( COURSE# IDENTIFIES COURSE
                       NULLS NOT ALLOWED )

STUDENT  ( COURSE#, OFF#, EMP#, GRADE )
         PRIMARY KEY ( COURSE, OFF#, EMP# )
         FOREIGN KEY ( COURSE#, OFF# IDENTIFIES OFFERING
                       NULLS NOT ALLOWED )
```

Sample values:

COURSE	COURSE#	SUBJECT	OFFERING	COURSE#	OFF#	LOCATION
	C1	Algebra		C1	O1	MIT
	C2	Calculus		C1	O2	UCLA

STUDENT	COURSE#	OFF#	EMP#	GRADE
	C1	O1	E1	A
	C1	O1	E2	B

As in Example 3, it is possible for some COURSE# value to appear in COURSE and not in OFFERING, but not conversely; i.e., COURSE and OFFERING satisfy a subset constraint. Likewise, it is possible for some (COURSE#,OFF#) pair to appear in OFFERING and not in STUDENT, but not conversely; i.e., OFFERING and STUDENT also satisfy a subset constraint.

Now suppose we wish to construct "the outer natural join of COURSE, OFFERING, and STUDENT over course numbers and offering numbers." As in Example 3, we can construct the outer natural join of COURSE and OFFERING over course numbers (relation XNCO). Then we can form the outer natural join of XNCO and STUDENT over the attributes (COURSE#,OFF#), namely relation XNCOS:

XNCOS	COURSE#	SUBJECT	OFF#	LOCATION	EMP#	GRADE
	C1	Algebra	O1	MIT	E1	A
	C1	Algebra	O1	MIT	E2	B
	C1	Algebra	O2	UCLA	?	?
	C2	Calculus	?	?	?	?

SQL solution:

```
SELECT  COURSE.COURSE#, SUBJECT, OFFERING.OFF#, LOCATION,
        EMP#, GRADE
FROM    COURSE, OFFERING, STUDENT
WHERE   COURSE.COURSE# = OFFERING.COURSE#
AND     OFFERING.COURSE# = STUDENT.COURSE#
AND     OFFERING.OFF# = STUDENT.OFF#

UNION

SELECT  COURSE.COURSE#, SUBJECT, OFFERING.OFF#, LOCATION,
        NULL, NULL
FROM    COURSE, OFFERING
WHERE   COURSE.COURSE# = OFFERING.COURSE#
AND     NOT EXISTS
      ( SELECT *
        FROM    STUDENT
        WHERE   STUDENT.COURSE# = OFFERING.COURSE#
        AND     STUDENT.OFF# = OFFERING.OFF# )

UNION

SELECT  COURSE.COURSE#, SUBJECT, NULL, NULL, NULL, NULL
FROM    COURSE
WHERE   NOT EXISTS
      ( SELECT *
        FROM    OFFERING
        WHERE   OFFERING.COURSE# = COURSE.COURSE# )
```

Like Example 3, this example involves primary-key/foreign-key joins. However, it is more general than Example 3, in that it involves three relations instead of two. Again we need to be able to preserve information for *combinations* of relations. To be specific, we need to preserve information for (a) COURSEs having no OFFERINGs, plus (b) matching (COURSE,OFFERING) pairs having no STUDENTs. The information preserved under (b) here is not just OFFERING tuples that do not participate in the inner natural join, but such OFFERING tuples in combination with matching COURSE tuples.

We conclude this section by remarking that, although all our examples concern themselves with outer equijoins or outer natural joins, it is of course important to be able to handle arbitrary outer theta-joins. Equijoins and natural joins just happen to be important special cases in practice.

A CONCRETE PROPOSAL

In this section we present a multipart proposal for expressing outer joins in a relational language. We express our proposal in the form of a set of extensions to the language SQL, in order to facilitate comparisons with (a) the examples of the previous section, and (b) Chamberlin's proposal [2], described in the next section. Our proposal:

- Is easily adaptable to other languages such as QUEL [10].

- Handles simple cases simply.

- Is completely general; it handles outer natural join and all flavors of outer theta-join (left, right, and symmetric forms, with arbitrary join predicates, and including in particular outer equijoin).

- Allows any outer join, involving any number of relations, to be represented as a single SELECT-expression.

- Allows most outer joins to be expressed quite succinctly (certainly more succinctly than either the UNION-style approach shown in the previous section or the proposals of [2] discussed later).

- Involves a set of extensions to SQL that (a) are reasonably slight, (b) do not do violence to the spirit of the existing language, and (c) to some extent are desirable anyway, regardless of their usefulness in connexion with outer join.

For expository reasons we proceed one step at a time, instead of presenting the entire proposal at once. The steps we consider are as follows (in order):

- Outer theta-join of exactly two relations (Example 1);

- Outer theta-join of more than two relations (Example 1A);

- Outer natural join of exactly two relations (Examples 3 and 2);

- Outer natural join of more than two relations (Examples 3A and 2A).

Outer Theta-Join of Two Relations

We start by considering the SQL expression SELECT-FROM-WHERE. That expression is semantically equivalent to a relational algebra expression of the form:

```
projection ( restriction ( product ) )
```

Here "product" represents the extended Cartesian product of the relations identified in the FROM clause; "restriction" eliminates tuples from that product that do not satisfy the predicate in the WHERE clause; and "projection" picks attributes out of that restriction as specified by the SELECT clause. (The "projection" may or may not be a true projection—i.e., duplicate tuples may or may not be eliminated. The distinction is irrelevant for present purposes.) The argument to "projection"—namely, the restriction of the product—is often loosely referred to as a join, so we may say that the original SELECT-expression is equivalent to:

```
projection ( join )
```

or (more precisely) to:

```
projection ( inner-join )   .
```

To handle *outer* join queries, therefore, we don't want the argument to "projection" to be just this inner join, but rather some kind of outer join—that is, we want the inner join to be *augmented* in a certain way:

```
projection ( inner-join union augmentation)
```

(where "inner-join" and "augmentation" have no tuples in common). To produce the result of Example 1 above, for instance (i.e., relation XSP), the "augmentation" we need is precisely:

S#	SCITY	P#	PCITY
S2	Paris	?	?
S3	?	?	?
S5	SFO	?	?
?	?	P2	Oslo
?	?	P3	?
?	?	P5	LA

For the left outer equijoin it is just the first three of these tuples, and for the right outer equijoin it is just the last three.

In the simplest case (which is all we are considering for the moment), the FROM clause will list exactly two relations, say relations R and S. Suppose we wish to preserve information for relation R in the result. Then the necessary augmentation for R consists of all tuples t satisfying the following:

(a) t is *union-compatible* with (loosely, is the same shape as—see [3], [4], or [6]) the tuples of "inner-join," where "inner-join" is as defined above;

(b) t consists of an all-null tuple in the relation-S position, concatenated with, in the relation-R position, a copy of a tuple from relation R that is such that it does not appear anywhere in the relation-R position within "inner-join."

This notion of augmentation is well-defined and is generalizable to any number of relations (though the foregoing is of course not the necessary precise definition; that definition is given later). The first part of our proposal is therefore as follows: We propose the introduction of a new clause into the SQL SELECT-expression, the PRESERVE clause, whose effect is to generate the necessary augmentation for the relation(s) identified in that clause. Relations may be identified in the PRESERVE clause (a) by their name or alias, or (b) by their ordinal position within the FROM clause. (We shall see the need for this latter kind of specification later.) Consider Example 1 once again.

- *Example 1* (suppliers and parts, outer equijoin):

```
SELECT    S#, SCITY, P#, PCITY
FROM      S, P
WHERE     SCITY = PCITY
PRESERVE S    /* or PRESERVE 1 */
```

Result: Left outer equijoin of S and P on SCITY and PCITY (information is preserved for S, i.e., every tuple of S appears in the result; information is not preserved for P).

```
SELECT    S#, SCITY, P#, PCITY
FROM      S, P
WHERE     SCITY = PCITY
PRESERVE P    /* or PRESERVE 2 */
```

Result: Right outer equijoin of S and P on SCITY and PCITY.

```
SELECT    S#, SCITY, P#, PCITY
FROM      S, P
WHERE     SCITY = PCITY
PRESERVE S, P /* or PRESERVE 1, 2 */
```

Result: Symmetric outer equijoin of S and P on SCITY and PCITY.

Any relation mentioned in the PRESERVE clause must previously have been mentioned in the FROM clause. For this reason, it might appear that a more succinct syntax would be as suggested by the following example (left outer equijoin of S and P over SCITY and PCITY):

```
SELECT    S#, SCITY, P#, PCITY
FROM      S AUGMENTED, P
WHERE     SCITY = PCITY
```

(Some people would prefer to spell AUGMENTED as " + " or " * ", etc.)
This syntax is intuitively unappealing, however, and indeed misleading, because nothing is being done to relation S; the augmentation is applied to
the result of evaluating the inner join expression

```
( S, P WHERE SCITY = PCITY )    ,
```

and hence the PRESERVE logically belongs after the WHERE. This is in
keeping with the general order of evaluation of clauses within a SELECT-
expression, except for the special case of the SELECT-clause itself, which
is anomalous.

Outer Theta-Join of More Than Two Relations

As indicated above, the PRESERVE approach does generalize to the case
of more than two relations. Unfortunately, however, that generalization is
not particularly straightforward. The reason for this state of affairs is as
follows. As shown earlier, the expression "outer theta-join of three (or
more) relations" is not well-defined. The ambiguity does not arise in the
definition of the operation, because that definition deals with the two-relation case only; i.e., the operation is defined as a binary operation only.
An outer join of more than two relations has to be formulated as a suitably
parenthesized expression representing a nest of such binary operations—
e.g., as follows (Example 1A):

```
( S [ SCITY *=* PCITY ] P ) [ SCITY *=* JCITY ] J
```

or

```
( S [ SCITY *=* PCITY ] P ) [ PCITY *=* JCITY ] J
```

(the * = * is merely notation, as usual). These two expressions represent two
different outer equijoins—the first corresponds to XSPJA and the second
to XSPJB, to use the naming introduced earlier. SQL does not currently
support such nesting. Hence the second part of our proposal is, precisely,
to introduce such nesting. A SQL version of the first of these two algebraic
expressions (the "XSPJA version") might then look as follows:

```
SELECT    S#, SCITY, P#, PCITY, J#, JCITY
FROM      ( SELECT    S#, SCITY, P#, PCITY
            FROM      S, P
            WHERE     SCITY = PCITY
            PRESERVE S, P ), J
WHERE     SCITY = JCITY
PRESERVE 1, 2
```

The "XSPJB version" would differ from the above only in that the outer WHERE clause would specify PCITY instead of SCITY.

Note that a syntax such as

```
SELECT   S#, SCITY, P#, PCITY, J#, JCITY
FROM     ( S, P ), J
WHERE    SCITY = PCITY AND SCITY = JCITY
PRESERVE 1, 2
```

does *not* work. In the example, it is not relations S and P that need to be bracketed together, but rather the entire expression "relations S and P where SCITY = PCITY, preserving S and P" (i.e., it is not the *product* of S and P that needs to be evaluated as an inner nested expression, but rather the *outer equijoin* of those two relations over SCITY and PCITY). In other words, while it is easy to define a PRESERVE clause that will preserve information for individual relations, it is not possible to extend that clause directly to preserve information for arbitrary *combinations* of relations—because such a combination must itself be defined by means of a FROM clause *and an appropriate WHERE clause and possibly a PRESERVE clause too.*

Note, too, that the expression

```
SELECT   S#, SCITY, P#, PCITY, J#, JCITY
FROM     S, P, J
WHERE    SCITY = PCITY AND SCITY = JCITY
PRESERVE S, P, J
```

does have a meaning (see the formal definition of PRESERVE, later), but that meaning is not the same as that of the earlier expression representing relation XSPJA (it is not an outer join at all, in fact). The value of this expression is:

S#	SCITY	P#	PCITY	J#	JCITY
S1	London	P1	London	J1	London
S2	Paris	?	?	?	?
S3	?	?	?	?	?
S4	NY	?	?	?	?
S5	SFO	?	?	?	?
?	?	P2	Oslo	?	?
?	?	P3	?	?	?
?	?	P4	NY	?	?
?	?	P5	LA	?	?
?	?	?	?	J2	Rome
?	?	?	?	J3	?
?	?	?	?	J4	SFO
?	?	?	?	J5	LA

Here information has been preserved for each of S, P, J *individually*. Contrast this relation with the outer join XSPJA shown earlier.

Semantics of PRESERVE

We can define the semantics of PRESERVE by means of a suitable pseu-docode algorithm, as follows. Note: The algorithm below is presented for definitional purposes only and is not intended to prescribe a specific manner of implementation.

Let the relations in the FROM clause, in order, be R1, . . ., Rn.

Let R be the extended Cartesian product R1 X . . . X Rn.

Let ri denote a typical tuple of Ri (i = 1, . . ., n). Then the *concatenated* tuple r = r1|| . . .||rn denotes a typical tuple of R.

Let p be the predicate in the WHERE clause.

Let J be the restriction (R WHERE p).

Let j be a typical tuple of J. Then j is a concatenated tuple j1|| . . .||jn, where each ji is some ri (i = 1, . . ., n).

Let the relations identified in the PRESERVE clause, in the order in which they appear in the FROM clause, be Rx, . . ., Ry (1 < = x < = y < = n).

Then the effect of the PRESERVE clause is as indicated below:

```
result := J ;
do for all i in set {x,...,y} ;
   do for all ri in Ri ;
   if ~ EXISTS j in J such that ji = ri then
      do ;
         do k := 1 to n ;
            if k = i
            then jk := rk ;
            else jk := nk ;
                 /* nk is a tuple that is union-compatible */
                 /* with Rk but consists of null values in */
                 /* every position                         */
         end ;
         j := j1||...||jn ;
         append j to result ;
      end ;
   end ;
end ;
```

We remark that if n = 1 (i.e., if there is only one relation mentioned in the FROM clause), then the PRESERVE clause has no effect.

Outer Natural Join of Two Relations

Now we turn our attention to the case of outer natural join. Again we consider the two-relation case first. It should be clear from what has been said so far that the PRESERVE extension is inadequate in itself to handle the general outer natural join of two relations (the PRESERVE clause allows us to construct an outer equijoin, and the SELECT clause then allows us to take a projection of such an outer equijoin, but, as we have pointed out several times already, the outer natural join is not in general a projection of an outer equijoin). However, PRESERVE *is* adequate for the case where the two relations in question satisfy an appropriate subset constraint

- *Example 3* (courses and offerings, outer natural join):

```
SELECT    COURSE.COURSE#, SUBJECT, OFF#, LOCATION
FROM      COURSE, OFFERING
WHERE     COURSE.COURSE# = OFFERING.COURSE#
PRESERVE COURSE
```

What about Example 2, where the subset constraint is not satisfied? To handle this case, we need a way of "coalescing" two attributes of the outer equijoin, which brings us to the third part of our proposal. Specifically, we propose the introduction of a new (scalar) binary operator "?" into SQL, with definition as follows. Let x and y be two scalar values. Then the value v of the expression

```
x ? y
```

(suggested pronunciation: "x coalesce y") is defined as follows:

- If x and y are both null, then v is null.
- If x is null but y is not, or vice versa, then v is equal to the nonnull value of the pair.
- If x and y are both nonnull, then v is equal to the lesser of the two values. (For the intended use, x and y will in fact be equal, but we have to define the general case. Picking the lesser value is arbitrary.)

The "?" operator is associative.

- *Example 2* (suppliers and parts, outer natural join):

```
SELECT    S#, SCITY ? PCITY, P#
FROM      S, P
WHERE     SCITY = PCITY
PRESERVE S, P
```

It would also be nice to be able to introduce a name for the attribute of the result corresponding to the expression "SCITY ? PCITY"—e.g., as follows:

```
SELECT    S#, ( SCITY ? PCITY ) AS CITY, P#
FROM      S, P
WHERE     SCITY = PCITY
PRESERVE S, P
```

Aside: This function (the ability to give names to the attributes of the result of a SELECT-expression) would be generally useful, quite apart from its usefulness in the present context. (By the same token, it would be useful to be able to specify a name for the overall result relation, but we do not propose any syntax here for such naming.)

Nested SELECT-Expressions Revisited

We remark in passing that a variation on Example 3 can be used to show once again the usefulness of nested SELECT-expressions. The same example also illustrates the need for naming the result of a SELECT-expression (see the aside under Example 2 above). Consider the following two queries.

```
1. SELECT   ALGEBRA.COURSE#, OFF#, LOCATION
   FROM   ( SELECT COURSE#
            FROM   COURSE
            WHERE  SUBJECT = 'Algebra' ) ALGEBRA, OFFERING
   WHERE    ALGEBRA.COURSE# = OFFERING.COURSE#
   PRESERVE ALGEBRA

2. SELECT   COURSE.COURSE#, OFF#, LOCATION
   FROM     COURSE, OFFERING
   WHERE    COURSE.COURSE# = OFFERING.COURSE#
   AND      SUBJECT = 'Algebra'
   PRESERVE COURSE
```

Each of these queries lists all algebra courses together with their offerings. The first also lists algebra courses that do not have any offerings, concatenated with null values in the OFF# and LOCATION positions; i.e., it preserves information for those courses. The second, by contrast, preserves information not only for those courses, *but also for all courses for which the subject is not algebra* (regardless of whether those courses actually have any offerings of their own). In other words, the first preserves information for algebra courses only (presumably as required); the second produces a lot of unnecessary output.

Outer Natural Join of More Than Two Relations

Nested expressions are required again here; so also may be the "?" operator, in general, though it is not needed for Example 3A.

- *Example 3A* (courses-offerings-students, outer natural join):

```
SELECT   XNCO.COURSE#, SUBJECT, XNCO.OFF#, LOCATION,
         EMP#, GRADE
FROM   ( SELECT   COURSE.COURSE#, SUBJECT, OFF#, LOCATION )
         FROM     COURSE, OFFERING
         WHERE    COURSE.COURSE# = OFFERING.COURSE#
         PRESERVE COURSE ) XNCO, STUDENT
WHERE    XNCO.COURSE# = STUDENT.COURSE#
AND      XNCO.OFF# = STUDENT.OFF#
PRESERVE XNCO
```

Now let us consider Example 2A. Our proposals so far are certainly capable of handling this problem:

```
SELECT    SPCITY ? JCITY AS CITY, S#, P#, J#
FROM    ( SELECT    SCITY ? PCITY AS SPCITY, S#, P#
          FROM      S, P
          WHERE     SCITY = PCITY
          PRESERVE S, P ) SP, J
WHERE     SPCITY = JCITY
PRESERVE SP, J
```

However, this formulation is not exactly "user-friendly." For one thing, it requires a slightly tricky use of naming (see the outer WHERE clause). More significantly, it involves an unpleasant degree of arbitrariness, in that it forces an essentially symmetric operation into an asymmetric mold: The user is forced to express what is basically a ternary operation (outer natural join of three relations) as a binary operation, in which one of the two operands is itself the result of another (nested) binary operation, even though the choice as to precisely which binary operation is to be performed first is in fact arbitrary.

Aside: Example 3A above also involves a certain amount of arbitrariness, but not so much as in the present case. To be specific, Example 3A *must* be formulated as a nested expression, because of the intrinsic asymmetry of the problem; however, it is a fact that there are two equally valid such formulations, neither of which is superior in any obvious sense to the other. The two formulations are:

1. The one shown above, which we may represent schematically as (COURSE *∧ OFFERING) *∧ STUDENT; and

2. Another which we may represent schematically as COURSE *∧ (OFFERING *∧ STUDENT).

(Recall that the notation "*∧" stands for left outer natural join.)

We therefore propose a shorthand syntax for problems such as that of Example 2A. To be precise, we propose the introduction of an explicit JOIN operation into SQL—where the keyword JOIN refers specifically to the (inner or outer) *natural* join of a set of relations over a set of attributes, one attribute from each relation, such that:

(a) The attributes concerned effectively constitute a *common* attribute for all the relations in the set (in the sense that attributes SCITY, PCITY, and JCITY, for example, constitute a common attribute for relations S, P, and J);

(b) The join can be evaluated by repeatedly replacing pairs of relations in the set by their join over the applicable attributes, until the set reduces to exactly one relation; and

(c) The sequence in which those pairwise joins are performed is arbitrary.

Using this operator, Example 2A can be expressed as follows:

```
OUTER JOIN S, P, J ( SCITY, PCITY, JCITY ) AS CITY
```

Here OUTER of course indicates that this is an outer instead of an inner join (INNER is the default); the parenthesized list indicates the attributes (one from each relation) over which the join is to be taken; and CITY is an introduced name, to be used as the name of the joining attribute in the result. Observe, incidentally, that there is now no need in this example for the user to be aware of the "?" operator at all.

Please note carefully that we propose the explicit JOIN operator as a *shorthand* merely. The definition of a given JOIN-expression is in terms of an expansion into a semantically equivalent SELECT-expression. The dangers of introducing special-case syntax for special-case situations are of course well-known: It is important to tread carefully on that slippery slope. But a shorthand that is defined in terms of a carefully thought out general-purpose language is not the same thing as an ad hoc extension. In the case of natural join specifically, we believe that the operation is sufficiently important in practice that such a shorthand is justified. This does not necessarily mean that we advocate an explicit JOIN operator that is completely general-purpose and covers all possible flavors of join.

SUMMARY OF SYNTAX

We present a BNF syntax for SQL queries that includes all aspects of our proposal.

```
query
    ::=  relation-expression

relation-expression
    ::=  select-expression | join-expression

select-expression
    ::=  select-clause
         from-clause
         [ where-clause ]
         [ preserve-clause ]

select-clause
    ::=  SELECT attribute-commalist

attribute
    ::=  scalar-expression [ AS introduced-name ]

scalar-expression
    ::=  ... includes new form:
         scalar-expression ? scalar-expression
```

```
from-clause
    ::=  FROM relation-commalist

relation
    ::=  relation-value [ [ AS ] relation-alias ]

relation-value
    ::=  relation-name ¦ ( relation-expression )

relation-alias
    ::=  introduced-name

where-clause
    ::=  ... as today

preserve-clause
    ::=  PRESERVE preserve-item-commalist

preserve-item
    ::=  relation-name ¦ relation-alias ¦ integer

join-expression
    ::=  [ OUTER ¦ INNER ] JOIN relation-commalist on-clause

on-clause
    ::=  ON ( attribute-commalist ) [ AS introduced-name ]
```

A COMPARISON WITH CHAMBERLIN'S PROPOSAL

An earlier proposal for incorporating outer joins into SQL is given by Chamberlin in reference [2]. In essence, that proposal involves (a) a syntactic convention—appending a plus sign to certain relation-names in the FROM clause, to indicate that the relations so marked should conceptually be extended with a single all-null tuple for the duration of the query; together with (b) the requirement that the user express the entire outer-join-defining predicate (making use of the introduced all-null tuples) in the WHERE clause. As Chamberlin points out in [2], this proposal:

- Provides "controllable asymmetry" (left, right, and symmetric outer joins can all be handled);

- Applies to arbitrary join conditions (i.e., arbitrary predicates in the WHERE clause);

- Does not interfere with other aspects of the language;

- Involves a comparatively slight syntactic extension.

    Let us consider our examples once again in the light of this proposal.

- *Example 1* (suppliers and parts, outer equijoin):

```
SELECT  SX.S#, SX.SCITY, PX.P#, PX.PCITY
FROM    S+ SX, P+ PX
WHERE   SX.SCITY = PX.PCITY
```

```
OR    (       PX.PCITY IS NULL
        AND SX.SCITY IS NOT NULL
        AND NOT EXISTS
          ( SELECT *
            FROM    P
            WHERE   PCITY = SX.SCITY ) )

OR    (       SX.SCITY IS NULL
        AND PX.PCITY IS NOT NULL
        AND NOT EXISTS
          ( SELECT *
            FROM    S
            WHERE   SCITY = PX.PCITY ) )
```

The expression

```
x IS [ NOT ] NULL
```

is the SOL version of the function reference

```
[ ~ ] IS_NULL ( x )     .
```

See the "Note on Null Values" earlier in this paper.

- *Example 1A* (suppliers-parts-projects, outer equijoin):

```
SELECT SX.S#, SX.SCITY, PX.P#, PX.PCITY, JX.J#, JX.JCITY
FROM    S+ SX, P+ PX, J+ JX
WHERE   (       SX.SCITY = PX.PCITY
          AND SX.SCITY = JX.JCITY )

OR    (       SX.SCITY = PX.PCITY
        AND JX.JCITY IS NULL
        AND NOT EXISTS
          ( SELECT *
            FROM    J
            WHERE   JCITY = SX.SCITY ) )

OR    (       SX.SCITY = JX.JCITY
        AND PX.PCITY IS NULL
        AND NOT EXISTS
          ( SELECT *
            FROM    P
            WHERE   PCITY = SX.SCITY ) )

OR    (       PX.PCITY IS NULL
        AND JX.JCITY IS NULL
        AND SX.SCITY IS NOT NULL
        AND NOT EXISTS
          ( SELECT *
            FROM    P
            WHERE   PCITY = SX.SCITY ) )

OR    (       SX.SCITY IS NULL
        AND JX.JCITY IS NULL
        AND PX.PCITY IS NOT NULL
        AND NOT EXISTS
          ( SELECT *
            FROM    S
            WHERE   SCITY = PX.PCITY ) )
```

```
OR    (        SX.SCITY IS NULL
        AND PX.PCITY IS NULL
        AND JX.JCITY IS NOT NULL
        AND NOT EXISTS
            ( SELECT *
              FROM    S
              WHERE   SCITY = JX.JCITY ) )
```

The above represents the "XSPJA version." The "XSPJB version" is left
as an exercise.

- *Example 2* (suppliers and parts, outer natural join):

The proposals of [2] do not help with this problem.

- *Example 2A* (suppliers-parts-projects, outer natural join):

The proposals of [2] do not help with this problem.

- *Example 3* (courses and offerings, outer natural join):

```
SELECT COURSE.COURSE#, SUBJECT, OX.OFF#, OX.LOCATION
FROM    COURSE, OFFERING+ OX
WHERE   COURSE.COURSE# = OX.COURSE#

OR    (        OX.COURSE# IS NULL
        AND NOT EXISTS
            ( SELECT *
              FROM    OFFERING
              WHERE   OFFERING.COURSE# = COURSE.COURSE# ) )
```

- *Example 3A* (courses-offerings-students, outer natural join):

```
SELECT COURSE.COURSE#, SUBJECT, OX.OFF#, OX.LOCATION,
        SX.EMP#, SX.GRADE
FROM    COURSE, OFFERING+ OX, STUDENT+ SX
WHERE   (        COURSE.COURSE# = OX.COURSE#
          AND OX.COURSE# = SX.COURSE#
          AND OX.OFF# = SX.OFF# )

OR    (        COURSE.COURSE# = OX.COURSE#
        AND SX.COURSE# IS NULL
        AND SX.OFF# IS NULL
        AND NOT EXISTS
            ( SELECT *
              FROM    STUDENT
              WHERE   STUDENT.COURSE# = OX.COURSE#
              AND     STUDENT.OFF# = OX.OFF# ) )

OR    (        OX.COURSE# IS NULL
        AND NOT EXISTS
            ( SELECT *
              FROM    OFFERING
              WHERE   OFFERING.COURSE# = COURSE.COURSE# ) )
```

By comparison with our proposal, the proposal of [2]:

- Is quite complex, even in simple situations (see Example 1, for instance).

- Is error-prone. The differences between the expression shown under Example 1A (for instance) and some other expression that represents some distinct outer join, or some other result that is not an outer join at all, are extremely subtle. The chances of the user making a mistake are correspondingly high.
- Does not help with outer natural join (general case).
- Does not lead to particularly succinct expressions.
- Requires extremely careful use of relation-names and aliases (again see Example 1A, for instance).
- Is intuitively difficult to apply. Consider Example 3, for instance. Here it is the COURSE relation for which information is to be preserved, yet it is the OFFERING relation that has to be marked with the plus sign. In Example 3A, by contrast, it is COURSEs and OFFERINGs for which information is to be preserved, and OFFERINGs and STUDENTs that have to be marked. Thus there is no immediately obvious rule or correspondence connecting relations that need to be "preserved" and relations that need to be marked.
- Involves the (temporary) introduction of an all-null tuple into a relation, thereby (temporarily) violating the constraint that the primary key of a base relation cannot accept null values. Although this fact is not important in itself, it could be puzzling to the user.

CONCLUSION

We have presented a three-part proposal for supporting the outer join operation in a language such as SQL. We have shown that all three components of the proposal are necessary, in general. It is our belief that the proposal can easily be adapted for incorporation into other relational languages. In QUEL, for example [10], the effect of nesting could be obtained by allowing the scope of a tuple variable (defined via a RANGE statement) to be an arbitrary relation-expression, instead of just a single relation.

We may briefly summarize the three components of our proposal as follows:

1. The PRESERVE clause allows the user to specify that information be preserved for either or both of the relations in a two-relation theta-join.
2. Nesting SELECT-expressions within the FROM clause allows the construction of outer joins involving any number of relations.[1]

---

[1]The ability to nest SELECT-expressions in this sense is desirable anyway, quite apart from its utility in connexion with the outer join problem.

3. The "?" (coalesce) operator allows the construction of outer natural joins where the relations concerned do not satisfy an appropriate subset constraint.

We have also proposed a syntactic shorthand (the explicit JOIN operator) to simplify the formulation of certain queries that we believe occur frequently in practice—namely, queries that involve natural joins (either inner or outer), where the relations to be joined all share a common attribute and the join is to be taken over that common attribute. We remark that using the explicit JOIN operator is likely to improve the chances of the system implementing the join in an optimal or near-optimal manner.

ACKNOWLEDGMENTS

I am grateful, first of all, to Don Chamberlin, conversations with whom regarding his own outer join proposal made me aware of some of the difficulties inherent in the problem and led me, indirectly and belatedly, to the proposals of this paper. I would also like to acknowledge the helpful comments, criticisms, and suggestions of several friends and colleagues: Don Chamberlin (again), Ted Codd, Bob Engles, Phil Shaw, Jim Strickland, Irv Traiger, and George Zagelow.

REFERENCES

1. D. D. Chamberlin et al., "SEQUEL 2: A Unified Approach to Data Definition, Manipulation, and Control," *IBM J. R&D* 20, No. 6 (November 1976).

2. D. D. Chamberlin, "A Summary of User Experience with the SQL Data Sublanguage," *Proc. International Conference on Databases,* Aberdeen, Scotland (July 1980).

3. E. F. Codd, "Extending the Database Relational Model to Capture More Meaning," *ACM TODS* 4, No. 4 (December 1979).

4. C. J. Date, *An Introduction to Database Systems: Volume II* (Reading, MA: Addison-Wesley, 1982).

5. C. J. Date, "Referential Integrity" (in this volume).

6. C. J. Date, "A Formal Definition of the Relational Model" (in this volume).

7. C. J. Date, "Null Values in Database Management" (in this volume).

8. I. J. Heath, IBM internal memo (April 1971).

9. M. Lacroix and A. Pirotte, "Generalized Joins," *ACM SIGMOD Record* 8, No. 3 (September 1976).

10. M. R. Stonebraker, E. Wong, P. Kreps, and G. D. Held, "The Design and Implementation of INGRES," *ACM TODS* 1, No. 3 (September 1976).

17

Updating Views

ABSTRACT

We present a discussion of the view update problem. For reasons of familiarity the discussion is presented in terms of SQL, but the ideas are quite general and apply with only syntactic changes to any relational language. However, we do assume that the language in question provides full support for primary and foreign keys, along the lines suggested in reference [8]; such support is prerequisite to proper view update support. We also assume that the language provides direct support for the outer join operation along the lines sketched in reference [11].

The paper deliberately does not aim to cover all possible types of view, but it does address what are probably the commonest cases, including in particular various kinds of join view.

COMMENTS ON PUBLICATION

This paper has not previously been published. It nevertheless still seems appropriate to make a few introductory remarks about it here, analogous to the "Comments on Republication" on other papers in this collection.

Previously unpublished.

The ability to update views is of course a well-known requirement, and many systems do already support it in some shape or form. However, that support is usually quite ad hoc in nature. Typically, restriction and "projection" views ("projection" in quotes because duplicates are probably not eliminated) are handled by the base DBMS itself, and join views are handled—if they are handled at all—through some kind of frontend system (e.g., an application generator). In other words, systems have a builtin (albeit imperfect) understanding of what it means to update a restriction or a "projection," but must be explicitly told what it means to update a join. Note, moreover, that they must be told explicitly what it means to update *each specific* join; it is not possible to tell them once and for all what "updating a join" means in general terms.

The proposals of this paper, by contrast, provide a basis for handling all such views (restrictions, projections, and joins) directly at the base DBMS level. More specifically, they allow the system (a) to improve its imperfect understanding, and therefore its treatment, of the restriction and projection cases, and (b) to gain an understanding of the join case, so that it can apply the same generic approach to joins as it does to the other cases, instead of requiring explicit join-by-join instructions on what to do as at present.

INTRODUCTION

Support for the updating of views is both severely limited and extremely ad hoc in most, if not all, relational systems currently available. The principal reason for this state of affairs is that the systems in question have by and large failed to recognize the fundamental importance of primary and foreign keys (in this area as in so many others). The basic point is that updatability is a *semantic* issue—it requires some knowledge of what the data means; and primary and foreign keys, being semantic constructs, can provide some of that necessary knowledge. Part of the purpose of this paper is to justify this claim.

To achieve that purpose, the paper proceeds by considering, specifically, the relational language SQL—but a dialect of SQL that is assumed to include primary and foreign key support, along the lines suggested in, for example, reference [8]—and showing what the effect of updates on certain kinds of view should be in terms of that language. In other words, the paper can be regarded as a "view update" proposal for SQL. Note, however, that although the discussion is thus somewhat SQL-specific at the detail level, the underlying ideas are quite general and apply with only trivial changes to all relational systems and languages.

Note, too, that the proposals of this paper are definitely not ad hoc. They are intended to fit into the framework of a general and systematic approach to the whole question of view updating.

Numerous other view updating proposals have already appeared in the literature [3–6,12–19]; however, the present proposal, while perhaps not fundamentally different in philosophy from those others, is at least superficially different in its general approach. To be specific, the present proposal:

1. Is presented in a fairly informal (albeit rigorous) manner;

2. Is expressed in terms of the familiar relational model, not some less well-known and less well-defined "entity-relationship" or other model;

3. Can be seen as a logical consequence of the prescriptions of the relational model;

4. Explicitly recognizes the fundamental importance of primary and foreign keys in this context;

5. Includes a discussion of views that are defined as outer as well as inner joins;

6. Applies to "views on views" (i.e., it includes consideration of views whose constituent relations are themselves views);

7. Does not usurp very general terms such as "physical," "logical," and "virtual" and give them very special and unmemorable meanings (for example, there is no such thing in this proposal as a "delete rule of virtual").

The paper is *not* intended to be a totally complete treatment of the subject. Instead, it deliberately limits itself to restriction, projection, and join views only. In other words, we effectively assume that the available SQL dialect supports only these three operations of the relational algebra. Note: The term "join" here and throughout this paper means specifically the *natural* join (either the inner or the outer variety [11]); it does not mean a general theta-join. Note that we are therefore also assuming that SQL has been extended to provide the necessary outer join support, along the lines indicated in reference [11]. Direct support for outer join is desirable in this context because it simplifies the system's task of recognizing an outer join operation for what it is—in particular, in the definition of a view. In the absence of such direct support, the system would have to disentangle possibly quite complex circumlocutions in order to perform that necessary recognition.

SCOPE OF THIS PAPER

The paper falls into five broad parts:

1. An informal statement of the requirement, with examples and justification (two sections);

2. A more formal examination of base tables, views, and relations (one section);

3. A discussion of restriction and projection views, with some formal proposals for supporting updates on such views (two sections);

4. A discussion of join views likewise (four sections);

5. A summary (one section).

WHAT IS VIEW UPDATING FOR?

The principal advantage of being able to update views is of course that it enhances logical data independence [9], thus making it possible (among other things) to make changes in the logical structure of the database without necessitating corresponding changes in programs. Here are some examples, all of them involving join views specifically. Analogous examples involving projection and restriction views instead can easily be given, of course.

1. A base relation R is replaced by two of its projections R1 and R2 in such a manner that R can be reconstructed by taking some join of those projections. In SQL today (and in many other systems) retrieval operations against R can continue to work if we define that join as a view and give it the same name R. It would be nice if the same could be said for update operations (at present, of course, it cannot).

2. The normalization guidelines for database design suggest that if there is a one-to-many relationship between (say) departments and employees, then there should be two relations in the database, one for the "one" side of the relationship and one for the "many" side. Those relations will typically be in third normal form (3NF). However, a user may wish to view those relations joined together as a single (non3NF) relation. It is easy to satisfy such a requirement so far as retrieval operations are concerned; again it would be nice if updates worked too—i.e., if updates could be directed to the non3NF view and mapped through automatically to the 3NF relations underneath.

3. Imagine a full-screen (forms-based) frontend to the system—either a generalized query interface such as Query-By-Forms [2] or a specialized interface tailored to the particular requirements of some application. A common requirement for such a frontend is to be able to display an arbitrary relation (base relation or view) on the screen and to allow the end-user to update that relation by making changes to it directly on the screen. The implementation of such a frontend would obviously be simplified if the

underlying DBMS supported view updates (especially join view updates) directly.

Let us examine a more specific version of the first of these three examples. Suppose we are given an employee base relation, EMP say, with SQL definition as follows:

```
CREATE TABLE EMP ( EMP# ... ,
                   ENAME ... ,
                   DEPT# ... ,
                   SALARY ... )
          PRIMARY KEY ( EMP# ) ;
```

(Note the explicit PRIMARY KEY clause [8].) Now suppose that EMP is to be replaced for some reason by two of its projections EES and ED:

```
CREATE TABLE EES ( EMP# ... ,
                   ENAME ... ,
                   SALARY ... )
          PRIMARY KEY ( EMP# ) ;

CREATE TABLE ED  ( EMP# ... ,
                   DEPT# ... )
          PRIMARY KEY ( EMP# ) ;
```

Then we can create a view called EMP that is effectively identical to the old base relation EMP:

```
CREATE VIEW EMP ( EMP#, ENAME, DEPT#, SALARY )
     AS SELECT EES.EMP#, EES.ENAME, ED.DEPT#, EES.SALARY
        FROM   EES, ED
        WHERE  EES.EMP# = ED.EMP# ;
```

This definition represents the (inner) natural join of EES and ES over EMP#. A program that previously issued SELECT operations against base relation EMP can now execute unchanged against view EMP. But a program that previously issued INSERT, DELETE, or UPDATE operations against base relation EMP will no longer work, because SQL currently does not support such operations on join views. If we were allowed to "update the join," however, that program could continue to work.

As a matter of fact, it is easy to see that INSERT, DELETE, and UPDATE operations *could* all be supported in this example. Informally:

1. Inserting a new tuple *t* into view EMP maps into the insertion of appropriate subtuples of *t* into each of base relations EES and ED.

2. Deleting a tuple *t* from view EMP maps into the deletion of corresponding subtuples of *t* from each of base relations EES and ED.

3. Updating an attribute *a* of a tuple *t* in view EMP maps into an update of the corresponding attribute of the corresponding subtuple of *t* in

whichever of base relations EES and ED happens to contain that at-tribute—or, if attribute *a* happens to be EMP#, then the update maps into an update of EMP# within two subtuples, one in each of base relations EES and ED.

The reason that updating the join is feasible in this example is of course that the join in question is a join of two relations on their primary keys—i.e., a "(PK,PK)-join" (see later). Updates to the join can be mapped through to updates on the underlying relations because, for any given tuple of the join, the corresponding underlying tuples can be pinpointed (i.e., uniquely identified) via their primary keys. The example thus highlights the crucial importance of the primary key concept in this whole area; more precisely, it shows why (in this context, among others) it is important for the system to be able to recognize primary keys and to understand their implications.

Note: The foregoing explanation does, however, gloss over one important point. Once base relation EMP has been split into base relations EES and ED, there is no a priori guarantee that those latter two relations will remain in synch. For example, it may now be possible to insert a tuple into relation EES for some employee *e*, say, without at the same time in-serting a tuple for *e* into ED (indeed, this possibility may have been the motivation for the split in the first place). If it is indeed possible that EES and ED may be out of synch in this sense, then view EMP should be defined as the *outer* join of EES and ED over EMP#, not (as above) the inner join, and the implications for update operations would then be rather different. It follows that any proposal for updating views should be prepared to deal with outer as well as inner joins.

SOME PRELIMINARY REMARKS

First, a few general principles:

1. The overall objective is to make a view look like a base relation, insofar as possible.
2. Side-effects are to be avoided; i.e., updating one tuple in a view should not cause other tuples in that view to change simultaneously and ap-parently unpredictably.
3. The effect of updating a view should be definable in terms of a small set of generally applicable rules; it should not be wildly different for views that are at least superficially similar. *In other words, we are look-*

*ing for automated (system-supported) solutions, not an "exit routine"
approach.*

4. Every update operation must be atomic (all or nothing) from the user's
   perspective, even if it maps to many updates under the covers. SAVE
   and RESTORE operations (as provided by, e.g., System R) can (and
   must) be used to achieve this effect, in general. Such operations are not
   shown explicitly in the algorithms given in this paper, however.

Now, it is well known that some views are *inherently* nonupdatable (in
the sense that they cannot be updated at all without violating one or more
of the principles listed above). For example, let relations R and S be as
follows:

```
    --- ---                  --- ---
R    A   B          S         B   C
    --- ---                  --- ---
     a   b                    b   c
     x   b                    b   z
```

Let V be a view that is defined as the (inner) natural join of R and S
over B:

```
    --- --- ---
V    A   B   C
    --- --- ---
     a   b   c
     a   b   z
     x   b   c
     x   b   z
```

Here are some examples of updates that cannot be supported on view
V:

1. It is not possible to delete just one tuple from V, say the tuple (a,b,c),
   because the relation that would remain would not be the join of any
   relations R and S whatsoever.

2. It is not possible to update the tuple (a,b,c) to, say, the tuple (a,b,d),
   for the same reason.

3. It is not possible to insert the tuple (a,b,d), say, for the same reason
   once again.

However, it is possible to perform certain updates on certain views—
in particular, on certain join views—when the system has the necessary understanding of what is going on (i.e., the necessary intelligence to understand the user's intent). And, as already indicated, it is primary and foreign
keys that provide the basis for that necessary understanding. The proposals
that follow therefore rely very heavily on these constructs.

BASE TABLES, VIEWS, AND RELATIONS

Base tables and views are not necessarily relations in SQL (nor are they in most other current systems, in fact). A relation can be regarded as a table that has a primary key, and thus does not contain any duplicate rows. *The proposals that follow apply to relations only, not to tables in general. As far as this paper is concerned, a table that does not have a primary key is not updatable.* What is more, it is not sufficient that a table merely *be* a relation in order to be updatable—it must be *known to the system* to be a relation (see paragraphs 3, 5, and 8 below for a definition of what "known to the system" means here). Henceforth, we will use the term "relation" to mean a table that is known to the system to be a relation—i.e., a table that has a system-known primary key. We will assume that any other table can at least potentially include duplicate records, and is therefore at least potentially not a "genuine relation."

More terminology: We will use the term "base relation" for a relation that is a base table, the term "derived relation" for a relation that is derived from one or more other relations by means of some SQL expression, and the term "virtual relation" for a *named* derived relation. (In other words, a virtual relation is a view—but not all views are virtual relations, since some views are not relations at all.)

1.   We assume throughout this paper (without loss of generality) that all primary and foreign keys are single-attribute. Paragraphs 8, 10, and 11 below show that this assumption is a reasonable one, in that it does not lead to any inconsistency. Extension to the multiattribute case is tedious but straightforward.

2.   Let V be a derived relation. For the purposes of this paper, V is assumed to be exactly one of the following:

(a)   A restriction of some relation R;

(b)   A KP-projection of some relation R;

(c)   An inner or outer (PK,PK)-join of two relations R and S;

(d)   An inner (PK,FK)-join of two relations R and S.

(The terms restriction, KP-projection, (PK,PK)-join, and (PK,FK)-join are defined later.)

In cases (a) and (b), relation R is the (only) *immediate participant* relation for V. In cases (c) and (d), relations R and S are the (only) immediate participant relations for V. Note that there is no requirement for an immediate participant to be a base relation, or even a named relation.

3.   A base table is known to the system to have a primary key—i.e., is a

base relation—if and only if an explicit declaration to that effect has been made.

4. A base table is known to the system to have a foreign key if and only if an explicit declaration to that effect has been made.

5. A view is known to the system to have a primary key—i.e., is a virtual relation—if and only if a primary key is inherited as explained in paragraph 8 below from (one of) the immediate participant(s) in the view.

6. A view is known to the system to have a foreign key if and only if a foreign key is inherited as explained in paragraphs 10 and 11 below from (one of) the immediate participant(s) in the view.

7. The constraint that no primary key value can be null does not apply to derived relations (but see paragraph 9 below). However, it is of course still the case that no relation can contain two tuples with the same primary key value—i.e., duplicate primary key values are not allowed. For this purpose, the definition of "duplicate" is extended, as follows [10]:

- The scalar values x and y are considered to be duplicates of one another if and only if either (a) x = y or (b) x and y are both null.
- The tuples $(x1,x2,...,xn)$ and $(y1,y2,...,yn)$ are considered to be duplicates of one another if and only if xi and yi are duplicates of one another for all i $(i = 1,2,...,n)$.

This is effectively the way duplicates are defined in SQL, incidentally.

8. Let R be a relation with (system-known) primary key Rp, and let V be a derived relation for which R is (one of) the immediate participant relation(s). Then relation V has a system-known primary key Vp, defined as follows:

(a) If V is a restriction of R, then Vp is the attribute of V that corresponds to Rp in R.

(b) If V is a KP-projection of R, then Vp is the attribute of V that corresponds to Rp in R.

(c) If V is an inner or outer (PK,PK)-join of R with some relation S (with system-known primary key Sp), then Vp is the attribute of V that corresponds to Rp in R (equivalently, to Sp in S).

Note: The primary key of an arbitrary outer (PK,PK)-join is the combination of all attributes of the relation, in general (see the discussion of this topic near the end of this paper). However, we impose certain constraints on R and S to ensure that Vp is in fact as defined here, even in the outer case. Specifically, we do not allow R or S to be an outer (PK,FK)-join. See paragraph 9.

(d) If V is an inner (PK,FK)-join of some relation S with R (i.e., the join is taken over the primary key Sp of S and some matching foreign key Rf in R), then Vp is the attribute of V that corresponds to Rp in R.

Each of these cases is amplified later. In all cases, Vp is said to be *derived from* Rp (loosely, "is the same as" Rp). To simplify subsequent discussion, it is convenient to consider the original primary key Rp itself as also being derived from Rp (via an identity derivation). The significance of this notion of derivation is made clear in paragraph 11.

9. Observe that the case in which V is an outer (PK,FK)-join is specifically excluded from (a)–(d) under paragraph 2 above, and therefore also from cases (a)–(d) under paragraph 8. *For the purposes of this paper, we do not consider an outer (PK, FK)-join to be a relation*: It does not possess a system-known primary key. We adopt this position in order to avoid having to consider outer joins in which one of the immediate participants is an outer (PK,FK)-join. We will justify this position later. Here we simply state that it leads to an important simplification, namely as follows: We never need to consider the possibility of updating a relation in which nulls are allowed for the primary key.

10. Let R be a relation with (system-known) primary key Rp, and let S be a relation with a (system-known) foreign key Sf matching Rp. Let V be a derived relation for which S is (one of) the immediate participant relation(s). If V includes an attribute Vf corresponding to Sf in S (note that the only case in which it does not is when V is defined as a projection of S and attribute Sf is not preserved in that projection), then V has a system-known foreign key, namely Vf, matching the primary key Rp in R.

11. Let R be a relation with (system-known) primary key Rp, and let S be a relation that includes an attribute Sf. Then Sf is a system-known foreign key matching Rp if and only if Sf is a system-known foreign key matching some primary key from which Rp is derived.

We are now in a position to define, in a recursive fashion, the effect of each of the update operations INSERT, DELETE, and UPDATE on certain kinds of derived relation—namely, restrictions, certain kinds of projection, and certain kinds of join.

Notes

1. The only kind of derived relation that can be updated *explicitly* is of course a *named* derived relation—i.e., a virtual relation. But the effect of updating a named derived relation may well have to be defined in terms of updating any number of *un*named derived relations (intermediaries be-

tween the named derived relation in question and the base relation(s) ultimately underlying that original named relation).

2. As stated earlier, we do not consider the question of updating views that are not relations. Our general feeling is that the existing SQL support for updating "row-and-column-subset" views [1,7] should be cleaned up, and that support for updates on join-style views that are not relations should not even be attempted.

3. All remarks in what follows regarding null values will require some slight modification if the system supports default values instead [10].

4. *Notation:* Throughout what follows, we assume the existence of relations R and S, with attributes as indicated:

```
R ( R1, ..., Rp, ..., Rm )
S ( S1, ..., Sp, ..., Sn )
```

Rp is the primary key of R and Sp is the primary key of S. We also assume where appropriate that S includes a foreign key Sf matching the primary key Rp of R. We do *not* assume that R and S are base relations, or even named relations.

Finally, we use *r-pred* to represent an arbitrary *restriction predicate*. (A restriction predicate is a predicate that can be evaluated for a given tuple by examining that tuple in isolation. Thus, given the SQL expression "SELECT * FROM R WHERE *r-pred,*" *r-pred* is a restriction predicate on R if and only if the only tuple variable it contains is R. We limit our attention to restriction predicates because they are the only kind we need for the limited set of operations we are considering, namely restriction, projection, and join.

RESTRICTION

Informally, a restriction is always updatable; updates simply map through directly into updates on the underlying relation. The only problem is ensuring that the resulting relation continues to satisfy the restriction predicate. We make these ideas more precise as follows.

A *restriction-expression* is an expression that evaluates to a restriction—in SQL terms, an expression of the form

```
SELECT R.R1, ..., R.Rp, ..., R.Rm
FROM    R
WHERE   r-pred ;
```

(or syntactic variation of the same that does not affect the meaning; note in particular that specifying DISTINCT preceding the SELECT-list is one such variation). If R is updatable and if V is defined (by means of a restriction-expression) as a restriction of R, then V is updatable as defined below.

INSERT on Restriction:

The operation

```
INSERT INTO V ( R1, ..., Rp, ..., Rm )
       VALUES ( r1, ..., rp, ..., rm ) ;
```

is defined to be equivalent to the sequence:

```
does the new tuple (r1,r2,...,rm) satisfy
                            the defining predicate for V ?
if not, ERROR ;
else
do ;
   INSERT INTO R ( R1, ..., Rp, ..., Rm )
          VALUES ( r1, ..., rp, ..., rm ) ;
   INSERT successful ? if not, ERROR ;
end ;
```

For generality we assume that the original INSERT supplies a value for every attribute of V (of course, supplying no value for some attribute is equivalent to supplying a null value for that attribute). The expansion shows the single-tuple case. The multi-tuple case INSERT ... SELECT is defined to be a shorthand for an appropriate series of single-tuple INSERTs, except of course that the entire operation should be atomic.

Note: SQL does provide some support for "INSERT on restriction" today, although of course it has no knowledge of relations as such. However, it does not currently support "INSERT on restriction" if DISTINCT appears in the SELECT-clause; also, the predicate check shown in the expansion above is currently optional in DB2, and can be applied only in certain special cases [1,7], and is not performed at all in SQL/DS [1].

DELETE on Restriction:

The operation

```
DELETE FROM V
WHERE   r-pred ;
```

is defined to be equivalent to the sequence:

```
DELETE FROM R
WHERE   r-pred-1
AND     r-pred-2 ;
DELETE successful ? if not, ERROR ;
```

Here *r-pred-1* is a predicate obtained from *r-pred* by replacing all references to V by references to R, and *r-pred-2* is the defining predicate for

V. The expansion shows the multi-tuple case. The single-tuple operation DELETE ... WHERE CURRENT is defined analogously.

Note: SQL does provide some support for "DELETE on restriction" today, but with the same shortcomings as noted under "INSERT on restriction" above.

UPDATE on Restriction:

The operation

```
UPDATE V
SET    R1 = r1, ..., Rp = rp, ..., Rm = rm
WHERE  r-pred ;
```

is defined to be equivalent to the sequence:

```
does the tuple (r1,r2,...,rm) satisfy
                       the defining predicate for V ?
if not, ERROR ;
else
do ;
    UPDATE R
    SET    R1 = r1, ..., Rp = rp, ..., Rm = rm
    WHERE  r-pred-1
    AND    r-pred-2 ;
    UPDATE successful ? if not, ERROR ;
end ;
```

For generality, we assume that the original UPDATE supplies a value for every attribute of V (of course, supplying no value for some attribute is equivalent to supplying a value for that attribute that is the same as the preUPDATE value). As in the DELETE case above, *r-pred-1* is a predicate obtained from *r-pred* by replacing all references to V by references to R, and *r-pred-2* is the defining predicate for V. The expansion shows the multi-tuple case. The single-tuple UPDATE ... WHERE CURRENT is defined analogously.

Note: SQL does provide some support for "UPDATE on restriction" today, but with the same shortcomings as noted under "INSERT on restriction" and "DELETE on restriction" above.

PROJECTION

Informally, a projection is updatable if and only if it preserves the primary key of the underlying relation, for then and only then can the system determine the precise tuple to be updated in that underlying relation. (Remember that projection involves duplicate elimination, in general; thus, if the primary key is not preserved, a given tuple of the projection may correspond to multiple tuples in the underlying relation.) We make these ideas more precise as follows.

A *projection-expression* is an expression that evaluates to a projection—in SQL terms, an expression of the form

```
SELECT DISTINCT R.Rx, R.Ry, ..., R.Rz
FROM   R ;
```

(or syntactic variation of the same that does not affect the meaning; note in particular that omitting DISTINCT if the SELECT-list includes Rp is one such variation). Rx, Ry, ..., Rz are attributes of R. No attribute can appear in the SELECT-list more than once.

If the primary key Rp is included in the SELECT-list, the projection is said to be a *key-preserving* projection (KP- projection). As already pointed out, DISTINCT need not be specified for a KP-projection, though it should not be disallowed. If R is updatable and if V is defined (by means of a projection-expression) as a KP-projection of R, then V is updatable as defined below.

INSERT on KP-Projection:

The operation

```
INSERT INTO V ( Rx, Ry, ..., Rz )
       VALUES ( rx, ry, ..., rz ) ;
```

is defined to be equivalent to the sequence:

```
INSERT INTO R ( Rx, Ry, ..., Rz )
       VALUES ( rx, ry, ..., rz ) ;
INSERT successful ? if not, ERROR ;
```

For generality, we assume that the original INSERT supplies a value for every attribute of V (of course, supplying no value for some attribute is equivalent to supplying a null value for that attribute). The expansion shows the single-tuple case. The multi-tuple case INSERT ... SELECT is defined to be a shorthand for an appropriate series of single-tuple IN-SERTs, except of course that the entire operation should be atomic.

Note: SQL does provide some support for "INSERT on projection" today, although of course it has no knowledge of relations as such. Loosely speaking, it supports "INSERT on *tuple*-preserving projections" (i.e., "projections" that do not involve DISTINCT) rather than key-preserving ones—with a "user beware" if the primary key is in fact not preserved.

Note also that if V is a KP-projection of a *restriction* R, and the definition of restriction R is of the form "... WHERE Ry = ry," and V does not include attribute Ry, then V cannot validly support INSERT operations at all. This is because attribute Ry will be set to null in the new tuple, thus violating the defining predicate for restriction R.

DELETE on KP-Projection:

The operation

```
DELETE FROM V
WHERE   r-pred ;
```

is defined to be equivalent to the sequence:

```
DELETE FROM R
WHERE   r-pred-1 ;
DELETE successful ? if not, ERROR ;
```

Here *r-pred-1* is a predicate obtained from *r-pred* by replacing all references to V by references to R. The expansion shows the multi-tuple case. The single-tuple operation DELETE ... WHERE CURRENT is defined analogously.

Note: SQL does provide some support for "DELETE on projection" today, but with the same shortcomings as noted under "INSERT on projection" above.

UPDATE on KP-Projection:

The operation

```
UPDATE V
SET    Rx = rx, Ry = ry, ..., Rz = rz
WHERE   r-pred ;
```

is defined to be equivalent to the sequence:

```
UPDATE R
SET    Rx = rx, Ry = ry, ..., Rz = rz
WHERE   r-pred-1 ;
UPDATE successful ? if not, ERROR ;
```

For generality, we assume that the original UPDATE supplies a value for every attribute of V (of course, supplying no value for some attribute is equivalent to supplying a value for that attribute that is the same as the preUPDATE value). As in the DELETE case above, *r-pred-1* is a predicate obtained from *r-pred* by replacing all references to V by references to R. The expansion shows the multi-tuple case. The single-tuple UPDATE ... WHERE CURRENT is defined analogously.

Note: SQL does provide some support for "UPDATE on projection" today, but with the same shortcomings as noted under "INSERT on projection" and "DELETE on projection" above.

JOIN

Now we turn to the question of join views. As indicated earlier in this paper, we deliberately do not consider all possible kinds of join. Instead, we restrict our attention to *natural* joins only (inner or outer); moreover, we consider only the case in which the attributes over which the join is taken are the primary key R.Rp of the one relation (R) and either the primary key S.Sp or a foreign key S.Sf matching R.Rp in the other relation (S). We refer to the first possibility as a (PK,PK)-join and the second as a (PK,FK)-join. We do not consider natural joins of any other kind, because we have already seen that the problem is unsolvable in more general cases, and because (PK,PK)- and (PK,FK)-joins represent the practical requirement. (By "unsolvable" here we mean "unsolvable without violating the principles established earlier"—e.g., the "no side-effects" principle.) We do not consider general theta-joins for the same reason.

Let R and S be two relations, some join of which we wish to be able to update. Either or both of R and S may be derived. However, for any given tuple of R or S, there exists some well-defined underlying tuple or set of tuples in some well-defined base relation(s), from which that tuple of R or S is ultimately derived. *We assume that R and S are such that there do not exist two distinct tuples, both in R or both in S or one in each, such that those two tuples have any underlying base tuples in common.* If this assumption is invalid, the result of an attempt to update an otherwise updatable join of R and S is unpredictable.

(PK,PK)-JOIN

Updates on a (PK,PK)-join map to corresponding updates to *both* of the participant relations (*very* loosely speaking). For example, deleting a tuple from such a join maps to a delete on both of the participants. We make these ideas more precise as follows.

Assume that R.Rp and S.Sp are comparable attributes. Then R and S are said to be (*PK,PK*)-*joinable*. A (PK,PK)-join of R and S is either an inner or an outer natural join of R and S over their primary keys Rp and Sp. Note: We assume that R.Rp is *not* a (system-known) foreign key matching S.Sp, and that likewise S.Sp is not a (system-known) foreign key matching R.Rp; for otherwise the join would be interpreted as a (PK,FK)-join (see later).

The *inner (PK,PK)-join* of R and S is the result of evaluating an expression of the form

```
SELECT R.R1, ..., R.Rp, ..., R.Rm, S.S1, ..., S.Sn
FROM   R, S
WHERE  R.Rp = S.Sp ;
```

(or syntactic variation of the same that does not affect the meaning). The SELECT-clause here is intended to list all attributes of relation R and all attributes of relation S except for attribute S.Sp, the primary key of S.

The *outer (PK,PK)-join* of R and S is the result of evaluating an expression of the form

```
SELECT   R.R1, ..., R.Rp ? S.Sp, ..., R.Rm, S.S1, ..., S.Sn
FROM     R, S
WHERE    R.Rp = S.Sp
PRESERVE R, S ;
```

(or syntactic variation of the same that does not affect the meaning). The SELECT-clause is intended to list all attributes of relation R and all attributes of relation S, except that attributes R.Rp and S.Sp are "coalesced" by means of the expression "R.Rp ? S.Sp". (See reference [11] for an explanation of the semantics of "coalesce," also of the PRESERVE clause. Note that the SELECT-expression shown above represents the "full" or symmetric outer join. If left and right outer joins are to be considered in addition, the proposals of this section will require a certain amount of modification.)

The primary key of an inner (PK,PK)-join is the attribute Vp of the result corresponding to attribute Rp of relation R. The primary key of an outer (PK,PK)-join is the attribute Vp of the result corresponding to the expression "R.Rp ? S.Sp" in the SELECT-list; in other words, it is (again) the attribute corresponding to attribute Rp of relation R, loosely speaking.

Note: As indicated earlier in this paper, our definition of "relation" guarantees that the foregoing statement is accurate in both the inner and outer cases. What is more, the primary key Vp is guaranteed not to contain any null values, even in the outer case.

If derived relation V is defined as a (PK,PK)-join of relations R and S and if R and S are both updatable, then V is updatable as explained below. Note: We assume that the attributes of V (in left-to-right order) are

```
V1,...,Vp,...,Vm,V(m+1),...,V(m+n-1)   ;
```

that is, attributes V1,...,Vp,...,Vm correspond to attributes R1,...,Rp,..., Rm of relation R, and attributes V(m+1),...,V(m+n-1) correspond to attributes S1,...,Sn (with attribute Sp omitted) of relation S.

One final preliminary remark: The expansions shown below are deliberately made general enough to deal with both inner and outer joins; some of the tests are in fact redundant for the inner join case. Indeed, the algorithms can probably be improved in many ways in any given situation.

INSERT on (PK,PK)-Join:

The operation

```
INSERT INTO V ( V1, ..., Vp, ..., Vm, V(m+1), ..., V(m+n-1) )
       VALUES ( v1, ..., vp, ..., vm, v(m+1), ..., v(m+n-1) ) ;
```

is defined to be equivalent to the sequence:

```
if vp is null, ERROR ;
if a tuple with Vp = vp already exists in V, ERROR ;
if a tuple with Rp = vp exists in R and
   no tuple with Sp = vp exists in S then
   /* applies to inner join only */
do ;
   if ~ (R1 = v1 and ... and Rm = vm), ERROR ;
   INSERT INTO S ( S1, ..., Sp, ..., Sn )
           VALUES ( v(m+1), ..., vp, ..., v(m+n-1) ) ;
   INSERT successful ? if not, ERROR ;
end ;
if a tuple with Sp = vp exists in S and
   no tuple with Rp = vp exists in R then
   /* applies to inner join only */
do ;
   if ~ (S1 = v(m+1) and ... and Sn = v(m+n-1)), ERROR ;
   INSERT INTO R ( R1, ..., Rp, ..., Rm )
           VALUES ( v1, ..., vp, ..., vm ) ;
   INSERT successful ? if not, ERROR ;
end ;
if no tuple with Rp = vp exists in R and
   no tuple with Sp = vp exists in S then
do ;
   INSERT INTO R ( R1, ..., Rp, ..., Rm )
           VALUES ( v1, ..., vp, ..., vm ) ;
   INSERT successful ? if not, ERROR ;
   INSERT INTO S ( S1, ..., Sp, ..., Sn )
           VALUES ( v(m+1), ..., vp, ..., v(m+n-1) ) ;
   INSERT successful ? if not, ERROR ;
end ;
```

The expansion shows the single-tuple case. The multi-tuple INSERT is defined to be a shorthand for an appropriate series of single-tuple INSERTs, except of course that the entire operation should be atomic.

DELETE on (PK,PK)-Join:

The operation

```
DELETE FROM V
WHERE   r-pred ;
```

is defined to be equivalent to the sequence:

```
CREATE TABLE TEMP ( Vp ) ;
INSERT INTO TEMP ( Vp )
       SELECT Vp FROM V
       WHERE  r-pred ;
DELETE FROM R
WHERE  EXISTS
     ( SELECT * FROM TEMP
       WHERE  TEMP.Vp = R.Rp ) ;
DELETE successful ? if not, ERROR ;
DELETE FROM S
WHERE  EXISTS
     ( SELECT * FROM TEMP
       WHERE  TEMP.Vp = S.Sp ) ;
DELETE successful ? if not, ERROR ;
DROP TABLE TEMP ;
```

The expansion shows the multi-tuple case. The single-tuple operation DELETE CURRENT is defined analogously.

UPDATE on (PK,PK)-Join:

The operation

```
UPDATE V
SET    V1 = v1, ..., Vp = vp, ..., Vm = vm,
       V(m+1) = v(m+1), ..., V(m+n-1) = v(m+n-1)
WHERE  r-pred ;
```

(where for generality we show all attributes being updated) is defined to be equivalent to the sequence:

```
if vp is null, ERROR ;
CREATE TABLE TEMP ( Vp ) ;
INSERT INTO TEMP ( Vp )
       SELECT Vp FROM V
       WHERE  r-pred ;
do for each tuple t in TEMP ;
   if a tuple r with r.Rp = t.Vp exists in R then
   do ;
       UPDATE R
       SET    R1 = v1, ..., Rp = vp, ..., Rm = vm,
       WHERE  R.Rp = t.Vp ;
       UPDATE successful ? if not, ERROR ;
   end ;
   else
   if ~ (v1 is null and ... and vm is null) then
   do ;
       INSERT INTO R ( R1, ..., Rp, ..., Rm )
              VALUES ( v1, ..., vp, ..., vm ) ;
       INSERT successful ? if not, ERROR ;
   end ;
   if a tuple s with s.Sp = t.Vp exists in S then
   do ;
       UPDATE S
       SET    V(m+1) = v(m+1), ..., V(m+n-1) = v(m+n-1)
       WHERE  S.Sp = t.Vp ;
```

```
      UPDATE successful ? if not, ERROR ;
   end ;
   else
   if ˜ (v(m+1) is null and ... and v(m+n-1) is null) then
   do ;
      INSERT INTO S ( S1, ..., Sp, ..., Sn )
              VALUES ( v(m+1), ..., vp, ..., v(m+n-1) ) ;
      INSERT successful ? if not, ERROR ;
   end ;
end ;
DROP TABLE TEMP ;
```

The expansion shows the multi-tuple case. The single-tuple UPDATE
CURRENT is defined analogously.

(PK,PK)-Join: Simplified Summary

INSERT: if key exists in R and not in S,
         (a) R-data must agree
         (b) insert into S
      if key exists in S and not in R,
         (a) S-data must agree
         (b) insert into R
      if key does not exist in either R or S,
         (a) insert into R
         (b) insert into S

DELETE: if key exists in R, delete from R
      if key exists in S, delete from S

UPDATE: if key exists in R, update R
      else insert into R
         (unless all nonkey R-attributes are null)
      if key exists in S, update S
      else insert into S
         (unless all nonkey S-attributes are null)

INNER (PK,FK)-JOIN

Informally, updating an inner (PK,FK)-join maps into an update on the
foreign key side only (except that INSERT may cause an insert on the primary key side too). For example, deleting a tuple from such a join maps
into either a delete on the foreign key side or an update to set the foreign
key to null, depending on whether NULLS NOT ALLOWED applies to the
foreign key in question (once again, very loosely speaking). We make these
ideas more precise as follows.

Let Sf be a foreign key in S that matches the primary key Rp of R. (For simplicity we assume that S has only one foreign key matching the primary key of R. This simplifying assumption does not materially affect the discussion in any way.) Then R and S are said to be (*PK,FK*)-*joinable* (over R.Rp and S.Sf). The *inner* (PK,FK)-join of R with S is the inner natural join of R and S over the primary key of R and and the matching foreign key of S; in other words, it is the result of evaluating an expression of the form

```
SELECT R.R1, ..., R.Rp,..., R.Rm, S.S1, ..., S.Sp, ..., S.Sn
FROM   R, S
WHERE  R.Rp = S.Sf ;
```

(or syntactic variation of the same that does not affect the meaning). The SELECT-clause here is intended to list all attributes of relation R and all attributes of relation S except for attribute S.Sf, the foreign key in S matching the primary key of R.

The primary key of the inner (PK,FK)-join is the attribute Vp of the result that corresponds to attribute Sp of relation S (i.e., it "is" S.Sp, loosely speaking).

The following diagram may be helpful. It is intended to represent both an inner *and an outer* (PK,FK)-join of relation R (primary key R.Rp) and relation S (primary key S.Sp). "PRESERVEd" tuples in the outer join are tuples from one of the input relations that have no match in the other. Note that the outer join can be regarded as the union of three pairwise-disjoint relations, corresponding (from top to bottom of the diagram) to "PRESERVE R," the inner join, and "PRESERVE S," respectively. As a help in interpreting this diagram, we also show a version with some data values filled in. In this latter version, relation R is the department relation DEPT (primary key D#), relation S is the employee relation EMP (primary key E#, foreign key D#). For generality, we assume that some DEPTs have no EMPs and that some EMPs have a null D# value, i.e., are currently assigned to no DEPT. Null values are shown as question marks.

If derived relation V is defined as an inner (PK,FK)-join of relations R and S and if R and S are updatable, then V is updatable as explained below. Note: We assume that the attributes of V (in left-to-right order) are

```
V1,...,Vp,...,Vm,V(m+1),...,V(m+p),...,V(m+n-1)    ;
```

that is, attributes V1,...,Vp,...,Vm correspond to attributes R1,...,Rp, ...,Rm of relation R, and attributes V(m+1),...,V(m+p),...,V(m+n-1) correspond to attributes S1,...,Sp,...,Sn (with attribute Sf omitted) of relation S. Attribute V(m+p) is the primary key of V.

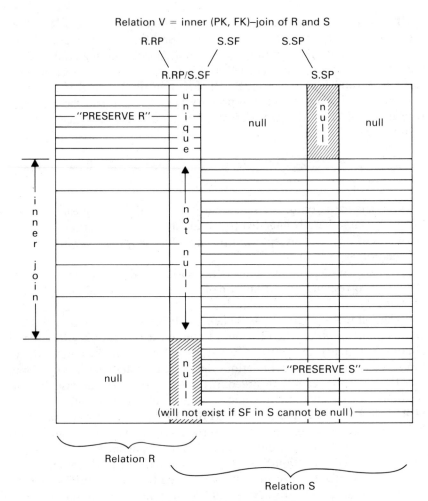

Inner/outer (PK,FK)-join of relations R and S

INSERT on Inner (PK,FK)-Join:

The operation

```
INSERT INTO V ( V1, ..., Vp, ..., Vm,
          V(m+1), ..., V(m+p), ..., V(m+n-1) )
     VALUES ( v1, ..., vp, ..., vm,
          v(m+1), ..., v(m+p), ..., v(m+n-1) ) ;
```

is defined to be equivalent to the sequence:

Relation DEPTEMP = inner (PK, FK)–join of DEPT and EMP

DEPT.D#   EMP.D#   EMP.E#

	D#		E#	
	D10		?	
	D11		?	
	D12	null	?	null
	D13		?	
	D14		?	
	D15		?	
	D1		E11	
	D1		E12	
	D2		E21	
	D2		E22	
	D2		E23	
	D2		E24	
	D3		E31	
	D4		E41	
	D4		E42	
	D5		E51	
	D5		E52	
	D5		E53	
	?		E61	
	?		E62	
null	?		E63	
	?		E64	
	?		E65	
	?		E66	

inner join

DEPT   EMP

Example: Inner/outer (PK,FK)-join of relations DEPT and EMP

```
if vp is null, ERROR ;
if v(m+p) is null, ERROR ;
if a tuple with V(m+p) = v(m+p) already exists in D, ERROR ;
if a tuple with Rp = vp exists in R and
    ~ (R1 = v1 and ... and Rm = vm), ERROR ;
INSERT INTO R ( R1, ..., Rp, ..., Rm )
      VALUES ( v1, ..., vp, ..., vm ) ;
INSERT successful ? if not, ERROR ;
if a tuple with Sp = v(m+p) exists in S then
do ;
   if Sf is not null, ERROR ;
   if ~ (S1 = v(m+1) and ... and Sn = v(m+n-1)), ERROR ;
   UPDATE S
   SET    Sf = vp
```

```
      WHERE   Sp = v(m+p) ;
      UPDATE successful ? if not, ERROR ;
   end ;
   else
   do ;
      INSERT INTO S ( S1, ..., Sf, ..., Sn )
             VALUES ( v(m+1), ..., vp, ..., v(m+n-1) ) ;
      INSERT successful ? if not, ERROR ;
   end ;
```

The expansion shows the single-tuple case. The multi-tuple INSERT is defined to be a shorthand for an appropriate series of single-tuple IN-SERTs, except of course that the entire operation should be atomic.

DELETE on Inner (PK,FK)-Join:

The operation

```
   DELETE FROM V
   WHERE   r-pred ;
```

is defined to be equivalent to the sequence:

```
   CREATE TABLE TEMP ( Vp ) ;
   INSERT INTO TEMP ( Vp )
          SELECT Vp FROM V
          WHERE   r-pred ;
   do the appropriate one of the following cases ;
      Case 1: DELETE CASCADES for S.Sf :
          DELETE FROM S
          WHERE   EXISTS
              ( SELECT * FROM TEMP
                WHERE   TEMP.Vp = S.Sp ) ;
          DELETE successful ? if not, ERROR ;
      end Case 1 ;
      Case 2: DELETE RESTRICTED for S.Sf :
          ERROR ;
      end Case 2 ;
      Case 3: DELETE NULLIFIES for S.Sf :
          UPDATE S
          SET     Sf = NULL
          WHERE   EXISTS
                ( SELECT * FROM TEMP
                  WHERE   TEMP.Vp = S.Sp ) ;
          UPDATE successful ? if not, ERROR ;
      end Case 3 ;
   end case ;
   DROP TABLE TEMP ;
```

The expansion shows the multi-tuple case. The single-tuple operation DELETE CURRENT is defined analogously.

UPDATE on Inner (PK,FK)-Join:

The operation

```
   UPDATE V
   SET     V(m+1) = v(m+1), ..., V(m+n-1) = v(m+n-1)
   WHERE   r-pred ;
```

(note that no R-attributes can be updated, and hence that S.Sf cannot be updated either) is defined to be equivalent to the sequence:

```
CREATE TABLE TEMP ( Vp ) ;
INSERT INTO TEMP ( Vp )
       SELECT Vp FROM V
       WHERE  r-pred ;
UPDATE S
SET    S1 = v(m+1), ..., Sn = v(m+n-1)
WHERE  EXISTS
       ( SELECT * FROM TEMP
         WHERE  TEMP.Vp = S.Sp ) ;
UPDATE successful ? if not, ERROR ;
DROP TABLE TEMP ;
```

The expansion shows the multi-tuple case. The single-tuple UPDATE CURRENT is defined analogously.

Inner (PK,FK)-Join: Simplified Summary

INSERT: if key exists in R, data must agree
      if key does not exist in R, insert into R
      if key exists in S,
        (a) Sf must be null
        (b) other data must agree
        (c) update Sf to nonnull
      if key does not exist in S, insert into S

DELETE: if nulls not allowed for Sf, delete from S
      if nulls allowed for Sf, set Sf to null

UPDATE: update S data => update S
      update R data => not allowed

OUTER (PK,FK)-JOIN

In this section we justify our position regarding outer (PK,FK)-joins. That position is as follows (to summarize):

(a) The primary key of an outer (PK,FK)-join is not "known to the system";

(b) Therefore an outer (PK,FK)-join is not considered to be a relation for the purposes of this paper;

(c) Therefore an outer (PK,FK)-join is not updatable;

(d) Therefore no object that is derived from an outer (PK,FK)-join is updatable either. More precisely, an outer (PK,FK)-join cannot be a participant in a derived relation, as that latter term is defined herein. Thus:

- A restriction of an outer (PK,FK)-join is not considered to be a relation and cannot be updated;

- A KP-projection of an outer (PK,FK)-join cannot even be defined, since there is no system-known primary key;
- No (inner or outer) (PK,PK)-join or (inner) (PK,FK)-join can have an outer (PK,FK)-join as a participant.

Note carefully that the foregoing does not mean that an outer (PK,FK)-join cannot participate in any further operations at all; it certainly can, and what is more that further operation might even be a join over (say) the primary key of the outer (PK,FK)-join and some matching foreign key somewhere; however, that primary key and that matching foreign key will not be recognized by the system as such, and so the result will not, by definition, be considered as a (PK,FK)-join, or indeed any kind of relation, and will not be updatable.

The principal reason for imposing the foregoing restrictions is that, out of the operations considered in this paper, *outer (PK,FK)-join is the only one that can introduce a (partly) null primary key value.* In fact, it is the only one that can introduce a composite (multiattribute) primary key. That is, the outer (PK,FK)-join of two relations having noncomposite primary keys is guaranteed to have

(a) a composite primary key, and

(b) at least one partly null primary key value,

except in degenerate cases (refer back to the diagrams shown earlier). Note, however, that if the participant relations do not include any all-null primary key values, then the result will not do so either.

Hence, by imposing the restrictions we do, we can guarantee that:

(a) If all base relations have noncomposite primary keys, then all derived relations will do so also—i.e., we do not have to consider composite primary keys at all;

(b) In particular, we do not have to consider composite primary key values in which the components are themselves composite and *each component* is partly but not wholly null;

(c) In fact, we do not have to consider primary key values that are (wholly or partly) null at all, and we can agree that any attempt to introduce such a value is an error;

(d) We do not have to define primary key inheritance rules for nonKP-projections—in particular, for projections that preserve part but not all of a composite primary key;

(e) We never need to eliminate duplicate tuples in the formation of an outer join (see below);

(f) We can guarantee that the primary key of an outer (PK,PK)-join is "the same as" that of the corresponding inner join (otherwise it would have to be the combination of all attributes in the relation).

To illustrate some of these points, assume first that R and S are as in the section "Inner (PK,FK)-Joins"—i.e., R has primary key Rp, S has primary key Sp and foreign key Sf matching R.Rp. The outer natural join of relations R and S over the primary key Rp of R and the matching foreign key Sf of S is the result of evaluating an expression of the form

```
SELECT    R.R1, ..., R.Rp ? S.Sf, ..., R.Rm,
          S.S1, ..., S.Sp, ..., S.Sn
FROM      R, S
WHERE     R.Rp = S.Sf
PRESERVE  R, S ;
```

The primary key of an outer (PK,FK)-join is the composite attribute that corresponds in the result to the combination of attributes (R.Rp ? S.Sf, S.Sp). Note: We are stating here what the primary key actually is; as explained earlier, we explicitly do not consider this primary key to be "system-known."

To see that the primary key must be this combination (i.e., must be composite), as we claim, the reader may find it helpful to refer back once again to the inner and outer join diagrams shown earlier in this paper. Those diagrams show why either component of a given value of such a primary key can be null. Moreover, if relation R includes a tuple in which Rp is wholly null, and/or relation S includes a tuple in which Sp and Sf are both wholly null, then the outer join will contain a tuple in which the primary key value is wholly null. Note in turn that this fact means that it may be necessary to apply duplicate elimination in the construction of an outer join. (It is never necessary in the construction of an inner join, of course.) For example, consider the outer join of R and S over Rp and Sf, where R and S are as follows:

```
         --              --
R        Rp       S      Sf
         --              --
         ?               ?
```

Neither of these two tuples matches the other, and so an intermediate result in the construction of the outer join is likely to be the following (note that it is of course not a relation):

```
         --      --
         Rp      Sf
         --      --
         ?       ?
         ?       ?
```

Consider also the following example. Let R and S be as follows:

```
        --   --                --   --
R       Ra   Rp        S       Sp   Sb
        --   --                --   --
        a1   p1                p1   b1
        a2   p2                p3   b3
        ?    ?                 ?    b2
```

R.Rp and S.Sp are the primary keys of R and S. The outer (PK,PK)-join of R and S is:

```
        --   --   --
        a    p    b
        --   --   --
        a1   p1   b1
        a2   p2   ?
        ?    ?    ?
        ?    p3   b3
        ?    ?    b2
```

What is the primary key of this join? It is not just p. It *could* be the combination (p,b), but only because R includes an all-null tuple and S does not; if the situation were reversed, then (p,b) could not be the primary key, though then (a,p) could. Since we obviously cannot have the primary key dependent on the chance distribution of data values, we have to say that the primary key is the combination of all attributes, in general.

SUMMARY

We have presented a proposal for updating certain kinds of view, namely restrictions, KP-projections, inner and outer (PK,PK)-joins, and inner (PK,FK)-joins, in a relational language such as SQL. We have also shown some of the difficulties inherent in updating certain other kinds of view, namely outer (PK,FK)-joins.

The proposal is not limited to SQL, of course; on the contrary, it can easily be adapted to other relational languages and systems. It is intended to serve as a basis for the incorporation of *automatic* support for view updating into the base DBMS; it is not an "exit routine," "frontend system," or other ad hoc kind of scheme. Instead, it uses the semantic notions of primary and foreign key to provide a systematic and generic approach to the problem. It is our feeling that support for view updating in existing systems should be tidied up (along the lines we have indicated) before any attempt is made to extend that support to other kinds of view.

REFERENCES

1. Information on DB2 and SQL/DS is available from IBM Corporation, Armonk, New York.

2. Information on Query-By-Forms is available from Relational Technology Inc., 1080 Marina Village Parkway, Alameda, California.

3. F. Bancilhon and N. Spyratos, "Update Semantics of Relational Views," *ACM TODS* 6, No. 4 (December 1981).

4. C. R. Carlson and A. K. Arora, "The Updatability of Relational Views Based on Functional Dependencies," *Proc. 3rd IEEE International Conference on Computer Software and Applications* (November 1979).

5. D. D. Chamberlin, J. N. Gray, and I. L. Traiger, "Views, Authorization, and Locking in a Relational Data Base System," *Proc. NCC* 44 (May 1975).

6. S. Cosmadakis and C. H. Papadimitriou, "Updates of Relational Views," *Proc. 2nd ACM SIGACT-SIGMOD Symposium on Principles of Database Systems* (March 1983).

7. C. J. Date, *A Guide to DB2* (Reading, MA: Addison-Wesley, 1984).

8. C. J. Date, *An Introduction to Database Systems: Volume I,* 4th edition (Reading, MA: Addison-Wesley, 1985).

9. C. J. Date and P. Hopewell, "File Definition and Logical Data Independence," *Proc. 1971 ACM SIGFIDET Workshop on Data Description, Access, and Control* (November 1971).

10. C. J. Date, "Null Values in Database Management" (in this volume).

11. C. J. Date, "The Outer Join" (in this volume).

12. U. Dayal and P. A. Bernstein, "On the Correct Translation of Update Operations on Relational Views," *ACM TODS* 7, No. 3 (September 1982).

13. R. Fagin, J. D. Ullman, and M. Y. Vardi, "On the Semantics of Updates in Databases," *Proc. 2nd ACM SIGACT-SIGMOD Symposium on Principles of Database Systems* (March 1983).

14. A. L. Furtado and M. A. Casanova, "Updating Relational Views." In *Query Processing in Database Systems* (eds., W. Kim, D. Reiner, and D. Batory). Springer Verlag, 1985.

15. A. L. Furtado, K. C. Sevcik, and C. S. dos Santos, "Permitting Updates Through Views of Data Bases," *Information Systems* 4, No. 4 (1979).

16. A. M. Keller, "Updates to Relational Databases Through Views Involving Joins." In *Improving Database Usability and Responsiveness* (ed., P. Scheuermann), (New York: Academic Press, 1982).

17. A. M. Keller and J. D. Ullman, "On Complementary and Independent Mappings on Databases," *Proc. 1984 ACM SIGMOD International Conference on Management of Data* (June 1984).

18. I. M. Osman, "Updating Defined Relations," *Proc. NCC* 48 (1979).

19. S. J. P. Todd, "Automatic Constraint Maintenance and Updating Defined Relations," *Proc. IFIP Congress,* 1977.

18

A Note on
the Parts Explosion Problem

ABSTRACT

The parts explosion problem, which arises quite frequently in practical contexts, is well known as a problem that is beyond the capabilities of classical relational algebra. In this paper we discuss two approaches to extending a relational language such as SQL in order to address that problem. The first involves a comparatively minor extension to the cursor mechanism of embedded SQL; it is quite general, in that it allows arbitrarily complex programs to be written, but on the other hand it does not directly help the user who wishes to perform parts explosions interactively from an online terminal. The second approach is much more ambitious—in particular, it does help the end user as well as the professional programmer—but unfortunately it also involves some comparatively major extensions and revisions to the SQL language. Then again, those changes can be seen as generally desirable in any case, quite apart from their usefulness in regard to the parts explosion problem specifically.

Previously unpublished.

COMMENTS ON PUBLICATION

This paper has not previously been published. As with the "View Updating" paper, however, it nevertheless seems appropriate to make a few introductory remarks about it here, analogous to the "Comments on Republication" on other papers in this collection.

As indicated in the abstract, the paper contains two principal ideas. The first is not really all that new; it consists basically of an elaboration of an idea previously sketched by the present writer in *A Guide to DB2* and (in a little more detail) in *An Introduction to Database Systems: Volume I* (4th edition). Essentially the same idea was independently proposed in a paper by Chamberlin [2], and a similar scheme was in fact implemented in the Peterlee Relational Test Vehicle [13]. In all cases, the basic idea was (and is) simply to make it easier to write a procedural parts explosion *program*; there was no attempt to address the question of formulating an interactive SQL query to do the same job.

By contrast, the second part of the paper does deal with this latter problem. While it certainly does not present a definitive solution to that problem, it does point out some of the difficulties involved, and I hope it gives some insight into ways in which those difficulties might be addressed. In particular, it shows some of the problems inherent in trying to extend a standalone data sublanguage like SQL to perform a task that really requires the facilities of a general-purpose programming language. Note, however, that there is at least one commercially available SQL system, namely ORACLE [1], that does provide some facilities in this area—though there is some question in my own mind as to how general, and how extendable, those facilities are in practice.

INTRODUCTION

The parts explosion problem can be explained as follows. A given database contains a parts inventory relation P (P#, . . .), together with another relation PP showing which parts contain which other parts as immediate components:

```
PP   ( MAJORP#, MINORP# )
     PRIMARY KEY ( MAJORP#, MINORP# )
     FOREIGN KEY ( MAJORP# IDENTIFIES P ... )
     FOREIGN KEY ( MINORP# IDENTIFIES P ... )
```

A given part may contain any number of other parts as immediate components and may itself be an immediate component of any number of other parts. In other words, relation PP represents a many-to-many relationship between parts and parts. Here are some sample values:

```
            -------   -------
PP   MAJORP#   MINORP#
            -------   -------
     P1        P2
     P1        P3
     P1        P4
     P2        P3
     P2        P5
     P3        P5
     P3        P6
     P4        P3
     P4        P6
     P7        P8
     P7        P9
```

For simplicity, we ignore the fact that relation PP would undoubtedly include additional attributes in practice—e.g., a QUANTITY attribute, indicating how many instances of a given MINORP# are required as immediate components of a single instance of a given MAJORP#.

The parts explosion problem can now be stated as follows:

- Find the components of some given part (say part P1) to all levels.

Or equivalently:

- Produce the *bill of materials* for that given part.

Note: Although we explain the problem in terms of parts and their components, it is of course of much more general applicability. The parts-to-parts structure PP can be regarded as the prototype for a wide class of such structures—family trees, organization charts, entity type hierarchies, and so on. An interesting example is provided by the catalog structure needed in DB2 and other SQL systems to represent the granting of authorization privileges [6] (since a given privilege can be granted to a given user by any number of users and can also be granted by that user to any number of users); such systems must by definition include internal code to perform parts explosions and similar functions, but that code is not usually accessible to the user.

Now, it is well known that it is impossible to formulate a parts explosion as a single expression in the relational algebra or relational calculus. What is perhaps less well known is that, in many languages, including in particular SQL, it is also very awkward—though of course not impossible [2,6]—even to write a program to do the same thing. This paper discusses the possibility of:

(a) Extending the cursor mechanism of embedded SQL to address the latter problem;

(b) Extending the function of the SQL SELECT operation to address the former problem.

Of course, if extension (b) turns out to be possible then extension (a) may not be necessary. Even if this turns out to be the case, however, extension (a) can be regarded as providing the basis for implementing extension (b), and for that reason it is still worth discussing. (Also, of course, extension (a) is much less ambitious, and thus much easier to implement, since it requires much less by way of revision to the SQL language—though as a result it offers less potential for optimization.) We therefore discuss extension (a) first. Before we can do that, however, it is first necessary to define the notion of a *tree-structured relation.*

TREE-STRUCTURED RELATIONS

A relation such as the parts-to-parts relation PP of the previous section can be regarded as a collection of *trees*, in the following sense: The immediate components of a given part, together with the immediate components of those components, the immediate components of *those* components, and so on, can be represented diagrammatically as a tree structure. For example, given the sample data values shown earlier, relation PP can be regarded as consisting of two such trees, one for part P1 and one for part P7. Here is the tree for part P1:

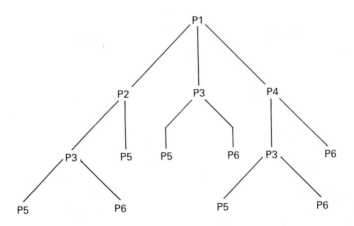

Note that the tree for any given part will contain duplicate nodes, in general. For example, the node "P5" appears four times in the tree for part P1.

We now define a *tree-structured relation* to be any relation, such as relation PP, that can be regarded as a collection of trees in the above sense. In the next section we proceed to discuss the first of our two proposals for extending SQL to deal with such relations.

EXTENDING THE SQL CURSOR MECHANISM

The basic difficulty with the parts explosion problem can be explained as follows:

1. We need to "explode" the given part to n levels—or, equivalently, in terms of the tree representation discussed above, we need to perform a tree search operation of depth n;

2. We therefore need a way of holding n distinct positions in the database (corresponding to n distinct levels in the tree) simultaneously;

3. The object that is used in (embedded) SQL to hold a given position in the database is the *cursor*, and so we need n cursors;

4. Since the value of n is unknown at the time of writing the program, those n cursors cannot readily be predeclared. It follows that we need a way of creating new cursors at run time.

Our first proposal is thus precisely to be able to create cursors dynamically—more exactly, to be able to define a *stack* of instances of a given cursor, and push and pop cursor instances on to and off that stack as necessary.

A PL/I EXAMPLE

Here is an example, expressed in PL/I. We use PL/I for this first example because the data structure—i.e., relation PP—is recursive, and the code therefore needs to be recursive too (either implicitly or explicitly), and PL/I provides direct support for such recursion.

```
BILLMAT1 : PROC ( MAJORP# ) RECURSIVE ;

    DCL MAJORP# ... ;
    DCL MINORP# ... ;

    EXEC SQL DECLARE C REOPENABLE CURSOR FOR
             SELECT MINORP#
             FROM   PP
             WHERE  MAJORP# = :MAJORP#
             ORDER  BY MINORP# ;

    output MAJORP# ;

    EXEC SQL OPEN C ;

    DO WHILE ~ ( not found ) ;
        EXEC SQL FETCH C INTO :MINORP# ;
        CALL BILLMAT1 ( MINORP# ) ;
    END ;

    EXEC SQL CLOSE C ;

END ;
```

The procedure BILLMAT1 is invoked initially with the part number of the given part as its argument. It returns as its result a list of all components of that given part, to all levels. The (new) specification REOPENABLE on a cursor definition means that multiple instances of that cursor can be open simultaneously; in other words, it is legal to issue an OPEN operation for such a cursor even if that cursor is already open (such an operation is an error otherwise). The effect of such an OPEN is to create a new instance of the cursor, using the current values of any host variables referenced in the cursor definition, and to push that new instance on to the top of the stack. References to that cursor in other manipulative statements such as FETCH are references to the current instance of the cursor (i.e., the instance on top of the stack). CLOSE destroys that instance and reinstates the previous instance as the current instance; in other words, CLOSE serves as the pop operator for the stack, just as OPEN serves as the push operator.

A COBOL EXAMPLE

Here is a COBOL version of the problem (the recursion now being dealt with by "hand coding" instead of by explicit language support):

```
01 STACK-DEPTH ...
01 MAJORP#      ...
01 MINORP#      ...
EXEC SQL DECLARE C REOPENABLE CURSOR FOR
         SELECT MINORP#
         FROM   PP
         WHERE  MAJORP# = :MAJORP#
         ORDER  BY MINORP#
END-EXEC

MOVE ZERO TO STACK-DEPTH
MOVE given part number TO MINORP#

PERFORM BILLMATSUB

PERFORM UNTIL STACK-DEPTH = ZERO
   EXEC SQL FETCH C INTO :MINORP# END-EXEC
   IF fetch successful
      PERFORM BILLMATSUB
   ELSE [ if this is "end of file" at the current level ]
      EXEC SQL CLOSE C END-EXEC
      SUBTRACT 1 FROM STACK-DEPTH
   END-IF
END-PERFORM .

BILLMATSUB.
   MOVE MINORP# TO MAJORP#
   output MAJORP#
   EXEC SQL OPEN C END-EXEC
   ADD 1 TO STACK-DEPTH .
```

Explicit manipulation of STACK-DEPTH could be avoided if the CLOSE operation were extended to return a count of the number of instances of the cursor in question that remain open after the CLOSE.

DISCUSSION

In this section we use the PL/I version of the parts explosion program (i.e., BILLMAT1) to illustrate a number of additional points, refining that program as we go. This discussion will pave the way for the analysis of the following section and the detailed proposals of the rest of the paper.

First we repeat the tree structure for part P1, for ease of reference:

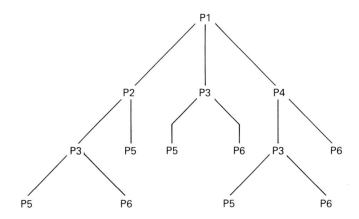

Given this tree and the input "P1", the BILLMAT1 program will produce the following output:

```
P1, P2, P3, P5, P6, P5, P3, P5, P6, P4, P3, P5, P6, P6
```

—i.e., a list of part numbers, in depth-first (top-to-bottom, left-to-right) order. Here is a slightly more readable version (table RESULT) of the output, in which for clarity we show the original part number as well as the part numbers for its components:

RESULT	MAJORP#	MINORP#
	P1	P2
	P1	P3
	P1	P5
	P1	P6
	P1	P5
	P1	P3
	P1	P5
	P1	P6
	P1	P4
	P1	P3
	P1	P5
	P1	P6
	P1	P6

(We now deliberately do not show part P1 as a component of itself.) We remark, incidentally, that the RESULT table is *not* identical to the transitive closure [4,12] of the original PP relation; neither is it derivable from that closure in any obvious manner. For interest, that transitive closure—relation TC, say—is shown below:

```
            -------   -------
     TC     MAJORP#   MINORP#
            -------   -------
            P1        P2
            P1        P3
            P1        P4
            P1        P5
            P1        P6
            P2        P3
            P2        P5
            P2        P6
            P3        P5
            P3        P6
            P4        P3
            P4        P5
            P4        P6
            P7        P8
            P7        P9
```

In fact, table RESULT is not even a relation—it is a *list*, involving both duplicate elements and essential ordering [5]. We will return to this point in a moment.

A point of more immediate concern is that the RESULT table is not actually all that useful as it stands; although it does show the components of the given part (P1), it does not properly show the *structure* of that part. For example, it is not clear from RESULT whether P6 is a component of P1 at the same level as P5. We therefore modify the BILLMAT1 program so that, along with each output minor part number, it also produces an indication as to the *level* of that component with respect to the structure of the given part. For clarity we also list the corresponding major part number in every case (as in the RESULT table above). The modified program is BILLMAT2:

```
BILLMAT2 : PROC ( GIVENP# ) ;

    DCL GIVENP# ... ;

    CALL BILLMAT2SUB ( GIVENP#, 0 ) ;

    BILLMAT2SUB : PROC ( MAJORP#, LEVEL ) RECURSIVE ;

        DCL MAJORP# ... ;
        DCL MINORP# ... ;
        DCL LEVEL   ... ;

        EXEC SQL DECLARE C REOPENABLE CURSOR FOR
                 SELECT MINORP#
```

```
                    FROM    PP
                    WHERE   MAJORP# = :MAJORP#
                    ORDER   BY MINORP# ;

           IF LEVEL > 0
           THEN output GIVENP#, MAJORP#, LEVEL
                /* as  MAJORP#, MINORP#, LEVEL respectively */ ;

           EXEC SQL OPEN C ;

           DO WHILE ~ ( not found ) ;
              EXEC SQL FETCH C INTO :MINORP# ;
              CALL BILLMAT2SUB ( MINORP#, LEVEL + 1 ) ;
           END ;

           EXEC SQL CLOSE C ;

        END ;

   END ;
```

Given the input value "P1", program BILLMAT2 will produce the following output:

```
-------   -------   -----
MAJORP#   MINORP#   LEVEL
-------   -------   -----
P1        P2        1
P1        P3        2
P1        P5        3
P1        P6        3
P1        P5        2
P1        P3        1
P1        P5        2
P1        P6        2
P1        P4        1
P1        P3        2
P1        P5        3
P1        P6        3
P1        P6        2
```

Note very carefully, however, that RESULT as shown is still not a relation—as pointed out earlier, it is a *list*, with both duplicate elements and essential ordering (the ordering in question is represented above by the top-to-bottom ordering of the rows, of course). Equivalently, RESULT can be regarded as an (*ordered*) *tuple*, each element of which consists in turn of an ordered triple

```
< major part number, minor part number, level >   .
```

Note: Throughout this paper we will reserve the term "tuple" to mean an ordered tuple (or list) specifically.

Of course, RESULT can be *converted into* a relation by appending a unique sequence number to each row. The effect of such numbering is to convert the essential ordering referred to above into an inessential one. In fact, those sequence numbers represent, precisely, the sequence obtained by numbering the arcs of the tree in depth-first (top-to-bottom, left-to-right) sequence, beginning with one. The resulting relation is

```
---     -------    -------    -----
ARC     MAJORP#    MINORP#    LEVEL
---     -------    -------    -----
  1     P1         P2             1
  2     P1         P3             2
  3     P1         P5             3
  4     P1         P6             3
  5     P1         P5             2
  6     P1         P3             1
  7     P1         P5             2
  8     P1         P6             2
  9     P1         P4             1
 10     P1         P3             2
 11     P1         P5             3
 12     P1         P6             3
 13     P1         P6             2
```

And of course it is highly desirable that the final result in fact be a relation, in order that the relational closure property be preserved. The corresponding program (BILLMAT3) is a trivial modification of BILLMAT2:

```
BILLMAT3 : PROC ( GIVENP# ) ;

    DCL GIVENP# ... ;
    DCL ARC      ... ;

    ARC = 0 ;

    CALL BILLMAT3SUB ( GIVENP#, 0 ) ;

    BILLMAT3SUB : PROC ( MAJORP#, LEVEL ) RECURSIVE ;

        DCL MAJORP# ... ;
        DCL MINORP# ... ;
        DCL LEVEL   ... ;

        EXEC SQL DECLARE C REOPENABLE CURSOR FOR
                 SELECT MINORP#
                 FROM   PP
                 WHERE  MAJORP# = :MAJORP#
                 ORDER  BY MINORP# ;

        IF LEVEL > 0
        THEN
            DO ;
                ARC = ARC + 1 ;
                output ARC, GIVENP#, MAJORP#, LEVEL
                /* as  ARC, MAJORP#, MINORP#, LEVEL respectively */ ;
            END ;

        EXEC SQL OPEN C ;

        DO WHILE ~ ( not found ) ;
            EXEC SQL FETCH C INTO :MINORP# ;
```

```
            CALL BILLMAT3SUB ( MINORP#, LEVEL + 1 ) ;
        END ;

        EXEC SQL CLOSE C ;

    END ;

END ;
```

ANALYSIS

In the previous section we showed how a program (BILLMAT3) could produce as output a relation representing the parts explosion for some given part (part P1 in the example). Suppose BILLMAT3 were to be executed multiple times, once for each distinct part number appearing in either of the columns MAJORP# and MINORP# of relation PP. The result would be a collection of relations, EXP1, EXP2, . . ., EXPn, say, all having the same general form (i.e., all union-compatible [9]) and no two having any rows in column. Now define EXP to be the union of all of those relations. (Note: The primary key of EXP is the composite attribute (ARC,MAJORP#).) If relation EXP were explicitly available, a parts explosion query could be expressed in SQL very simply:

```
SELECT  *
FROM    EXP
WHERE   MAJORP# = given part number ;
```

Of course, relation EXP is *not* explicitly available. We therefore proceed to define a new relational operator, EXPLODE, whose input is a tree-structured relation such as PP and whose output is the corresponding EXP relation. (A somewhat more precise definition of EXP is given in the next section.) We also assume that the FROM clause in the SQL SELECT statement can accept relation-valued expressions as well as simple relation-names as its arguments (we have argued elsewhere [8] that such a facility is desirable anyway for other reasons). Then the SQL version of the parts explosion query becomes

```
SELECT  *
FROM    EXPLODE ( PP )
WHERE   MAJORP# = given part number ;
```

EXTENDING THE SQL SELECT OPERATION

With the foregoing by way of motivation, we now start again at the beginning. Our aim is to present a step-by-step buildup to the definition of the EXPLODE function sketched in the previous section. We use a pidgin form of SQL (SQL pseudocode) to illustrate the ideas—a pidgin form only, because it turns out that we need to take a large number of liberties with the existing language. Indeed, the proposal does considerable violence to SQL as currently defined. The parts explosion problem illustrates rather clearly how difficult it is to extend data sublanguages in general, and the SQL data sublanguage in particular, for certain applications. (The problem is that we need to make extensive use of certain constructs, such as conditional expressions, that are a normal feature of general-purpose languages but not of data sublanguages.)

1. First, note that any tree can be regarded as a recursively nested tuple:

```
< root, < immediate dependents > >
```

For example, the tree for part P1 ("P1-tree") can be represented as:

```
< P1, < P2-tree, P3-tree, P4-tree > > ,
```

where each of "P2-tree," "P3-tree," and "P4-tree" in turn has the same kind of structure. The complete nested tuple (i.e., the complete tree) for part P1 is:

```
<P1,<<P2,<<P3,<P5,P6>>,P5>>,<P3,<P5,P6>>,<P4,<<P3,<P5,P6>>,P6>>>>
```

2. Next, note that the SQL SELECT-list construct can be regarded as representing a tuple (remember that tuples are always considered to be *ordered* in this paper). For example, in the SELECT statement

```
SELECT MAJORP#, MINORP# ... ;
```

the symbol string "MAJORP#, MINORP#" represents a tuple of two scalar values. Our first extension to SQL is to require such symbol strings to be enclosed in tuple brackets, though for compatibility we will also allow those brackets to be omitted at the outermost level (only) if the SELECT keyword is specified (see paragraphs 4 and 5 below). For example:

```
SELECT < MAJORP#, MINORP# > ... ;
```

3. Next, if all we want to do is SELECT a single tuple, rather than a whole relation, we will allow a SELECT clause to appear in isolation—i.e., with no accompanying clauses at all, not even a FROM clause. For example:

```
SELECT < 3, 4, 5 > ;

SELECT < 4 > ;

SELECT < 2 + 2 > ;

SELECT < 3, AVG ( EMP.SALARY ) , 2 + 2 > ;
```

Note: Each of these could equally well be written without the tuple brackets.

4. Next, we will meet situations (see paragraph 5 and elsewhere) where we need to specify tuple-valued expressions nested within other expressions. In such contexts—in fact, in most contexts, except at the outermost level of the statement in question, and usually there too—the keyword SELECT is obtrusive and redundant [8]. We therefore allow that keyword to be omitted in such contexts. Thus, the tuple examples above in paragraph 3 can be simplified to

```
< 3, 4, 5 > ;

< 4 > ;

< 2 + 2 > ;

< 3, AVG ( EMP.SALARY ) , 2 + 2 > ;
```

5. Next, we allow an element of a tuple to be a tuple in turn (in other words, we allow tuples to be nested to arbitrary depth). For example:

```
< 3, < AVG ( EMP.SALARY ) , 2 + 2 > , 58 > ;
```

We note in passing that nested tuples are desirable anyway as a basis for composite field support [7], quite apart from their usefulness in the present context.

6. We note next that a SELECT operation that includes an ORDER BY specification can and should be regarded as returning a *list*—i.e., an (ordered) tuple of tuples—rather than a relation. We therefore allow nested SELECT operations to include an ORDER BY clause if the context requires a tuple value rather than a relation value. (Note, however, that the tuple represented by a SELECT . . . ORDER BY is necessarily *homogeneous*, in the sense that all of the component tuples in that tuple must be union-compatible [9].)

7. Next, we allow functions to return tuple values. We also assume that function definitions can be recursive; this is not (yet) a SQL extension per se, because function definitions are not (yet) considered as being expressed in terms of SQL operations—but see the comments on this point at the very end of this section (paragraph 12).

8. Next, we define a function TREE, whose purpose is to produce the nested tuple version of the tree for a given part. Pseudocode definition:

```
TREE : PROC ( GIVENP# ) ... ;

      DCL GIVENP# ... ;

      IF ~ EXISTS ( SELECT *
                    FROM    PP
                    WHERE   MAJORP# = :GIVENP# )
      THEN RETURN ( GIVENP# ) ;
```

```
        ELSE RETURN ( < GIVENP#, SELECT TREE ( MINORP# )
                                 FROM    PP
                                 WHERE   MAJORP# = :GIVENP#
                                 ORDER   BY MINORP# > ) ;

    END ;
```

The nested SELECT . . . ORDER BY returns a tuple of subtrees, not a relation. Note: For simplicity, we show the TREE function as referring explicitly to relation PP. In practice, of course, it is desirable that the argument relation be specified as a parameter to the function invocation, and we will assume such a capability later.

9. Next we define a function TUPTOREL, whose purpose is to convert the nested tuple version of a given tree into a relation with attributes ARC, MAJORP#, MINORP#, and LEVEL (with meanings as defined earlier in the paper). Pseudocode definition:

```
TUPTOREL : PROC ( GIVEN ) ... ;

        DCL GIVEN TUPLE ... ;
        /* assume TUPLE consists of a string of "tokens" */
        /* -- i.e., tuple brackets and atomic components */
        /* (ignore commas for simplicity)                */

        DCL RESULT RELATION ... ;

        DCL ARC ... , LEVEL ... :
        DCL MAJORP# ... , MINORP# ... ;

        RESULT = empty ;
        ARC = 0 ;
        LEVEL = 0 ;

        DO for each token t in TUPLE ;

            CASE n OF :

                1. t is 1st token ("<") : ignore t

                2. t is 2nd token : set MAJORP# = t

                3. t = "<" :
                   if previous token was "<", ignore t ;
                   if previous token was ">" or a component,
                      LEVEL = LEVEL + 1 ;

                4. t = ">" :
                   if previous token was ">", ignore t ;
                   if previous token was "<" or a component,
                      LEVEL = LEVEL - 1 ;

                5. t is a component :
                   ARC = ARC + 1 ;
                   MINORP# = t ;
                   append ( ARC, MAJORP#, MINORP#, LEVEL )
                                             to RESULT ;
```

```
        END CASE ;

        END DO ;

        RETURN ( RESULT ) ;

   END TUPTOREL ;
```

Again we will assume a generalized version of this function later.

10. Next we define, for each part number Pi appearing in either of the columns MAJORP# and MINORP# of relation PP, the relation EXPi = TUPTOREL (TREE (Pi)).

11. Finally, we define the relation EXP to be the union of the relations EXPi defined in paragraph 10, and we define a builtin function EXPLODE that, given as argument a tree-structured relation PP, produces the corresponding "exploded" relation EXP. Then (as promised earlier) we can express a parts explosion query in SQL as:

```
SELECT  *
FROM    EXPLODE ( PP )
WHERE   MAJORP# = given part number ;
```

12. We conclude with the following observations. It is convenient for reasons of both usability and efficiency (i.e., optimizability) to provide a builtin function for the parts explosion problem—also for certain other common problems, such as the "where used" problem (for a given part, find all parts in which that part appears as a component, at any level), for which an IMPLODE function is obviously required. However, it is also desirable for users to be able to define their own functions. The reason is, of course, that "parts explosion" and "where used" are only special cases of a whole class of tree-traversing problems. Another such problem is the following: Suppose the PP relation includes a QUANTITY attribute, indicating the quantity of MINORP# required in the construction of MAJORP#. Then a user may well wish to compute the total quantity of some given part Py required for the construction of some other given part Px (the "gross requirements" problem). The discussions of this paper should serve to suggest an overall approach to such problems, but of course much additional work remains to be done.

SUMMARY

In this paper we have sketched two general approaches to extending a relational language such as SQL to deal with the parts explosion problem. The first involves a comparatively slight extension to the embedded SQL cursor mechanism—namely, "reopenable cursors." The second involves a new builtin function EXPLODE, whose purpose is to "explode" a tree-structured relation into another relation from which the bill of materials for a given part can easily be derived. We have shown how EXPLODE might be defined in a step-at-a-time fashion, using a variety of extensions to existing SQL. We have also suggested that users should be able to define their own functions in an analogous manner. Of course, we do not claim that the proposals of this paper are in any sense complete; our purpose has been merely to indicate the difficulties inherent in the parts explosion problem (and related problems), and to suggest some approaches for tackling some of those difficulties.

ACKNOWLEDGMENTS

The ideas presented in this paper have benefited from a study of several published discussions of the "parts explosion" problem and related matters —especially the presentations of the transitive closure operation in Zloof [12] and Codd [4] and the discussions of record-at-a-time (procedural) approaches to the problem in Huits [10] and Schmitz [11].

REFERENCES

1. Information on ORACLE is available from ORACLE Corporation, 2710 Sand Hill Road, Menlo Park, California.

2. D. D. Chamberlin, "A Summary of User Experience with the SQL Data Sublanguage," *Proc. International Conference on Databases (ICOD),* Aberdeen, Scotland (July 1980).

3. E. F. Codd, "A Data Base Sublanguage Founded on the Relational Calculus," *Proc. ACM SIGFIDET Workshop on Data Description, Access, and Control* (November 1971).

4. E. F. Codd, "Extending the Database Relational Model to Capture More Meaning," *ACM TODS* 4, No. 4 (December 1979).

5. E. F. Codd and C. J. Date, "Interactive Support for Nonprogrammers: The Relational and Network Approaches" (in this volume).

6. C. J. Date, *A Guide to DB2* (Reading, MA: Addison-Wesley, 1984).

7. C. J. Date, *An Introduction to Database Systems*: *Volume I*, 4th edition (Reading, MA: Addison-Wesley, 1985).

8. C. J. Date, "A Critique of the SQL Database Language" (in this volume).

9. C. J. Date, "A Formal Definition of the Relational Model" (in this volume).

10. M. H. H. Huits, "Requirements for Languages in Data Base Systems." In *Data Base Description* (eds., Douque and Nijssen), *Proc. IFIP TC-2 Special Working Conference on Data Base Description* (January 1975). North-Holland (1975).

11. Peter Schmitz, "Using INGRES for Bill of Materials Problems," Relational Technology Inc. (December 1981).

12. M. M. Zloof, "Query-By-Example: Operations on the Transitive Closure," *IBM Research Report RC5526* (July 1975).

13. PRTV Development Team, *User Manual for the Peterlee Relational Test Vehicle,* Technical Note 34, IBM UK Scientific Centre, Peterlee, England (July 1975).

## PART IV

DATABASE DESIGN

19

A Practical Approach
to Database Design

ABSTRACT

We present a practical approach to the database design problem, one that is specifically suited to a relational system and even more specifically to a SQL system (though many if not most of the ideas are applicable to other systems also, relational or otherwise). Most database design methodologies rely heavily on the well-known but somewhat abstract normalization discipline; ours does so too, but to a somewhat lesser extent than usual and in a somewhat disguised and more user-friendly manner. The methodology is referred to as *the synthetic approach*. That approach forms the principal topic of the paper; however, a brief description of the complementary *analytic* approach is also included, and the paper concludes with a discussion of a number of miscellaneous design topics of a rather more detailed nature.

A preliminary version of this paper was published as an IBM Technical Report, No. TR 03.220, under the title of "A Practical Guide to Database Design" (December 1982). A greatly condensed version subsequently appeared as Appendix B (pp. 277–293) of *A Guide to DB2*, by C. J. Date, copyright 1984, Addison-Wesley, Reading, Massachusetts. The primary and foreign key recipes were given in *An Introduction to Database Systems: Volume I* (4th edition, pp. 323–325), by C. J. Date, copyright 1986, Addison-Wesley, Reading, Massachusetts. Reprinted with permission.

417

Readers are assumed to be professionally interested in database design and to have at least an elementary understanding of the concepts of the relational model.

COMMENTS ON REPUBLICATION

I have been teaching the methodology described herein for some time as part of a series of seminars on database technology. The approach has been used in practice (successfully), both by myself and by other people, and in fact now forms the basis of a methodology taught to IBM customers as part of one of the IBM database administration classes. The approach differs from many others in the heavy emphasis it places on foreign keys; I have therefore retained all of the explanatory material on foreign keys (and on primary keys), even though those explanations duplicate material found elsewhere in the present volume, in order to preserve the self-contained nature of this part of the book.

The methodology is derived in large part from Codd's extended relational model RM/T. References to further reading on RM/T appear within the body of the paper.

SECTION ONE: PROLOGUE

The field of database design cannot by any stretch of the imagination be said to suffer from underpublication. Scarcely a week goes by in which an article on the subject does not appear in one or other of the trade journals; numerous design methodologies have been described in numerous technical papers (of varying degrees of readability), and several entire books, some of them admirable, others less so, have been published on the subject. Moreover, a number of "data models" have been constructed, and documented, with the express purpose of attacking the database design problem. It is therefore not without some trepidation that I venture to add to this already extensive literature. Certainly I feel that anyone who does produce yet another paper in this already overloaded area owes it to the reader to explain just how that paper differs from everything that has appeared previously. So here goes:

1. First, and perhaps most significant, the paper is specifically oriented toward database design in a relational system. This consideration is important because relational systems are beginning to have a significant im-

pact in the marketplace; the demand for a good relational design methodology is therefore naturally growing too, and fast.

2. Even more specifically, the techniques presented are generally expressed (where appropriate) in terms of the "Structured Query Language" SQL, since it is clear that SQL is well on its way to becoming the de facto standard for relational systems. However, it would be a simple matter to translate the SQL rules and formulations of this paper into their equivalents in some other relational language.

3. The paper discusses two somewhat different aspects of design:

- The first, and most important, concerns an *overall approach* to the design problem. Broadly speaking, it regards database design as a modeling process: There is some real "microworld" that must be represented in the database, and the problem is to build a model (i.e., a database representation) of that microworld whose behavior, both static and dynamic, mimics that of the microworld in question. Like almost every other publication in this area, therefore, the paper inevitably discusses this aspect of design in terms of "entities," "associations," and similar abstractions; however, it does so *without radically departing from the prescriptions of the familiar relational model* (unlike many other publications on this topic).

    Note, incidentally, that many published methodologies concern themselves solely with the *static* structure of the microworld in question. By contrast, it is my belief that it is just as important to address the dynamic behavior of that microworld also—and of course that belief is reflected in the methodology described in the paper.

- The second aspect is concerned with a much lower level of detail. It addresses a number of very specific, detailed decisions on such questions as naming (for example) that must be made when the overall design is mapped into the constructs supported by the database system at hand (which is assumed to be a SQL system, where it makes any difference).

4. With regard to the first of the two aspects of design mentioned above, the paper (as indicated in the Abstract) stresses a *synthesizing* approach, in which the final detailed design is gradually built up, or synthesized, from a series of less detailed (or at least less complete) intermediate designs. This approach contrasts with that presented in much of the literature, where a preliminary *detailed* design is gradually refined through an analytic process to produce the final design. This analytic approach is in fact complementary to the synthetic approach, as we will see; in other words, both are needed

in practice. However, the synthetic approach has the advantage that it deals quite explicitly with certain kinds of real-world relationship—represented in the relational model by means of foreign keys—that the analytic approach does not deal with at all.

A few further points of an introductory nature:

1. The reader will probably have realized already that I am using the term "database design" to mean, specifically, *logical* design. This paper does not concern itself at all with questions of physical design (physical data placement, etc.), except in one or two minor and isolated areas. Of course, this omission does not mean that I think that physical design is unimportant. On the contrary, I think it is very important—but it is a separate problem that can and should be separately addressed. Indeed, it is one of the major contributions of relational technology that the twin activities of logical and physical design can be separately addressed in this manner. It is that separation that provides the basis for the high degree of data independence, and the consequent high level of productivity, that can be achieved in relational systems.

2. Despite the claims made earlier to the effect that the paper is specifically concerned with relational design, many of the points discussed are in fact relevant to the design of other kinds of database also. Certainly the overall approach is suitable as the first stage in the design of any kind of database. In a nonrelational system, however, that first stage would then have to be followed by a stage in which the relational design is mapped into whatever data structures (e.g., hierarchies) the system in question does support.

3. Please note that the paper is intended purely as a *guide* to database design. The presentation is aimed at practitioners rather than theoreticians and is intentionally tutorial (and somewhat repetitive) in nature. I deliberately do not set my sights too high. Specifically, I do not claim that the approach is in any way a "theory" of database design, nor that it is "complete" in any formal sense. What is more, I do not mean to suggest that the approach is the only one possible—merely that it is one technique that seems to work well in practice.

4. The paper deliberately does not include large numbers of references to other work in the field. This is not because I wish to ignore that work, but rather because I have drawn on so many different sources that it would be difficult to name them all and invidious to mention just a few. However, a few specific references (ones that are especially relevant to the specific approach described) are mentioned within the body of the paper.

STRUCTURE OF THE PAPER

The paper is divided into five major sections, as follows:

- Section One: Prologue

Contains material of an introductory nature—in particular, a set of sample designs, and a brief discussion of synthesis vs. analysis.

- Section Two: The Synthetic Approach

The most important part of the paper. Describes the synthetic approach in detail, with a preliminary overview of the topic to indicate its scope and a final summarizing checklist of steps in the design process.

- Section Three: The Analytic Approach

A comparatively brief examination of further normalization and the analytic approach, with emphasis on how that approach can be used to complement the synthetic approach already discussed.

- Section Four: Miscellaneous Topics

An open-ended list of miscellaneous tips and hints to assist with various detailed aspects of the practical design process.

- Section Five: Epilogue

Summary and conclusions.

A WORD OF WARNING

I have a concern, and the concern is as follows. Database design can be *simple*. One of the advantages frequently claimed for relational systems— and I believe fairly—is precisely that database design is easier than it is in a nonrelational system. And just to show how simple it is, here is a paper of some 50 or so closely printed pages to explain how it is done. . . . If it's so simple, then why not five pages? Or two, or even one?

The problem is that the subject of database design has the property that (in simple cases at least) it is often easier just to do it than to try and articulate exactly what it was you did. If you glance at the examples in the next section, you will readily see that the database designs shown there are "obviously" right, and you will probably agree that they are the designs that any competent person would come up with after a few moments' thought. But if you were to ask exactly why those designs are right and how they were arrived at, it is likely that that same competent person would have some difficulty in explaining it to you. The fact is that (as already

mentioned) it is necessary when discussing database design in the abstract
to introduce corresponding abstract terms, such as "entity," "association,"
and so on—and it is precisely that fact that makes explanations and descriptions difficult to read and difficult to follow. Papers on this topic are
notoriously difficult to read. But it is my belief that this fact stems more
from the abstract nature of the terminology than from any fundamental
difficulty with the subject matter. In this paper, therefore, I will do my best
to stay out of the realms of abstract terminology as much as I can; but it
is impossible to avoid such terminology altogether. The reader is warned.

EXAMPLES

Before getting into any details of the design process per se, it is convenient
to present a set of sample databases (that is, sample *designs*), to be used as
the basis of the examples (or, at least, most of the examples) later in the
paper. Those databases are intended to be sufficiently simple that the
"right" design is intuitively obvious in each case[1].

Note: In preparing this paper, I considered the possibility of having a
single comprehensive example that illustrated all of the design points I
wished to make. However, the example quickly became so complex that it
was difficult to get the overall picture—too much detail kept getting in the
way. Thus, I decided to use several smaller examples, each one illustrating
only a few aspects of the total problem. Furthermore, even those examples
will be changed slightly from time to time in order to illustrate certain additional points.

- *Example 1* (departments and employees)

```
DEPT ( DEPT#, DNAME, MGR_EMP#, BUDGET )
EMP  ( EMP#, ENAME, DEPT#, SALARY )
```

Departments (DEPTs) have a department number (unique), a name, a
manager (represented by his or her employee number), and a budget. Employees (EMPs) have an employee number (unique), a name, a department
number, and a salary. Note that field DEPT.DEPT# (that is, field DEPT#
of table DEPT) is the primary key of the DEPT table; similarly, field
EMP.EMP# is the primary key for the EMP table. Furthermore, field
EMP.DEPT# is a foreign key in the EMP table matching the primary key
DEPT.DEPT# of the DEPT table; similarly, field DEPT.MGR_EMP# is a
foreign key in the DEPT table matching the primary key EMP.EMP# of

---

[1]It would be more accurate to say that the databases are *unrealistically* simple. But they are
realistic enough for the purposes of this paper.

the EMP table. Primary and foreign keys are crucially important to the synthetic design process, as we will see.

- *Example 2* (courses, offerings, and "enrollees")

```
COURSE    ( COURSE#, SUBJECT )
OFFERING  ( COURSE#, OFF#, DATE, LOCATION )
ENROLLEE  ( COURSE#, OFF#, EMP#, GRADE )
```

Each course has a course number (unique), a subject, and a set of offerings; each offering has an offering number (unique within course), a date, a location, and a set of "enrollees" (enrolled students); and each enrollee has an employee number (unique within offering) and a grade. Primary and foreign keys for this example will be specified later (but you may like to take a moment now to work them out for yourself).

- *Example 3* (suppliers and parts)

```
S  ( S#, SNAME, STATUS, CITY )
P  ( P#, PNAME, COLOR, WEIGHT, CITY )
SP ( S#, P#, QTY )
```

Each supplier (S) has a supplier number (unique), a name, a status, and a city (supplier location). Each part (P) has a part number (unique), a name, a color, a weight, and a city (location where parts of this kind are stored). Each shipment (SP) represents an association between a certain supplier and a certain part: The meaning of an SP record is that the indicated supplier (S#) is supplying, or shipping, the indicated part (P#) in the indicated quantity (QTY). We assume that each supplier supplies many parts and that each part is supplied by many suppliers. For the sake of the example, we also assume that (at any given time) no two shipments involve exactly the same part and the same supplier. Again, primary and foreign keys for this example will be specified later.

These examples allow us to introduce a couple of terms that will be useful in subsequent discussion. Clearly, the end product of the design process consists of a set of tables, each involving a set of fields, together with a corresponding set of primary and foreign key specifications. *Each table will be said to represent some type of "entity," and each field to represent some kind of "property" for the entity type in question.* For example, the EMP table represents entities of type "employee," and the fields of that table (EMP#, ENAME, DEPT#, and SALARY) represent four properties of that entity type. Thus, the design process can be seen as an attempt to represent in the database certain entity types from the microworld of interest, together with certain properties of those entity types; and it is up to the database designer to decide exactly what it is that constitutes an entity, and what it is that constitutes a property of such an entity, in that micro-world.

Notice, incidentally, how some properties (the EMP# property in the example quoted above) serve to *identify* the entity in question; others (e.g., the DEPT# property in the EMP example) serve to *reference* some other, related entity; and still others (e.g., the SALARY property in the EMP example) simply "stand for themselves." The identifying properties, of course, correspond to primary keys and the referencing properties to foreign keys. We will have more to say on these points later in the paper.

DISCLAIMER

This paper assumes for the most part that you already have a pretty good idea of what it is you want to model in your database—i.e., you already have a good understanding of your particular microworld. In other words, we are totally ignoring what is probably the most difficult part of the entire design process!—namely, arriving at that good understanding in the first place. To arrive at such an understanding, it is generally necessary to go through an extensive *data gathering* activity. Now, the activity of data gathering typically involves much hard thinking, a good deal of negotiation with users, and usually a lot of iteration; and the methodology presented in this paper will not help you with this process at all. (Well, perhaps this last statement is a little too strong; the methodology does after all provide a formal framework, which might be useful in helping you to structure your thinking somewhat. But its primary purpose is merely to help you convert the results of the data gathering activity into a formal relational representation, nothing more.)

One further point: The recommendations of this paper are by and large only guidelines, not unbreakable rules. Most of them can be ignored under appropriate circumstances. However, we do recommend that whenever you choose to ignore one of the guidelines, then you also document your reasons for doing so very carefully.

SYNTHESIS vs. ANALYSIS

As already indicated, it is possible to distinguish two complementary approaches to the overall database design problem, the synthetic approach and the analytic approach. (In practice you will certainly need to employ a mixture of both—see later—but for tutorial reasons it is convenient to treat the two separately, at least initially.)

- The synthetic approach is applicable when you are designing a brand new database from scratch. Broadly speaking, it involves deciding what

entities you need to represent in the database, deciding what relationships exist among those entities, deciding what properties those entities
have, and so on, and thus gradually building up or *synthesizing* an
appropriate relational structure to reflect all of those decisions.

- The analytic approach, by contrast, applies when you already have an
existing design (perhaps an existing body of data also, in some form
or other), and it is necessary to *analyze* that design in order to understand it properly before possibly recasting it into some more desirable
form. The discipline of normalization (third normal form, etc.) is relevant here.

Please note again that the two approaches are not that easily distinguished in practice, as will in fact become clear as we get into detail in the
next section of the paper.

SECTION TWO: THE SYNTHETIC APPROACH

The synthetic approach is the largest and most significant topic of this paper. This preliminary section provides a brief overview of the topic in order
to indicate its overall scope and to simplify later discussions. Subsequent
sections then present the approach in detail. A final summarizing section
provides a checklist of the steps involved in the synthetic design process.

Note: It is precisely in this area that abstract terminology first rears its
ugly head, as you will quickly see. However, each abstraction will be illustrated in as concrete terms as possible, and as quickly as possible, in the
sections that follow.

As already indicated in Section One, the synthetic approach is built
around the concept of "entity." The term "entity" is used to mean *any
distinguishable object*—where the object in question can be as concrete or
as abstract as we please. Examples of entities are persons, places, airplanes,
flights, jazz, the color red, and so on. In a database context, of course, the
entities we are principally interested in are those objects about which we
wish to record information in the database. For each such entity, there will
be some unique record in the database whose function is to represent that
entity (and only that entity). The function of that "entity record" is to
represent

(a) the *existence* of the entity in question, together with

(b) certain *single-valued properties* of that entity.

The "entity record" for a given entity serves as a kind of central anchor
point for all references to that entity from elsewhere in the database. (Such

references will be represented by foreign keys, of course.) For example, in the departments-and-employees microworld, departments would be regarded as entities of interest, because for each department we wish to record that department's name, budget, and so on. References to a given department from elsewhere in the database will be represented by references to the (unique) "entity record" for that department. We would not normally regard (say) department budgets as "entities of interest" (though there may be nothing wrong in doing so), because we do not wish to record any additional information about budgets in the database.

Entities can be grouped into entity *types*. For instance, every employee is an instance of the "employees" entity type. The purpose of such grouping is to enable us to impose a simple regular structure on the database: Entities of the same type have certain properties in common (for example, all employees have an employee number, a name, a department, and a salary), and hence we can factor out that commonality and achieve some (fairly obvious) economies of representation.

Perhaps the most important aspect of the synthetic approach is its *entity classification scheme*. Three classes of entity are defined: *kernels, associations*, and *characteristics*. Briefly, a kernel is an independent entity (it has independent existence); an association is a many-to-many (or many-to-many-to-many, etc.) relationship among two or more other entities; and a characteristic is an entity whose sole purpose (within the microworld of interest) is to describe or qualify some other entity. The purpose of this classification scheme is to provide a framework within which questions of design and related matters can be discussed in a precise and systematic manner. More explicitly, the purpose is to help the designer impose some structure on the microworld of interest (which might otherwise appear overwhelmingly unstructured). A corollary objective is to help the designer decide what integrity constraints apply to that microworld.

Examples:

kernels	suppliers, parts, employees, departments, courses
associations	shipments
characteristics	offerings (whose sole purpose is to describe a "superior" entity, namely a course), enrollees (whose sole purpose is to describe an offering)

To repeat, kernels have independent existence. Associations and characteristics do not, because they presuppose the existence of some other entity or entities to be associated or "characterized."

In more detail:

- Kernels
  Kernel entities are "what the database is all about." They have independent existence—that is, they do not depend for their existence on the existence of any other entity. In the three sample databases, the kernel entities are employees, departments, courses, suppliers, and parts.

- Associations
  An associative entity (or simply an association) is an entity whose function is to represent a many-to-many (or many-to-many-to-many, etc.) relationship among two or more other entities. For example, a shipment is an association between a supplier and a part. Each participant in an association—that is, each entity that is related to one or more other entities via an association—can be a kernel, or a characteristic, or another association.

- Characteristics
  A characteristic entity is an entity whose sole function (within the microworld of interest) is to qualify or describe or "characterize" some other entity (which may be a kernel or an association or another characteristic). For example, offerings are characteristics of courses; a given offering makes sense only as an offering of some particular course, it is meaningless by itself. Likewise, enrollees are characteristics of offerings. To state matters more precisely, characteristics are *existence-dependent* on the entity they characterize. Entity type B is said to be existence-dependent on entity type A if it is impossible for an instance of B to exist while no corresponding instance of A exists. ("Existence" here of course means existence within the microworld under consideration.) For example, an offering cannot exist if there does not exist any corresponding course; likewise, an enrollee cannot exist if there does not exist any corresponding offering.

Note: These three categories are not necessarily disjoint, as we shall see in Section Four of this paper. For example, a given entity might be regarded as an association by some users but as a characteristic by others.

An entity, then, can be a kernel or a characteristic or an association. But that is not all. Any entity, regardless of its classification, can additionally "designate" some other related entity, as (for example) an employee designates a corresponding department, or a flight designates a corresponding airline. A designation can be thought of as a many-to-one relationship between two entities.

Finally, each entity, again regardless of its classification, and regardless of whether it is also designative, will have a number of "properties." A property is a piece of information that describes an entity in some way. A given property may serve to *identify* the entity in question, as (for example) an employee's employee number identifies that employee; or it may serve to *reference* some related entity, as (for example) an employee's department number references that employee's department; or it may simply "stand for itself," as (for example) an employee's salary does. Other examples of properties that simply "stand for themselves" are department budgets, offering locations, enrollee grades, and shipment quantities. Of course, a property such as "department budget" might *become* a referencing property if an entity type "budgets" were to be subsequently introduced into the database, with properties of their own. Fortunately, however, this fact does not affect the design procedure in any significant way.

Note: Although it is convenient in some contexts to treat identifying properties and referencing properties just as special cases of the all-embracing concept of "properties," it is common in informal discussion to restrict the term "property" to mean, specifically, a property that stands for itself. This usage will normally be followed in the present paper.

Given the foregoing classification scheme as background, we are now in a position to understand in outline how the synthetic design approach proceeds. Briefly, it is a top-down process. The designer starts by identifying the kernel entities; these might be thought of as initial nodes in some kind of (mental) graphical representation of the database. Next, associations and designations are identified that connect various entities together; these are like edges or arcs that connect together the aforementioned nodes. Third, characteristic entities and properties are identified; these are like little local accretions that are closely attached to the entity nodes.

Of course, you must realize that (for example) associative entities *are* entities and can therefore have properties of their own, participate in other associations, etc., all of which means that any such graphical representation is likely to be very complicated in practice, much more complicated than the foregoing simple outline might indicate. We certainly do not mean to suggest that the graph should be physically created—merely that it might serve as a useful mental picture of the manner in which design proceeds. Also, of course, the whole process is highly iterative, so the steps might not actually be executed in the precise order stated, and it is quite likely that you will have to repeat each of them several times.

One last preliminary remark: You should be warned that the terminology of "kernel," "characteristic," etc., is by no means universally employed. The fact is, there simply does not yet exist a universally accepted set of terminology in this area. Thus, for example, other writers use "relationship" to mean what we have called an association. The only rule we have followed in choosing the terms of this paper is: Do not introduce any terms that conflict with those of the basic relational model (since that is what the methodology is building on).[2]

The next few sections now present the basic steps of the synthetic approach in detail. To recap, those basic steps are (very informally):

1. Decide the kernels;
2. Decide the associations;
3. Decide the designations;
4. Decide the characteristics;
5. Decide the properties;
6. Iterate until the design is complete.

KERNEL ENTITIES

Kernel entities are the fundamental entities of the microworld of interest. As stated earlier, they are "what the database is all about." They have independent existence. The kernel entities in the sample databases of Section One are departments, employees, courses, suppliers, and parts. In terms of SQL, each kernel entity type will eventually be represented by its own separate *base table*. In the examples, the kernel base tables are DEPT, EMP, COURSE, S, and P, respectively.

Note 1: A base table is a table that is directly stored in the database—as opposed to (e.g.) a view, which is a table that behaves like a base table in some respects but is materialized only when necessary and is not directly stored.

Note 2: As we will soon see, *every* entity type, kernel or otherwise, will in fact be represented by its own separate base table. But kernel entities are the only ones under discussion at this particular juncture.

Now, the single most important aspect of entities in the real world is their *distinguishability* (i.e., every entity has its own identity). Thus, when we consider the question of representing entities in the database, the single most important question to answer is "How are those entity *representatives*

---

[2] By and large, in fact, the terminology follows that of the *extended* relational model RM/T —see the paper by E. F. Codd in the *ACM Transactions on Database Systems,* Volume 4, No. 4 (December 1979). A brief tutorial on RM/T can be found in *An Introduction to Database Systems: Volume I,* 4th edition (Addison-Wesley, 1985), and a more extensive one in *An Introduction to Database Systems: Volume II* (Addison-Wesley, 1982).

distinguished from one another?''—i.e., how are entities identified in the database? In the relational model, the identification function is performed by primary keys. Thus, the first question to answer for each kernel entity type (and indeed for other entity types also) is "What is the primary key?" The following are the primary keys for the kernel entity types in the three sample databases:

- Departments and employees:

DEPT	—DEPT#	(department number)
EMP	—EMP#	(employee number)

- Courses, offerings, and enrollees:

COURSE#	—COURSE#	(course number)

- Suppliers and parts:

S	—S#	(supplier number)
P	—P#	(part number)

Here are two definitions—one informal, the other formal—for the relational concept "primary key."

Primary key (informal definition):

The primary key of a table is a field or field combination of that table that can be used as a unique identifier for the records of that table.

Primary key (formal definition):

The primary key of a table T is a set K of fields K1, K2, . . ., Kn of T (n > 0) having the following two time-independent properties:

1. Uniqueness:
At any given time, there cannot exist two distinct records of T having the same value for K1, the same value for K2, . . ., and the same value for Kn.

2. Minimality:
None of K1, K2, . . ., Kn can be discarded from K without destroying the uniqueness property.

In the case of base tables (which is all that we are concerned with here), primary keys cannot be null—that is, none of the fields participating in the primary key of a base table is allowed to take on null values.

A DIGRESSION: RECORDING DESIGN DECISIONS

As you go through the design procedure, it is of course necessary to record the decisions you make—that is, to document, preferably in some more or less formal manner, the kernels, associations, etc., to be represented in the database, their manner of representation, and other relevant information. The question is, what formalism should be used in this activity?

There are many possible answers to this question, none of them obviously preferable to all the rest; to some extent it is purely a matter of personal preference. Moreover, the various possibilities are by no means mutually exclusive. Some of those possibilities are:

- Natural language prose
- Functional dependency diagrams
- Data structure diagrams
- Bubble charts
- Entity-relationship diagrams
- Data definition statements

Of these, we would probably all agree that natural language should be used only as an adjunct to one of the others, since too often it is ambiguous or insufficiently precise when used in isolation. Data definition language statements (DDL statements) would appear to be a strong candidate, since such statements must eventually be constructed anyway when the design is converted into a database definition. Unfortunately, DDL statements alone are inadequate for the task in a SQL environment, for the important reason that they do not support certain concepts—specifically, primary and foreign keys—that (as we have stated) are absolutely crucial to the design process. This paper therefore uses a formalism that might be called "pseudoDDL."

PseudoDDL is based on the regular SQL DDL, but includes direct support for the missing concepts. Consider the kernel entity type "employees," for example. We have already seen that each entity type will map into a SQL base table. Thus, we might write the pseudoDDL statement

```
CREATE TABLE EMP                        /* employees (kernel) */
        FIELDS ( EMP# ... )
        PRIMARY KEY ( EMP# ) ;
```

to record the fact that a base table called EMP exists, it represents the kernel entity type "employees," and it has primary key EMP#. EMP# is of course a field of the EMP table. Later on we will come back to add further specifications to this statement to record further facts about this entity type. Ultimately, we will convert those statements into an appropriate set of genuine SQL DDL statements, for input to the database definition process.

To summarize: The proposal is to record design decisions in the form of pseudoDDL statements (including natural language comments where appropriate). The design process starts with the initial creation of those statements and continues by successively extending and revising them until they are eventually replaced by a corresponding set of genuine SQL DDL statements (plus certain constraint maintenance procedures—see later). The pseudoDDL statements should be kept in the form of a text file and a text editor used to maintain that file as design proceeds.[3]

ASSOCIATIONS

To return to the synthetic approach per se: The next step is to decide the associations. An association is a many-to-many (or many-to-many-to-many, etc.) relationship among two or more other entities (not necessarily distinct or of distinct types). For example, a shipment is an association between a supplier and a part; it is many-to-many, because each supplier can supply many parts and each part can be supplied by many suppliers, in general.

Diagrams can help in understanding associations:

Read the diagram as follows: "For one supplier there are many shipments (but for one shipment there is exactly one supplier); similarly, for one part there are many shipments (but for one shipment there is exactly one part)." In other words, suppliers to shipments are 1-to-M, and shipments to suppliers are M-to-1; and similarly for parts.

Note 1: In the phrases "many-to-one" (M-to-1) and "one-to-many" (1-to-M), "many" (or "M") is always understood to include the possibil-

---

[3]PseudoDDL can be regarded as a language for defining what is usually called the "conceptual schema." The syntax used for that language in this paper is deliberately somewhat wordy and repetitive, however; it would need a certain amount of refinement if it were ever to be considered as a serious candidate for implementation. On the other hand, it can certainly be regarded as a first approximation to what would undoubtedly be a very desirable set of extensions to existing SQL.

ities of one and zero. "One," by contrast, is sometimes taken to mean "*exactly* one," sometimes "one or zero." This lack of precision is regrettable but widespread. In the shipments example, "one" means "exactly one."

Note 2: The lines connecting the boxes in the diagram in fact represent designations, as will be made clear in the next section. The fact is, an association can always be thought of as a combination of at least two designations—usually, however, with the additional constraint that no two instances of the association involve exactly the same combination of instances of the designations. (This is a somewhat abstruse point, and may not make much sense until you have a thorough understanding of the entity classification scheme.) For example, no two shipments involve exactly the same combination of supplier and part.

Note 3: Although the example (shipments) is of a two-participant association (i.e., it is a *binary* association), do not lose sight of the fact that in general an association might involve any number of participants. For example, the shipments example might be extended to involve *projects* also: Each shipment is a shipment by a certain supplier of a certain part to a certain project. For simplicity, however, we will restrict our attention in this paper to binary associations only, for the most part.

Each associative entity type maps into its own base table. For example, the association type "shipments" is represented by table SP. Now, the most important question to ask about an association is, of course, "What are the entities being associated?"—i.e., what are the participants in the association? In the relational model, participants in an association are identified by foreign keys within the table representing that association. For example, the participants in shipments (namely, suppliers and parts) are represented by foreign keys S# and P#, respectively, within the table representing shipments, namely table SP. (Note carefully that identifying participants in associations is certainly not the only use for foreign keys, as the other two sample databases have already shown.) Thus we might write (pseudoDDL again):

```
CREATE TABLE SP              /* shipments -- associate S and P */
      FIELDS ( S#, P# ... )
      FOREIGN KEY ( S# IDENTIFIES S ... )
      FOREIGN KEY ( P# IDENTIFIES P ... )
```

S# and P# (or, to give them their fully qualified names, SP.S# and SP.P#) are fields in table SP; values of SP.S# are constrained to match values of the primary key S.S# of table S, values of SP.P# are constrained to match values of the primary key P.P# of table P.

Here are two definitions—one informal, the other formal—for the relational concept "foreign key."

Foreign key (informal definition):

A foreign key is a field or field combination in one table whose values are required to match those of the primary key of some other table (or possibly of the same table).

Foreign key (formal definition):

Let T be a base table with primary key the combination K1, K2, . . ., Kn (n > 0). Let U be a base table (T and U not necessarily distinct), and let L1, L2, . . . , Ln be fields of U satisfying the time-independent constraint that, for every record u of U, either u.L1, u.L2, . . . , u.Ln are all null, or there exists a record t of T such that u.L1 = t.K1, u.L2 = t.K2, . . . , u.Ln = t.Kn. Then the combination (L1,L2, . . . , Ln) is said to be a foreign key in U matching the primary key (K1,K2, . . . ,Kn) of T.

Thus, in considering the problem of how associations (and also designations—see the next section) are to be represented in the database, the basic question to be answered is "What are the foreign keys?" Such foreign keys must be specified in the pseudoDDL for the association (or designation) in question, as shown in the SP example above. But that is not the end of the story. For each foreign key it is necessary to consider three further questions:

1. Can that foreign key accept null values? In other words, is it possible for an instance of the entity type to exist for which the target of the foreign key reference is unknown? In the case of shipments it probably is not possible—a shipment for an unknown supplier or an unknown part does not make much sense—but cases do exist where it might well make sense. A simple example (involving a designation rather than an association, however) is provided by the departments-and-employees database: If it is possible for some employee to be currently assigned to no department at all, then the DEPT# field (which is a foreign key) would be null in the EMP record for that employee. So the general rule for foreign keys is as stated in the *formal* definition above: For a given foreign key, each value of that

foreign key either (a) is null (i.e., *wholly* null) or (b) matches some existing value of the corresponding primary key.

Note clearly that the answer to this question (as to whether nulls are allowed for a given foreign key) depends, not on the whim of the database designer, but on the policies in effect in the microworld under consideration. In other words, the answer corresponds to some predefined *business rule* in that microworld. Note, too, that the answer will typically be different for different foreign keys, even within a single microworld. Similar remarks apply to questions 2 and 3 below, of course.

2. What should happen on an attempt to delete the target of a foreign key reference?—for example, an attempt to delete a supplier for which there exists at least one matching shipment? For definiteness let us consider this case explicitly. In general there are three possibilities:

- CASCADES— The delete operation "cascades" to delete those matching shipments also
- RESTRICTED—The delete operation is "restricted" to the case where there are no such matching shipments (it is rejected otherwise)
- NULLIFIES— The foreign key is set to null in all such matching shipments and the supplier is then deleted (of course, this case could not apply if the foreign key cannot accept null values)

3. What should happen on an attempt to update the primary key of the target of a foreign key reference?—for example, an attempt to update the supplier number for a supplier for which there exists at least one matching shipment? For definiteness, again, we consider this case explicitly. In general there are the same three possibilities as for DELETE:

- CASCADES— The update operation "cascades" to update the foreign key in those matching shipments also (this is much the most likely possibility in practice)
- RESTRICTED—The update operation is "restricted" to the case where there are no such matching shipments (it is rejected otherwise)
- NULLIFIES— The foreign key is set to null in all such matching shipments and the supplier is then updated (of course, this case could not apply if the foreign key cannot accept null values)

For each foreign key in the design, therefore, the database designer should specify, not only the field or field combination constituting that foreign key and the target table that is identified by that foreign key, but also the answers to the foregoing three questions (i.e., the three constraints that apply to that foreign key). For example (pseudoDDL again):

```
CREATE TABLE SP               /* shipments -- associate S and P */
       FIELDS ( S#, P# ... )
       FOREIGN KEY ( S# IDENTIFIES S
                     NULLS NOT ALLOWED
                     DELETE OF S CASCADES
                     UPDATE OF S.S# CASCADES )
       FOREIGN KEY ( P# IDENTIFIES P
                     NULLS NOT ALLOWED
                     DELETE OF P RESTRICTED
                     UPDATE OF P.P# RESTRICTED ) ;
```

As already stated, each associative entity type maps into a base table, just like a kernel entity type. In fact, of course, associations are regarded as entities also (though not as kernels, since they do not have independent existence): They can have properties and characteristics and can participate in other (higher-level) associations, just like kernels. More fundamentally, since they are entities, they must be mutually distinguishable, and thus must have their own unique identifier or primary key. So we are faced with the question: What constitutes the primary key for an association?

Now, for a given association, it will often be the case that the combination of all foreign keys for participants in that association will have the uniqueness property. In table SP, for example, the combination (SP.S#,SP.P#) does have the uniqueness property, because no two shipments are allowed to exist simultaneously for the same supplier and the same part. If that constraint did not hold, then some additional field—say a SHIP_DATE field—would be needed to distinguish one shipment from another (if the shipments in question were otherwise indistinguishable), and the combination (S#,P#,SHIP_DATE) would then have the uniqueness property. Either way, there must be *some* combination of fields that could serve as the primary key. For example (assuming again that the combination (SP.S#,SP.P#) is unique):

```
CREATE TABLE SP               /* shipments -- associate S and P */
       FIELDS ( S#, P# ... )
       PRIMARY KEY ( S#, P# )
       FOREIGN KEY ( S# IDENTIFIES S  etc. )
       FOREIGN KEY ( P# IDENTIFIES P  etc. )
```

However, there are good arguments for avoiding composite primary keys (see Section Four of this paper for further discussion). Therefore, whenever such a key appears during the design process, you may wish to consider the introduction of another, noncomposite field to serve as the primary key instead—for example, a SHIP# (shipment number) field, in the case of table SP. For the time being, however, we will simply assume that associations—and also characteristics (see later)—will have composite primary keys. Note, however, that such an assumption implies that nulls *cannot* be allowed for a foreign key that identifies a participant in an association. Thus we are actually giving up a small amount of representational power by making such an assumption.

Note: Suppose again for the moment that the combination (SP.S#,SP.P#) requires a SHIP_DATE to make it unique. It could then be argued that shipments should be considered as associations involving *three* participants (suppliers, parts, and dates). However, one of those participants (dates) would be represented, not by a foreign key, but by a property that simply "stands for itself." SHIP_DATEs are not "entities of interest," as we interpret that term (i.e., entities about which we wish to record information). We choose to stay with our definition of an association as a relationship among *entities* (meaning "entities of interest"). Thus, we would continue to regard shipments as an association involving two entities, not three, but would recognize that in this case the combination of foreign keys identifying participants in the association is not adequate by itself to serve as the primary key. Please understand that we are not saying that the alternative interpretation is incorrect—merely that it is different, and that it leads to a different formulation of the overall methodology.

DESIGNATIONS

The next step in the design process is to decide designations. A designation is a many-to-one relationship between two entities (not necessarily distinct or of distinct types). For example, employees designate departments—for each employee, there is a single corresponding department. Likewise, departments designate managers (who of course are also employees in turn). Diagrammatically:

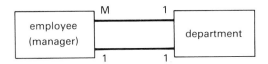

We assume that no employee can simultaneously manage more than one department, so that department-to-manager is in fact one-to-one (1-to-1). In this methodology "1-to-1" is not given any special treatment, being regarded merely as a particular case of many-to-one (M-to-1). "Many" (or

"M") here includes the possibilities of one and zero, as usual; the three "ones" in the diagram are interpreted as follows:

(a) In the relationship "employees-to-departments," "one" means "zero or one" (it is possible for some employee to have no corresponding department).

(b) In the relationship "departments-to-managers," every department must have a manager, but not all employees are managers. The left hand "one" therefore means "exactly one," the right hand "one" means "zero or one."

Designations do *not* normally map into base tables of their own (though it would not be wrong to do so; see the further discussion of this point below). Instead, each designation typically maps into a field—in fact, a foreign key—in the the base table corresponding to the designat*ing* entity type. For example:

```
CREATE TABLE EMP     /* employees (kernel) -- designate DEPT */
       FIELDS ( EMP#, DEPT# ... )
       PRIMARY KEY ( EMP# )
       FOREIGN KEY ( DEPT# IDENTIFIES DEPT ... ) ;

CREATE TABLE DEPT  /* departments (kernel) -- designate EMP */
       FIELDS ( DEPT#, MGR_EMP# ... )
       PRIMARY KEY ( DEPT# )
       FOREIGN KEY ( MGR_EMP# IDENTIFIES EMP ... ) ;
```

For each designation foreign key it is necessary to consider exactly the same three questions as for association foreign keys, namely:

1. Can that foreign key accept null values?
2. What should happen on an attempt to delete the target of the foreign key reference?
3. What should happen on an attempt to update the primary key of the target of the foreign key reference?

The possible answers to all three questions are the same as they were in the case of associations. Thus, for example:

```
CREATE TABLE EMP     /* employees (kernel) -- designate DEPT */
       FIELDS ( EMP#, DEPT# ... )
       PRIMARY KEY ( EMP# )
       FOREIGN KEY ( DEPT# IDENTIFIES DEPT
                     NULLS ALLOWED
                              /* it is legal for an employee to */
                              /* belong to no department        */
```

```
                    DELETE OF DEPT NULLIFIES
                        /* deleting a department leaves    */
                        /* any corresponding employees     */
                        /* currently unassigned            */
                    UPDATE OF DEPT.DEPT# CASCADES ) ;
                        /* changing a department number    */
                        /* causes the same change to be    */
                        /* applied to all corresponding    */
                        /* employees                       */

     CREATE TABLE DEPT  /* departments (kernel) -- designate EMP */
          FIELDS ( DEPT#, MGR_EMP# ... )
          PRIMARY KEY ( DEPT# )
          FOREIGN KEY ( MGR_EMP# IDENTIFIES EMP
                    NULLS NOT ALLOWED
                        /* every department must have a    */
                        /* manager                         */
                    DELETE OF EMP RESTRICTED
                        /* managers cannot be fired (they  */
                      . /* must be demoted first)          */
                    UPDATE OF EMP.EMP# CASCADES ) ;
                        /* changing a manager's employee   */
                        /* number causes the same change   */
                        /* to be applied to the corresp.   */
                        /* department record               */
```

We stated earlier that designations do not usually map into base tables of their own. In general, that statement is accurate. However, if there is any possibility that a given designation might at some point in the future evolve into an association—i.e., if a relationship that is currently many-to-one might eventually become many-to-many—then it would be better to represent it as a separate table right away, in order to avoid future disruptive changes to the design. In fact, designations, or many-to-one relationships, can be divided into two kinds: those that are *inherently* many-to-one, and those that simply happen to be many-to-one currently but are not guaranteed always to remain so. Inherent designations are those that result from inherent limitations of the real world—for example, a child has one mother, an object cannot be in two places at once, and so on. Other designations are merely the result of some policy decision—for example, the company policy that a given employee can be assigned to no more than one department at a time. If the policy is susceptible to change, then the designation might become an association, and (as stated above) it might be better to deal with it as an association right away.

One last point concerning designations: A designating entity type can be a kernel or an association or a characteristic (characteristic entity types are discussed in the next section). That is, the question of whether a given entity type is designative is independent of (or *orthogonal to*) the question of what kind of entity type (kernel, associative, or characteristic) that entity type happens to be.

CHARACTERISTICS

A characteristic is an entity whose sole function (within the microworld of interest) is to describe or qualify or "characterize" some other entity. For example, offerings are characteristics of courses—for each course, there is a set of offerings, each of which serves solely to provide further information concerning that course. Likewise, enrollees are characteristics of offerings. Diagrammatically:

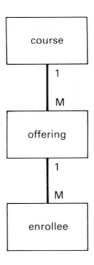

The relationship between a characteristic entity type and the entity type it characterizes is many-to-one, as the diagram indicates. (The "one" here means "exactly one," incidentally.) That relationship thus looks like a designation—and so it is, with this important proviso: The foreign key specifications that go with that designation *must* specify

```
NULLS NOT ALLOWED
DELETE OF target CASCADES
UPDATE OF target.primary-key CASCADES
```

to represent the existence dependence of the characteristic entity type on the entity type it describes. In other words, a characteristic entity type is simply a special case of a designating entity type, in which that designating entity type is existence-dependent on the corresponding designated entity type. It maps into a base table of its own, just like a kernel or an association. For example:

```
CREATE TABLE OFFERING
                    /* offerings -- characteristic of COURSE */
        FIELDS ( COURSE# ... )
        FOREIGN KEY ( COURSE# IDENTIFIES COURSE
                      NULLS NOT ALLOWED
                      DELETE OF COURSE CASCADES
                      UPDATE OF COURSE.COURSE# CASCADES ) ;
```

NULLS NOT ALLOWED must be specified because it would make no sense to have an offering for an unknown course. Similarly, deleting a course, or updating the course number of a course, must cascade, for essentially the same reason.

A characteristic entity type, of course, *is* an entity type—it can have properties of its own, it can participate in associations, and so on; indeed, it can have (lower-level) characteristics of its own, as OFFERINGs have ENROLLEEs. What constitutes the primary key for a characteristic? Inspection of the example above shows that we are faced with the same kind of choice here as we were with associations—namely, should we use the combination of the foreign key and the field that guarantees "uniqueness within entity described" (that combination is guaranteed to be unique), or should we introduce a new, noncomposite primary key instead? As in the case of associations, we defer detailed discussion of this question to Section Four of the paper, and assume for now that we stay with composite keys. Thus we might have:

```
CREATE TABLE COURSE                        /* courses (kernel) */
        FIELDS ( COURSE# ... )
        PRIMARY KEY ( COURSE# ) ;

CREATE TABLE OFFERING
                    /* offerings -- characteristic of COURSE */
        FIELDS ( COURSE#, OFF# ... )
        PRIMARY KEY ( COURSE#, OFF# )
        FOREIGN KEY ( COURSE# IDENTIFIES COURSE
                      NULLS NOT ALLOWED
                      DELETE OF COURSE CASCADES
                      UPDATE OF COURSE.COURSE# CASCADES ) ;

CREATE TABLE ENROLLEE
                    /* enrollees -- characteristic of OFFERING */
        FIELDS ( COURSE#, OFF#, EMP# ... )
        PRIMARY KEY ( COURSE#, OFF#, EMP# )
        FOREIGN KEY ( ( COURSE#, OFF# ) IDENTIFIES OFFERING
                      NULLS NOT ALLOWED
                      DELETE OF OFFERING CASCADES
                      UPDATE OF OFFERING.(COURSE#,OFF#)
                                              CASCADES ) ;
```

See the next section (third and fourth subsections) for further discussion of characteristics.

PROPERTIES

Note: It is in this area that the most direct overlap occurs between the synthetic and analytic approaches. A hint of things to come.

A property is a piece of information that describes an entity in some way. As explained earlier, a given property may identify the entity in question, or it may reference some other entity, or it may simply "stand for itself." In this section we are principally concerned with the last of these three cases (although in fact the ideas presented do apply to the other two cases also; but the point is that those two cases have already been discussed, in effect, in the preceding sections). Examples of properties that "stand for themselves" are department budgets, part weights, shipment quantities, and enrollee grades. The entity described by the property can be a kernel, an association, or a characteristic. It may also be designative.

Generally speaking, properties map into fields within base tables, as the examples just given indicate. Unfortunately, matters are not quite as simple as this statement suggests (neither are they very complex, however, we hasten to add); in fact, there are four distinct cases to consider, each of which requires its own special treatment. But the overall objective in each case is to map the property in question into a single field in some base table somewhere. The problem is just one of finding the right table.

The four cases are as follows.

Case	immediate	single-valued
1	yes	yes
2	no	yes
3	yes	no
4	no	no

We examine each in turn.

- *Case 1*: immediate, single-valued (this is the simple case)

A property is *immediate* if it genuinely is a property of the entity in question and not of some related entity. For example, "part color" is an immediate property of parts; it is not an immediate property of shipments, even though every shipment does have a unique corresponding part color, because (as already stated) it is really a property of a related entity, namely the part involved in that shipment. By contrast, "shipment quantity" is an immediate property of shipments.

A property is *single-valued* if each instance of the entity it describes has exactly one instance of the property. For example, "part weight" is a single-valued property of parts: Each part has one weight. By way of a counter-example, suppose that parts came in multiple colors. Then "part color" would be a multivalued property of parts.

Immediate, single-valued properties map directly into fields in the base table for the entity type concerned. For example:

```
CREATE TABLE P                              /* parts (kernel) */
       FIELDS ( P#, PNAME, COLOR, WEIGHT, CITY )
       PRIMARY KEY ( P# ) ;

CREATE TABLE SP /* shipments -- association between S and P */
       FIELDS ( S#, P#, QTY )
       PRIMARY KEY ( S#, P# )
       FOREIGN KEY ( S# IDENTIFIES S  etc. )
       FOREIGN KEY ( P# IDENTIFIES P  etc. ) ;
```

- *Case 2*: nonimmediate, single-valued

If you find you are dealing with a nonimmediate property and you do not yet have an entity for which that property is immediate, it simply means that you have not yet recognized the existence of that other entity. For example, suppose that "supplier status" is a function of "supplier city"—i.e., the status of any given supplier is determined entirely by where that supplier is located:

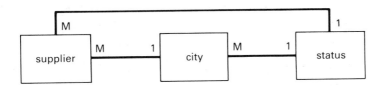

(The "ones" here mean "exactly one.") Although it is true that status is single-valued per supplier, the M-to-1 relationship from supplier to status is *transitive*—it can be deduced as a logical consequence from the other two M-to-1 relationships shown. In fact, what we really have here (as the diagram suggests) is two kernel entities, supplier and city, with a designation from the first to the second and an immediate, single-valued property for the second:

```
CREATE TABLE S           /* suppliers (kernel) -- designate C */
       FIELDS ( S#, SNAME, CITY )
       PRIMARY KEY ( P# )
       FOREIGN KEY ( CITY IDENTIFIES C  etc. ) ;

CREATE TABLE C                              /* cities (kernel) */
       FIELDS ( CITY, STAUS )
       PRIMARY KEY ( CITY ) ;
```

- *Case 3*: immediate, multivalued

For the sake of this subsection, suppose that parts come in multiple colors. Suppose also that parts are stored in multiple cities. Then "part color" and "part city" are examples of immediate but multivalued properties for parts. Each immediate, multivalued property for a given entity type is treated as a *separate characteristic* of that entity type and thus maps into its own separate base table. For example:

```
CREATE TABLE PCOLOR    /* part colors -- characteristic of P */
       FIELDS ( P#, COLOR )
       PRIMARY KEY ( P#, COLOR )
       FOREIGN KEY ( P# IDENTIFIES P
                     NULLS NOT ALLOWED
                     DELETE OF P CASCADES
                     UPDATE OF P.P# CASCADES ) ;

CREATE TABLE PCITY     /* part cities -- characteristic of P */
       FIELDS ( P#, CITY )
       PRIMARY KEY ( P#, CITY )
       FOREIGN KEY ( P# IDENTIFIES P
                     NULLS NOT ALLOWED
                     DELETE OF P CASCADES
                     UPDATE OF P.P# CASCADES ) ;
```

In fact, as the examples show, characteristics are the way the synthetic approach deals with what are usually referred to as repeating groups.

- *Case 4*: nonimmediate, multivalued

This last case is just a combination of preceding cases. Consider the course-offering-enrollee database. "Offering location" is a nonimmediate, multivalued property of courses; but it is an immediate, single-valued property of offerings, which are characteristics of courses. Likewise for "offering date." Hence:

```
CREATE TABLE COURSE                        /* courses (kernel) */
       FIELDS ( COURSE#, SUBJECT )
       PRIMARY KEY ( COURSE# ) ;

CREATE TABLE OFFERING
                 /* offerings -- characteristic of COURSE */
       FIELDS ( COURSE#, OFF#, DATE, LOCATION )
       PRIMARY KEY ( COURSE#, OFF# )
       FOREIGN KEY ( COURSE# IDENTIFIES COURSE
                     NULLS NOT ALLOWED
                     DELETE OF COURSE CASCADES
                     UPDATE OF COURSE.COURSE# CASCADES ) ;
```

Likewise, enrollee grade is a nonimmediate, multivalued property of offerings, but an immediate, single-valued property of enrollees, which are characteristics of offerings:

```
CREATE TABLE ENROLLEE
                    /* enrollees -- characteristic of OFFERING */
        FIELDS ( COURSE#, OFF#, EMP#, GRADE )
        PRIMARY KEY ( COURSE#, OFF#, EMP# )
        FOREIGN KEY ( ( COURSE#, OFF# ) IDENTIFIES OFFERING
                    NULLS NOT ALLOWED
                    DELETE OF OFFERING CASCADES
                    UPDATE OF OFFERING.(COURSE#,OFF#)
                                        CASCADES ) ;
```

A RECIPE FOR PRIMARY KEYS

We have now completed our presentation of the synthetic approach per se. We have stressed the crucial importance of primary and foreign keys to that approach. SQL, however, provides no direct support for those constructs (nor indeed do most other relational languages at the time of writing). We therefore present, in this section and the next, recipes by which you can enforce the primary and foreign key disciplines for yourself. The recipes are (obviously) somewhat SQL-specific but can readily be adapted to a nonSQL system.

First, primary keys. For each primary key in your design:

PK1. Specify NOT NULL for each field in the primary key.

PK2. Create a UNIQUE index over the combination of all fields in the primary key.

PK3. Ensure that this index is in existence whenever a record is inserted into the table or the primary key of a record in the table is updated. In practice, this typically means creating the index at the time the table itself is created, and "never" dropping that index.

PK4. Keep the PRIMARY KEY specifications from the pseudoDDL either as a comment in the catalog or in some separate user-defined table (which can then be logically regarded as an extension to the catalog).

Note that the last of these recommendations means that it will be possible to interrogate the catalog regarding primary keys, even though the system itself has no knowledge of such keys.

A RECIPE FOR FOREIGN KEYS

For each foreign key in your design:

FK1. Specify NOT NULL for each field in the foreign key, if and only if NULLS NOT ALLOWED applies to that foreign key.

FK2. Consider the merits of creating an index (probably not UNIQUE) over the combination of all fields in the foreign key. (Such an index usually will be desirable for performance reasons, since it is likely that the foreign key and its matching primary key will often be used as the basis for join operations. But performance considerations are generally beyond the scope of this paper.)

FK3. Use the authorization mechanism to prohibit all on-line operations that could violate the constraints that apply to this foreign key. By "on-line operation" here we mean a SQL operation, such as INSERT or DELETE, that is issued by an end-user rather than by an application program. Specifically, prohibit on-line:

- DELETE on the referenced table
- UPDATE on the referenced table primary key
- INSERT on the referencing table
- UPDATE on the referencing table foreign key

For example, consider the suppliers-and-parts database. Here S is a referenced table and SP is the referencing table. An on-line SQL user cannot be allowed to INSERT a shipment (for example), because there is no way to force that user to check that the supplier number for that shipment does currently exist in the shipments table. Similar remarks apply to the other prohibitions listed above.

FK4. Take the foreign key constraints as part of the requirements specification for database maintenance programs. Ideally, have exactly one such program for each foreign key (this does not mean that one program cannot deal with multiple foreign keys, only that one foreign key should not be maintained by multiple programs). Use the authorization mechanism to prevent all other programs from executing any operations that could violate those constraints (see paragraph FK3).

FK5. Keep the FOREIGN KEY specifications from the pseudoDDL either as a comment in the catalog or in some separate user-defined table (which again can then be regarded as a logical extension of the catalog). Note that—as in the case of the analogous rule for primary keys—this recommendation means that it will be possible to interrogate the catalog regarding foreign keys, even though the system itself has no knowledge of such keys.

Finally, as an independent (and conservative) measure:

FK6. Write a utility program to be run periodically to check for and report on any constraint violations. Note: If the FOREIGN KEY specifications are kept in the catalog in stylized form, as recommended under paragraph FK5, then this utility can be generalized—i.e., driven off the catalog—instead of having to be specifically tailored to the particular foreign keys defined for a particular database.

A couple of additional remarks regarding paragraphs FK3 and FK4:

- First, on-line SQL users will still be able to perform *some* SQL update operations. For example, inserting a new supplier record cannot cause any referential integrity problems. The same goes for deleting a shipment, or changing a supplier city or a shipment quantity (etc.).

- Second, on-line users will of course still be able to perform the other functions also, but *not via the SQL interface*. Instead, a user who (for example) wishes to insert a new shipment will do so by invoking the appropriate installation-written application program and supplying the "new shipment" details to that program. That program in turn will perform the necessary checks to ensure that (for example) the corresponding supplier already exists, before allowing the new shipment record to be created. Thus the recipes do not really take any function away from the end-user; they merely impose additional responsibilities on the application programmer. Eventually, of course, when the system itself assumes those responsibilities, the application programmer also will be able to devote more time to solving real application problems, instead of having to spend time remedying system deficiencies.

THE SYNTHETIC APPROACH: A CHECKLIST

The synthetic design procedure can be regarded as involving *three levels of abstraction*. At the top level, entities are identified and classified into kernels, characteristics, etc., and their properties are identified. At the next level, those entities and properties are mapped into pseudoDDL (i.e., CREATE TABLE statements, with explicit primary and foreign key specifications). At the third level, that pseudoDDL is mapped into real SQL DDL, plus procedures to maintain the foreign key constraints. By way of summary, we now present a checklist of the principal steps in the synthetic design process. Note: For brevity, in what follows we use "entity" to mean entity *type*.

1. Represent each kernel (independent entity) as a base table. Specify the primary key of that base table.

2. Represent each association (many-to-many, or many-to-many-to-many, etc., relationship among entities) as a base table. Use foreign keys within that table to identify the participants in the association. Specify the constraints associated with each of those foreign keys. Specify the primary key of the table—probably the combination of all participant-identifying for-

eign keys (but see the section on ''Composite Keys'' in Section Four of this paper).

3. Represent each characteristic (designating entity that is existence-dependent on the corresponding designated entity) as a base table with a foreign key identifying the entity described by the characteristic. Specify the foreign key constraints for existence dependence. Specify the primary key of the table—probably the combination of the foreign key and the property that guarantees ''uniqueness within entity described'' (but see the section on ''Composite Keys'' in Section Four of this paper).

4. Represent each designation (many-to-one relationship between two entities) not already dealt with under 3. above as a foreign key within the base table representing the designating entity. Specify the constraints associated with each such foreign key.

5. Represent each single-valued property as a field within the base table representing the entity most immediately described by that property.

6. Apply the recipes for primary and foreign keys.

7. Apply the procedures discussed in Section Three of this paper to ensure that the design does not unintentionally violate any of the normalization guidelines.

8. Iterate until your design is complete and all pseudoDDL has been converted into real SQL DDL, plus appropriate constraint maintenance procedures.

SECTION THREE: THE ANALYTIC APPROACH

By following the design procedure outlined in the previous sections, we will always finish up with a design that conforms to the following simple pattern:

Each table consists of:

(a) a primary key, representing the unique identifier for some particular entity type;

together with

(b) zero or more additional fields, each representing an immediate, single-valued property of the entity type identified by the primary key.

("Property" here includes the case of a referencing property, i.e., a property that is represented by a foreign key.)

Such a design is *clean*, in the sense that each table contains information about one entity type and one entity type only. That design will be easier to understand, easier to use, and (most important) easier to extend when new information is added to the database later on, than a design in which (e.g.) information about multiple entity types is bundled together into a single table. In other words, the design is *stable* and will be a good foundation for future growth.

Another way of expressing the clean design objective is: *One fact in one place.* Each fact (for example, the fact that a certain supplier has a certain city) appears at exactly one place in the design. Yet another way of characterizing it (very informally) is: *Each field represents a fact about the key, the whole key, and nothing but the key* (where "key" is shorthand for "entity identified by the primary key of the table that contains the field in question").

Clean design is also the objective of the *analytic* approach. The analytic approach, under the heading of "normalization," or more accurately *further* normalization, has been extensively discussed in numerous books and theoretical papers. In fact, the methodology discussed in this paper so far and the normalization discipline are complementary, in the sense that (as already explained) you will almost certainly find yourself employing them both in practice. However, normalization is frequently discussed in the literature as if it were the only design tool necessary; our feeling, by contrast, is that (as already suggested) its principal usefulness is as a final check on the design methodology already presented. It is certainly not a panacea. That is why we devote only a comparatively small part of this paper to it.

In brief, the idea of normalization is as follows. Any table that satisfies the condition that, at every row-and-column position within the table, there is always a single atomic value, never a set of such values, is said to be *normalized*. (In fact, *un*normalized tables—equivalently, tables that contain repeating groups—are not even permitted in a relational database.) Now, every normalized table is automatically considered to be in *first normal form* (abbreviated 1NF); that is, "normalized" and "first normal form" mean exactly the same thing, strictly speaking (but in practice the term "normalized" is often taken to have the narrower meaning of "fully normalized," in the sense that the design does not violate any of the normalization guidelines discussed below).

The reason that first normal form is called "first" is that it is possible to define further levels of normalization, over and above 1NF—second normal form (2NF), third normal form (3NF), and so on. Basically, a table is in 2NF if it is in 1NF and also satisfies a certain extra condition (which will not be spelled out here); it is in 3NF if it is in 2NF and also satisfies yet another extra condition; and so on. Thus each normal form is in a sense more restrictive than the one before. More significantly, each normal form is generally more *desirable* than the one before, also. This is because "(N + 1)st normal form" does not possess certain unattractive features that "Nth normal form" does. The whole point of the extra condition imposed on (N + 1)st over Nth is precisely to eliminate those unattractive features. For example, here is a table—table SPSC, primary key the combination (S#,P#)—that is in first normal form and not in second:

```
          --  --  ---  ------
SPSC  S#  P#  QTY  SCITY
          --  --  ---  ------
          S1  P1  300  London
          S1  P2  400  London
          S2  P1  200  Paris
          S2  P2  400  Paris
```

The "unattractive feature" of SPSC is obvious: Field SCITY (supplier city) contains a lot of redundancy. That redundancy in turn will lead to update and consistency problems (e.g., supplier S1 might be shown as having city London in one record and city Paris in another, unless appropriate controls are exercised). Intuitively, field SCITY is in the wrong place. A better design is:

```
        --  --  ---                   --  ------
SP  S#  P#  QTY              SC  S#  CITY
        --  --  ---                   --  ------
        S1  P1  300              S1  London
        S1  P2  400              S2  Paris
        S2  P1  200
        S2  P2  400
```

These tables are in 2NF (in fact, they are also in 3NF and 4NF and 5NF; 5NF is the "ultimate" normal form, in a very specific sense which unfortunately it is beyond the scope of this paper to discuss).

The overall purpose of the further normalization discipline is to eliminate redundancies such as that illustrated in this example. That discipline provides a set of guidelines by which a table that contains such redundancies can be broken down into smaller tables that do not. The ultimate objective, as already stated, is to come up with a design in which each fact appears in one and only one place. But of course this is the objective of the synthetic approach also. In fact, *the further normalization guidelines are in essence nothing more than the guidelines already given for dealing with properties (the four cases) in our earlier discussion of the synthetic approach.* Therefore, we do not treat them in detail here, but content ourselves with a superficial examination of the principal points. A detailed (but still tutorial) treatment can be found in *An Introduction to Database Systems: Volume I*, 4th edition (Addison-Wesley, 1985).

First we need to introduce the notion of *functional dependency* (FD). Field B of table T is said to be functionally dependent on field A of table T if and only if it is the case that, for each distinct value of field T.A, there is necessarily exactly one distinct value of T.B (at any given time). For example, in table SPSC above, field SCITY is functionally dependent on field S#—for each supplier number, there must be exactly one city (e.g., every time S1 appears as the supplier number, London must appear as the city). Note that fields T.A and T.B are allowed to be composite in this definition: For example, in table SPSC again, field QTY is functionally dependent on the composite field (S#,P#). We write:

```
S#        -->   SCITY

(S#,P#)   -->   QTY
```

Now comes the crucial point. If the database design satisfies the "one fact in one place" objective, *the only functional dependencies in any table will be of the form K → F, where K is the primary key and F is some other field*. Note that it follows from the definition that K → F always holds for all fields F in the table. "One fact in one place" says that no *other* functional dependencies hold. The purpose of the normalization discipline is to get rid of all "other" FDs, i.e., FDs that are not of the simple form K → F.

There are basically two cases to consider:

1. The table has a composite primary key, of the form (K1,K2) say, and also includes a field F that is functionally dependent on part of that key, say on K2, instead of on the whole key. (This was the case illustrated in the SPSC example above.) In this case the guidelines recommend forming another table containing K2 and F (primary key K2) and removing F from the original table:

Replace	T(K1,K2,F),	primary key (K1,K2), with FD K2 → F
by	T1(K1,K2),	primary key (K1,K2)
	and T2(K2,F),	primary key K2

2. The table has primary key K, a field F1 that is (of course) functionally dependent on K, and another field F2 that is functionally dependent on F1. (This case was illustrated in our discussion of nonimmediate, single-valued properties in Section Two of this paper, where we assumed for the sake of the example that supplier city was functionally dependent on supplier number and supplier status was functionally dependent on supplier city.) The

solution here is essentially the same as before—we form another table containing F1 and F2 (primary key F1), and remove F2 from the original table:

Replace	T(K,F1,F2),	primary key K, with FD F1 → F2
by	T1(K,F1),	primary key K
and	T2(F1,F2),	primary key F1

Given any table as input, repeated application of these two rules will (in almost all practical situations) eventually yield a set of tables that are in the "ultimate" normal form and thus do not contain any FDs not of the simple form K → F.

To recap, the normalization discipline involves reducing large tables to smaller ones. Loosely speaking, it assumes that you already have some small number of large tables as input, and it manipulates that input to produce a large number of small tables as output. But it does not say anything about how you arrive at those large tables in the first place. The synthetic approach, by contrast, addresses exactly that problem. That is why we claim that the two approaches complement one another. Our overall suggested design procedure thus consists of:

1. Using the synthetic approach to generate tables representing kernels, associations, etc.; and then

2. Using the analytic approach to verify that those tables do not unintentionally violate any of the normalization guidelines.

To conclude this part of the paper, a few final remarks on normalization:

- The lower normal forms such as 2NF are not particularly important in themselves other than as stepping-stones to the final normal form.

- Tables that are in 3NF but not in 4NF or 5NF, though theoretically possible, are very unlikely to occur in practice. This is why you hear people talking about third normal form, rather than fourth or fifth, as if it were the only and final goal; in practice, this is usually a justifiable simplification.

- A question that frequently arises is: Could the normalization procedure be mechanized? In other words, would it be possible to construct a program (i.e., a database design aid) that would "automatically" generate tables in the ultimate normal form? The answer is yes, it certainly would be possible. But would it be worthwhile? Consider what the input to such a program would be. Clearly, it would have to consist of some specified initial table or set of tables, *together with some specified set of functional dependencies* (for there is no way the program could determine those dependencies for itself). Unfortunately, it is precisely the step of determining the dependencies that is the difficult part of the job (normalization per se is almost trivial, once you know the dependencies). Thus, an "automatic normalizer" design aid would really only be automating the easy part of the task.

SECTION FOUR: MISCELLANEOUS TOPICS

We have now completed our broad look at the synthetic and analytic approaches to database design. The remainder of this paper is concerned with a variety of miscellaneous topics, some of them still of a fairly fundamental nature, others at a very detailed level, but all of them significant in a practical design context. The topics we discuss are as follows:

- Entity classification (again)
- Alternate keys
- Composite keys
- Entity supertypes and subtypes
- Domains
- Overnormalization
- Denormalization
- Null values
- Vectors
- Codes and flags
- Field overloading
- Individual user views

ENTITY CLASSIFICATION

The reader should not get the impression that the entity classification scheme sketched in Section Two of this paper is a totally rigid thing. For example, a given entity may be perceived as a characteristic by one user but as an association by another. Of course, the two perceptions must be compatible, in the sense that they must both involve the same foreign key constraints. In the association/characteristic example, the foreign key constraints must be those required by the rules for characteristics; for otherwise the given entity obviously could not be regarded as a characteristic at all.

Here is a concrete example of such a situation. Suppose again (as in Case 3 under "Properties" in Section Two of this paper) that parts are stored in multiple cities, and suppose also that cities form a separate kernel entity type, represented by a base table called C. Then we will have:

```
CREATE TABLE PCITY                              /* part cities */
        FIELDS ( P#, CITY )
        PRIMARY KEY ( P#, CITY )
        FOREIGN KEY ( P# IDENTIFIES P  etc. )
        FOREIGN KEY ( CITY IDENTIFIES C  etc. ) ;
```

But is PCITY a characteristic of parts, with PCITY.CITY as a multivalued part property, or is it an association linking parts and cities as equal partners? Well, let us complete the foreign key specifications, e.g., as follows:

```
CREATE TABLE PCITY                              /* part cities */
        FIELDS ( P#, CITY )
        PRIMARY KEY ( P#, CITY )
        FOREIGN KEY ( P# IDENTIFIES P
                      NULLS NOT ALLOWED
                      DELETE OF P CASCADES
                      UPDATE OF P.P# CASCADES )
        FOREIGN KEY ( CITY IDENTIFIES C
                      NULLS NOT ALLOWED
                      DELETE OF C CASCADES
                      UPDATE OF C.CITY CASCADES ) ;
```

With these specifications, PCITY could be regarded either as a characteristic of parts (designating cities) or as an association between parts and cities—or, for that matter, as a characteristic of cities (designating parts). If any portion of the foreign key specification for PCITY.CITY were to be changed, however, then PCITY could no longer be regarded as a characteristic of cities, though the other two interpretations would remain valid.

We remark in passing that one of the goals of good database design, and of a good database design methodology, should be precisely to support such alternative interpretations. In other words, it should be possible for different people to perceive the same microworld in different ways, much as different people can perceive the same database in different ways in relational systems today (by virtue of the relational view mechanism).

ALTERNATE KEYS

Consider the DEPT table from the departments-and-employees database once again:

```
CREATE TABLE DEPT  /* departments (kernel) -- designate EMP */
        FIELDS ( DEPT#, DNAME, MGR_EMP#, BUDGET )
        PRIMARY KEY ( DEPT# )
        FOREIGN KEY ( MGR_EMP# IDENTIFIES EMP
                      NULLS NOT ALLOWED
                      DELETE OF EMP RESTRICTED
                      UPDATE OF EMP.EMP# CASCADES ) ;
```

Within this table, no two DEPTs can have the same MGR_EMP# value (because of our assumption that no employee can manage more than one department at a time). To reflect this constraint in our design, we need to add the specification

```
ALTERNATE KEY ( MGR_EMP# )
```

to the pseudoDDL for DEPT (between the PRIMARY KEY and FOREIGN KEY clauses). An alternate key is a field or field combination that obeys the same uniqueness and minimality constraints as the primary key but is not the primary key.

As another example (perhaps simpler), suppose the EMP table is extended to include a social security number field SS#. Then SS# might be an alternate key for the EMP table.

Alternate key uniqueness can be enforced in SQL by creating a UNIQUE index over the field or field combination concerned. Barring explicit specifications to the contrary, an alternate key (unlike a primary key) is allowed to accept null values. Note, however, that a UNIQUE index in SQL does not enforce the constraint "unique unless null"—it enforces the constraint "unique, with at most one null."

COMPOSITE KEYS

We suggested a couple of times in Section Two of this paper that composite (i.e., multiple-field) keys suffer from certain disadvantages. One problem is simply that a multiple-field key is generally rather awkward to use (and the more fields there are, the worse it gets, of course). Consider the course-offering-enrollee database once again. Table OFFERING has a composite primary key (OFFERING.COURSE#,OFFERING.OFF#), and table ENROLLEE has a matching composite foreign key (ENROLLEE.COURSE#, ENROLLEE.OFF#). As a result, users will find themselves writing numerous WHERE clauses of the form

```
WHERE   OFFERING.COURSE#  = ENROLLEE.COURSE#
AND     OFFERING.OFF#     = ENROLLEE.OFF#
```

Such clumsy formulations do not represent any kind of fundamental problem, of course, but they can be awkward and tedious for the user. It would be nice if the system allowed composite fields to be given noncomposite names, so that the above WHERE clause could be simplified to (e.g.)

```
WHERE   OFFERING.CO# = ENROLLEE.CO#
```

where CO# stands for the combination of the COURSE# and OFF# fields. Unfortunately, however, few systems today provide any kind of composite field support.

A more significant problem is that composite keys can lead to redundancy. For example, if offering 3 of course 86 has 20 students enrolled, then the fact that course 86 *has* an offering 3 appears 21 times—once in an OFFERING record and 20 times in an ENROLLEE record. It might be better to introduce a new, noncomposite key—OKEY, say—for OFFERING, and then to use OKEY in the ENROLLEE record, as follows:

```
CREATE TABLE OFFERING
       FIELDS ( OKEY, COURSE#, OFF#, DATE, LOCATION )
       PRIMARY KEY ( OKEY )
       ALTERNATE KEY ( COURSE#, OFF# )
       FOREIGN KEY ( COURSE# IDENTIFIES COURSE  etc. )

CREATE TABLE ENROLLEE
       FIELDS ( EKEY, OKEY, EMP#, GRADE )
       PRIMARY KEY ( EKEY )
       ALTERNATE KEY ( OKEY, EMP# )
       FOREIGN KEY ( OKEY IDENTIFIES OFFERING  etc. )
```

We have also introduced a noncomposite key EKEY for the ENROLLEE table. Note the ALTERNATE KEY specifications.

The introduced keys OKEY and EKEY do not need to have any intrinsic meaning, of course. For example, the program that creates OFFERINGs can simply maintain a counter in the database, increasing that counter by one each time a new OFFERING is created in order to generate a new OKEY value. One advantage of this technique is that there would never be any need to update field OFFERING.OKEY at all, which in turn means that the UPDATE portion of the foreign key rules for field ENROLLEE.OKEY would be irrelevant and need not be specified (and hence that database maintenance programs would be simplified). Another advantage is that disk space requirements are likely to be reduced. On the other hand, there is a significant disadvantage also—namely, more joins will now be needed. For example, the query "List course numbers for courses attended by employee E5" will now require a join operation, whereas previously it did not. (It is true that a view could be defined to conceal the join from the user, but of course the join would still be there; furthermore, the system would probably not allow that view to be updated.)

One final point on this subject: We have tacitly been assuming so far that composite keys arise only in the context of characteristics and associations, not in the context of kernels. But it is quite possible for a kernel to have a composite key also. For example, suppose that cities are regarded as kernels, and cities are identified by their name together with the name of their containing state, as in, e.g., "Portland, Oregon." *Recommendation*: Kernels, at least, should always be given noncomposite keys. For example, introduce a noncomposite "city number" and treat city and state names just as properties of the entity identified by that city number.

ENTITY SUPERTYPES AND SUBTYPES

Consider the following example:

```
        ----   ----------   ------   ----------
EMP     EMP#   JOB          SALARY   COMMISSION
        ----   ----------   ------   ----------
        E1     Salesman        80K         25K
        E2     Accountant     100K          -
        E3     Programmer      25K          -
        E4     Salesman        85K         40K
        E5     Accountant     100K          -
```

The property COMMISSION applies only to salesmen, not to other kinds of employee. As a result, the COMMISSION field will be null for all nonsalesmen. Note, incidentally, that these nulls should be interpreted, not as "value unknown," but rather as "property inapplicable"—though at the time of writing few systems, if any, actually make any operational distinction between these two different kinds of null.

The example illustrates a situation that arises very frequently in practice, to wit: We are given a set of entities of some specific type (a set of employees, in the example), all of which therefore have some set of properties in common (for example, all employees have a salary); in addition, certain members of that set (the salesmen, in the example) have certain special properties of their own (salesmen have a COMMISSION property, but employees in general do not). If we represent the given entities by a single table, as in the example above, then that table will involve a certain number of explicit nulls, as we have seen. If on the other hand we represent the given entities by two tables, one containing the common properties and one the special properties, then those explicit nulls can be eliminated. For instance:

```
        ----   ----------   ------              ----   ----------
EMP     EMP#   JOB          SALARY   SALESMAN   EMP#   COMMISSION
        ----   ----------   ------              ----   ----------
        E1     Salesman        80K              E1            25K
        E2     Accountant     100K              E4            40K
        E3     Programmer      25K
        E4     Salesman        85K
        E5     Accountant     100K
```

One advantage of this latter representation is thus simply that it avoids the need for certain explicit nulls (and we will argue later in this paper that avoiding null values is generally a good idea). Perhaps more significantly, it captures the true semantics of the situation in a slightly clearer form (it is an arguably "better" representation of the microworld of interest). The point is, employees and salesman should both be regarded as entities—both can have properties, both can have characteristics, both can participate in associations, etc.—but the entity type "salesmen" is a *subtype* of the entity type "employees"; equivalently, entity type "employees" is a *supertype* of entity type "salesmen." Definition:

- Entity type B is a subtype of entity type A (and entity type A is a supertype of entity type B) if and only if every instance of B is necessarily an instance of A.

Subtype-supertype relationships such as that between SALESMAN and EMP can be represented diagrammatically by means of a *type hierarchy*. For example:

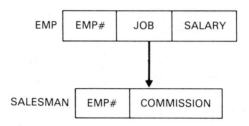

Type hierarchies are known by a variety of different names, including:

- *Generalization hierarchies* (an employee is a generalization of a salesman);
- *Specialization hierarchies* (a salesman is a specialization of an employee);

and

- *"Is-a" hierarchies* (every salesman "is a" employee).

In this paper we will stick to the term "type hierarchy." Note carefully that a type hierarchy is *not* an IMS-style hierarchy. It is not a data structure, in the sense that the hierarchies of IMS are data structures. Also, there is no notion of a given EMP record having multiple corresponding SALESMAN records; on the contrary, a given EMP record has at most one corresponding SALESMAN record, as the sample data shown earlier makes clear.

Let B be a subtype of supertype A. Then every property that applies to A automatically applies to B; for example, every SALESMAN automatically inherits the SALARY property from its superior EMP. (The converse is not true, of course; for example, EMPs do not inherit COMMISSIONs.) Likewise, every characteristic of employees is automatically a characteristic of salesmen, but salesmen may have characteristics of their own that do not apply to employees in general; every designation that applies to employees automatically applies to salesmen, but salesmen may have designations of their own that do not apply to employees in general; and every association that employees participate in automatically applies to salesmen, but salesmen may participate in associations of their own that do not apply to employees in general.

The EMP/SALESMAN example is very simple, of course. We might extend it by adding further subtypes of EMP called ACCOUNTANT, PROGRAMMER, etc. (assuming now that each job type has its own special properties that do not apply to the others). In addition, we might *also* divide EMPs into (say) MANAGERs and NON_MANAGERs (if each of those subtypes again has properties of its own); and so on. Furthermore, each subtype might in turn divide into lower-level subtypes; for example, PROGRAMMERs might divide into COBOL_PROGRAMMERs, FORTRAN_PROGRAMMERs, etc. Thus, in general, entity type A might divide into subtypes B1, B2, etc. according to one categorization (such as job type), into subtypes C1, C2, etc. according to another, and each of B1, B2, C1, C2, etc. may in turn further subdivide, and so on. If such a situation were represented by a single table, that table would be very sparse (in the sense that it would contain many nulls).

In the database, supertype-subtype relationships are represented (of course) by foreign keys. For example:

```
CREATE TABLE EMP                          /* employees (kernel) */
       FIELDS ( EMP#, SALARY ... )
       PRIMARY KEY ( EMP# ) ;

CREATE TABLE SALESMAN           /* salesmen -- subtype of EMP */
       FIELDS ( EMP#, COMMISSION ... )
       PRIMARY KEY ( EMP# )
       FOREIGN KEY ( EMP# IDENTIFIES EMP
                     NULLS NOT ALLOWED
                     DELETE OF EMP CASCADES
                     UPDATE OF EMP.EMP# CASCADES ) ;
```

(The foreign key rules are the same as for characteristics, but note that the foreign key is also the primary key for the subtype table and therefore possesses the uniqueness property.)

A disadvantage of this representation is thus that it introduces some additional foreign key constraints that need to be maintained. In fact it also introduces another integrity constraint that (given the state of systems today) will also have to be enforced by application code, namely that a given employee number must appear in the SALESMAN table if and only if that employee has job 'Salesman' in the EMP table. Nevertheless, it is still the case that the representation is logically cleaner than that involving just a single table.

We conclude this section by remarking that tables EMP and SALES-MAN can each be obtained from the original table by taking a restriction of that table followed by a projection, and that the original table can be reconstructed from EMP and SALESMAN by means of an outer join. It is thus conceivable that a new kind of normalization theory might be developed (and some corresponding new normal forms defined), based on restriction/projection as the reduction operator and outer join as the reconstruction operator. ("Classical" normalization theory is of course based on projection as the reduction operator and natural join as the reconstruction operator.)

DOMAINS

A domain is a conceptual pool of values from which one or more fields in the database draw their actual values. For example, in the suppliers-and-parts database, fields S.S# and SP.S# both draw their values from the domain of supplier numbers; fields S.CITY and P.CITY both draw their values from the domain of city names. If two fields are defined on (i.e., draw their values from) the same domain, then comparisons involving those two fields—and hence joins, unions, etc. based on those two fields—make sense. Conversely, if two fields are defined on different domains, then such operations normally do not make sense.

As you proceed with your design, you should identify the domains involved in the database and, for each field, name the underlying domain for that field. This activity is particularly important in the case of primary and foreign key fields (which are the fields over which most joins—though not necessarily all joins—will be done): A foreign key and its matching primary key should be defined on the same domain. For example (pseudoDDL once again):

```
CREATE DOMAIN S# CHAR(5) ;                    /* supplier numbers */

CREATE TABLE S
       FIELDS ( S# DOMAIN ( S# ), ... )
       PRIMARY KEY ( S# ) ;

CREATE TABLE SP
       FIELDS ( S# DOMAIN ( S# ), ... )
       PRIMARY KEY ...
       FOREIGN KEY ( S# IDENTIFIES S  etc. ) ;
```

When you map the pseudoDDL into real SQL DDL, the CREATE DOMAIN statements and the "DOMAIN (domain-name)" clauses will disappear entirely (SQL currently provides no support for domains at all). However, we recommend that you keep the domain specifications for each field in the catalog somehow. A good (recommended) way of doing this is as follows: *Whenever possible, give every field the same name as the underlying domain.* When it is not possible (which can be the case only if the same domain is used more than once within the same table, as in the case of, e.g., a bill-of-materials structure), give the field the name of the domain prefixed by some distinguishing qualifier to make it unique (within its containing table). Thus, for example, use S# or S_S# or SP_S# (etc.) as names of fields containing supplier numbers; do *not* use (e.g.) S# in one table and SNO in another and SNUM in a third, etc.

One reason for this rule is that it makes life easier for the user (fewer distinct names to remember, less arbitrariness). Another, much more significant, is that it allows you to interrogate the catalog about domains, even though the system does not understand domains. For example, to find all uses of the supplier number domain in the suppliers-and-parts database:

```
SELECT FIELDNAME, TABLENAME
FROM   SYSFIELDS
WHERE  FIELDNAME LIKE '%S#' ;
```

(where we assume that SYSFIELDS is a catalog table listing all fields in the database, together with their containing table in every case). If supplier numbers have to be increased from six characters to eight, for example, a query such as this one can help you locate all portions of the database that need to be changed.

Another recommendation: When you reach the level of detail in the design procedure at which individual field data types (DECIMAL(5), CHARACTER(4), etc.) need to be specified, specify those data types at the domain level and then allow each field to inherit its data type from the corresponding domain. In this way you can guarantee that most run-time field comparisons—and therefore most joins, unions, etc.—will not involve the overhead of any data conversion operations. (Most systems will allow such run-time conversions, but it is desirable to avoid them for performance reasons.)

OVERNORMALIZATION

The overall objective of normalization, as stated in Section Three of this paper, is to reduce redundancy. This objective is achieved by a process of successive refinement, in which at each step tables that contain such redundancy are replaced by smaller tables that do not. Ultimately, each table should consist of "properties of the key, the whole key, and nothing but the key." Once this stage has been reached, however, the normalization process should *stop*. For example, the table

```
EMP ( EMP#, ENAME, DEPT#, SALARY )
```

already satisfies the stated objective (it is in fact in fifth normal form). It *could* be reduced further; in the extreme, it could be reduced to a collection of binary relations:

```
EN ( EMP#, ENAME )
ED ( EMP#, DEPT# )
ES ( EMP#, SALARY )
```

However, there seems little to be gained from such further reduction. Moreover, while it is true that the original table EMP can be recovered by joining EN, ED, and ES back together again over EMP#, those joins will cause run-time overhead; also, of course, the joined table could not be updated in SQL because (as stated earlier in this paper) SQL does not currently support "update of join." Thus, our overall recommendation for normalization is as follows: Normalize all the way to the point where the "no redundancy" objective has been achieved, *but no further*.

Note: This recommendation is related to the next one. See below.

DENORMALIZATION

In a sense, the normalization discipline can be regarded as *optimizing for update at the expense of retrieval*—a fully normalized database tends to require less processing on update but more on retrieval. To put this another way, normalization reduces redundancy, and though redundancy is bad for update it may be good for retrieval. Instead of simply trying to avoid all redundancy, therefore, maybe what we should be doing is trying to avoid *harmful* redundancy. *Controlled* redundancy may be all right. This fact suggests another design guideline: If two items of information are very frequently retrieved together and are only very infrequently updated, and if full normalization would separate those two items, then maybe the design should be "denormalized" slightly to bring those items back together again.

An example will help to make this point clearer. Consider the table

```
NADDR ( NAME, STREET, CITY, STATE, ZIP )
```

in which we assume that, in addition to the functional dependencies implied by the primary key NAME (such as the dependency NAME $\rightarrow$ STREET), we also have the dependency

```
ZIP --> ( CITY, STATE )
```

The normalization guidelines would suggest that this table be broken down into the two tables

```
NSZ ( NAME, STREET, ZIP )
```

and

```
ZCS ( ZIP, CITY, STATE )
```

with primary keys NAME and ZIP, respectively. But since STREET, CITY, and STATE are almost always required together, and since zipcodes do not change often (well, not *very* often), it seems unlikely that such a decomposition would be worthwhile.

Denormalization is a slippery slope, however. It smacks very heavily of allowing physical performance considerations to influence the logical database design, which historically has always led to trouble in the long run. As a general rule, we would advocate normalizing "all the way" (as defined in the previous section), and then denormalizing only when there is a very clear advantage to doing so, and *documenting carefully* the reason for each such departure from the fully normalized position.

One further argument (perhaps slightly academic) in favor of "normalizing all the way" first, even if you finish up with a somewhat denormalized final design, is as follows: The denormalized tables in your final design may well be different from the ones you passed through as you went on down through the original normalization procedure. That is, full normalization followed by selective denormalization may lead you to consider design possibilities that would never even have arisen if you had simply stopped short during the original normalization process.

NULL VALUES

Null values in SQL exhibit very arbitrary and inconsistent behavior and can be the source of a lot of difficulties. An extensive discussion of this topic can be found in the paper "Null Values in Database Management" (in this volume). For example:

- Two null values are considered to be duplicates of each other for the purposes of DISTINCT and UNIQUE and ORDER BY but not for the purposes of WHERE or GROUP BY.

- The builtin functions COUNT, SUM, and AVG are not guaranteed to satisfy the requirement that the average be equal to the sum divided by the count (in the presence of null values).

- If F1 and F2 are fields, the expression SUM(F1) + SUM(F2) is not guaranteed to be equivalent to the expression SUM(F1 + F2) (in the presence of null values).

As a result, it is quite possible to obtain unexpected or even incorrect results from the database unless you have a thorough understanding of how the system works in this area (and "you" here may be "the naive end user," remember, not necessarily a DP professional).

For such reasons, you should consider very carefully whether you want to allow null values for any fields in the database at all. It may well be the case that using certain nonnull but "illegal" values, such as -1 for an HOURS_WORKED field, will serve your purposes better. (Of course, if you do choose to go this route, then the primary and foreign key recipes given earlier in this paper will require some revision.) Note, however, that there are three points at which the notion of null is woven into the very fabric of the SQL language. To be specific, SQL (at the time of writing):

- *Insists* on allowing nulls for any field added to a table via ALTER TABLE;
- *Generates* null as the result of applying a function such as AVG to an empty set;
- *Generates* null for any unspecified field on INSERT.

Further discussion of this topic is beyond the scope of the present paper.

VECTORS

We use the term "vector" to mean a one-dimensional array of n simple data values, where the value of n is known at design time (i.e., the array is fixed-length). We insist on the fixed-length requirement because in this case there is a choice as to how best to represent the array (namely, row-wise vs. column-wise). If the array were variable-length, then there would be no choice—it would have to be represented column-wise (this is what first normal form is all about; in fact, "variable-length array" is just another name for what is more commonly referred to as a repeating group). We shall argue that fixed-length arrays (vectors) should normally be represented column-wise also; but the arguments are not particularly overwhelming. Our main purpose here is simply to identify some of the factors that need to be taken into account when trying to make such a decision.

Consider, for example, the question of representing a set of sales items x, y, ..., z, together with their sales figures for each of the twelve months of last year. The obvious representations (with some sample values) are:

1. Row-wise:

```
       ----   -------   -------          -------
SALES  ITEM   JAN_QTY   FEB_QTY   ...    DEC_QTY
       ----   -------   -------   ---    -------
        x         100        50   ...        360
        y          75       144   ...         35
        .                     .   ...          .
        z         212        98   ...        401
```

2. Column-wise:

```
       ----   -----   ---
SALES  ITEM   MONTH   QTY
       ----   -----   ---
        x      Jan    100
        x      Feb     50
        .       .       .
        x      Dec    360
        y      Jan     75
        y      Feb    144
        .       .       .
        y      Dec     35
        .       .       .
        z      Dec    401
```

Advantages of the row-wise representation:

- One advantage is that all twelve sales figures for a given item can be inserted via a single INSERT operation. As a result, data entry is liable to be easier than with the column-wise representation.

- Another advantage is that it is likely to occupy less space on the disk.

- Another—possibly the most important in practice—is that it may be a requirement to produce row-wise reports from the data. If the available report writer is not sophisticated enough to produce such a report from a column-wise representation, then there is no real choice.

Advantages of the column-wise representation:

- To find the total sales for the year of item X, the row-wise representation requires

```
SELECT JAN_QTY + FEB_QTY + MAR_QTY + APR_QTY +
       MAY_QTY + JUN_QTY + JUL_QTY + AUG_QTY +
       SEP_QTY + OCT_QTY + NOV_QTY + DEC_QTY
FROM   SALES
WHERE  ITEM = X ;
```

whereas the column-wise representation requires

```
SELECT SUM ( QTY )
FROM   SALES
WHERE  ITEM = X ;
```

The SQL functions are all column-oriented, not row-oriented.

- The column-wise representation greatly simplifies the formulation of generalized queries (canned procedures). Consider, e.g., the problem of comparing the sales of item X for month M with the sales of item Y for month N, where X, Y, M, and N are all parameters. Such a problem is trivial with the column-wise representation—it basically involves a couple of simple SELECTs and a comparison:

```
SELECT QTY                    SELECT QTY
INTO   Q1                     INTO   Q2
FROM   SALES                  FROM   SALES
WHERE  ITEM = X               WHERE  ITEM = Y
AND    MONTH = M ;            AND    MONTH = N ;

              compare Q1 and Q2 ;
```

With the row-wise representation, however, the problem is much harder. In fact, it will almost certainly require the use of the so-called "dynamic" features of SQL (PREPARE and EXECUTE), which means that (a) the program will be orders of magnitude more difficult to write, and (b) it will also be significantly less efficient, since it will involve run-time compilation.

- If the vector in fact represents a time-series (e.g., the last twelve months' sales, instead of the sales for the twelve months of last year), then month-end processing is very clumsy with the row-wise representation but comparatively straightforward with the column-wise representation.

- If requirements subsequently change, so that sales figures are required for (say) eighteen months instead of twelve, then it is easier to change the column-wise design (changing a column-wise design basically means adding rows, whereas changing a row-wise design means adding columns, and it is easier to add rows than columns).

(Of course, the "correct" solution to the vector representation problem is for the system to provide a vector data type—but most systems currently do not. As a consequence, the considerations sketched above are relevant.)

CODES AND FLAGS

Note: Most of the ideas of this section and the next, and most of the examples, are taken (with permission) from a paper entitled "Data Analysis," by John Widger, dated 22 December 1980 and published by IBM United Kingdom.

For reasons of control and brevity, it is frequently desirable to represent properties in an encoded form in the database. For example, the property "car color" might be encoded as follows:

```
----  -------
CODE  MEANING
----  -------
  01  Red
  02  Blue
  03  Yellow
  04  Brown
```

It is important to keep code values mutually independent. For instance, consider the following example, in which the property being encoded is "type of location":

```
----  ------------------------
CODE  MEANING
----  ------------------------
  01  Warehouse
  02  Retail outlet
  03  Plant
  04  Warehouse / Retail outlet
  05  Plant / Warehouse
```

The ambiguities and problems here are obvious. For example, it is not clear whether code 04 includes the meaning of code 02. To find out whether a retail outlet exists at a given location, does the user have to test for both codes or only one? And if only one, then which one? Does code 02 exclude the possibility of a retail outlet location also being a warehouse location? (Etc., etc.)

The information is far better represented by three mutually independent yes-or-no *flags*:

Is it a warehouse?

Is it a retail outlet?

Is it a plant?

All possible combinations are now handled unambiguously.

FIELD OVERLOADING

Every field should have a single meaning. If it does not, then it is *overloaded*. For example, the "purchase-order quantity" field clearly applies to purchased parts only, so it *could* be used to represent "work-in-progress quantity" for parts that are manufactured in-house. But such a design leads to programming complexity, difficulty in understanding system documentation, and severe problems if it is ever decided both to manufacture and purchase the same part.

As another example, consider the coded property "car color" from the previous section. Suppose it becomes necessary to record the additional property "type of gearbox" (automatic or manual). Instead of going to the trouble of adding a new field to the table, it is tempting to make use of the spare color codes, as follows: Use the existing codes (1,2,3,4) to mean red, blue, yellow, and brown (as before), but with the additional meaning of "manual gearbox"; use four new values (5,6,7,8) to mean red, blue, yellow, and brown also, but with an automatic gearbox. This approach requires no database or definitional changes, but it leaves the database in an unnnecessarily confused state. Future maintenance is more complicated, owing to that increased confusion. Furthermore, if more car colors are introduced, we will run out of available codes twice as quickly as we would otherwise have done. "In other words, the redesign and restructuring is merely postponed, not avoided. When it does come, the real damage has already been done" (paraphrasing Widger's paper).

Primary keys are particularly prone to such overloading. To paraphrase Widger again: "For example, manufactured parts [might be] given part numbers below 5000, and [purchased parts] numbers 5000 and above. One danger [of such a scheme] is that the allocated range may be inadequate; for example, if the business decides to subcontract most of its parts manufacturing, it may become necessary to assign codes below 5000 to purchased parts. More importantly, if application programs have become dependent on the ranges, the problem is compounded because the cost of changing the code structure may become prohibitive. For example, when purchased parts are assigned numbers 4500 and 4501, programs that include the test

```
IF P# > 5000
```

have to be changed to say

```
IF P# > 5000 OR P# = 4500 OR P# = 4501
```

This sort of data corruption creates systems that eventually become unmaintainable and hopelessly dependent on specific experienced personnel who happen to be familiar with the corruptions. It is also a nightmare for users, who need to understand the meaning of the data in the database."

Finally: "It is possible that some such corruptions already exist, with a considerable investment in program logic dependent on them. The best solution in this case is to leave the existing codes as they are, but to add new fields to the database to reflect each separate meaning. In the case of the part number example above, two new flags—"Is it purchased?" and

"Is it manufactured?"—should be defined." New programs should use those new fields. When it becomes necessary (for other reasons) to change existing programs, they too can be revised to use the new fields.

INDIVIDUAL USER VIEWS

Finally, a few more words on the topic of normalization. Almost all of our discussion prior to this point has been concerned with base tables; and we have agreed that such base tables should generally be in (at least) third normal form. However, there is no requirement that *views* be in 3NF, even if the base tables are, and indeed they frequently will not be. The design procedure we have been advocating is, to a large extent, *application-independent*; we have simply been saying "Decide what entities you are interested in, decide what relationships exist among them, and so on," and we have totally ignored the question of how that information is going to be used later. It is possible (to some extent) subsequently to tailor, restructure, and slant that application-independent design to meet the needs of individual applications, via the relational view mechanism. However, that tailoring activity is very much a secondary consideration. The primary objective is to get the independent design right in the first place.

We remark also that individual user views are the logical place to keep derived or computed fields, although in some cases it may be desirable to represent such fields at the base table level for performance reasons.

SECTION FIVE: EPILOGUE

Database design has traditionally been regarded as a very difficult task, requiring very specialized skills. Relational technology simplifies that task somewhat in three different ways:

1. By decoupling the logical and physical levels of the system to a greater extent than did previous technologies, and by bringing the logical level closer to the real-world level of entities, properties, and so forth, it simplifies the process of mapping a "real world level" design into a structure that the system can directly support.

2. Because the relational structure itself is conceptually simple, it becomes feasible to implement small and/or simple (and therefore easy-to-design) databases, such as personal or departmental databases, that would never even have been considered as candidates for implementation in older, more complex systems.

3. The theory and discipline of normalization can help by showing precisely what goes wrong if relations are *not* structured in the "obvious," commonsense way.

Nevertheless, relational technology is not a panacea. Large, complicated databases can still present a difficult design problem. In this paper we have outlined a set of principles that can be used to approach that problem in a systematic manner and can help to impose some structure on the overall design task. We have also provided a number of miscellaneous (but still practical and still important) tips and hints to assist with various detailed aspects of the design process.

ACKNOWLEDGMENTS

I have been influenced by many people in writing this paper. Chief among them are Ted Codd, whose work on RM/T forms the basis for the material presented in the sections on the synthetic approach; John Widger, from whose *Data Analysis* document I took much of the material on "Codes and Flags" and "Field Overloading"; and Bill Kent, who tried very hard to persuade me to adopt a different approach entirely (although he was unsuccessful in this attempt, his arguments led me to make numerous improvements in the presentation of my own methodology). I am also grateful to the following people for their helpful comments on early drafts of this paper: Paula Capello, Ted Codd (again), Jnan Dash, Paul Higginbotham, Walt Roseberry, Phil Shaw, Jim Strickland, and George Zagelow. Of course, I do not mean to suggest that these people endorse the paper in any way; on the contrary, the paper, together with all its shortcomings, is entirely my own responsibility.

The Relational Future

COMMENTS ON REPUBLICATION

This appendix consists of the edited transcript of an interview I gave to *Data Base Newsletter* in 1983. I have included it here because it touches on so many of the topics that are treated at greater length in the body of the book—database design, data integrity, null values, concerns regarding the SQL language, the possibility of building a relational frontend to a non-relational system, misconceptions about the relational model, and so on—plus certain additional topics, such as database machines and distributed systems.

As so often in such cases, the style of the original interview (published version) ranged all the way from the excessively chatty to the extremely stilted. I have made some slight revisions in the version printed here in order to remove the worst stylistic offenses, but I fear that the style of the revised version is still somewhat uneven. More importantly, I have also taken the opportunity of clarifying a few of my original responses. Indeed, I was sorely tempted in one or two cases to change those responses entirely (par-

Originally published in two parts. Part I appeared in *Data Base Newsletter 11,* No. 5 (September/October 1983), Part 2 in *Data Base Newsletter 11,* No. 6 (November/December 1983). Reprinted with permission of Database Research Group, Inc., Boston, Massachusetts, Ronald G. Ross, Editor/Publisher.

ticularly in the database machine section, where I now feel my comments were perhaps excessively negative), but all such temptations were firmly resisted.

RELATIONAL SYSTEMS TODAY

Newsletter: Many people saw 1981, with the release of IBM's SQL/DS and Ted Codd's Turing Award, as a watershed for the commercial emergence of the relational model. With IBM's recent DB2 announcement, we might amend that now to 1983. In your view, where are we today with the relational model?

Date: Indeed, as you suggest, I believe relational technology has now finally made a significant breakthrough into the commercial marketplace. If you review the huge number of database product announcements during the last three or four years, you find that almost every one is either for a new relational DBMS or for a relational-like frontend to one of the older systems. This is true across the board, from the smallest micro to the largest mainframe.

Newsletter: Do you have any idea how many relational systems are now available?

Date: Even though I try to keep a record of the announcements, it's almost impossible to keep up. My best estimate is that there are currently at least 40 systems that are truly relational.[1] Beside these, there are also many inverted list systems that seem to be trying to cash in on their relational-like flavor, as well as hierarchical or network systems now attempting to develop relational frontends. I think it's fairly clear now, especially with companies like IBM announcing DB2 and Cullinet announcing IDMS/R, that most hardware and software vendors feel relational database is the trend—it is the way they should be going.

Newsletter: So you feel that relational systems now represent a fully viable commercial technology?

Date: Absolutely.

Newsletter: Do you still nonetheless find significant misconceptions about what "relational" really is?

Date: The situation is improving, but unfortunately there is still much confusion. The most common misconception that still persists is that people frequently see the relational model as just flat files and focus exclusively on just that one aspect—the data structure aspect.

---

[1]This was in 1983. The figure now (1985) is well in excess of 100.

I can't say this too strongly—the relational model is *not* just data structure. It is data structure plus other things—in particular, the relational operators such as join, select, project, and so on. Without those operators, you're left with something that's not very useful; it's as if you had a database, but no processing you could do on that database.

Newsletter: Other misconceptions?

Date: I think it's important to make a distinction between something being complicated and something being powerful. The relational model, for example, does not permit repeating groups. But it does that very deliberately, because there is nothing you can do with repeating groups that you can't also do without them. By discarding them, you simplify, but in no sense do you weaken. You simply eliminate unnecessary choices.

Newsletter: What do you have to say about a vendor who claims its DBMS is somehow better because it allows users to operate on both normalized and unnormalized data?

Date: They seem to be suggesting that this makes their system more powerful. It doesn't. But it does make it more complicated. The situation reminds me a little of the debates over structured programming a few years back. Some people argued that a language like PL/I, for example, was more powerful than a structured programming language because it not only supported the structured approach, but offered a GO TO as well. But this didn't really make it any more powerful, only more complicated. The situation with handling unnormalized data in a DBMS is much the same.

Newsletter: Any other misconceptions about the relational model?

Date: Yes, another misconception people sometimes have is that the relational model demands that the data be in third normal form, and also incidentally that third normal form is somehow "difficult," which it certainly is not. Third normal form is a good idea, but it is completely separate from the workings of the relational model itself. The relational model simply says that data must be structured in the form of tables.

Still another misconception seems to be the idea that relational systems are primarily aimed at supporting query requirements, and that consequently they are not well suited for full-scale application work involving heavy-duty production and transaction processing.

Newsletter: Isn't it true that if you examine those 40 or so relational systems on the market today that you will find that most are either private, unshared systems, or even in those systems which are not, that there are definite limits on the amount of production work or transaction volumes they can handle?

Date: Yes, that is true, but you must remember that I said those 40 systems range over a broad spectrum of machine sizes. At the large end, you will find products comparable in performance to all but a select few existing systems.

You won't find any relational product today that can perform as well as, for example, IMS Fast Path. But at this point in time, you really wouldn't expect that either. On the other hand, you do find relational products that perform very acceptably for significant, and sometimes surprising, amounts of production work.

Newsletter: Are there any inherent theoretical or practical reasons why relational systems cannot ultimately match the large-end performance of other database systems?

Date: None whatsoever.

Newsletter: Will relational systems require hardware breakthroughs, for example associative memories, to do so?

Date: Absolutely not. This is another misconception about relational systems.

DEFINING THE RELATIONAL MODEL

Newsletter: In practical terms, how do you define the relational model?

Date: The relational model is a way of looking at data, a prescription for how data can be represented and manipulated. This prescription has three pieces to it—a structural piece (basically tables), an integrity piece, and a manipulative piece.

The integrity piece says, for example, that every relation (i.e., table) should have a unique, nonnull primary key to identify table entries or rows. The manipulative piece consists of operators for processing tables. In Ted Codd's *Newsletter* interview last year, I believe he very aptly characterized this manipulative piece as being cut-and-paste operators for tables. There are many such operators in the complete model, but the most important ones are the familiar *select*, *project*, and *join*. Conceptually, these operators are very straightforward. The *select* operator picks out rows; the *project* operator picks out columns; and the *join* operator sticks two tables together. Among them, these three operators support most of the operations on data you need to do.

Newsletter: Is it accurate to say that the relational model is a prescription for how a DBMS should operate?

Date: Precisely.

Newsletter: You mentioned earlier that the relational model precludes support for repeating groups. Are there other criteria that define when a DBMS is relational and when it is not?

Date: When I say that a relational system is one in which the user sees tables, I mean just that—the user sees tables and nothing but tables. This precludes the user from seeing explicit connections or links between tables, or from having to traverse between tables on the basis of such links. It also precludes user-visible indexes on fields. Indeed, it precludes users from seeing *anything* that smacks of the physical storage level. Tables are a *logical abstraction* of what is physically stored.

Now, there are certain packages on the market today in which the user does see tables, but which place restrictions on what the user can do with those tables. For example, some products support stepping from one table to another only if there happens to be a physical pointer connecting them. What this really means is that the user must see, or be aware of, something else, some physical aspect of the way the data is stored, in addition to the basic tabular format itself.

When you write programs in such a system, you must conform to the underlying physical structure. If the structure happens to change, you're stuck with modifying the programs. This is one of the flaws in traditional database systems that the relational model originally set out to correct.

Newsletter: Is it correct to conclude that by limiting the user to seeing only tables, the relational model actually increases the power and flexibility associated with their use?

Date: Yes, but let me amplify that a little. The tables in a relational DBMS are a rather neutral structure. With systems like IMS or IDMS, by contrast, the database structure is biased toward certain applications—it includes certain built-in paths. For those particular applications, this makes those structures more powerful.

The relational model takes those paths out of the structure (and in doing so, actually reduces the power of the structure), but then gives that power right back in spades with the manipulative operators. Since the user is no longer limited to predefined paths, this enhances not only the overall power of the system, but its flexibility and productivity as well.

RELATIONAL DBMSs

Newsletter: Can a DBMS be classified as relational if it doesn't handle such basic data management functions as concurrency controls?

Date: The point at issue here is not "What is relational?", but rather, "What is a DBMS?".

Historically, databases have always been shared. This is because DBMSs are typically very large programs, operating therefore in a large machine environment, where by definition there were a large number of users to do the sharing. Since this environment was essentially a given, it naturally shaped our early ideas of what database meant.

The situation now, however, is changing radically. Although DBMSs are not getting any smaller, small computers—PCs, for example—have been steadily getting larger. As a result, the benefits of database management (ad hoc query, canned procedures, reports, etc.) can now be brought down all the way to the home computer user. These people don't need concurrency controls. Does that mean the data management system they use is not a DBMS?

Newsletter: Much of the true complexity in constructing DBMSs, relational or otherwise, is associated with automating all concurrency considerations. Don't implementers of private data management facilities—in spite of the need for innovations in user-friendliness—really face a much easier job than implementers of large, shared systems?

Date: Yes, there are very difficult problems associated with implementing concurrency controls, crash recovery, and so forth. This is one reason, incidentally, why a shared system like DB2 requires an MVS-size machine.

But there are other hard problems as well. If you accept the challenge of supporting the relational operators efficiently, for example, you must also undertake some very significant and difficult work on optimization.

Newsletter: Earlier you mentioned the development of relational frontends for certain existing nonrelational DBMSs. Do you feel this is really possible in the full sense of the relational model?

Date: Whenever I use the terms "frontend" and "relational" together in this context, I mentally put "relational" in quotes. However, I am not deeply familiar with any of the commercial products that purport to do this, so I'm not really in a position to offer a detailed judgment on individual cases. I can tell you, however, that there are severe technical problems involved in trying to build such a frontend.

In theory, there are two distinct types of frontends you might want to build. One type simply uses the existing DBMS, say IMS, as an access method to implement new databases. Although this is probably feasible, it's not particularly useful. Given the complexities and performance issues, you'd probably be better off rebuilding the "database engine" from scratch.

The second and more interesting case is to put a relational frontend onto an older DBMS to obtain relational-style access to *existing* databases. These databases might be currently stored under IMS, IDMS, or what have you. This case is much more difficult because these existing databases are much less disciplined than data under the relational model. For example, applications can bury information in the physical ordering of records. Once they do that, there's no way any process but the application itself can dig it back out.

Theoretically, it might be possible to do a 75 percent, or a 95 percent, or even 99 percent complete job. But frankly I'm not sure how useful anything but a 100 percent job really is.

Newsletter: Compared with traditional systems, how would you summarize the advantages of the relational model?

Date: It would take a long time, an hour or more, to answer that question properly. But one specific point I'd like to make is the following. With relational systems, unlike traditional DBMSs, the theory preceded any implementations. Given that a relational implementation conforms to this preceding theory, its behavior in any given situation will be completely predictable. Users can extrapolate with confidence from what they know to what they don't know. Under traditional systems, by contrast, so many things come as surprises or exceptions.

In principle, the manual for a relational system should be much thinner than one for its traditional counterpart. There is simply less to learn. Thus rather than complicating, the prior existence of a theory for relational systems actually makes life simpler, both for implementers and for all kinds of users.

Newsletter: Other conceptual differences from traditional DBMSs?

Date: Yes, another important characteristic is that the relational model was developed with the end-user in mind right from the word "go." An original objective, in fact, was to put the end-user directly in touch with the data without having to go through the DP department to get there.

Once the relational operators were defined, of course, it rapidly became apparent that they could be used to improve the productivity of professional programmers also. But it was definitely the end-user that originally motivated the model, not the professional programmer.

Newsletter: Do you have any first-hand experience concerning the difficulty of teaching end-users how to use relational facilities?

Date: I have to admit that systems available today are not quite as simple as I would like. On the other hand, the current success of systems like dBASE II for small machines is a good indication that end-users can learn these ideas fairly easily.

Newsletter: What impact are relational systems likely to have on the way database applications are developed?

Date: One obvious implication, and an extremely important one too, is that there will be many instances where no application development in the traditional sense will be required at all. Users will be able to deal with many of their own needs directly. In those remaining cases where application programs are still required, we can look forward to easier and quicker implementation, with significantly less subsequent maintenance.

Another important implication for application development is that with relational systems we will see more prototyping than ever before. Under a relational DBMS it is extremely easy to design and create a database, build some applications, and then run them, showing actual users the screens and reports they can anticipate. If they don't like them, you can change them—simple as that. And you can go round that loop as many times as you like.

Newsletter: For more complex systems, you're not suggesting that relational systems will permit us to eliminate all upfront analysis, are you?

Date: Of course not. For certain types of problems they will, but by no means for all.

Newsletter: With regard to relational theory, rather than implementations on the market today, do you see any applications or environments for which relational DBMSs do not appear suitable?

Date: None whatsoever.

RELATIONAL LANGUAGES

Newsletter: Besides host computer size, are there any classes or distinctions, perhaps based on language, among the 40 or so relational systems in the marketplace today?

Date: Yes, clearly there are. One large grouping is the SQL family, which includes both of IBM's large-scale relational products, SQL/DS and DB2. ORACLE is another SQL product. Most ORACLE sales are currently to DEC hardware users.[2] Fujitsu has announced a SQL product too. And there are several others.

The SQL language was developed in 1974 at IBM Research by Donald Chamberlin and others. First a minor prototype was developed, then the major prototype that most people have heard about, System R. The tech-

---

[2]No longer true (1985).

nology explored and developed in that prototype is basically the same that IBM subsequently exploited in both SQL/DS and DB2.

A second major grouping is those systems that support the QUEL language. QUEL was originally developed by Mike Stonebraker and others at the University of California at Berkeley round about 1974 as part of the INGRES system. INGRES is now marketed by Relational Technology Inc., principally for DEC hardware.[3] Tandem's ENCOMPASS system and Britton-Lee's IDM database machine both use QUEL-like languages. As an aside, implementers who come from a university background, as opposed to implementers in one of the longer-established commercial vendors, tend to build QUEL systems because their educational background is usually INGRES and QUEL.

A third language is QBE (Query-By-Example), developed by Moshe Zloof at IBM in 1974–75, which has been available in product form from IBM on the VM operating system for several years. Incidentally, IBM recently announced a QBE interface for its new product QMF, which will operate on top of either SQL/DS or DB2. For a lot of people's money, QBE (which uses a fill-in-the-blanks approach) is a much more user-friendly language than SQL. I believe Intel also has a QBE-style interface for one of its products; so does Honeywell; and there is at least one QBE-like product for micros.

Beside these more or less formal relational schools, there is also a loose collection of existing products that support what are sometimes called "fourth generation languages." I don't very much care for that term, and I certainly don't think that all so-called fourth-generation systems are relational, but I would like to say something about one such product, namely NOMAD2. Whereas by formal standards, NOMAD2 has certain characteristics that are nonrelational—for example, the system supports hierarchies in addition to relations—its thrust seems to be very much in line with relational objectives and approaches. Since the system has been in the marketplace for many years and has developed some very nice features that parallel the intent of the relational model, I regard it as being very much in the relational spirit.

Newsletter: How much difference is there between SQL and QUEL?

Date: In some ways you can regard them as dialects of a common language. They both support the principal manipulative operations of the relational model, though of course they do so in a different syntactic style. Conceptually, the effort required to switch from one to the other is roughly

---

[3]No longer true (1985).

equivalent to that needed to switch from one dialect of COBOL to another. It's not like switching from COBOL to FORTRAN. If you know SQL, it's very easy to become comparably proficient in QUEL, or vice versa.

Newsletter: Do any of those languages have clearcut advantages over the others?

Date: I'd rather avoid making any value judgments for now. From a pragmatic or economic point of view, however, there's no escaping the fact that SQL is going to be extremely important. Its endorsement by IBM in SQL/DS and DB2 will surely see to that.

Newsletter: What are the implications?

Date: I think we've already seen some. In fact, even before IBM's official endorsement, some other vendors perceived that was the way it would go and began rushing to build SQL-compatible products. Of the 40 or so relational products on the market, at least 15 have a SQL flavor.[4]

Another development worth noting is that there is a group within ANSI chartered with developing a relational standard. This group is using SQL as its starting point. Their target date for delivering a proposed standard for public comment is October 1984, a date they very probably will meet.[5]

Newsletter: So you're suggesting that we could end up either with an official or de facto relational standard based on SQL?

Date: Precisely.

Newsletter: Would that be bad?

Date: I'm not sure. Frankly, I'm not really much of a fan of standards in areas like these. Also, there are some technical and theoretical problems with SQL that concern me. But like it or not, it seems inescapable that SQL is going to be the COBOL of relational database. You can interpret that statement however you like.

Newsletter: What sort of things concern you about SQL?

Date: You remember I said earlier one thing wrong with traditional DBMSs is that their behavior is often rather unpredictable. Unfortunately, SQL has some of the same characteristics. There are some occasional surprises. For example, null values in SQL display very arbitrary and inconsistent behavior.

In that sense, and in spite of the many advantages it enjoys simply

---

[4]Now at least 25 (1985).
[5]It turned out to be May 1985.

because it is relational, I feel it has in some ways missed the relational boat. Incidentally, this is not a criticism of the System R people. In general, I think they did a fantastic job. In fact, System R probably contributed more to proving the viability of the relational model, and to developing practical implementation techniques, than any other prototyping work.

What I would criticize, however, is the process that takes a prototype system—that's what System R was—and directly elevates it to product status without first fixing the things that are wrong. With regard to SQL, many of those flaws had been identified in detail. But I suppose that when something new, like SQL, is so far ahead of what already exists—let's say DL/I in this case—it becomes very difficult to convince people that there are nonetheless still things wrong with it.

Newsletter: Is that a criticism of IBM?

Date: It's a criticism of the process, not necessarily of a particular company or group of people.

Newsletter: What are the probable long-term effects of the flaws in SQL?

Date: It's very difficult to predict. Perhaps problems in implementing still higher-level interfaces on top of SQL. Perhaps migration problems 10 or 15 years down the road that could have been avoided. Theoretical problems so often have a way of turning into practical problems later on.

Newsletter: You mentioned the contribution of System R. Could you single out anything particular in that work that was especially noteworthy?

Date: One of System R's most significant contributions was to treat database statements like any other high-level language statements—which is to say, it compiled them ahead of time and then used optimized object code at execution time. Add to that its checking just prior to run-time to see whether any of the physical database structures had changed—and automatically recompiling if they had—and you have a quite powerful technique that combines the performance of a compiling system with the flexibility of a late-binding system. This feature was picked up in both SQL/DS and DB2, and now there are several other vendors in the marketplace trying to change their proprietary packages to incorporate the same technique.

ON IBM'S DB2

Newsletter: In general what is your reaction to IBM's DB2 announcement?

Date: I am extremely pleased the product has been finally announced. I wouldn't want any of the comments or criticisms I have made prior to this point to suggest in any way that I'm not. Certainly I believe the emphasis on ease of use and ease of installation and operation is extremely nice. I'm also very pleased with QMF and with the fact that it offers a QBE interface. In general, I don't hesitate to predict that these will be excellent products.

Newsletter: Are you concerned about the lack of run-time bridges for IMS?

Date: No, not at all. Besides being technically difficult—and perhaps impossible at the 100 percent level—there seem to be other problems to solve that are far more important.

Newsletter: Can you give an example of why a bridge is difficult?

Date: Most of the reasons have to do with quirks in IMS. For example, IMS has a segment insert option of *"here."* The reason why a program might choose to insert a segment *"here,"* instead of over *"there,"* is buried within the logic of the program. But its decision has definite meaning— meaning that is unavailable to the relational system to emulate.

Newsletter: Do you anticipate users migrating or replacing DL/I applications onto DB2?

Date: I suspect some applications will go that route over time. This will be an interesting area to watch.

Newsletter: Won't there continue to be pressures for run-time bridges?

Date: Probably so, at least until users get an accurate picture of what it might cost.

Newsletter: Could a run-time bridge in any way diminish the relational characteristics of DB2?

Date: It's possible, and that's disturbing. Support for some of the undisciplined data types of IMS, for example, might lead to such an effect. Apart from specifics like that, anything that makes the system more complicated is essentially bad from a productivity point of view. From a reliability point of view too, maybe.

Newsletter: Does the reported size of DB2 concern you in any way?

Date: My understanding is that DB2 is a very large system, optimized to very large machines and databases. Given the target environment, as well as the anticipated rapid growth in hardware capacity, I'm sure this was the correct approach to take.

I do have one concern, however. When users first install the system, they may be reluctant to give it the full measure of resources and storage it requires. This, in turn, may act to degrade its performance and result in a reputation for poor performance it doesn't truly deserve.

Newsletter: Given the proper resources, do you think DB2's performance will be adequate?

Date: I believe it will. In any case, it can be enhanced over time.

The important thing about DB2 is that the *functionality* is there. When people concentrate too hard on machine performance, they tend to forget this. How much is it worth to the company to be able to develop new applications quickly and efficiently? If you have to pay a small price in machine overhead to get that, surely it's worth the cost.

With DB2, the bottom line is that because application development can be done so much more productively, your investment is smaller to begin with, and the returns start accruing much sooner. Even if the same application did eventually run more efficiently under a traditional system—when it was finally operational—it might still never catch up, economically speaking, with the relational version before it reached the end of its useful life. Furthermore, this argument applies with even more force if heavy subsequent maintenance is a factor.

Newsletter: Given the IBM view of the database world, we have production databases in the Development Center supported by IMS, and separate information databases in the Information Center supported by DB2. This means duplication of data and of databases. Isn't any type of data redundancy bad, even this type?

Date: First, let me object to the underlying assumption in your question, which is that IMS supports "production" databases, whereas DB2 supports something other than that. Like IMS, DB2 is a full DBMS and also supports production work.

Newsletter: But it's IBM itself that's promoting the opposing view, isn't it?

Date: Perhaps, but that's a different story.

To return to your question, redundancy as such is not always bad; rather, it is uncontrolled redundancy that is always bad. If you know what you're doing, redundancy can sometimes serve very useful purposes. Let me explain. The intent of the question, I believe, is to suggest that running relational queries directly against established databases, rather than first doing an extract of data into a separate database, might be desirable, because it avoids redundancy. Unfortunately, using that strategy you immediately encounter operational difficulties, which incidentally have little to do with relational systems per se.

In general, there are two kinds of database processing you must consider. The first kind, traditionally known as transaction processing, involves applications that individually touch only a tiny portion of the database—far less than one percent—but which are highly repetitive, sometimes recurring tens or even hundreds of times per second.

The second kind of processing is queries, which touch much more of the database—sometimes on the order of 10 percent or more—but which recur only infrequently in the same exact form.

Any time both of these kinds of processing must be accommodated for the same data at the same time, you can anticipate severe operational problems because by their very nature the two tend to be mutually disruptive. Often, the only viable solution is the extract mode. This is especially true if many of the queries are of the "what if" variety, or if end-users want time-summarized data. For these reasons, and apart from the relational issue altogether, I expect that extract strategies will therefore stay with us for a long time to come—although I might point out that extract mode operation is considerably simplified if the "extracted from" system and the "extracted to" system are in fact a single (relational) system.

Newsletter: You observe elsewhere in this interview that you anticipate relational catalogs expanding into full-scale dictionaries. Since IBM already has a dictionary product that runs under IMS, doesn't this present it with something of a dilemma?

Date: Yes. You could hardly expect a customer that buys only DB2 or SQL/DS to purchase IMS just to have a dictionary. On the other hand, the IMS dictionary is here to stay. I therefore believe separate and thriving dictionary systems in each of these environments is the most likely outcome.

Newsletter: Why did it take IBM so long to develop and announce DB2?

Date: The reasons had to do with marketing considerations. I wasn't party to them.

Newsletter: Given the existence of DB2, what do you predict for IMS in the long term?

Date: It will survive for the foreseeable future, until the year 2000 at least. IBM will presumably continue to enhance it, though it is difficult to see in what ways.

ANSWERING CRITICISMS

Newsletter: The relational model was first proposed by Codd in 1970. Why has it taken so long for anything commercially useful to emerge from it?

Date: The reasons were not wholly technical, but rather pertained to the economic importance of existing nonrelational systems, entrenched political and philosophical biases, and assorted other nasty reasons that are probably not worth discussing.

Newsletter: How do you respond to critics who say that the relational model really isn't all that different from other approaches?

Date: They miss the point entirely. We simply didn't have well-defined, high-level operators such as joins before the relational model came along. These operators are its distinguishing part.

Newsletter: The most frequent criticism of relational systems seems to be on the performance issue. For example, IBM's DB2 doesn't appear to have any specific or special devices aimed toward improving performance. Does this disappoint you?

Date: I interpret your question as referring to the fact that the set of performance tuning features in DB2 is rather small—though it is unfair to suggest that there are no such features at all. No one can realistically expect everything to be done in the first release of a new system. If you compare the first release of DB2 to the current release of IMS, of course you will find performance and tuning deficiencies—that's only natural. There are bound to be bottlenecks in any new system, but until you run it for a reasonable time you can't know where they are.

I have said many times that in the long run I fully believe that relational systems can achieve comparable, and perhaps superior, performance to any other DBMS. I think that systems like ORACLE, which has already undergone several releases, are already beginning to demonstrate this. For the present, perhaps a more realistic comparison of performance between DB2 and IMS would be against the *first* release of IMS fifteen years ago, with fair benchmark criteria. Of course, I don't mean by this to suggest that DB2 is 15 years behind!—rather, I mean that DB2 performance now is almost certainly *better* than that of IMS when it was first released. Furthermore, I think DB2 will catch up with IMS in terms of performance in considerably less than 15 years.

Newsletter: What do you mean by "fair benchmark criteria"?

Date: When people benchmark relational systems, they typically take a problem defined in the old way, and see how it will perform under the new. Unfortunately, doing this for relational systems ignores the new *types* of problems that the relational operators allow you to solve. These are problems that would give traditional systems fits, if in fact those systems could solve them at all.

Newsletter: You mentioned earlier in this interview that effective performance in relational systems used for production work can be achieved without hardware innovation. Wasn't the database community historically led to believe that such innovation would be required?

Date: I don't know about that. If so, that idea certainly didn't come from the researchers and developers actually working on relational systems.

Newsletter: Given the lack of special performance devices in current relational systems—of the hardware variety or otherwise—satisfying certain types of queries is going to prove either costly or lengthy, or both. One might surmise that after a time, users will discover which queries those are and will begin to create a mental map of the physical database structure to avoid them. Doesn't that defeat the whole intent of "relational"?

Date: Some users may begin developing such a map, but many others simply won't care about such issues. For those users, the relational system will open many new doors and provide the means to address altogether new types of business questions directly and productively.

   Incidentally, those more sophisticated users who do develop such a map must remember it may change from time to time as the physical database structures are tuned and modified. In other words, a "static" map may not do them much good. Another point to remember is that when physical database structures change under the relational model, this doesn't mean that the user's program or query must also change—in marked contrast to traditional systems.

Newsletter: But relational proponents have always insisted that users should not see—and perhaps we should add, *nor sense—any* physical database characteristics. Isn't this a hedge on the part of relational implementers?

Date: Given today's technology, there's no way to prevent the observant user from discovering certain physical characteristics of the database. The important thing, which relational implementers have achieved, is keeping that knowledge out of programs.

Newsletter: Another criticism sometimes aimed at relational systems on the market is that they have been slow to implement the dictionary concept. How do you respond to that?

Date: That's a very strange criticism. I would have thought it was exactly the opposite—it is the *non*relational systems that typically have no integrated dictionary. If you look at relational systems like INGRES or SQL/DS or DB2, you find they possess carefully integrated catalogs that can be accessed using the regular language facilities of those systems. This is one of their outstanding features compared with older DBMSs.

The problem with those catalogs today is that they lack specifications for things on the "outside," such as terminal networks and so on. I fully anticipate, however, that they will be expanded into all these other "dictionary" areas in the near future. In fact, customers are already doing this for themselves, even where the vendor hasn't.

Newsletter: A final criticism of the relational model is the lack of support for integrity constraints, which are supported within the data structures of hierarchical and network DBMSs. How do you defend the relational model on this point?

Date: Integrity constraints were prescribed in Codd's original work on the model. It's not the relational model itself that's weak, rather it's the existing implementations. There is no question, however, that this is the greatest deficiency in these systems today.

Newsletter: Why has this happened?

Date: I'm not quite sure. It's not really that it's a hard problem. Perhaps the early prototypers failed to perceive the full importance of the integrity rules.

NORMALIZATION

Newsletter: Do you feel that normalization is a good practical database design methodology?

Date: Yes, normalization is good as far as it goes. It may have been somewhat oversold by some people, however.

Newsletter: Oversold?

Date: In simplest terms, normalization requires that every fact should be put in one and only one place. Bill Kent said it very nicely, as follows: "Every fact is a fact about the key, the whole key, and nothing but the key."

In a sense, normalization optimizes update performance at the expense of retrieval performance. Sometimes, in order to improve retrieval performance, however, it may be desirable to put two facts in one place, or one fact in two places. If you follow normalization strictly, however, you're not allowed to make tradeoffs of that sort.

Newsletter: What does normalization do correctly?

Date: Basically, normalization helps you structure your thinking. It makes you aware of the problems that can occur when all the facts aren't sorted out and each one stored in one and only one place. It gives examples of the types of things that can go wrong if such a guideline is not followed.

I certainly believe that anyone doing database design should be familiar with normalization. But it should not be viewed as a panacea. There is a lot more to database design than just normalizing.

Newsletter: For example?

Date: In essence, normalization tells you how to derive better tables out of tables you have already. It doesn't tell you where those original tables come from. You need some other methodology for that.

Newsletter: What other type of methodology do you suggest?

Date: I prefer some type of top-down methodology based on such notions as entities and associations. First you translate your perceptions of these things into tables; then you use normalization to check and improve the results of the first step. Naturally, this whole process is very iterative. It sounds very simple and straightforward, but of course it may not be so in practice, if the database is complicated.

Newsletter: So the frontend methodology helps structure the original tables based on an entity orientation?

Date: Yes. Suppose you have information about departments. How do you know you should have just one table, DEPARTMENT, rather than a table for DEPARTMENT-1, a second table for DEPARTMENT-2, and so on? Normalization per se doesn't provide any answer for this; but if you perceive departments as an entity type, then you will probably realize that one table is the right approach.

Here is another example where normalization as such does not help much. Consider sales data that is accumulated monthly. Should you have one "item" table containing 12 individually named month attributes, or an "item, month" table where the 12 month values will be *occurrences* of the "month" attribute? Again, normalization per se provides no answer.

Newsletter: Traditional normalization also lacks an integrated element naming or definition philosophy. What do you recommend to designers in this regard?

Date: The relational model does include the concept of domains. Every attribute or field that corresponds to a given domain should generally be given the same name as that domain. When this is not possible—for example, because the domain is used twice in the same table, as in a bill-of-materials relation—then a distinguishing prefix should be added to the domain name.

Newsletter: What should be made of the fact that there seems to be no end to the new normal forms discovered beyond third normal form?

Date: In a theoretical and very precise sense, there is a final normal form in normalization—the fifth.

From a practical point of view, however, *third* normal form is the highest a designer should ever really need to worry about. If you create tables correctly and sensibly up-front, then by the time you reach third, you're almost automatically in fourth. And fifth normal form is really only important in a rather theoretical kind of way. For most practical design purposes, it can essentially be ignored.

Newsletter: What is the intention of some of the newer modeling work, such as Codd's semantics-oriented RM/T?

Date: The broad intention is to raise the level of the relational interface and to make the system generally more intelligent. Like the basic relational model, RM/T also has three parts—objects, operators, and integrity rules. The objects, however, are not simply tables, but higher-order objects (built out of tables) for describing things like entities and associations. Its operators and integrity rules are similarly extended.

Newsletter: What impact is RM/T likely to have?

Date: It's still in a very preliminary state. However, some of its concepts are already proving productive for database design, where higher-order notions for describing real world entities and associations are immediately useful.

I see a direct parallel, in fact, to the basic relational model, which was used for logical database design long before any relational DBMS was ever available. Even if no RM/T system per se is ever developed, its use in design may nonetheless prove an important contribution.

Newsletter: Are there any ways in which database design could be automated, or perhaps even eliminated, as a discrete task?

Date: I can imagine dialog-based tools that could help structure the design process somewhat better. Such tools might also automate the translation of the design into the definition specifics for a given DBMS and thus make that portion of the implementation activity transparent to the human designer.

It may also be possible to inspect sample data and automatically deduce possible dependencies for interactive inspection by designers. However, I'm not convinced this type of tool would prove in practice to be all that useful.

I really can't see database design *ever* being eliminated completely, however, even if tools such as these are developed. There is simply some point where significant human involvement will always be required to create databases properly.

DATABASE MACHINES

Newsletter: How do you define a database machine?

Date: A database machine can be defined as a dedicated, backend processor with storage, attached to one or more hosts running applications. It is usually perceived as a conventional processor running a stripped-down operating system and a full-fledged DBMS like INGRES or ORACLE. Associative disks may or may not be present; they can be viewed as an optional add-on.

Newsletter: So the crux of your definition has to do with the function of the processor in a network, rather than specialized hardware?

Date: Yes.

Newsletter: In the September, 1982 *Newsletter*, IBM's G. B. Ryan quoted you as saying that in order for a backend processor to be successful, it would have to be an order of magnitude faster than any frontend processor. What did you mean by that?

Date: Actually, that wasn't quite what I said. There is a rule of thumb for database machines, sometimes called the "offloading theorem" (though it isn't really a *theorem* at all), which says that for the backend configuration to be cost-effective, the amount of work offloaded should be at least ten times the cost of doing the offloading. For example, if you offload five seconds' worth of database searching, but the offloading itself costs you two seconds' worth of I/O communications to do it, you're losing. On the other hand, if the communications only take you one-tenth of a second, you're winning.

Newsletter: What's the implication?

Date: The conclusion would seem to be that the database machine concept is unlikely to provide better overall system performance.[6]

---

[6]See the "Comments on Republication."

Newsletter: Does this seem to be a prevailing opinion?

Date: It's the opinion of at least some of the experts who've been working in the area for some time. The original motivation for database machines was essentially to fix the performance problem. But they haven't really managed to do that.

Newsletter: Is there any other reason for database machines then?

Date: Database machines are good for sharing. A database server in a local area network, for example, has significant potential, especially if the hosts themselves may be of different types or brands. I believe the thrust of the database machine concept in the next few years will be toward this important area.

Newsletter: What do you see as the potential of associative disks?

Date: Associative disks seem to be good for a specific type of processing sometimes called the library search problem. This type of processing involves very complex queries, but these queries also have the property that every record can be identified as being, or not being, a hit by inspecting nothing else than just the record itself. An example of such a query might be the following: "Find all employees who have red hair, or who have been working for more than ten years and speak French, or have a degree in math, etc." All this information is in just one record type.

For more conventional applications, which involve queries that can only be satisfied by inspecting multiple record types, it really isn't clear that associative disks can prove their cost-effectiveness.

Newsletter: Isn't it true that most of the research work on database machines has been done using relational systems?

Date: Yes. Going back to the offloading theorem, one of the ways of cutting down on the number of times offloading occurs, and thus cutting down communication costs, is by ensuring that very high-level data requests go across the channel. That, in turn, suggests a relational system. Indeed, the large majority of both prototype and commercial database machines are relational.

Newsletter: What about distributed systems?

Date: The same holds true. With distributed systems a principal goal is again to minimize communication traffic.

However, that is only one of several characteristics that make the relational model an excellent choice for building distributed systems. Another is that the relational model makes it very easy to break tables apart into smaller pieces, either vertically or horizontally, which can be easily and cleanly distributed across the network. Having done that, an additional advantage is that you can then use the regular relational operators, such as joins and unions, to put those pieces back together again. Both of these are areas that present considerable difficulties for traditional systems. Remember also that the relational operators are extremely high-level, and precisely because of that, they can be optimized in ways essential for distributed access.

Index